Also by Ann Hagedorn

RANSOM: THE UNTOLD STORY OF INTERNATIONAL KIDNAPPING

WILD RIDE: THE RISE AND TRAGIC FALL OF CALUMET FARM, INC.,
AMERICA'S PREMIER RACING DYNASTY

ANN HAGEDORN

Beyond the River

THE UNTOLD STORY OF THE HEROES OF THE
UNDERGROUND RAILROAD

SIMON & SCHUSTER

New York   London   Toronto   Sydney   Singapore

SIMON & SCHUSTER
Rockefeller Center
1230 Avenue of the Americas
New York, NY 10020

SIMON & SCHUSTER and colophon are registered trademarks
of Simon & Schuster, Inc.

For information regarding special discounts for bulk purchases,
please contact Simon & Schuster Special Sales at
1-800-456-6798 or business@simonandschuster.com

Map © 2002 by Jeffrey L. Ward

Manufactured in the United States of America

2   4   6   8   10   9   7   5   3   1

Library of Congress Cataloging-in-Publication Data
Hagedorn, Ann.
Beyond the river : the untold story of the heroes of the
Underground Railroad / Ann Hagedorn.
        p.   cm.
Includes bibliographical references (p.   ) and index.
1. Underground railroad—Ohio.   2. Antislavery movements—Ohio—
History—19th century.   3. Abolitionists—Ohio—History—19th century.
4. Fugitive slaves—Ohio—History—19th century.   5. Rankin, John, 1793–1886.
6. Abolitionists—Ohio—Biography.   I. Title.
E450 .H165   2002
973.7'115—dc21   2002070645
ISBN 0-684-87065-7

To the people of Ripley,
then and now

CONTENTS

CONTENTS

Beyond the River

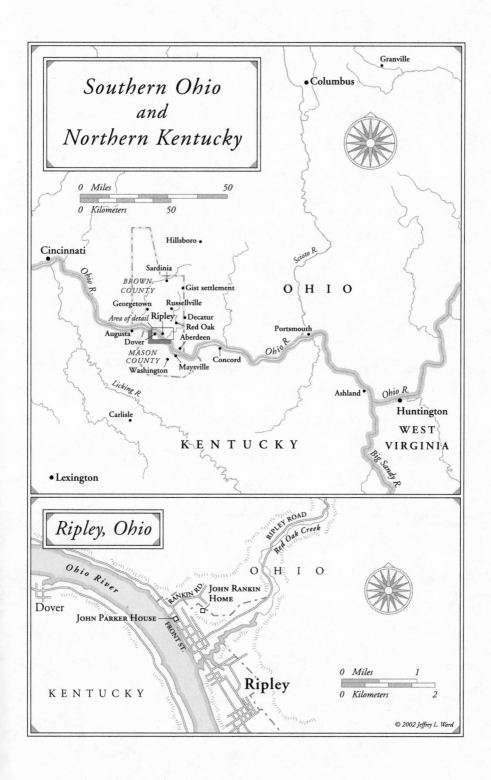

Southern Ohio
and
Northern Kentucky

0 Miles 50

0 Kilometers 50

Granville

• Columbus

Cincinnati

Ohio R.

Scioto R.

Hillsboro •

Sardinia •

BROWN
COUNTY

• Gist settlement

Georgetown • Russellville •

Area of detail Ripley • • Decatur

Augusta • • Red Oak

Dover • Aberdeen •

MASON
COUNTY

Washington • • Maysville • Concord

O H I O

Portsmouth •

Ohio R.

Ashland • *Ohio R.*

Huntington

WEST
VIRGINIA

Licking R.

Carlisle •

K E N T U C K Y

Big Sandy R.

• Lexington

Ripley, Ohio

Ohio River

Dover

JOHN PARKER HOUSE

RIPLEY ROAD

Red Oak Creek

O H I O

RANKIN RD.

JOHN RANKIN
HOME

FRONT ST.

Ripley

K E N T U C K Y

0 Miles 1

0 Kilometers 2

© 2002 Jeffrey L. Ward

Thus have I been attacked at midnight with fire and weapons of death, and nothing but the good providence of God has preserved my property from flames and myself and family from violence and death. And why? Have I wronged any one? No, but I am an ABOLITION-IST. I do not recognize the slaveholder's right to the flesh and blood and souls of men and women. For this I must be proscribed, my property burnt, and my life put in jeopardy!

Now I desire all men to know that I am not to be deterred from what I believe to be my duty by fire and sword. I also wish all to know that I feel it my duty to defend my HOME to the very uttermost, and that it is as much a duty to shoot the midnight assassin in his attacks as it is to pray.

—REVEREND JOHN RANKIN,
RIPLEY, OHIO, 1841

A Double Life

The people who lived on Front Street were the first to notice changes on the river. They knew when calm water began to churn, lapping loudly against the shore, or when boats stalled on shallow bends, as rains of warmer days turned to snow and water levels fell. And in the middle of the wintry night, when sheets of ice slid downriver, they could hear the high-pitched moan that some would say was the gradual grinding of the ice as floes collided and congealed; others would swear it was the sound of a human cry. For, as everyone in the town of Ripley knew, especially those who lived closest to the water, on Front Street things happened in the night when the river froze, things that some townsfolk tried hard to expose and others risked their lives to conceal.

In the winter of 1838, along the five bends visible from the highest point in Ripley, the Ohio River froze for nearly ten days. Ice floating down the river bore against the Kentucky and Ohio shores. As the level of the water fell day after day and temperatures plummeted, the ice spread, and what was once a river separating the North from the South, free states from slave, became a glassy road that seemed almost to connect them. In other years, the frozen surface heaved with ridges where floes had overlapped and formed a rugged mosaic. But so smooth was the river now that it lured every boy in town, skates slung over his shoulders, to its icy, snow-spattered banks. There they stood, in hushed awe, staring at the white expanse and watching each other, as if one of them could know whether the sheets of ice would now bear their weight. Even Jimmy Campbell, the best skater in the county, hesitated. So did John Rankin, Jr., and his brother Sam, both well practiced on the ice.

Behind the boys, along the river's edge, a crowd gathered. And just when it seemed that no one would venture onto the virgin ice, out of the cluster a boy darted. Skates firmly strapped, head bent close to the frozen ground, he dashed to the middle of the river and then turned a somersault. Like a gunshot starting a race, his move signaled the others. Soon, forty or more skaters took to the ice. But those who knew the river best, who watched its moods and its traffic, knew how perilous and unpredictable it could be. They cringed when they saw a horse and sleigh appear along the shore. The Campbell boy and others had persuaded two Ripley girls to ride in the sleigh onto the ice, though the ice was still settling and the river still falling. Tentatively the horse pawed the frozen ground, and then, urged on by the boys, it drew the sleigh out upon the slick surface. The sudden cracking sounded like "grinding bark," John Rankin, Jr., later wrote. Skaters fled. Spectators gasped. And the horse, with awkward strides, ice buckling beneath its hooves, hurried its precious cargo back ashore.

For many in Ripley, 1838 would stick in memory as the time when the frozen river hindered boat traffic for nearly two weeks, and as the only instance thus far in the town's history when a horse and sleigh rode upon the ice. For the Rankin boys and their father, for the father of Jimmy Campbell, Ripley's mayor, and for several of the Front Street dwellers, 1838 would be a striking year for other reasons. They were the men and women attuned to the traffic that picked up, rather than ceased, when the river froze: the human traffic of runaway slaves. For, somewhere on the other side of the river, on any given night, a slave, driven by the fear of capture, torture, and an endless future of bondage, was crossing a snowy field, wading an icy stream, dodging men and dogs to reach a river he or she had only heard of but never seen, to escape to the freedom beyond it.

One or more of the Ripley skaters testing the ice that day, looking for cracks, knew that the life of a runaway slave could depend upon the depth of the freeze. Some of them waited in the throng along the banks watching the events on the ice, all the while thinking about Kentucky and how close the shores of slavery now seemed. They thought too about the recently posted bounties for the assassination of John Rankin and other members of their underground band, and about a Ripley woman languishing in a Kentucky jail cell not far from the shoreline, a free black woman abducted from her home by slave catchers months ago.

Eighteen thirty-eight was a time of danger and conflict, a time to be wary of shadows in the alleys off Front Street, a time some in Ripley would remember for more than the horse and sleigh incident, the killing temperatures, and the brittle ice. For, although Ripley was a town of ordinary pleasures, it was also a town of extraordinary secrets, a town with a double life.

PART I

The War Before the War

There was a time when fierce passions swept this little town, dividing its people into bitter factions. I never thought of going uptown without a pistol in my pocket, a knife in my belt, and a blackjack handy. Day or night I dare not walk on the sidewalks for fear someone might leap out of a narrow alley at me. What I did, the other men did, walked the streets armed. This was a period when men went armed with pistol and knife and used them on the least provocation. When under cover of night the uncertain steps of slaves were heard quietly seeking their friends. When the mornings brought strange rumors of secret encounters the night before, but daylight showed no evidence of the fray. When pursuers and pursued stood at bay in a narrow alley with pistols drawn ready for the assault. When angry men surrounded one of the [Front Street] houses, kept up gunfire until late in the afternoon, endeavoring to break into it by force, in search of runaways. These were the days of passion and battle which turned father against son, and neighbor against neighbor.

—JOHN PARKER, FORMER SLAVE, FOUNDRY OWNER, INVENTOR,
UNDERGROUND RAILROAD CONDUCTOR ON THE RIPLEY LINE

The Kindling and the Spark

The town of Ripley lies on land wedged between the Ohio River and a steep, sprawling ridge in a region once known among frontiersmen as the Imperial Forest. Long ago, this vast expanse of green, fifty miles east of Cincinnati, 250 miles south of the Canadian border, and roughly a thousand feet from the Kentucky banks of the Ohio, was rich in hickory and elm, beech and oak, ash and walnut. Sycamores grew to forty-five feet around, so wide, it was said, that a horse and rider could stand in the hollow of a trunk. Thickets of grapevines entangled trees and shrubs in leafy mazes that blocked the sun.

The Shawnee and the Miami traversed these ridges and hollows, tracking bear and buck, ever wary of the panthers and wolves lurking in the shadows. Their villages lined the Scioto and Little Miami rivers, which bordered these verdant hills and fed the Ohio. And at a place where the Ohio narrowed to barely more than a thousand feet and flowed briefly northward, the place where Ripley would one day stand, they crossed the river to Kentucky to hunt more game and sometimes to steal horses. Then, back again, across the river they would come, with the horses they now claimed as their own, followed by the owners they had to outrun.

In the spring of 1804, two cumbrous flatboats moved slowly, like giant, eighty-foot arks, down the river from Mason County, Kentucky, taking most of a day to reach that narrow place where the river runs north, the place so often used for crossings. Colonel James Poage, a forty-four-year-old surveyor from Virginia, had come to claim his thousand acres on the new frontier: Military Warrant No. 14, Survey No. 416, "beginning at two sugar trees and a mulberry running down the river, crossing the mouth of Red Oak Creek to a sugar tree and two buckeyes on the bank of the river." One boat carried his wife, his ten children, and his possessions; on the other were his twenty slaves, whom he soon would set free.

By then, the Battle of the Fallen Timbers in 1794 and the Treaty of Greenville the following year were forcing the Indians northward and westward, marking the end of their lives in the Imperial Forest and tolling the death knell for much of the forest itself. The forest now stood in the midst of the Virginia Military District, a vast expanse of nearly four million acres between the Scioto and Little Miami rivers, thought to be the richest and fairest part of the region beyond the river. This was the land that, after the Revolution, Virginia refused to cede to Congress.

In those early years of the new nation, the fate of the Northwest Territory, of which Ohio was a significant part, emerged as a hotly contested issue. To whom did the bountiful Western domain now belong? In a nation poverty stricken after the Revolutionary War, every state envisioned revenue gushing from those lands for its own gain. The dense forests, the fertile soil, the abundant game, the river—all of it—conjured images of growth and profit. But a destitute Congress appealed to the states to relinquish their claims for the benefit of all; land sales would fill the government's coffers. The states conceded. Virginia, however, demanded to reserve a tract northwest of the Ohio River to pay its soldiers of the Continental Army. "In case the quantity of good lands on the southeast side of the Ohio, upon the Cumberland River, and between the Green River and the Tennessee River, which have been reserved by law for the Virginia troops of the Continental establishment, should prove insufficient for their legal bounties," the 1784 deed of cession read, "the deficiency should be made up to the troops in good lands to be laid off between the rivers Scioto and the Little Miami, on the northwest side of the river Ohio."

During the next three years, warrants issued to hundreds of ex-soldiers were laid upon the "good lands" between the Tennessee and Green rivers. There seemed little need for, or interest in, the reserve north of the river until the summer of 1787, when all of the so-called best lands had been claimed. In August of that year, a bureau opened in Louisville to encourage surveys into the Ohio territory. The early surveyors, knowing they could profit handsomely, returned from their missions with glowing accounts.

That same year, Congress passed the Northwest Ordinance—the first law in the new nation's history to ban slavery. "There shall be neither slavery nor involuntary servitude in the said territory otherwise than in the punishment of crimes," the sixth article of the law read. In Ohio, in its early years, slave owners could free their slaves without any liability. Other states, fearing that freed slaves would become wards of the state, required a bond. This new land of the free had particular appeal among those ex-soldiers of the Continental Army who had fought with the cause of liberty in their hearts and after the Revolution saw only hypocrisy in the slavery sanctioned by their home states.

So, by the early years of the nineteenth century, droves of Virginia's veteran soldiers, as well as speculators who had purchased the warrants from soldiers choosing not to move, were hastening to the land beyond the Ohio River, to this El Dorado of the West, a land where no man could be enslaved as the property of another.

Colonel James Poage, the man docking his flatboats, was one of them. Poage had served in the war, first as ensign in 1780 and then as lieutenant of militia in 1782. His title of colonel came out of his trailblazing years as a surveyor. Surveying in the unsettled Northwest was such a perilous job that parties of surveyors often banded together for protection, and when they did, the leader of the group was designated "colonel." Known for ambitious expeditions, a bold style, and a generous, egalitarian treatment of workers and slaves, Colonel Poage led large surveying bands into the wildest parts of Virginia, Kentucky, Indiana, Illinois, and Ohio throughout the 1780s and 1790s. In exchange for his work—nearly twenty years of it—he acquired parts of what he had surveyed: forty thousand acres, mostly in Virginia, Kentucky, and Illinois. When he retired from surveying, he first claimed land in Kentucky, where he lived in Ashland and then near Maysville, in Mason County. But it was his thousand-acre military warrant on the southernmost edge of the Imperial Forest that he chose for his permanent settlement.

Poage clearly recognized the potential his acreage held for riches from timber, agriculture, and the passing river traffic. But there was something else that lured the colonel, something pulling him to Ripley's shore like the spring sun drawing sap through the trees: He abhorred slavery. This loathing had risen within him during the Revolution and had grown with time, convincing him to renounce his own slaveholding and causing him to become dissatisfied with his life in Kentucky. In Ashland, he was in conflict with the slaveholders in his church, and in Mason County he couldn't bear the presence of slave traders or the sight of slave auctions. Once upon Ohio soil, he freed his slaves. He took apart his flatboats and built shelters from the logs. He called his settlement Buck's Landing.

In the months that followed, Poage renamed his plot, calling it Staunton, after the town in Virginia where he and many of his slaves had been born. Soon he and others tore the vines from the trees, hewed the hickory and beech, the ash and oak, and made paths through the remaining woods. Even the massive sycamores fell, one by one, as they cleared the land to build houses.

The others came slowly, year by year. There was Alexander Campbell, Ripley's first physician, who in 1804 migrated to Ohio from Kentucky, freed his slaves, and settled on Front Street. Born in Virginia and educated in Kentucky, Dr. Campbell was, by most accounts, Ohio's first abolitionist and soon to be one of the state's first two U.S. senators. James Gilliland, a Presbyterian minister ostracized in South Carolina for his antislavery views, arrived in 1805 and settled six miles north in Red Oak. Families from his congregation who shared his views, and friends from his hometown in North Carolina, soon followed and eventually joined him in the abolitionist underground. Thomas McCague, who would one day be a magnate in the nation's pork-packing industry, and his wife, Catherine, would also become active participants in Ripley's secret world, sharing their covert work with Front Street neighbors Nathaniel Collins, a carpenter and Ripley's first mayor; with three of his sons, Theodore, Thomas, and James; with the Beasley brothers, Alfred and Benjamin, both physicians; and with Dr. Campbell. From East Tennessee came Reverend Jesse Lockhart, who worked the Russellville, Ohio, link in the Ripley line, and Reverend John Rankin, whom William Lloyd Garrison would one day call his inspiration and teacher in the cause of ending slavery. Later would come John Parker, the free black abolitionist who distinguished himself by his daring forays into Kentucky to liberate slaves.

In the coming years, the growing community would attract more citizens of conscience whose abhorrence of slavery impelled them to uproot their families and to travel sometimes for months, often over rugged foothills and mountains, to a land they had never seen: Dr. Greenleaf Norton, Dr. Isaac M. Beck, Martha West Lucas, Sally Hudson and her brother John, the Pettijohns, the Cumberlands, and John B. Mahan among others. Some would live to see the end of slavery. Others would die in the struggle against it—casualties of the war before the war.

In 1812, Poage laid out his new town. Four years later, Staunton, population 104, became Ripley. A town farther north had already taken the name Staunton, and so the townsfolk changed theirs to honor General Eleazar Wheelock Ripley, a renowned American officer in the War of 1812. General Ripley had commanded the Second Brigade in the army of General Jacob Brown, for whom Ohio's Brown County had been named.

In the earliest plans for the town, there was always a road running parallel to the river with alleys branching out from it. At first, it seemed, the alleys provided comfortable distances between neighbors. Then, as more and more rooftops winked through the foliage and woodsmoke plumed over the town, horse-drawn wagons ambled along these narrow passages, leaving piles of wood at the side doors and back entrances of the riverfront houses. And as Ripley's double identity took shape, the alleys took on a new life—at night. Perpendicular to the river, they were conduits to the land beyond Ripley—extensions of the river as much as the ravines and streams flowing like tiny arteries around the heart of town. The alleys facilitated swift passage out the back doors of Front Street, up the steep hill behind the town, and onward to other towns and other hills. Dr. Campbell, Rankin, one of Rankin's sons, and others in the underground would build or purchase houses along the alleys.

By the 1830s, the alleys were well worn from the horse-and-wagon traffic of daily commerce and the human traffic that sometimes ran deep into the night. By then, Ripley was one of the busiest shipping points on the Ohio River. Stately brick row houses were replacing log cabins on Front Street. And on the many new streets in town, there were seven mercantile houses, three physicians, two attorneys, several cabinet shops, tan yards, groceries, millineries, shoemakers, wagon and carriage makers, a clockmaker, and a large woolen mill. Along the creeks were flour mills, and on the riverbank was a boatyard where flatboats and steamboats were built. By then, too, Ripley was second only to Cincinnati in the pork-packing industry. Farmers throughout the county brought their hogs to the Ripley market, where the animals were slaughtered and the lard was packed in kegs, the pork was pickled in barrels, and the slabs of cured hams and bacons were piled onto ships and sent east on the river via Pittsburgh or south to New Orleans.

The town was also known, at least among slaves and their masters in northern Kentucky, as a haven into which runaways seemed to disappear. In the early 1830s, a slave named Tice Davids had reached the Ohio River across from Ripley with his Kentucky master trailing so close behind him that Davids had not a second to search the shoreline for a skiff. And so he swam. His master, however, did spend time looking for a boat, and though he rowed swiftly and could see the head and arms of his slave thrashing through the water, he could not catch him. He watched as Davids climbed up the Ripley banks, then lost sight of him. He rammed his boat onto the shore and rushed up the steep bank to Front Street, where he asked everyone he saw about the black man who had just moments ago emerged from the river, clothes heavy with the weight of water. Had no one seen him? He walked the streets and searched the alleys, but he never found his slave. No one he asked in the entire town could recall seeing a man of Davids's description. Frustrated and confused, he returned to Kentucky, where he told everyone he knew that his slave "must have disappeared on an underground road."

Word of such a road began to spread, and Ripley's position along one of the narrowest bends of the Ohio was soon known among slaves in Kentucky. Many knew that a dry spell rendered the river so shallow that crossing at such a narrow stretch was more like wading a stream than navigating a river. For those who managed to cross at higher water, the network of streams and creeks bordering the town provided pathways away from the river and far beyond it—Eagle Creek, Red Oak Creek, Straight Creek, White Oak Creek, all wide enough for skiffs and even flatboats, depending on the season and the rainfall. The hounds of a slave hunter could not detect the scent of a man escaping by way of water. The streams cut through a complex terrain of hills and dales that could mask the sight of a horse and rider at every undulating curve or hollow. Just as important were the remnants of the Imperial Forest, the dense woods above the town, beyond the hill, and along the creeks—a thicket that, for those who knew it well and did not fear it, gave cover that would foil pursuit.

Also critical to Ripley's appeal as a gateway to freedom were the nearby free black settlements. In 1818, 950 freed slaves from Virginia had settled on twenty-two hundred acres north of town. These men, women, and children had labored for Samuel Gist, a British merchant of exceptional wealth who had died in London a few years before and had stipulated in his will that upon his death the slaves on his vast Virginia plantations would be set free. The proceeds from the sale of his Virginia lands were to be used to buy land in that state for the freed slaves, to build their houses, churches, and schools, and to pay their teachers and ministers. But when his daughters petitioned the Virginia legislature to approve the will, legislators balked at the notion of releasing so many slaves in their state—what would be one of the largest manumissions in the nation's history. No slaveholding Virginian could forget the recent slave rebellions throughout the Western world, sometimes led by bands of free blacks. Some legislators referred to the bloody Haitian revolt in 1791, in which slaves overthrew their white masters. Others spoke of the attempted rebellion of a slave named Gabriel, who enlisted the help of more than one thousand slaves in Virginia in 1800. The legislators cited an 1806 law that required freed slaves to leave Virginia within one year or face re-enslavement. And so the legislators voted to allow the manumission only if the freed slaves moved out of Virginia. Three hundred of the slaves left their homes in Virginia's counties of Hanover, Amherst, Goslin, and Henrico and, under the guidance of Gist's agents, resettled in Brown County, Ohio, in two communities. The remaining fifty came separately, stopping several places on the way and arriving more than a year later.

For slaves south of the river, the Gist settlements were Mecca. Escaping slaves naturally sought out free black communities as hideouts from slave hunters and masters. As the largest free black encampments in the region, the Gist communities increased the runaway traffic through Ripley, the main river town in Brown County. They also intensified the friction between Ripley and nearby towns, where abolitionists were often despised and Gist settlers treated like an Old Testament pestilence. For, despite the antislavery sentiment in and around Ripley, the region, so close to the border of a slave state, was filled with indifference and sympathy for Southern slaveholding. In the summer of 1819, in a Southern Ohio newspaper, an unnamed citizen who called the settlements "camps" wrote to the editor: "Much as we commiserate the situation of those who, when emancipated, are obliged to leave their country or agin be enslaved, we trust our constitution and laws are not so defective as to suffer us to be overrun by such a wretched population. Ohio will suffer seriously from the iniquitous policy pursued by the States of Virginia and Kentucky in driving all their free Negroes upon us."

A year after the arrival of the Gist slaves, the Missouri Territory sought admission to the Union as a slave state—an issue that at first seemed unimportant to Ripley. If Missouri entered as a slave state, slaveholding interests in the U.S. Senate would have a voting margin over the free states. This would also facilitate the expansion of slavery into the rest of the unorganized lands of the Louisiana Purchase. The ensuing debate was so bitter as to threaten the life of the Union. Elihu Embree, a Quaker abolitionist from Tennessee, wrote, "Hell is about to enlarge her borders and tyranny her domain."

A compromise was fashioned and, to balance the slavery scale, Maine entered the Union as a free state. Under the Missouri Compromise, as it was known, slavery would be permitted south of latitude 36 degrees 30 minutes, and prohibited north of that line. Dissolution and war were averted, for the time, but the compromise sectionalized the nation as never before. John Quincy Adams presently called the compromise "the title page of a great, tragic volume." Newspapers in slaveholding states burst with commentaries ardently defending the institution of slavery. They saw the compromise, which prohibited slavery in a vast portion of the Louisiana Purchase, as a device to minimize the number of slaveholding states. And they claimed that "deluded madmen" were plotting to destroy their world. Abolitionists in slave states lost much of their support and migrated to free states, where antislavery sentiment was building. At the same time, antislavery forces saw the compromise as an indication that slaveholders in Congress—what they called the "slave power"—were shaping national policy and would be the architects of Western expansion. After numerous complaints about slave catchers roaming the banks of the river, Ohio legislators passed a law to punish the mercenaries who invaded the state to hunt down free blacks in order to collect slave owners' rewards for their recapture or to sell them downriver. In response, Kentucky legislators, in violation of the Constitution, passed a law bolstering the rights of slave owners to enter free states and reclaim their "property."

Along the river, tensions were rising and suspicions growing. The kindling of controversy was piled high. Ripley's role in this borderland war was becoming ever clearer. A single spark might unite Ripley in the cause of ending slavery and resisting the slave power. It came in the form of a Presbyterian minister named John Rankin.

As news of the Missouri Compromise reached Carlisle, Kentucky, where Rankin lived, and nearby Concord, where he preached, Rankin felt the pulse of his community quicken. He sensed the anger in the hearts of slave owners and the frustration among antislavery advocates when he stood at the pulpit seeking to prove that slavery was as great a crime against the laws of God as murder, and arguing that every slaveholder must free his slaves to adhere to the teachings of the Scriptures. At the same time, an economic downturn known as the Panic of 1819 was devastating the farmers and merchants of his community in north-central Kentucky. The majority of his antislavery congregation was moving northward, and those who remained could not afford to pay Rankin's $550 annual salary. The Kentucky Abolition Society, which he had helped to expand, was dwindling. And the newspaper that he zealously promoted, *Abolition Intelligencer and Missionary Magazine*, was failing.

Rankin could have endured the economic hardship, as he would at other junctures in his life. But what had inspired him to work in a slave state was the hope that his antislavery activism—his speaking, writing, and teaching against the evils of slavery—would help to transform Kentucky into a free state. The anger and fear that grew out of the Missouri Compromise intensified the opposition to his work and nearly extinguished his local support. Unable to provide for his family or to persuade slaveholders to free their slaves, he knew he must leave.

In December 1821, twenty-eight-year-old Rankin, with $50 in his pocket and his wife, three sons, and one daughter at his side, set out for the land beyond the river. Late on the eve of a new year, they arrived at the banks of the Ohio, only to find the river running with ice floes. The flatboat they had arranged to use was too large for the crossing. Only small skiffs could dodge the floes and find a path through the ice. They must depart at once before the ice coalesced. Leaving their horses and possessions with a friend until spring, they piled into two skiffs. "I can remember that crossing and how frightened we were when we were struck by a large field of ice which nearly upset our boats," Rankin's oldest son, Adam Lowry, wrote years later.

Early in the morning of January 1, 1822, they pulled their skiffs onto the banks at Ripley, and the kindling got its spark.

CHAPTER TWO

VISIONS AND IDEALS

In the unbroken wilderness of East Tennessee in 1793, in a log cabin at the headwaters of Assumption Creek, a midwife delivered the fourth son of Jane and Richard Rankin. The parents named the baby John, and they planned a simple life for him. But John was a boy who would know early what he believed and what he lived for. His life would never be simple.

John Rankin was born early in the evening of February 4, but on abolition's clock it was closer to daybreak. The sun was slowly rising on a new generation of crusaders who would exalt the laws of conscience and God over those of government and man. Their fathers had fought in the Revolution, and now they would seek to end the great hypocrisy that came out of it: the lie and the abomination that were slavery. They would do what most true believers only dream of doing. They would change the world into which they had been born.

In 1793, it was seven years before the births of both Nat Turner and John Brown; twelve years before the birth of William Lloyd Garrison; and George Washington had just begun his second term as president of the United States. In the week after Rankin's birth, the Second Congress of the new nation passed what would be known as the Fugitive Slave Act of 1793—a law Rankin would spend much of his life breaking. One reason for the new law was to carry out Article IV, Section 2, of the Constitution, which said that anyone held to service or labor in one state under the laws of that state escaping to another cannot be discharged from that service, but instead can be claimed by the person to whom the labor is due and returned to servitude. Despite its explosive potential, this clause of the Constitution generated no opposition whatsoever—unlike the articles regarding the slave trade, the regulation of commerce, and the taxation of exports. This so-called fugitive-slave clause was adopted unanimously. Either the framers were too exhausted for yet another strenuous debate, or the northern delegates may not have foreseen the dangers that could result from such a clause.

A challenge came quickly. Four years later, the governors of Virginia and Pennsylvania were enmeshed in a battle over the rights of three Virginians who abducted a black man, John Davis, from his new home in the free state of Pennsylvania to return him to servitude. President Washington was urged to clarify Article IV, Section 2. Thus came the law of 1793, which said effectively that slave owners and their agents—soon to be as familiar a sight on the northern banks of the Ohio as debris in the river after a storm—had the legal right to "seize or arrest" their slaves in free states, without a warrant and without the presence of a civil official. All that a slaveholder needed to do was to take the captured slave to a nearby circuit-court judge or the magistrate of a county, city, or town in which the seizure or arrest was made, and prove to the satisfaction of the judge, by either oral testimony or affidavit, that the slave belonged to the slaveholder. The black man or woman had no right to testify on his or her own behalf, and the word of the white man was automatically accepted. Worse still, the new law warned that obstructing a slave catcher in the act of apprehending a fugitive, no matter how violent and savage that act might be, and harboring or concealing a fugitive on the path to freedom, no matter how humane and justified that helping hand might be, were now illegal acts. The penalty could be as much as a $500 fine and a prison sentence of one year.

The Senate approved it without a single dissenting vote on January 18. The House passed it, forty-eight to seven, with so little discussion that no report was ever officially recorded. President Washington signed it on February 12, exactly sixteen years before the birth of Abraham Lincoln. Perhaps the Union was so new that a veil of naïveté prevented legislators from seeing the truth: that the flight to freedom would not stop, and that the intended interstate harmony would end the moment the South began to see its human property disappearing.

And so, with the passage of the law, the territories and states declared free under the Northwest Ordinance—Ohio, Indiana, Illinois, Michigan, Wisconsin—could never be true sanctuaries for escaping slaves. Only beyond international borders, in Mexico and Canada, where the law did not reach, could a runaway be assured of freedom from the fear of slave catchers and other mercenaries who profited handsomely by returning runaway slaves to their owners, or by selling them for even more money to slave traders who took them downriver into the Deep South. It was in that same year of 1793 that Eli Whitney patented his cotton gin, which soon would cause the demand for slaves to explode in the cotton-growing Southern states. As more slaves took flight, pathways between the South and foreign borders emerged, and those people sympathetic to the plight of slaves, those who ardently opposed slavery, those who stood on the high ground of the laws of conscience, assisted their escape when necessary, despite the laws. Ironically, the law that was intended to discourage the flight of slaves encouraged loosely organized networks of blacks and whites to guide runaway slaves to places of safety and freedom.

By 1793, thousands of white refugees from the slave revolt in Haiti had fled to the American South, often bringing their slaves, who eagerly told the story of black liberty unfolding on an island to the south. They talked about the mass meetings in forests during the days leading up to the first bloody moments of revolt. They described walls of fire under blackened skies as plantations burned, and they told of scenes of human carnage as slaves avenged two centuries of degradation and abuse. They spoke of the freedom and power they had learned from their leaders, whose words still rang in their ears with the clarity of church bells. They recalled the prayers of their leaders during the night that the terror began: "Throw away the symbol of the god of the whites who has so often caused us to weep, and listen to the voice of liberty, which speaks in the hearts of us all."

What happened in Haiti destroyed the image of harmony and peace that the slaveholders and their sympathizers wanted the nation to believe. Rebellion was sweeping across the South, and fear and paranoia were more prominent than ever before. "They write from Charleston (S.C.) that the NEGROES have become very insolent, in so much that the citizens are alarmed, and the militia keep a constant guard. It is said that the St. Domingo [Haitian] negroes have sown these seeds of revolt," reported *The New York Journal & Patriotic Register.*

For slaves, the message billowing in the smoke over Haiti was that victory over their oppressors was possible. For slaveholders, "What if?" had suddenly become "When?" Their response was to tighten restraints, to raise the walls of confinement higher, to argue for laws to protect their human property, and eventually to blame antislavery crusaders for fomenting revolt. But to block the flow of subversive ideas into the quarters of their slaves, to censure the Haitian slaves whose eyes now reflected the stars of liberty, or to destroy the dream of freedom was an impossible feat, one that no measure of beatings, whippings, or legal undertakings could ever accomplish.

The uprising in Haiti, the Fugitive Slave Act, and Whitney's new cotton gin seemed far away from the secluded cabin where Rankin was born. But the question of liberty and who was entitled to it would run through the lives of the generation coming of age in the early nineteenth century like a swollen river threatening to flood after each new rain.

Of the Southern states and territories in 1793, Tennessee had the smallest slave population, with roughly 3,500 slaves, compared with about 293,000 in Virginia and about 107,000 in South Carolina. Tennessee was more akin to Northern states such as Pennsylvania, which had about 3,700 slaves that year, or Connecticut, with about 2,700. And of all the regions in the state, East Tennessee held the fewest slaves of all—though one was too many for Rankin's parents.

East Tennessee lay between the valleys of the Cumberland and Tennessee rivers. It was largely unsuited for sprawling plantations of cotton—unlike the western portion of the state, which spawned a plantation economy. The Cumberland Plateau, an area of thin, sandy, unfertile land, formed its western boundary, and on the eastern side, in the Unaka region, the soil was equally rugged and unproductive, though interspersed with tillable patches. Barely half of the acreage of East Tennessee was arable land, largely in the river valleys, where buckwheat, corn, rye, and potatoes could grow, amid small fields of cotton. There were no cash crops. The uncertain terrain of the remainder of the region was used for grazing horses, sheep, mules, hogs, and cattle, or for mining coal, iron ore, zinc, and other minerals.

In the 1790s, antislavery advocates were not uncommon in East Tennessee. In 1797, the *Knoxville Gazette* ran a letter calling for "public spirited citizens" to join in the "gradual abolition of slavery of every kind." On February 25, 1815, Quaker citizens of Jefferson County gathered at the Lost Creek Meeting House to form the Tennessee Manumission Society. Its constitution called for each member to display in his home a sign reading: "Freedom is the natural right of all men; I therefore acknowledge myself a member of the Tennessee Society for Promoting the Manumission of Slaves." And the nation's first periodical to focus exclusively on the cause of ending slavery, the Quaker Elihu Embree's *Manumission Intelligencer,* later renamed *The Emancipator,* came out of that early stronghold of abolitionists in 1819. After Embree's death, another Quaker and early architect of the antislavery cause, Benjamin Lundy, came to East Tennessee to promote abolition and to publish his own paper, *Genius of Universal Emancipation.*

By 1793, John Rankin's father, Richard, owned a thousand acres roughly seven miles northeast of Dandridge, in Jefferson County. Eight years before, Richard Rankin and his wife, Jane Steele, had migrated from Augusta County, Virginia, her home and his place of apprenticeship in the blacksmith trade—also the county from which Ripley's founder, James Poage, emigrated. In Tennessee, Richard and Jane joined his five brothers and his father, Thomas, all of whom had come from Pennsylvania after the Revolutionary War. Richard and Jane Rankin would raise eleven sons and one daughter in Tennessee. Jane would outlive five of their sons.

The families of both Richard and Jane Steele Rankin had originated in Scotland. In 1727, Richard's grandfather John Rankin, a Calvinist, moved his family to the New World. There, in Carlisle, Cumberland County, Pennsylvania, on 150 acres on the south side of Yellow Britches Creek, he brought up his God-fearing, Scottish Presbyterian brood of two boys and eight girls. He died in 1749. Thomas, one of his sons, farmed the family's fertile Pennsylvania plot and brought up six daughters and six sons, one of whom was Richard Rankin. After the War for Independence, Thomas sold the farm to the government for what he likely did not know was worthless Continental money. The story handed down through generations was that Thomas Rankin never regretted the act of "giving" his land to the fledgling new Union.

Penniless after the sale, Thomas Rankin was forced to move his family to the frontier, to Tennessee, where land was cheap and bountiful. A year or so later, Richard, now nineteen, moved to Augusta County, Virginia, to work for Samuel Steele, whose daughter he married. The young couple moved back to Tennessee in 1786.

Richard's parcel in Tennessee was effectively a thousand-acre forest, for which he paid pennies per acre. Along a clear, cool creek, branching out from a tributary of the Tennessee River, he built a log cabin with a clay chimney and erected a blacksmith shop. But smithing was hardly a livelihood in a land where the few inhabitants had little if any money and no possessions of worth to barter. Worse still, commerce was nearly impossible because any goods produced or purchased had to be transported hundreds of miles in a wagon to reach a market.

An earnest, meditative, quiet man, Richard was fueled by the simple yet passionate hope that his children would survive the frontier and live to bear their own children. He was a keen reader of books, mostly theological, but he rarely discussed his ideas. Jane's dream exceeded her husband's, as did her habits of speech. She wanted her children to explore the vast frontier of their souls. She read to them as often as a mother of so many children could, and she openly expressed her views on every subject of humanity. She opposed drinking, dancing, smoking, and slavery. A native of one slave state and a resident for all of her life of another, she understood slavery's depravity and protested its evils. If asked, her husband acknowledged that he was an opponent of slavery, but he did not volunteer the sentiment. Jane, on the other hand, persistently pressed her antislavery beliefs upon her children, her neighbors, and her fellow church members. Only one of her children would ever own slaves, and he, at the insistence of his brother John, would eventually free them. "My mother was a woman of strong mental capacity, well able to give a reason for the hope that was within her," John Rankin said after her death, "a woman of remarkable intellectual culture for one brought up on the frontier [and whose] whole life was that of a pioneer."

For young John Rankin, it was a stark and rugged life branded with the stern imprint of Calvinism: thrift, hard work, austerity, control. Still, he was blessed with parents who believed in education and taught him to read as soon as he could understand enough words to listen. It was a time on the frontier when some settlers opposed the concept of education. Learning, they argued, bred a mentality of rogues. Some local preachers even believed that reading would block a spiritual calling inspired by the Gospel. Rankin was home-taught during most of his youth, aided by his parents' exceptional library. Dilworth's spelling book, the Bible, and works of Scottish theologians were the springboards for a lifetime of writing, lecturing, debating, and agitating. The school he attended during the winters of his early years was nearly three miles away, in a room with dirt floors, no windows, and three log walls. The fourth was a stone wall, against which a heap of wood was piled each morning and set ablaze, stoked by the schoolmaster as often as needed. There Rankin learned what were considered rudiments, one at a time: more of Dilworth's, then the New Testament and the Old Testament. When those were mastered, there were lessons in history and arithmetic. Rankin would later recall the hard slabs of timber on which he sat, the master with his long hickory switch, which he cracked freely across the hands of any idle child, and the long walk from home along a narrow rock-strewn path over high craggy hills. Each week, too, weather permitting, the Rankins walked seven miles to attend the Presbyterian church in Dandridge. There they sat on backless slabs of pine in a room with no fire to warm them for two one-hour sermons with an hour break between. One dreary winter day, John's father admitted to his children that in that church "no power of eloquence could warm up the heavens."

Cold. Bleak. Sullen. Severe. A lullaby of struggle. That was the life into which John Rankin was born. And then came the summer of 1800. By then Rankin, at age seven, was immersed in the routines of frontier life: a rigorous mix of learning how to read, write, and study, and how to hoe. When his father left for weeks with local men to fight Indians, he stayed home from school and worked in the cleared portions of the land, where small fields of corn and cotton grew. At night, he sat by the warmth of burning pine knots, studied the Bible, and contemplated what it might mean.

In Rankin's eighth summer, the religious revival known as the Second Great Awakening, which had begun in New England in the late 1790s, was moving westward to Kentucky and Tennessee. How startling it must have been for a boy accustomed to orderly days of religious restraint suddenly to witness the screaming and shouting of the fervent crowds. At tent meetings in forest clearings, spellbinding preachers unleashed the pent-up passions of masses of people who swayed and jerked like tree limbs in a strong, erratic wind. At night, the glare of hundreds of candles and torches cast long, distorted shadows across the assemblage of heads bowing, hands waving, and bodies shaking. The night wind carried the high-pitched shrieks, sobs, and chants for many miles as children, long tucked away in their beds, lay awake, the excitement wafting through their small, barren rooms and their hungry minds.

Richard Rankin took his family to camp meetings in the forests near Dandridge. "A wonderful nervous affection pervaded the meetings," John Rankin later wrote. "Some would tremble as if terribly frightened; some would have violent twitching and jerking; others would fall down suddenly as if breathless and lie there for hours. Some would laugh with a loud ha!! ha!!, others would form a ring and dance round awhile, then fall back on those who stood round to take care of them. There were some who would bark like dogs. Young as I was, my mind was much exercised on the subject of religion. My body too was agitated to some extent."

That same summer of agitation ended with the largest slave conspiracy in American history, in Virginia. As Rankin and his generation inherited the vision and ideals of the Revolution, those same ideals reverberated for another struggling group: the one-sixth held in bondage, the enslaved Africans. Throughout the summer and the previous spring, the slave named Gabriel had been hatching a plot to free the slaves of Virginia. Inspired by both the American Revolution and the more recent revolt in Haiti, Gabriel Prosser, a highly skilled blacksmith, recruited roughly a thousand slaves from ten Virginia counties to the cause. Liberty. Equality. Fraternity. Why were these the rights of white men and not of blacks? The rebels planned a long march on Richmond at midnight on August 30. Marchers intended to carry flags bearing the Haitian battle cry: "Death or Liberty." They were instructed to spare Quakers, Methodists, Frenchmen, and poor white women from the vengeance in their hearts. The goal was to rouse the fears of the white establishment enough to scare them into believing they could save their own lives only by freeing Virginia's massive slave population. But, of all things, the weather betrayed them. Torrents of rain washed out bridges over rivers and creeks that Gabriel's army needed to cross to begin their siege. The weight of water crushed their dream. Two slaves scared by the spiritual implications of the storm revealed the plot to authorities.

By early autumn, news of the failed rebellion and the executions of Gabriel and twenty-seven of his men was trumpeted throughout the South. Rankin's mother, an ardent yet nonviolent antislavery advocate, saw tragedy in the tale and blamed the evil of slavery. Gabriel's conspiracy was the logical consequence of holding down a race of people, and nothing in the Bible condoned such oppression. At the trial, in October, one of Gabriel's allies testified, "I have nothing more to offer than what General Washington would have had to offer, had he been taken by the British and put to trial by them. I have adventured my life in endeavoring to obtain the liberty of my countrymen, and am a willing sacrifice in their cause. . . ."

For Rankin, the events of his eighth year resonated deeply. In his memory, the story of a man losing his life in pursuit of freedom would always blend together with the many nights of divine manifestation in the woodlands of East Tennessee. There would come a time when enough years had passed that Rankin could look back and know that the passions of the summer of 1800 had inspired his own private awakening.

Revivals in Tennessee and Kentucky continued throughout the warm months of 1802 and 1803. When they ended, Rankin slipped into what he later called "a season of coldness. A state of darkness and doubt." It was a time of self-examination and questioning. What he had heard in the preaching and the exhortations were the requirements for becoming truly pious and the demands of faith and of perfection emanating from the Scriptures. He knew that he wanted to follow the Biblical teachings but felt inadequate and unfit. Moody and withdrawn, he told no one of his despair. Instead, he read and reread parts of the Bible, replayed the words he had heard about death, judgment, and eternity, and rehearsed his own interpretations of them. He struggled with the concept of eternal life and with God's gift of salvation. He was troubled by the book of Romans, in which the apostle Paul explains that grace and salvation do not have to be earned and that, in the fulfillment of God's purpose, even those who commit hostile or evil deeds will be brought into harmony with God for eternity. Good works, according to Paul, do not set a man apart. Worse still for Rankin, Paul instructs slaves and masters to accept their roles in life. For years, Rankin was unable even to read Romans—it so challenged his mission to justify his work as an activist with the teachings of God.

Into his teenage years, Rankin studied hard and spent long hours walking through woods and fields, speaking where no one could hear him about his understanding of the Gospel, practicing for a lifetime of oratory. It was then that he committed to memory long passages from the Bible, which would dazzle his audiences in future years. And it was then, at an age when other boys were climbing trees and rigging slingshots, that Rankin made his decision to devote his life to preaching the Gospel and to ridding the world of those things that contradicted the teachings of the Scriptures—such as slavery.

From pulpits in Tennessee, Kentucky, and Ohio, Rankin would one day recite with great excitation the passages from Exodus—"He that stealeth a man and selleth him, or if he be found in his hand, he shall surely be put to death"—and from Deuteronomy—"Thou shalt not deliver unto his master the servant which is escaped from his master unto thee. He shall dwell with thee, even among you, in that place which he shall choose in one of thy gates, where it liketh him best: thou shalt not oppress him."

"Death! Certain Death is the penalty which the Almighty has attached to the crime of depriving an innocent person of his liberty," he would tell his audiences. "And this awful penalty was annexed to the crime of enslaving the innocent at a period of the world when the ignorance of the rights of man tended much to mitigate the guilt of slavery. The criminality of slavery continually increases with the progress of knowledge."

CHAPTER THREE

ON THE WINGS OF HIS WORDS

In the hours before dawn on December 16, 1811, the people who lived in the valleys of the Mississippi and Ohio rivers and their tributaries, including the Tennessee and Cumberland rivers, felt a terrible trembling beneath them that no amount of praying could stop. Some were awakened by a sound like a thousand wagons rolling down the side of a mountain. In Knoxville, Tennessee, "There was a rumbling noise like the roaring of distant thunder or a storm rattling like the rolling of a heavy body over the floor of an adjacent room," one newspaper reported. In Cincinnati, there was a loud noise, first like the clashing together of rocks and then like the roaring of a furnace or the passing of a tornado.

In the long first seconds of the tumult, those who had lived through the Revolution thought it was the sound of soldiers marching onto their land; others were certain it was a band of thieves or Indians coming to take their possessions. Many more waited for the sound of trumpets, believing that the end of the world had finally come. They opened their doors and windows and looked with horror as they saw the agitated earth tossing and pitching, for nearly a minute in some places, then quivering in the aftermath like the body of a freshly killed animal. Hills shook. Rocks moved. Chimneys collapsed. The moaning and shrieking of cows and horses and dogs blended with the human cries that emanated from farmhouse to row house. Animals fell headlong into crevices that suddenly burst open. Buildings waved like leaves in a windstorm, some twisting free of their foundations and some simply falling down. Banks along the Ohio River slid into the water. The Mississippi River briefly reversed its course.

This violent movement of the earth, which would recur for at least three more months, was the largest earthquake in North American recorded history. It was centered at New Madrid, Missouri. Unlike most earthquakes, after which the shocks become less intense and less frequent with time, the New Madrid aftershocks grew in severity and frequency with each new strike. In late December and most of January, hundreds of aftershocks were felt throughout Missouri, Kentucky, Tennessee, Ohio, Illinois, Indiana, and as far east as Washington, D.C., and Boston. In Cincinnati, for the first three weeks after the December quake, there was at least one aftershock every day, and then one every other day, until the next big quake struck, on January 23. One man in Tennessee recorded five hundred aftershocks between January 23 and February 7, when the next one hit—the biggest of all, estimated now at 8.8 on the Richter scale. A year later, two more quakes occurred in the region, though far less severe. Aftershocks with diminishing strengths were reported until the winter of 1815.

"For several hours previous to the shock the most tremendous noise was heard from the neighboring mountains," wrote a Knoxville man after the February quake. "At intervals it was quiet but would begin with so much violence that each repetition was believed to be the last groan of expiring nature. I believe so many fervent prayers were never put up in this place as were on that fearful night and morning. I think what has been done may be termed a revival in religion."

Eerie and unnerving, the days and nights of repeated tremors sent people to church to pray for relief, even those who had never before turned to religion to understand their world. In the aftermath of months and then years, during which the earth still trembled now and again, churches were overrun with people who found little satisfaction in the scientific explanations for what they had felt and seen.

John Rankin was living at home, near Dandridge, when the first of the shock waves ripped through the valleys of the Tennessee and Cumberland rivers. "The inhabitants here were aroused by a dreadful sound that gave us all considerable alarm. Some took to prayer," wrote a man who lived a few miles east of Rankin's home. "The late appearance of a splendid comet and the blood-like color of the sun for several days before this had alarmed a great many people. They talked of war and all that was happening as an awful precursor to war and that the same had occurred before the war by which we gained our independence. The more courageous among us ventured to open our doors to discover what occasioned the noise. A sudden trembling of the earth, fresh terror and alarm from which we had not time to recover before we felt a violent shock which lasted about three minutes and was attended by a hollow rumbling noise, and ended with a dreadful crash leaving behind a strong sulphurous stench."

The need for ministers was suddenly as strong as it had been during the revivals earlier in the century, and it would increase in the months ahead, as it would throughout Rankin's lifetime, whatever the crisis or issue of the moment might be. For this was a time when churches and religion represented the ganglia of intellectual thought and social influence, making Rankin's calling one of the era's more powerful professions. During those early months of 1812, as the earth shook beneath him and a crisis rumbled through the countryside around him, Rankin kept a tight focus on his goals, studying hard, knowing that soon he would enroll at Washington College in nearby Jonesboro, a step closer to his ordination.

A few months after the last big quake, four of Rankin's brothers—Thomas, Samuel, David, and William—joined the forces to stop British interference with American trade. This was effectively the nation's second war for independence, the War of 1812. In the autumn of that year, as Rankin, who volunteered but was not called to serve, was taking notes at his first college class, his brothers were training for their first major battles.

Although Rankin's Calvinist training fueled a lifetime of hard work, it was likely the death of his brother David that drove him beyond that simple, diligent life his parents had envisioned to a place on higher ground, where he would risk his life for a cause. It happened on March 29, 1814, during Rankin's second year of college—when his money was running out. David, age twenty-three, was shot in the chest at the Battle of Horseshoe Bend, near the Tallapoosa River in Alabama. He died minutes later. Soon thereafter, Rankin's father told him that the government allowance granted to the family for the death of his brother would pay his college tuition.

Rankin believed in the power of God as the controller of all events, and that God used the free agency of man—such as David's voluntary commitment to the war—to achieve his own purposes. "All events are part of one great plan by which the greatest good will ultimately be accomplished," he wrote of his brother's death. From that day forward, Rankin never doubted that he was meant to devote his life to something far larger than himself—something worthy of his brother's sacrifice.

During the next year, Rankin boarded at the home of the daughter and son-in-law of Samuel Doak, Washington College's founder and president and one of the framers of the Constitution for the state of Franklin, the abortive effort of East Tennessee to gain admission to the Union separately from the rest of Tennessee. Born in Augusta County, Virginia, Doak was a 1775 graduate of the College of New Jersey—later known as Princeton College—and in 1778 became the first minister to settle in the territory that became the state of Tennessee. After three years, he built a log school-house that was the first educational institution in the region of the Mississippi Valley. He modeled his new school on his alma mater, and in his teachings he strongly encouraged students to think for themselves and to rely on their own investigations of the world to form their thoughts and opinions. As pastor of the Salem Presbyterian Church in Jonesboro, he was a member of the Abingdon Presbytery, a network of churches in East Tennessee and in nearby southwestern Virginia whose congregations were largely slaveholders. Doak too owned slaves, though he favored emancipation and taught his students that slavery was indeed evil. He and his fellow ministers did not believe there was a practical solution for ending the peculiar institution that had shaped and now seemed to hold together their world. By contrast, East Tennessee's Union Presbytery, which included the church of Rankin's youth, employed a coterie of antislavery ministers and had few slaveholders in its congregations. During the year that Rankin lived with Doak's son-in-law, the Union Presbytery entered a fierce theological battle with the Abingdon Presbytery regarding the teachings of Dr. Samuel Hopkins, who challenged certain teachings of John Calvin. In the mud-slinging that ensued, the Abingdon group called its Union brethren "Hopkinsites." And in response, for their unbending slaveholding adversaries, the Union pastors called their slaveholding coreligionists "Copperheads," after the venomous snake. It was an epithet that would endure throughout the antebellum years as a term for proslavers. Doak was dubbed "Father of the Copperheads." His son-in-law, Adam Lowry, was, however, an outspoken abolitionist who would not keep a slave. His wife supported his views, and they raised their five daughters and two sons in the belief that slavery must be abolished. Eventually, three of those daughters would marry three of Richard and Jane Rankin's sons—including John. And Lowry, the owner of a sawmill, a gristmill, a woolen mill, and a distillery, would one day persuade Doak to free his slaves.

The indemnity from David Rankin's death was nearly gone by the late autumn of 1815, and Rankin's parents struggled to sell enough corn and to shoe enough horses to carry their son through the last several months of college. They were doubtful that he could finish, and then Rankin surprised them—and everyone else. At Christmas that year, he announced to friends and family that he would marry Jean Lowry on January 2, 1816. In an unusual tone of excitement, he also told them that he would make his own wedding shoes while she was making his wedding coat. "My marriage was a matter of duty and interest as well as affection," he later wrote. "It was a matter of surprise to my friends and acquaintances because I was unaccustomed to associating with young ladies. It did not in the least interfere with my progress in college. Some perhaps thought it unwise in me to marry before I had studied my profession; but time fully justified my wisdom. It enabled me to study, and helped sustain me in the practice of it when completed. A more affectionate and industrious wife could not be found in any place."

Supported now by his wife and her family, Rankin was able to relieve his parents of the burden of his tuition and finish his college education. At the same time, he engaged in a private tutorial, for eighteen months, with his grandfather-in-law, Samuel Doak, whose teachings of fortitude and the independent spirit would have a permanent impact on Rankin. Adam Lowry bought the couple a small house nearby and furnished it. In the autumn of 1816, the first of John and Jean's thirteen children was born, Adam Lowry Rankin. And by spring, John Rankin was a licensed Presbyterian minister. Although ordination opened a career path for John Rankin, his views on perfecting life on earth, which included ending slavery, would throw many obstacles in his path.

From his student days through his ordination, the steadfast, driven Reverend Rankin inspired only skepticism among the churchmen of the Abingdon Presbytery. They qualified his entry into their virtuous realm by writing in his file that he was accepted "with suspicion and distrust because of his frequent expression of opposition to slavery." To be sure, by then he had been working for nearly two years with the Quaker minister Charles Osborne to expand the membership of their newly formed Manumission Society of Tennessee and to spawn antislavery societies in counties throughout East Tennessee—activities that must have tortured the Abingdon "Copperheads," whose allegiance to Doak stopped them from taking action against Rankin.

Rankin spent the early months of his new life as a minister practicing the fine art of oratory, this time not in the woods but, rather, with a real audience. He rotated from church to church, filling vacant pulpits, including the one from his boyhood years in Dandridge, and learning what it takes to preach two and three times a day, often to the same audience. His endless hours of studying the Scripture, from the time he was seven years old, benefited him now. Still, it was a very challenging time for someone as diffident in the pulpit as Rankin: Despite his occasional boldness in face-to-face encounters, he was tormented by his own perception of ineptitude before the public. At times he was so nervous in front of an audience that all moisture in his mouth would dry up, his tongue would stick to the roof of it, and his speech would sound garbled. He needed practice, and more practice. At first he tried the technique of memorizing every word of his sermons, which gave him some confidence, but as he quickly learned, this left little room for expressions of passion, and that in turn seemed to result in an outbreak of heavy eyelids in the congregations. In those early sermons, he never dared to mention the word "slavery," or even to mention the concept of oppression.

It would take him several years to perfect a style of extemporaneous speaking and to leave behind the lonely chill he seemed to carry with him to the pulpit. But it would be only a matter of weeks before he uttered the word "slavery" from the pulpit.

One summer day in 1817, at a church in the Abingdon group, he explained to his audience, with fierce certitude, that the mission of Christianity was to drive oppression from the earth, and that the Bible was opposed to "all forms of oppression." In the days that followed, he was told by the elders that his words were "incendiary." The slaveholders in the congregation feared that slaves might eventually hear such words and then be dangerously aroused. Rankin was told never to preach on the subject of oppression again. A few weeks later, Rankin was invited to speak at a church in the Union Presbytery where he knew there were very few slaveholders, and where antislavery sentiment was on the rise. That day, perhaps for the first time, Rankin, who in the spirit of a true activist had been inspired by the Abingdon rejection, felt the potential power in damning slavery from the pulpit. His piercing eyes looking out from lowered brows across the aisles and pews of the congregation, his broad forehead beaded with sweat, Rankin abandoned his orderly lecture and spoke spontaneously against the evils of oppression. He even used the word "slavery." To raise the curtain on the issue, to drop all pretense, all euphemisms, all subterfuge, to utter the word that would be his divining rod for many years to come, must have been a glorious release. Like an actor whose audience blurs before him as he immerses himself in the essence of his role, Rankin was unaware of the impact of his words, and possibly never doubted for a moment that the congregation was swept into the passion of his beliefs. He was flying on the wings of his own words. But no one else was. Expecting accolades, Rankin was stunned when, afterward, the church elders told him that he should consider leaving the state of Tennessee if he planned to preach against slavery ever again. Even though members of the church agreed with him that the Bible was opposed to slavery, to say it publicly was a radical move, he was told. These things were discussed only in parlors and offices, never from the pulpit. There were roughly sixty thousand slaves in Tennessee by then—up from the thirty-five hundred the year of Rankin's birth—and the white population, those who owned slaves and those who did not condone such ownership, feared that preaching against oppression and crusading for liberty could incite a revolt and thus endanger their lives.

It was clear now that if Rankin were to stay in Tennessee he would have to leave the ministry or suppress his antislavery convictions, which for him would be tantamount to abandoning his Christian faith. He was unwilling to compromise his beliefs. Time and again, his visions of equality would far exceed the understanding of those far more powerful than he, including the leadership of his church. His vision of a world without slavery would eventually force him, in a painful turn, to confront the doctrines of his church and even to endorse violence to end the evil. His path would forever be strewn with obstacles, but his objectives seemed as carefully laid out as the lessons of Scripture.

Within days of the Union Presbytery sermon, Rankin announced to friends and family that he and his wife had decided to move to the free state of Ohio. Through his mother's family back in Virginia, he had heard about a town called Ripley, where some antislavery Virginians had resettled. But his friends urged him not to go. The trip, across mountains and rivers, would be hard, especially for a woman and a baby. Ohio was still a wild, unsettled land, they warned. His father offered him a portion of his thousand acres and begged him to stay. But he had observed his son for twenty-four years, and he, of all people, knew that his son would not yield to the temptations of comfort and security.

Adam Lowry gave the young Rankins a horse, a two-wheeled carriage, and $70. A friend gave them $5 and an umbrella for their roofless carriage. And Rankin's father and mother gave them clothing and quilts, too much for their small carriage to hold. On the morning of their departure, his father did not come to breakfast and could not be found until the moment Rankin was set to leave. With the carriage packed and all the farewells spoken, Rankin, never looking back, steered the horse down the path he had so often walked as a boy. Seconds later, Richard Rankin mounted his horse and appeared alongside the carriage. For miles the father trotted his horse next to the son's carriage, looking straight ahead without saying a word. In a world where distances were long and lives were short, both father and son knew what their farewell meant. "The feelings of that parting moment I never can describe," John Rankin wrote later. "I felt we were to meet no more on this earth."

In the coming years, when escaping slaves sat by Rankin's hearth, he would know something of their pain in leaving their homes and families. He would also know how rugged the physical journey north to a free state could be, though his own was made without baying hounds and angry slaveholders trailing close behind.

It took the Rankins fifteen days to travel from Dandridge, Tennessee, to Lexington, Kentucky—a distance of two hundred miles. The uneven terrain often forced them to walk, with Rankin leading the horse, and his wife carrying their young boy. So precipitous was their path at some points that Rankin had to lash the wheels of the carriage to prevent the vehicle from overwhelming the horse. Once, the carriage tumbled down an abrupt two-foot drop, and the axle broke. With a steep mountain road behind them, Rankin chose to ride ahead in search of a blacksmith, carrying the broken axle and riding bareback for fifteen miles. Jean and the baby waited on the side of the road in the dark until the early hours of the morning, when Rankin finally returned.

In Lexington, they stopped for a few days while Rankin replenished his purse by giving three sermons, one on a Saturday evening and two on Sunday. Then, $20 richer, they headed for Ohio, moving along the winding roads from Lexington to Paris, Kentucky, where again he preached to pick up much-needed cash. In Paris, a Presbyterian minister informed him of a vacant pulpit at the Concord Presbyterian Church near Carlisle, Kentucky, some sixteen miles north of Paris and thirty-five miles from the Ohio River. This was on his way to Ohio, so Rankin agreed to deliver a few sermons. But when the Rankins arrived in Carlisle, their horse collapsed from exhaustion. The church was more than willing to employ him during the month the horse needed to heal. By the end of that month, the elders had invited him to be their permanent pastor. By then it was winter, and Rankin, impressed that there was only one slaveholder in the congregation, accepted the post, but only until the spring.

For decades, the Concord church had been a stronghold of antislavery sentiment in Kentucky, a slave state where the crusade to end slavery had emanated from the Presbyterian, Baptist, and Methodist churches, some of which boldly denied membership to slaveholders. As early as 1807, members of the Concord congregation and those of twelve other churches established the Kentucky Abolition Society—one of the first antislavery societies in the nation. Its constitution, written in 1808, called for an end to slavery, for antislavery sermons and speeches, for the education of black children in the state of Kentucky, and for "justice in favor of such negroes and mulatoes as are held in bondage." Rankin arrived at a moment in Kentucky's history when antislavery sentiment was rising to a peak it would never again reach. Not only was he allowed to expound on the evils of slavery from the pulpit as loudly and ardently as he wished, but he was encouraged by his antislavery colleagues to do just that. He was able to practice his antislavery oratory almost weekly, through either the church or the abolition society. And he found people and places to help him work around the law that prohibited teaching slaves to read. In the spring, the elders again asked him to stay, which he did.

During his four years in Kentucky, Rankin followed his instincts as a budding activist, finding every opportunity to write and speak against the inhumanity and sin of slavery, to challenge the laws and attitudes of a slave state, and to confront slaveholders, individually and in groups, with the immorality of their ways. In his early days in Kentucky, Rankin believed that he and other antislavery crusaders could actually persuade slaveholders to free their slaves. A year or more into the challenge, he began to believe that slaveholders needed the incentive of compensation from the federal government in exchange for freeing their "property." Whatever the remedy, the longer Rankin was in Kentucky, the closer he appeared to move to what would one day, in the 1830s, be called "immediate emancipation." He wrote later that he and his colleagues in the Kentucky Abolition Society promoted the concept that, "if the slave has a right to freedom at all, he has it now."

Rankin's quest drove him to the parlors of Southerners, where he never hesitated to share his views on slavery with some of the wealthiest slaveholders in the region. There he sat, a man of average height, clean-shaven, with keen eyes, a severe, firm jaw, and a kindly disposition, chatting about matters of local interest, and then slowly easing into the topic of slavery, introducing the slaveholders to his vision of the moral landscape of the times.

He even started a school for slaves—the first of several schools he would try to maintain in his lifetime to educate black men, women, and children.

His theory was that if blacks were educated they could be viewed as equals, and that if the prejudice and discrimination that held them down could be eliminated then slavery would lose its spurious justification. If he did not use books or written lessons, he was able to provide some education orally to slaves without breaking the Kentucky law that prohibited him from teaching them to read. And so he and his brother-in-law Samuel Lowry, who had followed Rankin to Carlisle, lectured to the slaves every Sabbath afternoon in a small log schoolhouse. For nearly a year, they were undisturbed. When local groups began to threaten the lives of both teachers and pupils, Rankin moved the school to an empty house that a member of his congregation donated for the cause. This gave them a few months of privacy and peace, until a mob broke through the doors one night and forced the slaves out of the house with clubs. They then moved the sessions to a friend's kitchen, hoping that the home of a local citizen, rather than an empty house, might discourage the mob from attacking. But the mob beat the slaves with clubs and guns as they walked home. After weeks of this, none of Rankin's students, despite their eagerness to learn about the world beyond their servitude, dared to return to his school. Rankin tried to persuade the slaveholders to allow their slaves to continue the lessons and to protect them from the mob. But the slave masters ignored his requests.

By the time Rankin closed his school, the first waves of the Panic of 1819 were surging through the Ohio Valley. And as bank failures and worthless notes hit the region, Rankin had just begun to build a house. "When I made my contract, the country was flooded with money of independent banks, but before a brick was laid those banks all failed, their bills were worthless, and large numbers of the people became bankrupt," he wrote later. "My salary could not be paid, hence I became deeply involved in debt." As soon as his carpenter completed the house, Rankin borrowed money against it. Though the property and house were valued at $2,000, he was only able to borrow $400, which he used to pay down his debts. A year later, after he had decided to leave the state, he still had debts of $1,000, of which he owed the carpenter $743. He ended up giving the property and the house to the carpenter to pay off the debt, and the carpenter gave him a note for $1,257 to be paid in carpentry and brickwork at a location of Rankin's choice within one year's time. The location, the carpenter said, could be no farther north than Ripley, Ohio.

On New Year's Eve in the year 1821, six Rankins—John, his wife, his three sons, and one daughter—with $50 and the carpenter's note, completed the journey that three of them had begun in the autumn of 1817:

the journey to a free state. In the four years it had taken Rankin to reach that land beyond the river, he had become a practiced and passionate orator, a facile writer, a fearless activist, and a well-known name. For slave traders and masters, it was a name synonymous with challenge and trouble; and for slaves, "Rankin" meant hope and liberation. Both slave master and slave would watch Rankin leave. And some, in the years ahead, would follow.

CHAPTER FOUR

RIVER OF ANGUISH

The carpenter from Carlisle rode to Ripley a week before his debt to Rankin was due. Back in Kentucky, Rankin had agreed to board the carpenter and a crew and to supply the raw materials for a house, but by 1823 he hadn't the money for either expense. Nor did he have a lot on which to build. And so he borrowed from a bank, as he had done in Kentucky and would have to do so often in his life—this time, for the purchase of a lot on Ripley's Front Street, for the shingles and planks, and for the workmen's lodgings. The timber for the interior came from beech trees on the outskirts of town. Workers in Ripley made the bricks. Eight months later, a new façade appeared on the banks of the Ohio: a two-story house measuring twenty-five by sixty feet, with one distinguishing characteristic. The house had three front doors.

Rankin and his family moved into the apartment on the north side of the building and leased out the other two. A local doctor moved into the middle unit, and David Ammen, the editor of the local newspaper, *The Castigator,* which would soon play a major role in Rankin's life, moved into the south side.

When the carpenter returned to Kentucky, news of his work in Ohio spread to fields and cabins where slaves lived and toiled, and where the Rankin name was sometimes known. The man who preached that slavery was evil and who believed that educating slaves was good, now lived in a brick house with three front doors somewhere beyond the river in the free state of Ohio. The words carried the tempting scent of freedom, touching the inner, unspoken lives of slaves who listened carefully and sent the news farther north, to slaves already moving toward the river. Some used the knowledge to begin plotting their own escapes.

By then thousands upon thousands of slaves had fled from captivity. These were men, women, and children who had spent their lives as human property of people who spoke to them through the sound of a bullwhip against their bare skin, who separated them from their sons and daughters, their fathers, mothers, and lovers, and who forced them to till the fields and build the structures of a new civilization while denying them the right to know their own children, the dream of ever owning the fields where they toiled, or the hope of ever improving their lives—unless, of course, they escaped. And if they escaped and were recaptured, which many were, they were beaten, tortured, and even killed. Some were "stript naked, stretched and tied across barrels, or large logs and tortured with the keenest lashes during hours and even whole days until their flesh is mangled to the very bones," wrote Rankin. Those who successfully escaped did so with little, if any, knowledge of the world outside their captivity. Slaves escaped over the sides of the vessels that transported them, out of the fields where they labored, and from the pantries and parlors where the myth of the contented slave was spawned.

At the same time, masters fabricated horrors of the life up north, warning their slaves that conditions would be far worse there. The climate was cold and the soil poor, the masters said, and the slaves would freeze to death or die from starvation. Worse still, the slaveholders asserted, white men in the free states would catch them and sell them to traders who would take them to the Deep South, where life was hardest for slaves. Yet, despite the propaganda against the North and the daunting fear of the unknown, by the 1820s, slaves had organized hundreds of revolts and executed thousands of escapes. An inherent will to be free and a desperate longing for something better were proving far more powerful than oppression.

Indeed, while slaves dreamed of freedom, the slavocracy—meaning the slaveholding class—was doing everything in its power to stifle initiative and hope. And, like all humans, slaves slipped into the habits of their surroundings. To flee family and familiarity required courage, a nearly impulsive spirit, or such deep emotional pain and frustration that to risk their lives for freedom seemed the only path left other than the ultimate escape of suicide. In 1822, John Finley Crowe, the editor of the *Abolition Intelligencer and Missionary Magazine,* wrote, "The rigor of oppression has broken the proud spirit of the man and transformed him into the obsequious slave."

Some escapes were planned for years, and runaways who succeeded rarely shared their plans with anyone. Provocation spanned the range of human emotions: anger, fear, pain, love. Many left after the news that their masters had died or were headed toward financial ruin, which meant they would likely be sold—a particular fear for slaves in the northern regions of the South. To be sold "downriver" into the Deep South, where overseers were known to whip their slaves to death to maintain competitive production levels, was tantamount to dying. Some fled when the opportunity presented itself, in a moment when an overseer looked the other way or a master sent a trusted slave across a border into a free state to run an errand. Others escaped out of anger after a brutal lashing or a torturous punishment. Fugitives frequently bore the crisscrossed scars of past whippings on their backs and chests; in some cases, a cat had been pulled by the tail across the back of a slave, leaving the imprint of its claws. Other slaves had had their fingernails ripped off. Some had cropped ears, branded cheeks, or missing eyes. Ever more restrictive rules and laws governing the behavior of slaves provoked some to flee. Sometimes the inducement was the news of successful escapes to places where a person of color could live without shackles and whips. Even when masters treated their slaves with some kindness, these men and women felt a powerful longing to take control over their own lives.

Pete Driscoll, a slave owner along the river in northern Kentucky, a few miles upriver from Ripley, often boasted that his slaves were so content that none would ever flee. "Not even 'Uncle Johnny' [Rankin] whom all niggers like, could persuade my niggers to leave me," he once said. Driscoll did give his slaves ample freedoms. When their work was done, they were allowed to go where they chose, and he often sent them to Ripley to run errands. In Ripley, they developed contacts and began to help slaves from other plantations escape across the river. Then, one day, after learning that Driscoll had been told about their ventures and was being pressured by other slaveholders to send his slaves south to be sold, they too escaped through Ripley. Driscoll pursued them all the way to Sandusky, where with great agitation he watched from a pier as they boarded a schooner and sailed across Lake Erie to freedom.

Rarely did runaway slaves have a plan more elaborate than to find the town they had heard would be safe, the place along the river where a skiff might be hitched, or a house known for sheltering runaways. Those running north sometimes knew to follow the brightest star near the Big Dipper. "The North Star was, in many instances, the only friend that the weary and footsore fugitive found on his pilgrimage to his new home among strangers," one runaway wrote in a letter to an antislavery newspaper. A white sailor who had labored on Southern plantations reputedly taught slaves the song "The Drinking Gourd" to deliver the message of traveling toward freedom by following the North Star, using the drinking gourd, the Big Dipper.

> *Follow the drinking gourd,*
> *Follow the drinking gourd,*
> *For the old man is a-waiting for to carry you to freedom*
> *If you follow the drinking gourd.*
> *The riverbank will make a very good road,*
> *The dead trees show you the way.*
> *Left foot, peg foot, traveling on.*
> *Follow the drinking gourd.*
> *The river ends between two hills.*
> *Follow the drinking gourd.*
> *There's another river on the other side.*
> *Follow the drinking gourd.*
> *Where the great big river meets the little river*
> *Follow the drinking gourd.*
> *The old man is a-waiting for to carry you to freedom*
> *If you follow the drinking gourd.*

"The slaves need no incentives at our hands," wrote abolitionist leader William Lloyd Garrison. "They will find them in their stripes—in their emaciated bodies—in their ceaseless toil—their ignorant minds—in every field, in every valley, on every hilltop and mountain, wherever you and your fathers have fought for liberty—in your speeches, your conversations, your celebrations, your pamphlets, your newspapers—voices in the air, sounds from across the ocean, invitations to resistance, above, below all around them! What more do they need?"

By the 1820s, the Ohio River was transporting ever-increasing numbers of slaves and slave hunters. Since the earliest days of slavery along its southern banks, the river that the French called La Belle Rivière and that some

Native Americans named Ohiopekhanne, meaning "a very white stream," had become the River Jordan to runaways and a symbol of anarchy to the slavocracy. Its shores were a place where slavery's twin cultures of resistance and oppression collided like sheets of ice grinding one against another. And it was a constant reminder of the insidious conflict that many Americans, in their zeal to explore and open the new frontier, chose to ignore. Those who lived on both shores knew the sounds of oppression and resistance, amplified and carried down- and upriver late at night as oars splashed, dogs wailed, and the wings of herons beat loudly, their peace disturbed by the hard, desperate landings of fugitives and slave hunters along the banks.

Long before runaways found their way to Front Street, before Rankin was known among the slaves of Kentucky, even before Poage arrived at Ripley's shores, slaves were braving the currents of the Ohio to join the Indians on the other side. When the Northwest Ordinance banned human servitude in 1787, word spread that north of the river was a place of freedom. Soon more slaves disappeared into the lush, feral hills of the Imperial Forest. And after the war of 1812, slaves who had never heard of Canada listened to the stories of returning soldiers who spoke of former slaves fighting with the Canadian troops. They learned that while they were abating their hunger by seizing morsels of bread or meat thrown to their masters' dogs, their brothers and sisters in Canada were eating the food grown in their own fields.

By the time Rankin arrived in Ripley, enough slaves were escaping northward, especially across the Ohio River, that the loss of slaveholders' property had become an issue in the border counties of Kentucky. Paths to the river's edge were wearing deeper, slaveholders were threatened, and a cottage industry of slave catchers was emerging. Newspapers in northern Kentucky announced county meetings of slaveholders "for the purpose of concerting measures for the better security of their property." In 1820, Kentucky even passed a law that gave slaveholders the right to "remove any slave from any state within the U.S. into this Commonwealth." In the June 22, 1820, edition of *Liberty Hall,* a Cincinnati newspaper, the editor wrote, "Between the slaveholding and non-slaveholding States along the river, there is a moral difference, a kind of instinctive antipathy [that] no political ties of the Union are strong enough totally to eradicate." So agitated were the slaveholders that in 1821 they pressed their politicians to present a resolution to Congress protesting Canada's willingness to accept American slaves and unwillingness to return them. Letters from Kentucky congressmen spoke of "the growing evil under which many of the Citizens of [Kentucky] labour from the countenance and protection which their fugitive slaves receive from the authorities of the government of upper Canada."

Slaves were escaping all along the river in Ohio, Indiana, and Illinois. In Ohio, they came to Cincinnati, New Richmond, Moscow, Manchester, Portsmouth, Ironton, Gallipolis, Point Pleasant, and Marietta, among others. And Ripley, with its network of creeks, its narrow crossing, and its alleys running straight from the river to the hills behind the town—one of which ran right next to Rankin's new house, and another next to Alexander Campbell's home—was fast becoming a favored passage.

But wherever slaves crossed, challenges abounded on the other side. Where to go. How to eat. Whom to trust. "They was all kinds of white folks, just like they is now. . . . Devils and good people walking in the road at the same time, and nobody could tell one from t'other," one former slave wrote. Ohio may have been the land of the free, but it was also a land filled with hateful racial prejudice. The Northwest Ordinance and Ohio's constitution banned slavery, but nothing had outlawed prejudice, which seemed only to intensify with time, and with more escapes. By 1807, the state had passed "Black Laws" that required blacks to post a $500 bond as a condition of residence to guarantee good behavior. These laws also prohibited blacks from testifying against white men in court, among other restrictions. Although so many of Ohio's early settlers from the South brought their intolerance, if not hatred, for slavery, many more staunchly defended it and sought to discourage blacks from entering the state. Just as abolitionists could be found in northern Kentucky, slave hunters and "nigger" haters were also common in Ohio's southernmost counties. Some even covertly kept slaves until they were exposed and forced by Ohio laws to free them. Others were indifferent to the cause and unwilling to risk their reputations and the legal penalties to help a runaway or to be associated with people like Rankin, who allowed runaway slaves to sleep in his house and share food with his children.

In the early days of Ripley, before the Underground Railroad developed, there were a few people Rankin knew he could trust. Thomas McCague moved to Ripley in 1820 from nearby Adams County to start his pork-packing business. A few doors down on Front Street, the Collins family had been hiding runaways in the corn shocks behind their house since around 1815. Upriver on Front Street was Dr. Campbell. Five miles into the hills behind Ripley, Reverend Gilliland, who had been preaching against slavery at the Red Oak Presbyterian Church since his arrival there in November 1806, was, like Rankin, always on call to assist runaways. And there were the men of the nearby free black settlements: among them, John Hudson and Moses Cumberland. But it would be several years before the Ripley line would be strong enough to pose a threat to the border counties south of the river—a threat great enough to provoke revenge. In the 1820s, John B. Mahan, who would settle north of Ripley, in Sardinia, was teaching in Bethel, in adjacent Clermont County. Jesse Lockhart, who would eventually work out of Russellville, Ohio, was not to leave his hometown in East Tennessee for six more years. Dr. Isaac Beck was studying medicine in Clermont County. Martha Lucas, who would one day be known for hiding runaways in the attic of her Russellville row house, was a toddler in the 1820s. John Parker had not yet been born. And Rankin's oldest son, Adam Lowry Rankin, who would someday take more than three hundred slaves to Canada, had been only seven years old when the family moved into the house with the three front doors.

CHAPTER FIVE

"My Dear Brother"

In the early 1820s, Ripley had not yet become the "abolitionist hellhole" Kentuckians would one day call it. A young, wild river town, it was simply a hellhole. Shootouts and fistfights were as common on the streets of Ripley as muddy wagon wheels on rainy days. There were more saloons than any other businesses. Jeering the new pastor in town was a local sport. And the crusade to end slavery was about as far from the hearts and minds of the majority of Ripley's 421 residents as the Greek campaign against the Ottoman Empire halfway around the world. Rankin's irksome stands against idleness, drinking, and slavery had inspired mostly enemies passionately devoted to his defeat.

During his first weeks in Ripley, when Rankin stayed at the home of Colonel Poage's son, drunken hecklers followed him each day as he left to walk into town or to his church. When he moved to a small log house on Second Street, anti-Rankin protesters gathered outside his windows, howling and beating on tin pans as the family prayed together before dinner. And when he broke ground for his new house on Front Street, showing the town his utter determination to stay, men rushed out of bars to shout obscenities as Rankin and his workmen carried boards and other materials through town to the construction site. "It seemed to be a question of endurance as to who should hold out the longest, father or the rabble," Adam Lowry Rankin later wrote.

Rankin, as if in training for his later challenges of confronting antiabolitionist mobs, faced the protests and moved forward. At one point he wrote his resignation from the Ripley church, but Jean Rankin persuaded him not to deliver it. Something good would eventually come from his work in Ripley, his wife believed. He might be able to make a difference. On August 17, 1824, the local newspaper, *The Castigator,* ran the first of a series of twenty-one letters from Rankin to his brother. The subject was slavery. It was the beginning of something that would indeed make a difference.

A few months after moving to the new house on Front Street, Rankin had received a letter from his brother Thomas, a merchant in Augusta County, Virginia. Unlike his other siblings, Thomas had acquired substantial wealth. In the letter, dated December 2, 1823—and received in early 1824—he announced to his brother that he had used some of his wealth to purchase slaves. Rankin was stunned that any of his brothers could ignore the teachings of their antislavery parents and be swept into the torrent of denial over slavery. For months, he was troubled over how to respond.

By 1823, the unraveling of the Union had already begun, though few people realized it. The Missouri Compromise in 1820, the growing numbers of slaves escaping north, and slave uprisings such as the Denmark Vesey slave conspiracy in 1822 were gradually dissolving the Union. In the aftermath of revolts, the slavocracy, like a threatened animal, became ever more protective and fierce. Slaveholders called for stricter laws and tightened controls over their slaves. Some killed rebellious slaves as if they were dogs gone mad. Slave owners sought safety in increased oppression—unable or unwilling to see that it was the oppression that had caused the resistance, rebellions, and escapes. Vesey's revolt, in which he plotted to free every slave in Charleston, South Carolina, as well as to massacre the white population, seize the harbor, and sail to the West Indies, if necessary, was especially frightening to slaveholders because of its scope and because Vesey was a free and educated black man. He knew several languages, was well read—especially in the Bible—and was highly respected among slaves and free blacks. His co-conspirators were artisans, for the most part, and slaves of high standing in the homes where they labored. Two of them worked for the South Carolina governor—an unnerving fact for those who clung to the illusion that the humans they enslaved were contented. In retaliation, 131 men and women were arrested, thirty-two were exiled, thirty-five were executed, twenty-six were acquitted, and thirty-eight discharged, though whipped mercilessly before their release. Twenty-two of Vesey's followers were hanged simultaneously from a platform that was not high enough to cause their necks to snap. Instead, they were suspended for hours between life and death as they suffocated from a slowly tightening noose. Eventually, a guard rode by and shot each of them in the head. "It is difficult to imagine what infatuation could have prompted you to attempt an enterprise so wild and visionary," the judge told Vesey at his trial.

Southern editorials called the executions "awful but necessary"; decried a system that had grown too lenient on slaves, especially house servants; and assailed the "general spirit of insubordination among our slaves and free Negroes—springing from the relaxation of discipline on the part of whites." One editorial, defending Northern criticism for the horrific hangings, reminded the public that in 1741 a New York court had burned, hanged, or exiled 120 slaves charged with conspiring to burn down the city. One writer in a Washington, D.C., publication called African Americans a "pampered race" and said that "if they meditate murder when thus indulged they must suffer for it." Just one "educated slave or colored freeman," said South Carolina legislator Whitemarsh Seabrook in 1825, was "capable of infusing the poison of insubordination into a whole body of the black population."

A flurry of pamphlets, published locally and reprinted in some cases for a national audience, debated the reasons for the terrifying conspiracy that came within a day of occurring. Some blamed the fact that these slaves were not only indulged by their owners but also "overeducated" and that they had therefore been more susceptible perhaps than others to the dangerous teachings of abolitionists. One blamed the event on "the fruits of abolitionists," who were "the worst enemy of man and destitute of every Christian principle." The diplomat Thomas Pinckney wrote in his pamphlet *Reflections Occasioned by the Late Disturbances in Charleston* that the "indiscreet zeal in favor of universal liberty, expressed by many of our fellow-citizens in the States north and east of Maryland," was "the most obvious cause" of the Vesey plot. William Desaussure, a South Carolina politician who was at one point the director of the U.S. Mint, referred to abolitionists as "bitter enemies" in his pamphlet *A Series of Numbers Addressed to the Public, on the Subject of the Slaves and Free People of Color.*

At a time when the walls protecting slavery seemed higher than ever, and when abolitionists were pushed right up against them, Rankin went on the offensive to help build the movement against slavery. He made the decision to use his response to his brother as an opportunity to reach a larger audience by writing a series of letters in which he explained why slavery was evil and destructive to the nation. For several months in 1824, the letters appeared in *The Castigator,* which was edited and published by his neighbor and tenant on Front Street, David Ammen.

Though he could not condone Vesey's violence, Rankin could understand Vesey's "infatuation." How was it possible not to understand the passion that "prompted" someone to seek freedom or to help others to attain it? In his years in Kentucky and thus far in Ripley, Rankin had witnessed horrible strife and pain because of the slavocracy. "Some of the keenest sensations of mental anguish I ever felt were occasioned by contemplating the cruelties inflicted upon slaves," he later wrote. Once, in Rankin's early Front Street years in Ripley, a former slave returned from Canada to retrieve his wife and two children and had to travel more than a hundred miles into Kentucky to reach them, which he did. But he was so closely followed in his flight to the river that he lost one child to his pursuers. When he arrived in Ripley, a free black man hid the family of three in the woods not far from town. While he sought assistance to take the family farther on their trip to Canada, a slave catcher found them, persuaded them that he was their friend, and then slapped their wrists with irons. The father was torn once again from his wife and child and sold back into slavery.

In another case that startled Rankin during those years, a slave who worked at the ferry across from Ripley on the Kentucky side, and who was known to Rankin and others in Ripley, had been told by his slave master that he would be sold unless he could buy his own freedom. The price was $500. He had saved a good portion of it, but the due date was drawing near and he needed more. And so he called upon his master's nephew who lived in Ripley, asking him to intercede for him and loan him the rest of the money. The nephew called upon Rankin and a few others in town who were sympathetic to the cause and knew the slave from their many trips on the ferry. Rankin himself contributed $25. The master was well aware of the campaign in Ripley to buy his slave. Then a strange thing happened. One day, just as the sun was setting upon the river, four men appeared at the slave's cabin, seized him, tied his arms at the elbow, and even shackled his wrists and ankles. "Oh I could bear it if it were not for my wife and children," he said to his captors. The slave master was able to get a better deal: $700 for his slave. And so he sold him to the Far South. The poor man was not even allowed to see his family one more time to bid them farewell. Rankin believed that slavery bred such betrayal as the master had exhibited.

Rankin's responses to his brother's letter allowed him to express his despair over slavery as he had witnessed it during his years in the South and thus far in Ripley. This was his chance, away from the constraints of the pulpit, to unleash his passions against the house of bondage that he hoped to bring down.

The first of the letters began:

My Dear Brother: I received yours of the 2d December with mingled sensations of pleasure and pain; it gave me pleasure to hear of your health, and pain to hear of your purchasing slaves. I consider involuntary slavery a never failing fountain of the grossest immorality, and one of the deepest sources of human misery; it hangs like the mantle of night over our republic, and shrouds its rising glories. I sincerely pity the man who tinges his hand in the unhallowed thing that is fraught with the tears, and sweat, and groans, and blood of hapless millions of innocent, unoffending people. A brother, who has manifested towards me a kind and generous heart, claims my strongest sympathies—then I see him involved in what is both sinful and dangerous. Shall I not strive to liberate him? Does he wander from the paths of rectitude, and shall not fraternal affection pursue him, and call him from the verge of ruin, and the unperceived precipice of woe, to the fair and pleasant walks of piety and peace? Shall I suffer sin upon my brother? No, his kindness to me forbids it, fraternal love forbids it, and what is still more to be regarded, the law of God forbids it. Though he has wandered for the moment, may I not hope to shew him his error, and restrain his wanderings? Under such views and feelings, I have resolved to address you in a series of letters on the injustice of enslaving the Africans.

For six months, on the second floor of Rankin's house, with seven-year-old Adam Lowry Rankin and Ammen's sons looking on, the young editor beat the ink boxes, inked the forms of his paper, and cranked the Romage press to roll out editions of *The Castigator* featuring Rankin's letters on slavery. Rarely before had the evils of slavery been so thoroughly and brutally dissected. Like all antislavery advocates, Rankin recounted gruesome incidents in which slaves were tormented and hurt. But, like few other writers before him, Rankin also showed how slavery, with or without physical cruelty, was wicked because it deprived the slave of his or her humanity and infected society with a poisonous retinue of wretched habits that would damage the nation for generations into the future.

In one letter, Rankin asked his brother to imagine what it would feel like to watch his own wife and child stripped bare and whipped to the point of near death. "How could you bear to see your daughter's tender skin cruelly torn by the torturing lash of a wicked master whose heart by cruel indulgence has become totally estranged from the feelings of compassion? Would not such a scene shock the whole current of your nature, and turn all the streams of tenderness into the channel of direful revenge, which even the fear of a most terrible death could scarcely restrain? Slavery is often clothed with such scenes of cruelty and blood and often sports with everything that is dear to man!—it breaks the most tender relations of life."

In another, he spoke of "the hand of oppression pressing the Africans down from the rank of men to that of beasts." God did not create Africans for slavery, he wrote, and because the ancestors of slaves were born free, the nation had sinned by enslaving them. Slavery induces immorality and idleness in the slaveholding class, increases the gap between rich and poor, and cultivates a spirit of cruelty and tyranny. At the basis of slavery is racial prejudice, but at the basis of that, he wrote, is the love of gain, which is, he wrote, "the polluted fountain whence issue all the dreadful evils that pervade our world. It gives energy to the tyrant's sword, it drenches the earth with blood, and binds whole nations in chains. The love of gain first introduced slavery into the world, and has been its constant support in every age. We often see the love of gain weighing down the finest feelings of soul, blunting the most acute powers of perception, crushing the strongest faculty of judgment, breaking the most powerful ties of humanity, falling upon the unhappy African, and binding him in chains of perpetual bondage!"

In the fifth letter, Rankin pleaded with his brother to "do justly, love mercy, break every yoke, and let the oppressed go free." In the next, he decried the evils of Kentucky's slave auctions and the greed of slaveholders. "It is well known that many masters are so avaricious that they cannot be satisfied with a reasonable quantity of labor. The manner in which these unfeeling monsters exact labor from their poor slaves may be illustrated by a single fact, the knowledge of which came to me from a respectable source." The source, a resident of Georgia, told him about a slaveholder from that state who demanded so much work from six slave girls that they "executed the dreadful design of hanging themselves!" After being beaten several times for failing to complete the tasks assigned them, they returned one morning "with sore backs and bleeding hands," Rankin wrote. "Their hoe handles were soon made red with their innocent blood and they labored with great assiduity, but they could not perform the unreasonable task, and consequently received an enlarged number of lashes!" Each day they returned to work, the overseer broadened their tasks, and so, by the last morning, "they commenced again, but the task was so very much enlarged that all hope of performing it was entirely precluded, and the enormously increased number of lashes became certain. The unhappy girls despaired of life and concluded that they must inevitably die under the torturing lash, unless they could despatch themselves of some other method. This appeared to them to be the only means of escaping the most terrible cruelty."

In another, he told the story of a Kentuckian who bought a chair, which his wife later broke in the presence of a neighbor. She blamed the damage on a seventeen-year-old slave girl, who declared her innocence repeatedly.

The brutish master, seized the poor unfortunate girl, drew her clothes up over her head, hanged her by them to the limb of a tree and in that shameful position whipt her several times very severely. By the extremity of torture she was sometimes forced to say that she did break the furniture but in the moment of respite she would honestly deny it again and this subjected her to more torture. Fortunately the gentleman who was present when the mistress broke the furniture happened to be passing by. He passed in utter amazement at the shocking scene; he soon discovered the cause of the cruelty. Indignation overcame him. He approached the brutish master and told him that his own wife had broken the furniture in his presence, and declared that if he did not cease from torturing the poor girl he would give him as much as he had given her. With this, the shameless monster thought it necessary to comply, and for that time the girl was released from his torturing hand. The gentleman who rescued the girl is now a resident of Ohio and is known to be a man of truth. It is painful to record such a shameful outrage upon decency and humanity; but it is necessary to do it in order to show the horrible extent of the slaveholder's power over his slaves. Every master has the power to strip his female slaves, and treat them in the same disgraceful manner, and thousands of them are base enough to put such power into exercise. It really grieves me to think that any government, and much more that our own does sanction such an abomination.

In one of the last letters, he warned the nation that, "even after a people, who have been long enslaved, are emancipated, it will require them to pass through several generations in order to regain their original strength of mind, and give the world a fair exhibition of the powers they really possess."

The last letter ran in *The Castigator* on February 22, 1825. Preceding it, Ammen wrote, "This day's paper contains the last of a series of letters, on slavery, published in this paper. Such are the ways of the world, that we have been censured by some, and applauded by others, for publishing them."

CHAPTER SIX

The Lantern in the Window

On the hot humid days of an Ohio Valley summer, clouds of mist sometimes hover above the river, their thin white wisps nearly touching the water like arms reaching out from bodies adrift in the air. They haunt the hollows between bluffs and linger for hours in the hills beyond the river—smoke from some primeval time. Early in the morning on one such steamy day in the summer of 1825, low-lying mist moved along the river near Maysville, Kentucky, but the wisps were gray this time, and ashes swirled around them. In Ripley, nine miles downriver, boatmen docking at dawn brought the news that a warehouse in Maysville had burned to its base. Its contents—including at least four hundred copies of a book of Rankin's letters—were completely destroyed. The cause was arson.

Shortly after Rankin's twenty-first letter had appeared in *The Castigator*, David Ammen reprinted the letters in a book entitled *Rankin's Letters on Slavery*. With the help of his sons, Ammen printed a thousand copies of the book at a cost of $80, and Rankin paid Ammen by releasing him from his rent until the debt was paid. Five hundred or so copies were bound by Edward Cox, an antislavery friend of Rankin's in Maysville, and many were sold in his Maysville bookstore. Others were sent to individuals Rankin knew, mostly in Ohio and Kentucky. Between four and five hundred copies were stored, unbound, at the warehouse in Maysville. The plan was to keep the books until Rankin could save enough money to have Cox bind and distribute them. The fire, as the arsonist intended, stymied the promotion of Rankin's work—but only temporarily.

Throughout 1825, Rankin's words, from both *The Castigator* and the book, shot through the valley with the intensity of a spark hitting gunpowder. The Vesey uprising was still fresh in people's minds; voices for and against slavery were growing louder; more slaves were escaping, and more slaveholders were blaming abolitionists for the loss. When people who lived along the river watched the sun sinking below the Kentucky hills, they thought not about the splendor of the bright reflection upon the water but rather about the bedeviling things that might occur after nightfall. What would this night bring? The arson in Maysville was just the beginning.

In early 1826, *The Castigator* reported:

We have it from undoubted authority that a slave was lately murdered in Henry County, Kentucky, in the following barbarous manner: The murderer had hired the slave, and treated him with intolerable cruelty. Of course, the slave ran away from him in order to gain a little respite from his sufferings. [The master] pursued him, took him, and tied him to his horse and when extremely heated, drew him through a creek of cold running water. The consequence was the unhappy creature soon became unable to keep on his feet, and when he fell to the ground, the unfeeling monster dismounted and beat him to death! The criminal was arrested; but the court of examination determined that it was a case of manslaughter and consequently bound him in a trifling sum to appear at the circuit court; and thus, he was let loose again. The most malicious, deliberate and barbarous murder of a slave is but man-slaughter!

There was more tragedy in the autumn in northern Kentucky, when five slaves were hanged in Bourbon County for murdering a slave trader and his crew. Forty-seven more slaves were sent downriver as punishment for conspiring to escape from the trader. The incident concerned Edward Stone, one of Kentucky's most notorious slave traders, who had been buying young slaves throughout Kentucky since 1816, "storing" them in the iron-barred cellar of his own home until he had enough to fill a boat, and then heading south to peddle his "stock." Late that September, Stone and four other men led seventy-seven slaves onto a flat-bottomed boat and started downriver. About ninety miles below Louisville, the slaves, armed with axes, knives, and billets of wood, rose up and killed their five captors, weighted the bodies, threw them into the river, sank the boat, then landed on the Indiana shore and marched through the countryside as free men—until they were caught.

That year, the runaway traffic provoked Southern legislators to lobby the federal government so intensely that the newly appointed "U.S. Envoy Extraordinary and Minister Plenipotentiary" to Great Britain, Albert Gallatin, was assigned to negotiate a "return policy" with Canada regarding runaways; the U.S. was seeking an extradition treaty with England for the return of the fugitive slaves. Such a deal was struck with the United Mexican States, but not with Canada. In 1827, the British envoy informed Gallatin that "it was utterly impossible for [the Canadians] to agree to a stipulation for the surrender of fugitive slaves."

Without the cooperation of the Canadian government in stopping up the hole into which their slaves seemed to be disappearing, slaveholders had to find someone to blame for the escapes, a target for their frustrations and anger, a new goal for legislative action. It could not be slavery itself, slaveholders told one another, for it was not evil. Slavery was a divine institution ordained by God for the best interests of the race it enslaved. Quoting Leviticus and other scriptures, they claimed that even the Bible supported it: "Thy bondmen and thy bondmaids which thou shalt have, shall be of the heathen that are round about you; of them shall ye buy bondmen and bondmaids. Moreover, of the children of the strangers that do sojourn among you, of them shall ye buy, and of their families that are with you, which they begat in your land. And they shall be your possession. And ye shall take them as an inheritance for your children after you, to inherit them for a possession they shall be your bondmen forever."

Could the inclination to escape and rebel come from the slaves themselves? Certainly not, for they were not smart enough to engineer their own escapes, slaveholders assured each other. Besides, their slaves were well cared for and content, especially those in the northern regions of the South. Slavery, after all, provided food, shelter, and work. It had saved the "wretched creatures."

What about those intrusive men and women who brainwashed slaves into believing they had a right to be free and should exercise it? What about the preachers and the crusaders who created the mirage that life was better out of servitude? As one Kentucky editorial put it, those "ignorant, infatuated barbarians [abolitionists] have violated the laws of God, and manifested an utter destitution of fellow feeling by scattering the firebrands of their iniquitous purpose. Was ever impudence so barefaced? Was ever wickedness so hypocritical? They talk of their attachment to the constitution and of their obedience to the precepts of humanity and religion. They, who secretly encourage an amalgamation of the whites and blacks, who support seminaries for the education of children of both colors, who abuse the freedom of the press by using it as an instrument of destruction to the peace and happiness of their fellow-citizens, who circulate publications of the most wicked and incendiary character, filled with ludicrous ends, well calculated to shake the obedience of the Southern slaves and excite them toward escape and rebellion . . ." And so the abolitionists were blamed—and despised—for the insurrections and the escapes.

The arsonist in Maysville was an early warning to Rankin and his compatriots that their passionate call for freedom and equality would be answered by an equally ardent demonstration of beliefs, in the form of violence. From the moment the Missouri Compromise was signed, what had begun as a moral dispute between neighbors who shared a river was evolving into a high-stakes, life-threatening duel that intensified throughout the 1820s. By the mid-1830s, it would prove to be nothing less than a war.

In one incident along the Ohio River near Ripley, a Presbyterian minister from Ohio was traveling downriver on a steamboat on which there were numerous slaves going south to be sold. The minister spoke to the slaves and told them that they were as free in God's eyes as any other men. Other white men on the boat, who saw what the minister was doing, ordered the captain to land his boat on the Kentucky shore. At first he refused, but they persisted, threatening violence. As he landed the boat, the men tied a rope around the neck of the preacher, which they then threw over the limb of a tree near the boat. Just as they were about to hoist the preacher off his feet and to his fate, his wife fainted at the feet of one of the men. This sight moved one of the witnesses from the boat to step forward and to tell the men, in reportedly eloquent terms, how wrong their tactics were and how righteous the minister had been in trying to help the slaves. The men stopped, and one said, "He must be thankful he was on Kentucky soil, for if he had been on the soil of some of the other States, eloquence would have availed him nothing in that crisis." Later, a slaveholding owner of two Mississippi plantations wrote a letter to the editor of a Kentucky newspaper which had reported the passenger's heroic intervention: "If you should be caught in any part of the South and the declarations you made should be proved against you, YOU WOULD BE HANGED WITHOUT JUDGE OR JURY, to the disgrace of your family."

The majority of Americans, in both North and South, viewed men like Rankin—who had been advocating immediate emancipation for more than a decade, and who were still a small minority during the 1820s—as members of a dangerous fringe population threatening to disrupt the social order and to deny white supremacy. To them, the notion of integrating Africans into American society was sheer madness. Americans who did acknowledge slavery's evils were in conflict over how to end it. The anti-slavery umbrella sheltered a diverse group within which, again, the abolitionists were in the minority. On the one extreme side were the people who said that slavery was evil but to end it would weaken, if not dissolve, the Union; some even went so far as to say that ending slavery would make the nation, if it were still a nation, vulnerable to a British takeover. Of those who sought solutions, some believed in gradual and partial emancipation and in government compensation of slaveholders for the cost of freed slaves. Others joined the American Colonization Society, formed in 1816, to promote the wholesale exportation of all free blacks in the U.S. back to Africa. Most antislavery advocates in the 1820s were more likely to link up with the colonization movement than to endorse some deranged advocate of equality of the races—that is, an abolitionist who believed that a multiracial society was possible. Many abolitionists, after all, were advocating that all white Americans undergo a revolution of the heart and eradicate the basis of slavery, which was racism. For most Americans, this required a personal awakening, a confrontation with an immense lie that had permeated generations, a confession of the sin of slavery.

By the time Andrew Jackson was elected president in 1828, abolitionists were increasingly threatened from all sides: from slaveholders, from proslavery Southern sympathizers in the North, and from colonization zealots. Theirs was a tiny, despised minority that sought to free the slaves, to educate them, and to help them assimilate into American society. And now came a president who would soon try to destroy abolitionism by, among other things, calling for severe penalties to suppress the movement's "unconstitutional and wicked" publications and activities.

Locally, the Jacksonian era began with the Kentucky legislature's response to popular demand for severe penalties against people who assisted slaves. For enticing a slave to leave his owner, for aiding in a slave's escape out of the state, for providing a forged paper of freedom, and for concealing a runaway, the punishment could range from two to twenty years in prison and a fine of $1,000. If a person was charged under this law and then acquitted, there was still a penalty of $500 to provide security against any future accusations of a similar nature. This was far more severe than the punishments outlined in the 1793 act.

Shortly after Jackson's inauguration, in the spring of 1829, Rankin decided that he must move his family away from Front Street. His deeds and writings were well enough known throughout the Ohio Valley—ignoble to some and heroic to others—that he was typically the first suspect when slave hunters and owners came to Ripley. At any time of the night, they could pound on his door, with their dogs and their suspicions and their indignation. This was no way to raise his family—which now included three daughters and six sons. On Front Street, he felt too vulnerable to the clashes along the river that he feared would increase in the years ahead. He also wanted farmland, forests, and fruit groves for sources of income. And so he purchased sixty-five and a half acres of thickly forested land on a hill that stood 540 feet above the town. On each side of the land were extensions of Red Oak Creek and another creek called Cornick's Run. Beyond were the billowing Appalachian foothills.

From the top of his hill, Rankin could see nearly five miles of the winding waterway that separated his world from the land of slavery. He could see the steamboats traveling with their human cargo from Maysville to the South. He could see the villages of Higginsport and Levanna on the Ohio side, the Kentucky towns of Dover and Charleston, and the cedar-covered bluffs just above the town of Augusta, seven miles downriver in Kentucky. He could see the alleys in the town below him that extended from the river to his hill. He could see the rooftops and backyards of the homes of the Collinses, Campbells, Beasleys, and McCagues. And he could see horsemen coming toward his hill, giving him ample time to prepare for their arrival. From any of the front windows of his house, he could see a stretch of land across the river that looked very much like the one on which he lived but was very different. He began each day now by looking at a vista of miles and miles of land where men and women were sometimes chained to cabin floors at night, where hickory branches broke upon the backs of aged women, and where the punishment for seeking freedom could be death.

The new property, with its timber and its fertile soil, quickly allowed Rankin to supplement his meager annual income from the church, which was now $350, down from $500. For his first seven years in Ripley, he had pastored another church nearby, a post he resigned in 1829, thus reducing his salary by $150. With the $350 he had to feed and clothe a family that would eventually expand even more. And he had to support his covert work of providing food, clothing, and often cash to fugitives, and of promoting his antislavery beliefs through publications and lectures.

To pay the $700 for the land, he put down $100 and borrowed the rest from a local bank, to be paid over the next five years. The first payment was deferred for a year to give him time, with the help of his older sons, to cut enough timber to make the payment. That spring and summer, his eldest son, Adam Lowry, drove a team of oxen into the town and sold wood for a dollar a cord to the steamboats, the local steam flour mill, and other businesses in town. Meanwhile, Rankin, who had built a log house for his family to live in temporarily, was working on a larger brick house at the very edge of the property. He paid for the materials by selling a third of the house on Front Street to one of his brothers, who would continue the tradition of sequestering runaway slaves, and he sold acreage on Zane's Trace, east of Ripley, that he had purchased in 1827 and that had originally been part of James Monroe's land grant in Ohio. At the end of the summer, he moved his family into its new home. The log house then became a barn—with a hidden cellar beneath the hay to sequester runaways.

To alert the slaves to the location of their new house, the Rankins placed a lantern in a front window every night—a ritual that over time would assume mythic status. Some people said that the light was so bright it could be seen for miles along the Kentucky shore, and even into the hills of Mason and Bracken counties. However deeply the twinkling lantern penetrated the hills on the other side, its radiance was amplified by the hopeful spirit it invoked among those who wanted to believe that there was a better life beyond the river. It was also a symbol of Rankin's resistance to the slavery sympathizers who attacked him. One Mason County slave, Arnold Gragston, who helped other slaves to escape across the river, would remember the light as "a big lighthouse in his yard, about thirty feet high and Rankin kept it burnin' all night. It always meant freedom for a slave if he could get to this light."

Rankin's move to the high hill over Ripley and his series of public letters in response to his brother's purchase of a slave were dramatic decisions that showed his intention to be aggressive, outspoken, and highly visible in his attack on slavery, to be a leader in the antislavery struggle.

After the fire—the Maysville arsonist was never found—Rankin was unable to subsidize the printing of a second edition of his *Letters on Slavery.* "I supposed it would never appear again," he later wrote. For five years, there were only six hundred copies in circulation nationwide, though they eventually had an impact in all the ways Rankin intended. For one, his brother Thomas came to Ohio and freed his slaves in 1827, the same year that their father died. Then, in 1830, Rankin received a letter from an antislavery man in New Jersey asking whether Rankin would give him the rights to reprint the letters. Rankin told the man, who was a Quaker, that he had only one purpose in publishing the book: to destroy slavery. If this man believed that reprinting his book would help in that crusade, Rankin said he would gladly permit as many editions to be published as possible. Financial gain, he stressed, was not his intention. Thus came *Rankin on Slavery*, the second edition of the letters. It was published by the Society of Friends in New Jersey. And, by a circuitous route, the second edition ended up in England, where a British publisher issued three more printings. This edition was in turn the basis for five printings from the American Anti-Slavery Society, which used the letters as a textbook for its lectures and as standard reading for its agents. Between 1833 and 1850, there would be as many as eighteen more editions of the letters.

Sometime during 1830, the second edition found its way to Boston and into the hands of the young abolitionist William Lloyd Garrison, who would serialize the letters in 1832 in his new antislavery newspaper, *The Liberator*. At a convention in Cincinnati in 1853, Garrison would credit Rankin with being "my anti-slavery father; his book on slavery was the cause of my entering the anti-slavery conflict." And when he gave a copy of his autobiography to Rankin, Garrison inscribed it: "Rev. John Rankin. With the profound regards and loving veneration of his anti-slavery disciple and humble co-worker in the cause of emancipation."

CHAPTER SEVEN

1831

"Wo if it come with storm, and blood, and fire; When midnight darkness veils the earth and sky! Wo to the innocent babe—the guilty sire—Mother and daughter—friends of kindred tie! Stranger and citizen alike shall die!" So wrote Garrison on January 1, 1831, in the first issue of *The Liberator.*

Eight months later, on August 21, 1831, in a remote region of southern Virginia, a slave did what Gabriel Prosser had tried to do in 1800 and Denmark Vesey in 1822, what slave owners feared and abolitionists such as Rankin continually warned that oppression would always provoke. He rose up against his master, and all masters of his enslaved race. On that day, Nat Turner and his co-conspirators Nelson, Jack, Will, Sam, Henry, and Hank provided an impassioned answer to the slavery dilemma: armed rebellion. In twenty-four hours, with a gathering force of sixty or more men, they killed at least fifty white men, women, and children in Southampton County, Virginia.

Turner was apprehended in October 1831, convicted on November 5, and hanged with fifteen of his co-conspirators six days later in Jerusalem, Virginia. Terror quickly turned to anger in the South as slave owners reacted against black people who read, prayed, preached, or convened. New laws were passed, old laws tightened, slave patrols expanded. No teaching. No preaching. No learning to read. From then on, every breeze that rustled through the limbs of plantation oaks, every leaf that crunched underfoot beneath a bedroom window, every skiff that pulled into the thickets along the banks of the Ohio would mean more than it did before. Suspicion and fear would fill the air. Violence would be the trademark of the 1830s. And Rankin and all who quietly understood the passions of men like Vesey and Turner would go about the work of building a movement to arouse the antislavery conscience of the nation. This would encompass the work not only to free the enslaved but also to educate them once they were free.

In 1831, the runaway slaves slipping through the alleys of Front Street, following the creeks to the cascade of hills behind the town, hiding in the cellar beneath the hay mound in Rankin's barn, riding in wagons or on horses with the sons of Collins, Campbell, Rankin, and Gilliland, challenged and mystified their irate owners more than ever before. This was the year when the owner of Tice Davids, the runaway slave who seemed to disappear somewhere in Ripley, took back to Kentucky the news that there must be some secret road in that town that only runaways knew. It was the year when residents of Ripley noticed more strangers on horseback coming from the other side of the river, riding in and out of the alleys and up and down the hills. This was also the year when Benjamin Franklin Templeton, a free young black man, came to Ripley to get his education, and Ripley got a taste of the racist violence that would permeate the decade.

Templeton was born into slavery on a cotton plantation in Spartanburg District, South Carolina, in 1809. His parents, Pompey and Terak, had worked for many years for Thomas and Sarah Williamson, the plantation owners. Sarah despised slavery and braved local critics and irate neighbors to teach her slaves all that she knew about reading and writing. When Thomas died in 1813, his will freed his twenty-seven slaves, all of whom— including the Templeton family—moved with Sarah to Adams County to live near one of her sons, the Reverend William Williamson. An ardent abolitionist and Presbyterian, Williamson had come north to Ohio in 1805 with a group of antislavery advocates that included Reverend James Gilliland, who was Rankin's counterpart in Red Oak, and Robert Wilson, who later became the president of Ohio University. In 1824, Benjamin's older brother, John, enrolled at Ohio University and worked as Wilson's house servant to pay his tuition. Four years later, he became the school's first African-American graduate, the fourth in the nation. An ordained minister, John spent some time after graduation working at the Chillicothe Presbytery and mentoring Benjamin. In 1831, the Presbytery agreed to raise enough money to pay a portion of Benjamin's tuition to go to college. Their choice was a school in Ripley, where they knew John Rankin would warmly receive him.

By 1831, Ripley College, despite a wobbly financial start in 1828, was running smoothly. Its nearly one hundred students came not only from Ohio and Kentucky but from as far away as Mississippi, Louisiana, and Tennessee. One day Ulysses S. Grant would attend the school. For now, the student roster included the sons of just about every abolitionist in the area—William Porter, Jimmy Campbell, Amos Huggins, Robert Poage, and Adam Lowry Rankin—as well as the sons of Southern sympathizers, such as Chancey Shaw. Classes ran in two sessions, beginning on the first Mondays of November and May and ending on the last Wednesdays of March and September. Tuition was $10 per session, paid in advance. The main prerequisite to attending, besides the tuition payment, was the ability to read.

Rankin was the school's founder and the chairman of the board of trustees. An ad in *The Castigator* in 1831 read: "The course of study is extensive, and, it is believed, well calculated to make thorough scholars. It is intended to comprise as much as students of good capacity and industrious habits can accomplish in four years; and yet to avoid the extreme of so crowding it with numerous, and unnecessary branches as to make students unavoidably superficial in almost every branch. It is designed to make practical men as well as theoretical scholars."

One of the features of the college was the debating club, known at first as the Buckeye Club and later renamed the Eromathean Society. Topics ranged from "Is Phrenology true as a science?," "Is there more pleasure in the married life or in the single life?," and "Are men raised to eminence more by circumstances than intellect?" to "Should capital punishment be inflicted in any case?," "Should foreign emigration to the U.S. be prohibited?," and "Have slaveholders the right to take back their fugitive slaves after they have escaped into the state of Ohio?"

The faculty consisted largely of men who took part in Ripley's double life; indeed, students sometimes engaged in the work of the Underground Railroad. And the doors of the school were wide open to free black men and women. Education was the key to equality, and Rankin, from his early antislavery advocacy in Kentucky, had tried to educate blacks every chance he could, whether through preaching, teaching, starting schools, running tutorials, speaking on tours, or writing pamphlets and editorials. Out of the more than ten thousand blacks in Ohio then, very few could read. For Rankin, Templeton's enrollment represented a passionate conviction put into motion.

Templeton adjusted well to the otherwise all-white school. Even the students from the South seemed to accept him. At first, with the sight of Templeton in the classrooms at Ripley College, it seemed to Rankin and his colleagues that the 1830s in Ripley might bring a bright new day. But in a few months, the Templeton experiment began to unravel.

Most townsfolk were indifferent to what Rankin and his inner circle were trying to accomplish regarding the education of blacks. Few understood what Templeton represented in the cause to end racial prejudice. They hauled their timber, built their boats, packed their pork, and let the rest of the world move past them as easily as a saw log drifting downriver. Live and let live—that was often the Ripley way, though not for everyone, and definitely not for Franklin Shaw.

Shaw was one of several sons of Peter Shaw, a local boatbuilder who was working on a steamboat called the *Champion* in 1831. He spent most of his time farming some land north and east of town, and a good deal of the rest of the time in the Ripley saloons. Franklin knew of Templeton because his brother Chancey had begun a course of study at Ripley College and then, for financial reasons, had had to drop out. Shaw may have been drunk when he wrote a note to Ripley College President Nathan Brockway demanding the dismissal of "the nigger" from the college. He stressed that, if his brother was too poor to go to college, how could Templeton have what Chancey had been denied? He threatened to "cowhide the nigger" if his demand for dismissal was not granted.

Templeton remained at Ripley College. But for a time after receiving the note, President Brockway or one of the Ripley instructors accompanied the tall, soft-spoken young black man as he walked to and from his boarding house downtown and the school building half a mile away. After a few weeks of no notes, no threats, no signs of violence, Rankin and others felt it was safe for Templeton to resume his student life without bodyguards. But on the second day of this new freedom, Templeton was leaving the college and walking along Second Street in the middle of the afternoon when Shaw approached him, cowhide in hand, vengeance coursing through his alcohol-filled veins. He pulled Templeton into a side alley, tore off his shirt, and lashed him repeatedly until the young black man was nearly unconscious. Shaw stood above the body, frozen either with fear or with the satisfaction of having possibly eliminated the source of his outrage. He was arrested and fined $10, then he moved across the river to Mason County, never to return to Ripley.

Templeton recovered. For weeks, the townsfolk in and out of the college talked of nothing but Templeton. Some folks saw what had happened as part of the retribution that communities across the North as well as the South were experiencing in the aftermath of the Turner revolt. Others attributed the incident to nothing more than what they saw: some drunken citizen who should have behaved better. The question now was what to do about Templeton. The issue divided the town. And it exposed the ramifications of slavery as clearly as the river that ran between the slave and free states. At meetings in town, both secret and open, the events of the previous few weeks were replayed, and opinions burst forth like underbrush in the spring.

At the college, the Southern students, now a sizable portion of the student body, threatened to withdraw if Templeton did not leave the school. Because of this, a majority of the board of trustees favored Templeton's dismissal. They did not want the scandal of having the Southern students walk out, and they feared a recurrence of violence, either of which could discourage future enrollments. At the same time, a public dismissal would stigmatize the school among liberal-minded individuals in the area who donated money to keep the school running. And most of the school's backers—such as the wealthy Thomas McCague, Alexander Campbell, and others with an abolitionist point of view—were outspoken about wanting Templeton to stay.

Caught in the middle of the two arguments, Rankin sought a compromise solution. If the board agreed to allow Templeton to remain at the college, then Rankin would physically withdraw the young man from classes and take him into his home, where he would tutor Templeton in the same courses he had been taking. The board agreed, and Templeton became one of several young black men whom through the years Rankin would teach in his home.

Rankin decided to tutor Templeton through the spring-1832 session and then to send him to Hanover College in Indiana, a place where he felt the young man could be safe from the growing animosity toward blacks and abolitionists near Ripley. Templeton would go on to attend the Lane Theological Seminary, where his years would overlap with those of Adam Lowry Rankin. He would be ordained as a minister in the Ripley Presbytery in 1838, later pastoring his own churches in Pittsburgh and Philadelphia.

Rankin's decision took the heat off Templeton, and by mid-December 1831, townsfolk in Ripley had turned their attentions from racial unrest to the river, which had frozen over on December 2. In the next few weeks, nine steamboats were destroyed by the crashing blows and the jagged edges of the grinding ice that broke up, refroze, and violently broke up again. On January 8, 1832, the river began to move again, and for a few weeks the rhythm of the river towns returned to normal. But there would be little that was normal about 1832. By the end of January, no matter how often and intensely people prayed, life along the river seemed to be spinning out of control.

CHAPTER EIGHT

Speak Truth to Power

The floods in Ripley begin in the creeks that surround it. Eagle Creek and Red Oak Creek reach capacity, and water rushes onto the land, down Main Street, the alleys, Market Street, to the river. At the same time, waves of water come out of the creeks to crash upon the river, spinning in endless circles, as if waiting to ride the torrents that will soon rip downriver. The creeks overflow in the time it takes to say the word "flood," but the river takes days to make the transformation from friend to foe.

By the end of the first week of February 1832, the river had begun to rise. Merchants and residents of Ripley loaded their wagons with furniture, portraits, linens, and china and headed for higher ground. By February 9, the river was higher than it had ever been since records had been kept, which by most accounts began with the flood of 1755, noted by British traders living near the mouth of the Scioto River. By February 17, the river had risen dramatically to what would be its highest mark, at Maysville: sixty-five feet and five inches. What floated downriver was the proof of its rage: parts of barns, fences, outhouses, stables, and houses swept in their entirety from their foundations, the carefully sewn curtains still hanging, soaked and torn. Clusters of hay and corn entangled with saw logs and stumps of trees that floated like hellish rafts on the River Styx, sometimes colliding into horses, sheep, hogs, or cattle from farms as far upriver as

Portsmouth or Ironton. In Ripley, the centennial of Washington's birth—
on which there was to be a big local celebration—was spent returning to
stores encrusted with mud, to streets coated with brown slop, and to
homes filled with despair.

For months, the town struggled to pull itself back together. But by the
time the days were longer and warmer, fans were fluttering, and daily routines had resumed, another danger loomed—cholera—the first attack ever
in the U.S. On June 27, the disease hit New York City with epidemic
vengeance. By the end of July, it had spread to Philadelphia; by September,
to Louisville. On September 30, the first cases were reported in Cincinnati.
Cholera's passage to the Midwest was thought to have begun on a ship
from England that had arrived at Quebec in early June. From there the ship
traveled up the St. Lawrence to Montreal with the infected voyagers on
board; it passed down the Champlain Canal—by then, infected individuals were on the canal boats—along the Erie Canal, then across the Great
Lakes in steamboats and into the Upper Mississippi. The scourge arrived in
Louisville before Cincinnati, in Cincinnati before Wheeling, and in
Wheeling before Pittsburgh. Although Pittsburgh was only four hundred
miles from Philadelphia, the cholera had taken a circuitous watercourse of
three thousand miles between the two cities.

By the end of the first week of October 1832, cholera had arrived on the
shores of Ripley. President Brockway of Ripley College was the first victim.
Adam Lowry Rankin wrote, "My father and mother were constantly in at-
tendance on the sick. The people were greatly alarmed and it was difficult
to get for the sick the attention they needed. For a time, there averaged four
deaths a day for two weeks, one hundred and fifty cases at one time. I shall
never forget the dismay it produced. Every business was closed and the
stillness of death seemed to pervade the whole town."

James Simpson, professor of languages, succeeded Brockway as the
young college's president. But Simpson soon resigned, and before the end
of the year Rankin's board urged him to take the post. Preacher, activist, ed-
ucator, writer, speaker, Underground Railroad conductor, husband, and at
this time father of ten children (the youngest child born two weeks before
the cholera outbreak), Rankin was hesitant to add the responsibilities of
college president. Moreover, the flood and the cholera had stolen time
from all of his devotions. Nonetheless, he accepted the job. It was a call to
duty, which he seemed unable to resist. But now his antislavery work
would infringe on the college as well as the church. His new job began at

about the same time that the antislavery crusade was entering a new phase, in which Rankin's involvement would profoundly expand.

In late August 1832, Garrison began to publish Rankin's letters on slavery in *The Liberator*. Several months later, Rankin was summoned to Philadelphia as a "friend of immediate emancipation to meet on the 4th of December to form a NATIONAL ANTI-SLAVERY SOCIETY," according to the invitation. Rankin went to the convention, and shortly thereafter the new society reissued the second edition of his letters and advertised it regularly in antislavery publications nationwide. Out of all of this came new connections for Rankin throughout 1832 and 1833, including the Connecticut-born abolitionist Theodore Dwight Weld, whose efforts to inspire a virtual army of antislavery crusaders in Ohio would affect both Ripley's and Rankin's roles in the cause.

After nearly twenty years of preaching immediate emancipation to a small audience of true believers, Rankin was now going to witness the stunning emergence of a national movement that endorsed his antislavery devotion. The despised abolitionist minority, which was barely a flickering ember in the 1820s, was about to become a bonfire in the 1830s. And Weld was one of the reasons.

A tall, untidy-looking man with thick, tousled hair and disheveled clothes, Weld was a former member of the Holy Band of followers of the evangelist Charles Finney, who was the moving force behind the Great Revival of the later 1820s through 1830. Finney and his followers condemned the bleak Calvinist concept of original sin. All God's children were not damned at birth, they believed. Mankind was not doomed; rather, it could be saved. And with the enthusiasm and the endless energy that come with youth, the new converts channeled their benevolence into the cause of unsaved mankind, focusing on issues such as temperance and education. Thanks to the vast network of state and local temperance societies, the influence of people like Weld, and the newly founded Lane Theological Seminary in Cincinnati, many devotees would soon begin to turn their attention to the crusade to end slavery as part of their mission to save humanity.

In 1830, inspired by a fellow Finney disciple, Charles Stuart, who returned to England in 1829 to fight slavery and wrote to Weld, begging him to enlist in the "sacred cause," and with the promise of a hefty endowment from a wealthy New York merchant, philanthropist, and antislavery advocate named Arthur Tappan, Weld ventured west in search of a school that could become a training center for young evangelists inspired by the Great Revival. Graduates would then be expected to convert and "save" the West and all its new territories and states. Neither Stuart's plea nor Tappan's antislavery advocacy was far from Weld's thoughts as he came to Ohio and discovered a small seminary in Cincinnati. Founded in 1829 with a donation of $5,000 from two local merchants, Ebenezer and William Lane, the school, also called Lane, consisted of one main building, a few smaller, unfinished structures, and some wooded acreage in a section known as Walnut Hills, two miles north of the city. With the help of additional funding from Tappan, the buildings were completed and the school was expanded. Lyman Beecher, a highly regarded clergyman from New England, came west with his family, including his daughter Harriet, to assume the presidency of the new institution. And Weld enrolled, quickly becoming the student-body president. Among his fellow students were William T. Allan, the son of a Presbyterian minister in Alabama; James A. Thome, heir to a wealthy planter family across the river from Ripley in northern Kentucky; Asa Stone, a teacher from Mississippi; Huntington Lyman, from a slaveholding family in Louisiana; Andrew Benton, from the distinguished Benton family of Missouri; and Henry B. Stanton, who came to Cincinnati with a few other new enrollees from New York on a raft down the Ohio River from Pittsburgh, and who would one day serve in Lincoln's Cabinet.

Weld's class consisted of forty students, thirty of whom were over the age of twenty-six. Most were college graduates. Some were from the South, though most had come from upstate New York and New England. One was a black man from Guinea who had purchased his freedom. Few, if any, were engaged in the antislavery cause when they entered Lane. Most believed the abolitionists to be fanatics and thought that the only solution to slavery was either gradual emancipation or colonization or both. But soon Weld would change that.

Weld, who had promised the fervent abolitionist Tappan that he would promote the discussion of the abolition of slavery at the new school, was quietly proselytizing in an effort to generate enough controversy to organize a debate. In February 1834, the students indeed decided to hold a public discussion on slavery. The so-called debate began with the question, "Ought the people of the slaveholding states abolish slavery immediately?" The students met eighteen times between February and April to discuss the slavery issue. John Rankin, James Gilliland, and Jesse Lockhart were among those who attended.

During the first two nights, William Allan, who had grown up in the midst of slavery in Alabama, explained the reasons for his conviction regarding immediate emancipation:

> At our house, it is so common to hear their screams from a neighboring plantation, that we think nothing of it. The overseer of this plantation told me one day that he laid a young woman over a log and beat her so severely that she was soon after delivered of a dead child. A bricklayer, a neighbor of ours, owned a very smart young negro man, who ran away; but was caught. When his master got him home, he stripped him naked, tied him up by his hands, in plain sight and hearing of the academy and the public green, so high that his feet could not touch the ground; then tied them together and put a long board between his legs to keep him steady. After preparing him in this way, he took a paddle, bored full of holes, and commenced beating him with it. He continued it leisurely all day. At night his flesh was literally pounded to a jelly. It was two weeks before he was able to walk. No one took any notice of it. No one thought any wrong was done.

Other students from the South then added their own keen observations on the cruelty of slavery. Andrew Benton from Missouri told the story of "a young woman who was generally very badly treated," and who,

> after receiving a more severe whipping than usual, ran away. In a few days, she came back and was sent into the field to work. At this time, the garment next to her skin was stiff like a scab from the running sores made by the whipping. Towards night, she told her master that she was sick and wished to go to the house. She went; and as soon as she reached it, laid down on the floor exhausted. The mistress asked her what the matter was? She made no reply. She asked again; but received no answer. "I'll see," said she, "if I can't make you speak." So taking the tongs, she heated them red hot and put them upon the bottoms of her feet; then upon her legs and body; and finally in a rage took hold of her throat. This had the desired effect. The poor girl faintly whispered, "Oh, missee, don't—I am most gone," and then expired. The woman yet lives there and owns slaves.

Some students retold the stories passed on by antislavery advocates of harsh life in the Deep South, though they themselves had never observed it. After several nights, a few confessed profound guilt over the existence of such a system in a Christian land. Former slave James Bradley brought his classmates to tears as he spoke of his experience on a slave ship as a child. Those who had grown up in the border states, such as Kentucky, talked of the slave trade and the horror of the auctions of human flesh. Weld spoke with immense compassion, and eloquence, for the oppressors as well as the oppressed. By the ninth night, the students voted unanimously for the immediate end of slavery. By the end of the eighteenth evening, the students had voted down the colonization society and had formed their own anti-slavery society. William Allan became the society's president. And every officer of the society came from the South: Alabama, Tennessee, Kentucky, Missouri, and Virginia. Weld wrote to Tappan, "The Lord has done great things for us here."

The students, as part of the work in their new society, raised hundreds of dollars among themselves to start a library, a reading room, and several schools—all for the purpose of educating Cincinnati's free black population. Using a system of rotation devised by Weld out of respect for the students' own classwork, they conducted reading classes every evening during the week, and during the days they taught geography, science, grammar, and arithmetic. Classes were so crowded that some days people were turned away. Finding that many of the city's three thousand free blacks had no access to religious instruction, the students also organized three Sunday schools and numerous Bible classes. Some may have begun work on the Underground Railroad, referred to secretly as "the business of Egypt." Every minute that they could spare from their studies, the students devoted to their cause.

The Lane example of conviction put into action thrilled abolitionists nationwide. And because so many of the newly converted students were from the South, there was a feeling in the antislavery community that perhaps the very conversion of the South had begun. But the citizens of Cincinnati, even in the city churches where a few people of color had been brave enough to enter, were not pleased. One church member protested in the *Cincinnati Journal* about blacks daring to mingle with whites in "our temple of God." A mob threatened to tear down the seminary.

The trustees of Lane, the faculty, and President Beecher, an antislavery advocate who favored colonization, were distressed, to say the least, mostly over the actual contact between the students and the black community. Trustees, fearing there would be violence, felt blessed when the school closed for the twelve weeks of summer vacation. Now there was time to consider the next move. While Beecher went east on a fund-raising expedition, Weld and some of the students continued their work in the city, sometimes bringing people of color onto the Lane campus. And two of the students attended the anniversary celebration for the American Anti-Slavery Society in New York, where they captivated members with their stories of life at Lane.

By the time classes resumed, the executive committee of the Lane board of trustees—in the absence of Dr. Beecher, who was still out east—responded to the student body by passing resolutions and new regulations, which included the abolition of the students' antislavery society. They also gave themselves the power to dismiss students and to censor any student discussions and activities of which they did not approve. Their intent was likely to expel Weld and Allan, to stop the students' work in the free black communities of Cincinnati, and to prohibit any future discussions of slavery. Although violence was avoided, what they chose to do condemned the students' spirit of learning. "Far better for the Seminary and the religion, had the mob torn the building to the ground," Rankin wrote in an editorial after the news of the board's decision. "It could have been reared again as a standing monument to integrity."

The majority of the trustees supported the new rules and upheld the sentiments of their board, as did most of the faculty. Upon their return for the fall term, the students asked the faculty if they could discuss the new rules imposed upon them, and were told they could not. Weld wrote a statement on behalf of the students and signed by fifty-one of them. And then, in one of the great moments in America's history of protest movements, the students who signed Weld's impassioned statement simply walked out the doors of Lane.

Rankin was well acquainted with most of the Lane board members. He knew Dr. Beecher quite well. That autumn, Beecher and his daughter Harriet—who at the time described Rankin as a "handsome, modest, amiable-looking young man"—had been the house guests of the Rankins during the meeting of the Cincinnati Synod of the Presbyterian Church in Ripley. And Rankin esteemed as his brethren most if not all of the faculty.

Still, Rankin was compelled to support the students ardently. For a man so true to his beliefs, this meant speaking out against men who believed he was their friend and writing about the importance of the students' anti-slavery rebellion to the causes of free inquiry and abolition. "The Society was right in itself," he wrote in a letter to the *Cincinnati Journal,* and later published by himself in pamphlet form.

It was founded in the noblest feelings of the human heart, and in opposition to one of the blackest sins that ever stained human character. . . . How could the humane heart resist such a call? . . .

"Oppression maketh a wise man mad," whether he endures it himself or sees it inflicted on others. This is the only subject upon which madness is considered as evidence of wisdom. Powerful minds take the deeper hold upon every subject they contemplate, and consequently are the more sympathetic, and easily driven to madness. If the students were driven to madness by the enormities presented they should have been the objects of pity rather than of severity!

Rankin particularly took offense at the faculty's comment about the students doing "violence to public sentiment reckless of consequences." "But was public sentiment right?" he said.

Was it in accordance with the Gospel? The history of the world shows that public sentiment has been oftener wrong than right. Many of the greatest enormities ever witnessed on earth have been sanctioned by public sentiment. In the judgement of many of the wisest and best men of the nation, public sentiment is wrong, egregiously wrong. The object of the students in their society was to cooperate with similar institutions to change what they deemed wrong in public sentiment. This they and all others had a right to do. Without such right there could be no public reform. To attack public sentiment when wrong, with arguments and example is no violence, else the Savior and his Apostles did violence to public sentiment. They attacked it both with argument and practice, and were charged with turning the world upside down. It is no violence to do what is our duty. Public sentiment assumes the chair of the Pope when it places itself above investigation, and meets opposing arguments with clubs and stones.

Eventually, fences were mended, and in the years to come, three of Rankin's sons would attend Lane. The Lane Rebels, as they would be known, scattered about the country and carried the torch of abolition into some of the nation's darkest corners of racial prejudice. Of the fifty-one who walked out, only four asked to be readmitted. Several went to other seminaries such as Yale Divinity School. Some continued their work with free blacks in Cincinnati, which, by most accounts, included assisting runaway slaves. Dozens stayed in Cincinnati for the remainder of 1834 and then, in 1835, followed Asa Mahan to northern Ohio, where Mahan had become president of the new Oberlin College on the condition that it be opened to students of color.

Weld, whose critics accused him of intentionally going to Lane to stir up trouble, enlisted immediately as a full-time agent of the American Anti-Slavery Society. His first mission as an agent was to "abolitionize Ohio" and to put into motion his firm belief that organizers must first convert the rural areas and small towns. With a strong foundation in the countryside, it would be harder for the cities to generate successful opposition to the abolitionist forces.

And so, in November 1834, from Rankin's pulpit in Ripley, Weld launched what would be a legendary year-long speaking tour in Ohio. For eleven consecutive nights, like a wave breaking upon the emotions of his audience, Weld spoke in that impassioned, selfless way that was his gift. His appeal was the intimate, personal challenge of the evangelist and activist. With his words, he hoped to organize but also to invigorate, for the power of conviction was as important to him as the power of numbers.

If your hearts ache and bleed, we want you, you will help us; but if you merely adopt our principles as dry theories, do let us alone: we have mill-stones enough swinging at our necks already. Further, if you join us merely out of a sense of DUTY, we pray you KEEP ALOOF and give place to those who leap into our ranks because they can not keep themselves out; who instead of whining about duty, shout "privilege," "delight"! . . .

Every man knows that slavery is a curse. Whoever denies this, his lips libel his heart. Try him; clank the chains in his ears, and tell him they are for him; give him an hour to prepare his wife and children for a life of slavery; bid him make haste and get ready their necks for the yoke, and their wrists for the coffle chains, then look at his pale lips and trembling knees, and you have Nature's testimony against slavery.

What had brought Weld to Ripley was Rankin. He stayed at the Rankins' and spoke for long hours with the man whose *Letters* he had read. Everyone in Weld's circle seemed to know and admire Rankin for his devotion to ending slavery.

Until Weld's two-week visit, Rankin had spoken against slavery only from the pulpit. Now, as he witnessed the impact of Weld's lectures, he felt inspired to do what Weld was doing: lecture from town to town, in meeting halls and anywhere else he could speak, as well as churches. Within the next two years, Rankin would rearrange his life, putting aside his roles as college president, preacher, father, husband, to become an agent of the American Anti-Slavery Society. Lunging at an enemy that many Northerners had thus far been unable or unwilling to see, he, like Weld, would summon hundreds of new recruits to the cause in Ohio and launch dozens of new antislavery societies. A few weeks after Weld left Ripley, Rankin would be surprised to learn that the newest soldier in the antislavery movement was his eldest son, Adam Lowry.

CHAPTER NINE

FAMILY

By the time he was eighteen years old, Adam Lowry—born on November 4, 1816, and known to his friends as "Lowry"—had no intention of joining the ministry or participating in the Underground Railroad any more than what was required of him at home as a member of his family. To be sure, he had drunk deeply from the cup of his father's convictions, but no matter how often he had listened to his father or other local abolitionists speak out against slavery, no matter how many times he had rushed to the barn late at night to saddle up a horse and transport a waiting runaway to a safe house farther north, no matter how often his father had urged him to join the ministry and the cause, Lowry would not concede.

From his childhood onward, he had delighted in the use of all sorts of tools and spent his playtime building little boats to sail on the river as well as wagons and sleds. Once, his father sent him on an errand to a wool mill that was driven by a horse walking up an inclined wheel. After he returned home, he built the same sort of wheel device, though his favorite cat replaced the horse. His dream was to develop what he called his "mechanical tastes" and to become a carpenter. In 1829, Lowry enrolled in Ripley College's charter class and remained there until the spring of 1833 when he dropped out. Not yet seventeen, he worried about the pressures and expectations that would be thrust upon him if he graduated that spring. He had no desire to enter a profession and still wanted only to become a carpenter. An apprenticeship in Ripley had just become available with an architect and carpenter from Scotland, William McNish, who had married one of Lowry's aunts. Lowry wanted to take it. His father, expressing many objections, urged him to graduate with his class and not to pursue the work. It had been his "cherished desire," Rankin told his oldest son, to see him enter the ministry, and if not the ministry then another profession, such as medicine.

But when Lowry refused, his father consented, saying, "Unless you have a love of the work of the gospel ministry, and though I shall feel greatly disappointed, I will not insist." Lowry agreed to return to college when his apprenticeship ended.

The apprenticeship began almost immediately that spring. It would end on his nineteenth birthday, in 1835. From the time he entered the apprenticeship, Lowry spent most nights studying architectural drafting. During his days, he worked with the architects and builders of Ripley who constructed steamboats, specializing in the building of steamboat cabins. For eighteen months, he progressed predictably in his rhythm of study and practical application, and then, one December afternoon in 1834, his plans abruptly changed.

Lowry had a vivid memory of the New Year's night in 1822 when his father rowed the boat conveying his mother, his little sister, his two younger brothers, and himself across the Ohio River. He remembered the howling mob that gathered night after night outside the Rankins' log house on Second Street as his father began the evening worship. He recalled the hours he spent watching Mr. Ammen beat the ink boxes to prepare for the printing of *The Castigator*. And he remembered how, in the early days of steamboats, the whole town crowded the riverbank peering over each other's shoulders in hushed anticipation of the next boat. But his most powerful memory of Ripley would always be the docking of the *Uncle Sam*. Reputed to be the largest steamboat in the nation in 1834, the *Uncle Sam* docked at the Ripley wharf that December.

That morning, Lowry was working on the intricate molding for the cabin of a steamer called *Fair Play*, under construction for nearly a year in Ripley. At noon, his uncle told the staff that the *Uncle Sam* had docked at the Ripley wharf and was contracted to take five hundred barrels of pork from Ripley to New Orleans. Knowing that the *Uncle Sam* was twice as large as any boat on the Ohio or the Mississippi, all hands were eager to walk her decks and tour her cabins. McNish announced that his staff could stop work at 4 p.m. and spend the rest of the day on the "big boat." With little but carpentry on his mind, Lowry boarded the steamer.

His first stop was the cabin, where he and others inspected the floors, the configuration of windows and walls, the brasswork and the woodwork. Then he visited the lower deck, first the engine room and then aft, toward the stern. There he saw something that aroused more than his passion for the building of a mighty vessel: two groups of slaves, about fifty in all, chained to each side of the deck, the men on his left and the women on his right. The antislavery sentiments that Theodore Weld had aroused in him two weeks before, suddenly surfaced from deep within him, bursting forth in a way that he would never forget.

In his own words:

I saw two long chains, extending from the forward to the rear of each side of the steerage deck. The ends were bolted to the sides of the boat about four feet above the deck floor. To these chains, at about equal distances apart, were attached twenty-five shorter chains with a handcuff attached to the loose end. The handcuff was locked on the wrists of the right arm of each slave. The short chain was just long enough to enable the slave to sit or lie down on the deck, and in weight and size was that of the ordinary chain used in plowing with horses. No seat or bed was provided; they were compelled to use the deck floor. When I came on the scene some were sitting as best they could on the floor, others were lying down and some were standing. It was an unpleasant picture.

The men were of sullen countenance and the women appeared to be stricken with a hopeless grief. Farther from them at my right at the extreme end of the long chain was a woman, young, not more than twenty. She had a pretty face, it might with propriety be called beautiful. She had long, fine, wavy, shiny black hair put up with care and taste and she was as white as any woman of my acquaintance, requiring the closest scrutiny to detect the least touch of African blood.

I said to myself, "Can it be possible that she is a slave, bound for a Southern slave mart to stand on the auction block and be knocked down by some brutal auctioneer to the highest bidder. Yes, that handcuff and chain proclaim that she is a slave, a young woman, beautiful in feature and form that has no more rights of person and soul than the beasts of the field."

As I leaned against a stanchion for support I asked myself why let all my sympathies be expended upon that one woman. Were the women, her companions in slavery, though they be of a darker hue than she, any less the daughters of the Lord Almight? Were they not as well as their white sisters the objects of Christ's redeeming love? For a time all I had forgotten of Theodore Weld's descriptions a few weeks before of the horrors of American slavery came vividly to my mind as I looked at the picture before me. Yet I might have gone away with my dislike of slavery a little more intensified and nothing more had I not caught a fragment of a conversation between two men who were approaching.

The words I heard were, "Ain't she a beauty?" The men passed by me, scarcely noting my presence, and stopped in front of the woman I have just described. One of the men was coarse and hard featured. He carried in his hand a small rawhide cane that could be used in the place of the common "rawhide." He was the owner of the slave and had the usual characteristics of the "negro trader," fond of whisky, rough, profane and unchaste in conversation, brutal, and passionate in disposition. They were a class of men that were a product of slavery, dreaded by the slaves and despised by the slaveholders. He wore heavy woolen clothes, the trousers loosely pushed into the tops of cowhide boots with heavy soles. His hair was worn long in regulation style and was topped by the broad-brimmed hat of the Southern "Overseer." The other was a tall, well-dressed young man, not bad in feature, passably good looking, with a little outcropping of the sensual. Under proper influences he might be an honorable, moral man who would command the respect of the good. I gathered from the conversation that he was a single man, engaged in some business in New Orleans, and the son of a Southern planter. His conversation was free of profanity and obscenity. As far as the circumstances would admit I inferred from the first part of the conversation that he had some conscience about the propriety of the business in hand, the purchase of the woman.

I decided not to leave my post but to watch the transaction. The trader used the vilest language, proposing the woman as a mistress for the young man and insisting she was worth more than he asked, $2,500, and swearing he could get $3,000 for her in New Orleans. He knew young men, he said, who would jump to get such a well made and good looking woman as she was.

All the time she had her face covered with her hands and was crying as if her heart would break. The other women were crying also and more than one man muttered curses and I saw clenched fists and angry eyes, all showing how helpless they felt to protect the women. As the trader, with an oath, said, "No more of that, you black sons of ———," he struck the woman on the shoulder and ordered her to take her hands from her face and stop her crying or he would half-kill her. She obeyed, and after a little more talk the young man offered $2,000. This was rejected at this stage of the proceedings and the trader played what might be called the last card in his game of debauchery.

He asked the young man if he was the only occupant of his stateroom, receiving an affirmative reply. He then said, "How fortunate. You have to go to your room by the door that opens on the deck and no one will be the wiser and you can have a splendid time. It will cost you nothing. I have paid her passage and bond."

The young man was evidently tempted but shook his head. The trader then ordered the woman to unfasten the front of her dress. She declined, but a stroke on the shoulder brought a reluctant obedience; a second expedited the work. When done, her hands lingered, but pushing them away he exposed her bosom to view and induced the young man to feel of her breast, then of her thighs. By this time the young man was carried to the point of yielding and the money paid, the woman relieved of her chain, followed her new master to his room.

As I left the boat my indignation reached the boiling point over the wicked transaction and, lifting my right hand toward the heavens, I said aloud, "My God helping me, there shall be a perpetual war between me and human slavery in this nation of which I am a member and I pray God I may never be persuaded to give up the fight until slavery is dead or the Lord calls me home."

I thought I was alone with God in the evening gloom and was a little startled at hearing a young friend call, "Lowry, what is the matter, do I hear you swearing?"

"Yes, what of it? I have taken a solemn promise that I will fight slavery until it is dead."

"Oh, that is all right but I guess you will die long before slavery is killed," was his laughing reply as he left me.

On reaching my uncle's I found all the others had been to supper and my aunt had been waiting three-quarters of an hour for me wondering if I had gone to father's. I had no appetite and uncle asked if I was unwell. I said I had seen enough to make a strong man sick, much less a boy.

"What is that?" he asked, for he had not visited the boat.

"Fifty chained slaves, borne like hogs to market, and I am angry."

"Let not the sun go down on your anger, my boy," he replied.

"I guess, uncle, your advice has come too late in the day as aunt's patiently waiting supper for me testifies," I laughingly replied as I went to my room.

In his room, Lowry returned to the shadows of his private thoughts. Sitting at his drafting board, he stared at an unfinished drawing of a stairway. He was trying to configure the staircase in a given imaginary space where it would be very difficult to build one, but he could not concentrate on the assignment. The scene on the *Uncle Sam* still gripped his mind and heart. He paced the floor. "What of it, yes, that is the question," he said out loud. "What of it? You made today a most solemn vow before God. Now what are you going to do about it? Will you settle down and drift with the popular current and be satisfied with an expression of your abhorrence of slavery in idle words?"

He struggled all night long, and by morning he had decided to abandon his carpentry career when his apprenticeship was over, return to college as his father had asked him to do, and enter the ministry with the intention of dedicating his life to fighting slavery.

Throughout his apprenticeship with his uncle, Lowry engaged more and more in antislavery work. He was a charter member of the Ripley Anti-Slavery Society and attended meetings of the state society. On many controversial issues regarding slavery and free blacks, he publicly stood with his father. And he engaged in a different kind of apprenticeship, a secretive one with his father and his father's co-conspirators, learning all he could about the Underground Railroad.

Around the time of Lowry's conversion, the movement was gaining momentum nationwide, and as it did, animosities were heating up along the river about as quickly as fire in a hay barn. What Gilliland and Campbell, then Collins and Rankin, had begun years ago in Ripley, Red Oak, and beyond was becoming increasingly dangerous. Still, the numbers were growing of people willing to work in the underground and unwilling to accept the notion that the North had no responsibility with regard to slavery. Lowry had plenty of mentors.

For some people, the strongest reason to join the cause was the church and Scripture. It was in the churches, after all, that the antislavery agitation had begun, long before *The Liberator* and Garrison had even contemplated "immediatism." For others, a single event caused a dramatic change in their lives, much like Lowry's afternoon on the lower deck of the *Uncle Sam*. Witnessing slavery for the first time and experiencing it firsthand were often inducements. For many others, fighting slavery was simply part of family life.

Along the river, the antislavery crusade was mostly a "family business" that had begun at the moment of exodus from the slave states of Virginia, Tennessee, the Carolinas, and Kentucky during the late eighteenth and early nineteenth centuries. By the time Lowry entered this risky business, there were already two or three generations in some families who had lived the double life of "conductors." They knew by the blaze of the moonlight through the woods, by the time of year, by the weather, by recent threats, and by local events just where to go next. They knew who had a concealed room beneath the hearth, who had a cellar in the barn, who had a hay wagon with a secret compartment, who had a fast horse, a proslavery neighbor, a secure garret.

Families were large. The Rankins would raise at least twenty-two children: thirteen of their own; a niece they adopted after the death of the child's parents; two children of one of their sons who died of typhoid fever; five of Jean Rankin's siblings' children; one adopted black girl named Catherine McCaskey, who had been born into slavery in Alabama and possibly another black girl, Mary Donahoo Rankin. There were eight Collinses, five Gillilands, and ten Beasleys, all active on the line in Ripley. Brothers working together were common: the McCague brothers, Thomas and James; the Mahans, John B. and William; the four Kincaid brothers, the Moores, the Pangburns, and the McCoys. At the Gist settlements, there were thirty-four Hudsons in seven Hudson families, fifty-one Cumberlands in eight families, and twenty-seven Johnsons in four families. The membership of the Ripley Anti-Slavery Society included twelve Salisburys, fourteen Hopkinses, half a dozen Snedakers, Shepherds, Sutherlands, Evanses, and Porters. In and around Sardinia, on the northern portion of the line, there were dozens of Pettijohns and nearly as many Hugginses. Over the northern boundary of Brown County, in Highland County, there were Van Pelts, Nelsons, Smalleys, among others who were active on the line.

For these families, the risks of the underground became a way of life, as common to the children of "conductors" as learning to skate on the frozen river. Often abolitionists' children intermarried. Rankin and two of his brothers married daughters of a Tennessee antislavery man. John B. Mahan and his brother married the Curtis sisters, all raised in antislavery households. The sister of abolitionist Jacob Ebersole, in nearby Moscow, Ohio, married the ardent antislaver Robert Fee in Batavia—both conductors on the Underground Railroad. In one of the free black settlements, a Cumberland married a Hudson. In Ripley, a Gilliland married a Collins. In Sardinia, a Pettijohn married a Huggins.

By the mid-1830s, the Ripley line into which Lowry had been inducted was well established. In Ripley, the Collins brothers—Theodore and Thomas—continued the work of their father, Nathaniel, at the family home on the corner of Front and Mulberry streets. Theodore also owned property behind Rankin's hilltop land, on the way to Red Oak, which came in handy on many a night. Thomas, with the help of his wife, sometimes sequestered runaways in the coffins that he made in his workshop at the back of the Front Street house. Others in Ripley included the sons of Nathaniel Beasley, who had left Virginia with his family at the age of fifteen, in 1789, and settled in Decatur, northeast of Ripley. From the 1830s onward, one of his sons practiced medicine in Ripley and worked closely with Rankin and the Collinses. In Red Oak, Gilliland, his five children, and his wife had run one of the most active stations in the region, in their home and in the old stone church, for nearly thirty years. In Russellville, the Reverend Jesse Lockhart, a cousin of Rankin who, like him, was born in 1793 in East Tennessee, opened the doors of his home and his church to fugitives from the moment he settled there in the late 1820s. In Decatur, a physician, Greenleaf Norton, also born in 1793, had been helping fugitives since at least the 1820s, when he immigrated to Ohio from Maine. Also in the countryside near Decatur and Russellville were the McCoys, who had come to Ohio from Kentucky in 1811 and would work in the underground for more than twenty years.

Fugitives coming through Ripley found their own way up to Rankin's house or were guided up the hill by someone in town. From there, one or more of Rankin's sons would take them in a wagon or on horseback to Red Oak, where the Gillilands or other families, such as the Hopkinses, would shelter them and make the choice to send them on either to Decatur, which was east of Red Oak, or to Russellville, almost directly north. Sometimes they were taken to a stagecoach stop outside of Decatur, a small building with two rooms for overnight stays built on a slight promontory in the middle of a large expanse of open fields, from which horsemen could be seen long before the pounding of their horses' hooves could be heard. From Decatur, which was only a few miles from the Adams County border, runaways sometimes went to houses in West Union, in Adams County, or directly north, to one of the free black settlements.

Slaves leaving Russellville typically traveled north to the new town of

Sardinia, not far from the border of Highland County. From there they found their way or were led to a farm several miles northeast of the border—four miles from Hillsboro, Ohio—owned by John M. Nelson, a Virginian who had been raised in a household with many slaves and who had come to Ohio to fight slavery. He and his son Marshall worked closely with John Rankin and his sons, from the late 1820s onward. Many slaves went on to a Quaker settlement at New Petersburg, and then to the town of Greenfield, where there were several safe houses. If these routes were too dangerous at a particular time, there were always alternatives, such as sending the fugitives west into Clermont County, or as far as Cincinnati. From Cincinnati, they would then move north to towns such as Lebanon and Springboro, where there were Quaker safe houses and Presbyterians active in the underground, or even into Indiana and then north.

Hiding and helping runaways was an inexact science based on the instincts and knowledge of the conductors and the specific circumstances of the night. Sometimes, because of the information that conductors might have about slave hunters or slave owners in pursuit, the fugitive was given a cryptically written note about the conductor's opinion regarding the safest route for him. Other times, one conductor might send a note in advance to alert those in the next house of the imminent arrival of a runaway. One such note out of Greene County, Ohio, farther to the north, read: "Dear Sir: By tomorrow's mail you will receive two volumes of the 'Irrepressible Conflict' bound in black. After perusal, please forward and oblige."

The Rankins kept as many as twelve fugitives at a time on some nights, putting a few in the barn and a few others in the house. Jean Rankin fed them all. Sometimes the warmth they experienced made them want to stay. "A young man came to my house on his way to Canada," Rankin later wrote. "He said that in Kentucky there were twenty men after him in a wheat field and they were so near him he thought they would hear his heart beat. He said the Kentuckians had told him the Abolitionists took the runaway slaves to some place and sold them but, said he, 'I was sold anyhow and I thought I would try it.' When some young men came to take him to another depot he bade me farewell and said, 'Oh, how good to find friends. Can't I come back from Canada and see you all?' 'No,' I said, 'the laws are against you. You cannot come back.' "

With the Rankins, the underground work was always a family event, and each escape presented its own peculiar set of challenges that often required members of the family to change their plans abruptly. At dawn one summer day in the 1830s, a young black woman, around sixteen or seventeen, arrived at the house with the three front doors, about which she had heard in Maysville, where she lived. She had taken a skiff and rowed her way to Ripley's shores. One of Rankin's brothers answered the door and quickly pulled her inside the house. The sun had risen and so it was too late to take her to the house on the hill. Instead, he sent one of his sons with a note up the hill to tell his brother what had happened and to seek his advice on how to proceed. Upon receiving the note, John Rankin hiked down the hill to his old house on Front Street. He spoke to the girl and assured her that all was fine, and that if she simply did what he said she would soon be on the path north, "where you will always be free." Then he sat down with his brother and sister-in-law to discuss what he had in mind. The girl was light-complexioned and the size of Rankin's teenage daughter, Julia. Julia was planning to go to the Kincaid family's apple-picking that very day. It was a big event in which there would be two great kettles of apple butter; all the teens in town would be there. Instead, Rankin said, Julia would now come to the house on Front Street, walk in the door, and give her clothes to the runaway slave, who would walk out the door in her place. Rankin returned home and told Julia the plan, which she immediately agreed to.

To enhance the reality of the scene and to supply an armed escort for the slave, Rankin asked his son Richard Calvin to ride next to the girl as she left town. All went smoothly, and Richard Calvin rode with the girl as far as Alexander McCoy's house, about seven and a half miles from Ripley. There McCoy's red-headed twin daughters, Bessie and Becky, took the girl in and found rugged clothes for her for the next leg of her journey. That night, William and James McCoy took her on a two-day trip north. Julia, meanwhile, missed her big day at the Kincaids', but, as her brother Samuel would later say, "Julia would deny herself any kind of pleasure to give a helping hand to the slaves."

Often, those who stopped at the Rankin home were women. From the accounts of John Rankin:

There was a slave woman, a member of the Presbyterian church, who was sold out of a Presbyterian into a Methodist family. She nursed the children of this family. After the children were grown up the old people permitted her to live as a free woman and she was highly esteemed as a pious woman. When the old people died some of the heirs determined to have her sold. Augusta, Kentucky was her home and the people of that place could not see her sold. She was concealed till she could be taken away. A free colored girl of Ohio took a skiff and brought her away in the night to my house. I cannot express the mental exercises I had when I looked upon her calm and benevolent countenance. Here was a woman, fifty years of age, a member of the Lord Jesus Christ, under my roof, concealed from pursuers, and she had to travel by night, hundreds of miles to a foreign land to escape being sold like a beast of the field, to the highest bidder. And I, for giving her shelter, if it were known, was liable to suffer the heaviest penalty of a most diabolical law.

A gentleman in Maysville, Kentucky hired a young slave woman to wait on his sick wife. Before her time was up a slave driver bought her and came for her. The gentleman refused to let her go till her time was up. When the man had gone he told the young woman, "You are sold and I cannot keep you. If you have any desire to go to Canada now is the time." She replied, "Your wife is sick. How can you do without me?" He said he would do the best he could about that and she left and came to our house and then went safely, by the aid of benevolent persons, to Canada.

A Kentucky slave mother having been harshly treated by her mistress, took her child in her arms and in the night started for Canada. She came to the house of an old Scotchman who lived on the Ohio River. She asked him what was best for her to do. My house being on top of a high hill he pointed to it and said, "A good man lives in that house. Go to it and go in and you will be safe." The river was frozen over and a thaw had come so the water was running over the ice, which was just ready to break up. She waded across and went to my house, went into the kitchen, made a fire and dried herself. Then she waked up two of my boys and they conveyed her to another depot the same night. The lakes being frozen over she could not get to Canada till spring. She passed the winter at Greenfield. Her husband, who was also a slave, followed her there. Some men went to the house to tell her that her husband had come and inquired for her. She, believing them to be slave catchers, took her child, ran out and wandered about in a cold night until they both nearly perished. She was forced to go to a house, which happened to be of the right sort. Next morning her husband was brought to her. When spring came they were safely conveyed to Victoria's dominion.

Another young slave woman came from Maysville to my house. She was beautiful and accomplished in her manners and but slightly colored. She was a seamstress and, as such, had intercourse with the highest class of ladies, from whom she gained much knowledge and learned politeness. She would have been glad to make her home with my family but that could not be done. The slave catchers would soon have found her and taken her back to slavery. Several fugitive slaves were with her, one of whom intended to make her his bride after getting to Canada.

Slave hunters often followed their prey for days, some venturing as far as the Canadian border. The reward for returning a runaway in the state of Kentucky was usually $100, and it was twice that if the slave had crossed the river into a free state. This meant that sometimes slave catchers drove runaways, like cattle, into Ohio, then cornered them and took them back, in order to reap the larger reward. It also meant that men in Ohio often engaged in slave hunting to collect the reward. They joined packs of Kentucky slaveholders to round up runaways, knowing they could get a share of the reward.

Throughout the 1830s, clashes between slave hunters and abolitionists along the Ohio River were increasing, simply because there were more of both. In Ripley, that knocking at the door in the middle of the night could be friend or foe. On other stops along the line, especially those near the free black settlements, the battles sometimes erupted into gunfights between two groups of mounted horsemen—one trying to protect the slave and the other trying to catch him. In the years ahead, the area around the new town of Sardinia and the conductors there would be caught in numerous skirmishes, largely because of its proximity to the largest of the free black settlements in Brown County and because of the aggressive participation of several of Sardinia's citizens in the underground, mainly Dr. Isaac Beck and John Bennington Mahan.

Around the time Lowry became active in the underground, Sardinia had emerged as an important stop. It was laid out along the east branch of White Oak Creek, about twenty-five miles north of Ripley, in 1833 by a small group of men, mostly of antislavery persuasion and mostly Methodists. One of them, Dr. Beck, named the town after his favorite Methodist hymn. Born in Bethel, Ohio, not far from Ripley, Dr. Beck was Sardinia's first physician and one of the state's most ardent abolitionists. His uncle was Thomas Morris, the U.S. senator from Ohio who would one day risk his career to speak out against slavery on the floor of the U.S. Senate. Both of his parents were raised in the South and yet believed in immediate emancipation as early as Rankin had advocated it. All eight of Dr. Beck's children labored in the antislavery crusade.

Dr. Beck and his family worked frequently with the Pettijohn clan of twelve households, all from Virginia—some doctors, some merchants, some preachers, and all Presbyterians willing to hide, feed, and transport runaways—and with the Huggins families, also Presbyterians, who had followed Reverend Gilliland from North Carolina, leaving the South because of slavery. The two Huggins brothers, Robert and William, settled at first in Ripley and Red Oak, and then purchased considerable tracts on the north fork of White Oak Creek, outside of Sardinia. Robert had five sons, including another William and Milton, and then William, his brother, had numerous sons, including James. These three—William, Milton, and James—late at night, sometimes rode to a place in the hills halfway between Ripley and Sardinia to meet Lowry Rankin, at least one runaway slave, and one or two of Lowry's brothers. The Hugginses then hid the slaves beneath hay or fodder piled high on their wagons, and typically took them to a cabin on Robert's farm near Sardinia. On the farm was a house where Robert had built a false hearth that could be raised to expose a space large enough for the slaves to hide for a few hours if slave hunters were nearby.

Dr. Beck's closest colleagues on the line, however, were John D. Hudson, a free black man, and Mahan, a Methodist minister. Around the time of the arrival of the *Uncle Sam* riverboat in Ripley, Mahan had just opened the first tavern in Sardinia in a large brick building that had rooms for overnight visitors and a publike eatery that did not serve liquor. Known as a "temperance tavern" among the locals, it was soon known also as a safe stop for runaways. Mahan was born in Kentucky in 1801 to Martha Bennington and Jacob Mahan, a Baptist minister from Pennsylvania whose father had come to America from Ireland in the eighteenth century. Both parents abhorred slavery, and in 1804 they moved their sons and daughters from Kentucky to the Ohio town of Bethel in Clermont County. In the early 1820s, Jacob became a member of the United Brethren Church, and, being an articulate man known for his clear, strong sermons, he took to the road as a missionary in the new territories, mainly Indiana. Part of his personal mission was to use the pulpit to spread the word against slavery. But his mission was cut short. In 1828, he was traveling on horseback some miles below Crawfordsville, Indiana, when heavy rains caused a flash flood in the stream he was trying to cross. Swept off his horse and thrust into the top of a fallen tree, he remained there for hours in the wet and cold, until two men rescued him. He died shortly afterward from exposure. Dramatically affected by their father's death, all six of his children took aggressive stands against slavery.

John Mahan and his younger brother, William, married sisters Cassandra and Mary "Polly" Curtis in the 1820s and settled on 160 acres on a little stream called Bell's Run in Highland County, only four or so miles north of the Brown County border. A few years later, in the early 1830s, John bought land on White Oak Creek, not many miles into Brown County, and there he would remain for the rest of his life. Though trained as a schoolteacher and a Methodist minister, Mahan helped to organize the Presbyterian church in Sardinia, where he preached frequently against slavery, with the power and eloquence he had inherited from his father. By the time he opened the tavern, he had built a sawmill, purchased several pieces of property in the area, and was working on plans for a dry-goods store. All of his properties were used for hiding runaways. A tall, muscular, swarthy man, Mahan was a highly respected citizen of Sardinia, though he inspired his share of enemies in and around the town among those who strongly suspected that he was feeding fugitives.

Mahan knew Rankin well. Both lectured throughout the countryside, launched antislavery societies, and strongly advocated immediate and total emancipation. Both also worked with the Quaker Levi Coffin, who then lived in Indiana. Mahan, who likely made the Coffin connection through his father in the 1820s, was one of the early links between Rankin and Coffin. Mahan also worked with Lowry on numerous occasions, with Nelson up in Highland County near the home of his brother, with the Pettijohns, and with the Huggins brothers. In the nearby free black community, where Mahan was a familiar figure, he forged a bond with a black man, John Hudson—a bond that made the Ripley line all the more formidable to those who tried to fit together the pieces of the underground puzzle.

Free blacks were often suspicious of the white community, for good reason, but in Brown County, perhaps because of the Gist communities, the two groups came together as whites and blacks rarely had. Mahan and Beck were especially close to Hudson, who was highly respected on the Underground Railroad. Born into slavery in Virginia, he was a boy of nine or ten when he came to Ohio with his parents, who were among the freed slaves of Samuel Gist. His mother taught him the importance of learning to read, which he did by befriending white people in Brown County who took the time to teach him. A tall, robust man with a reputation for fearlessly confronting and outsmarting slave catchers, Hudson began helping runaways in the 1820s. After Dr. Beck, Mahan, and others moved into the area in the 1830s, Dr. Beck arranged that Hudson be paid for his high-risk underground work. At least three men—Beck, Mahan, and one of the Pettijohn brothers—contributed 25 cents each to pay Hudson for transporting runaways to the next stop. For years Beck told people up and down the line that Hudson was "the man who guided more [runaways] than any other." Hudson was the man who Mahan, Beck, and Rankin knew could always be depended upon to help run off slave hunters, and who often hid runaway slaves at the Gist camps—an increasingly dangerous scheme, because slave hunters were drawn to the free black communities like hounds to the scent. Said Beck, "Fugitives were very likely to hear of the abolitionists or the 'nigger camps' and to endeavor to find one or the other immediately after crossing the river. If they landed at the camps, which was common, they were often helped to our neighborhood for the colored people soon came to believe that the runaways were safer among the whites than with themselves."

Hudson helped a slave named Ike escape from his pursuers by following closely behind the slave hunters and tooting a conch shell to warn Ike and his guide of the hunters' location. When asked if he was not afraid to arouse the hunters' wrath, he said, "No. The knots on the shell would hurt a fellow's head very bad."

There were other free blacks on the Ripley line, including Moses Cumberland, Billy Marshall, and Polly Jackson, who was known to throw pans of boiling water at inquiring slave hunters who got too close. In Maysville, in the mid-to-late 1830s, a black barber worked with Rankin, Mahan, and perhaps others to guide slaves across the river and up Rankin's hill. But on the Ohio side it was Hudson who most often appeared as the slave catchers closed in on their prey. Few could match his courage in Brown County's underground.

CHAPTER TEN

AGITATION

In the summer of 1835, one of the Lane Rebels, Amos Dresser, was traveling throughout the South selling Bibles to raise funds for his education. At the same time, Dresser was distributing a variety of antislavery publications. His inventory included several copies of the American Anti-Slavery Society's new edition of Rankin's letters, which was now contraband material in a large portion of the nation. After leaving Cincinnati on July 1, Dresser rode through Kentucky and Tennessee, where, in Sumner County, he sold a copy of the letters. With a carriage full of the literature of dissent, he arrived in Nashville on July 18. The August 25 issue of the *Cincinnati Gazette* carried his account of what happened next:

> As my name has obtained an unexpected notoriety, I ask the public attention to my own account of the transactions that have given me celebrity.
>
> On the first of last month I left Cincinnati for the purpose of selling the "Cottage Bible," to raise funds sufficient to enable me to complete my education. The largest portion of my books were sent to Nashville by water. I took several copies of the Bible with me, besides a considerable number of the little work, entitled, "Six months in a Convent." In packing them into my trunk and the box of my barouche [carriage], a num-

ber of pamphlets and papers of different descriptions were used to prevent the books from injury by rubbing, intending to distribute them as suitable opportunities should present. Among them were old religious newspapers, anti-slavery publications, numbers of the Missionary Herald, Sunday school periodicals, temperance almanacs, &c. &c.

At Danville, K., where a state anti-slavery society had been organized some months before, and where the subject of emancipation seemed to be discussed without restraint, besides selling several copies of my books, I parted with a large share of my anti-slavery publications. In travelling through that state, I distributed most of my temperance almanacs and other papers above mentioned, including a few tracts on slavery, given to those who were willing to receive them. I gave none of these to any person of color, bond or free, nor had I any intention to do so.

Near Gallatin, in Sumner Co., Tenn., I sold a copy of Rankin's Letters on Slavery. I arrived at Nashville on Saturday the 18th of [July], and took lodgings at the Nashville Inn. The young man who accompanied me, in bringing into the house my books from the box of the barouche, omitted the anti-slavery tracts and other pamphlets. Their being overlooked did not occupy the attention of either of us, and on Monday morning the barouche was taken to the shop of Mr. Stout to be repaired. In the course of the day, Mr. S. remarked to his workmen, as he afterwards informed me, that perhaps, as I came from Cincinnati, I was an Abolitionist. On this, one of them commenced rummaging my carriage. In the box he found, among the other pamphlets, a February No. of the Anti-Slavery Record, with a cut representing a drove of slaves chained, the two foremost having violins, on which they were playing—the American flag waving in the centre, whilst the slave driver, with his whip, was urging on the rear. This added considerably to the general excitement, which I afterwards learned was prevailing in relation to slavery—and in a short time it was noised about that I had been "circulating incendiary periodicals among the free colored people, and trying to excite the slaves to insurrection." So soon as the report came to my knowledge, I went to Mr. Stout and explained to him how it was that the pamphlets had been left in the barouche. I then took into my custody the remainder of them, and locked them up in my trunk. Mr. S., on this occasion, told me that the scene represented in the cut was by no means an infrequent occurrence—that it was accurate in all its parts, and that he had witnessed it again and again. Mr. S. is himself a slaveholder, though, as he says, opposed to slavery in principle—a member, if not an elder, in the Presbyterian Church, and one of the committee of vigilance which afterwards sat in judgment upon me.

The excitement continued to increase, and it was added to the report, that I had been posting handbills about the city, inviting an insurrection of the slaves. Knowing all the charges to be false—feeling unconscious of any evil intention, and therefore fearless of danger, I continued the sale of my Bibles in and around the city, till Saturday, the 18th of the month, when, as I was preparing to leave town to attend a camp-meeting, held some 8 or 10 miles distant, a Mr. Estell, formerly an auctioneer and vendor of slaves, at public outcry in Alabama, met me at the door and demanded "those abolition documents" I had in my possession. I replied, he should have them and proceeded to get them for him. When he made the demand he was under the influence of very highly excited feelings—his whole frame indicated agitation, even to trembling. On presenting the pamphlets, I requested him to read them before he condemned them. This seemed greatly to inflame his rage.

I then proceeded to the camp-ground where, about two hours after my arrival, I was taken in charge by Mr. Braughton, the principal city officer. I take pleasure here, in stating of Mr. B. that, allowing his conduct to be strictly official, he exhibited to me, throughout the whole of this melancholy affair, the kindest and most delicate deportment. I immediately accompanied him to town, where, on arriving at my boarding-house, I found the mayor, Mr. John P. Erwin, waiting for us. He remarked, he was afraid I had got myself into difficulty, and wished me to appear before the committee of Vigilance. To this I replied, it would give me pleasure to do so, as I wished it understood just what I had done, and what I had not done. He then asked me if I had any witness I wished to have called. My reply was, I knew not what need I had of witnesses, till I had heard the charge brought against me—that I supposed it would be necessary to prove me guilty of some misdemeanor, and not that it should be upon me to prove that I had broken no law. To his demand, if I was ready for trial, I answered, I wished it to take place immediately as I was anxious to return to the camp-ground. We repaired to the court-room, which was at once crowded full to overflowing. The roll of the Committee (60 in number) was called, and the names of the absentees proclaimed.

The meeting being called to order, the mayor stated that he had caused me to be arrested, and brought before the Committee, in consequence of the excitement produced by the periodicals known to have been in my possession; and that he had also taken in his charge my trunk, which he had delayed opening till my return. The trunk was then produced before the Committee, and a motion made and carried, that I should be interrogated as to its contents before opening it. On being interrogated accordingly, I replied, as the trunk was before them, I preferred they should make the examination for themselves. It was then resolved, (the whole house voting) that my trunk should be examined. The officer first laid before the committee a pile of clothing, which was examined very closely—then followed my books, among which was found, one copy of the "Oasis," one of "Rankin's Letters on Slavery," and one of "Bourne's Picture of Slavery in the United States." These, I informed the Committee, I had put in my trunk for my own perusal, as I wished to compare what had been written with the result of my own observation while in the slave States and that no individual had seen them besides myself. A careful inspection was made of the books also. Then was presented my business and private letters, which were read with eagerness, and much interest. Extracts were read aloud.

Among them was one from a letter received from a very aged and venerable lady, running thus—"Preached a stream of abolition two hundred and fifty miles long," in travelling from Cincinnati to Cleveland. Great importance was attached to this. Another spoke of the "inconsistency of celebrating the 4th of July, while so many among us were literally in bondage." Another, from a letter of Mr. Ensign, (a gentleman well known to entertain no very favorable sentiments for Abolitionism) which, after urging me to diligence in the sale of my Bibles, (obtained from him) jestingly concluded, "Now don't spend more than half your time among the niggers." This was cheered by the crowd. The last was from a friend of mine, a minister of the gospel, who remarked that on visiting his friends in the east, abolition had been the principle topic of conversation that day, and he had preached on slavery at night!

Great stress was laid on these extracts, and I was questioned very minutely, as to the authors of the letters. They labored much to prove I was sent out by some society, and that I was, under the guise of a religious mission, performing the odious office of an insurrectionary agent.

My journal was next brought into review, but as it had been kept in pencil mark, the memoranda short and hastily written, it served them very little purpose. It was laid down again by the Mayor who had attempted to read it aloud with this remark—"It is evidently very hostile to slavery."

A witness was now called forward by whom it was proved, that an anti-slavery periodical of some kind had been left by some individual on the counter of the Nashville Inn. That it was left with a copy of the Cottage Bible, at the time I arrived. On being questioned by me, it turned out to be a number of the "Emancipator," [a newspaper] used as an envelope, or wrapper to the Bible. Other witnesses were called, but this was the substance of all they proved against me.

It was conceded without hesitation on my part, that I had sold a copy of "Rankin's Letters," in Sumner Co. and that I had read to Mr. Cayce, at his request, the number of the "A[nti-]S[lavery] Record" before mentioned, which he said contained nothing that any candid man, and especially any Christian could gainsay. The chairman of the committee, asked me if I remembered the places where I had circulated anti-slavery tracts. Thus, by the form of the question, as well as by the manner, making the impression I had circulated them somewhere and that the fact of my having done so was known to the committee. To this I replied that what I did, I did openly—that I had not distributed any anti-slavery publications whatever in Tennessee, except the one above mentioned, and that, if any had been found under circumstances calculated to throw suspicion on me, it was a device of my enemies. On being interrogated as to my former connexion with Lane Seminary, I informed the committee that I had been a member of that institution as well as of the A[merican] [Anti-]S[lavery] Society, formed there more than a year ago; and that I had voluntarily withdrawn, and had received an honorable dismission from the same.

A handbill was next produced, and I was asked if I had ever seen it. After having examined it, I replied I never had. I was then asked with strong emphasis if I was sure I never had seen a copy of it. I again replied I was sure I never had. I was asked a third time, with a provoking and still stronger emphasis, if I was positively sure I had never seen any thing of the kind. I again took it into my hand and after examining it more minutely, again replied, I was positively sure I had never seen anything of the kind.

The trial continued from between 4 and 5 o'clock, p.m., till 11 o'clock at night when I was called up for my own defence. The perplexity I must have felt in making it may well be imagined, when it is recollected that I was charged not with transgressing any law of the state or ordinance of the city, but with conduct to which, if the law had attached the penalty of crime, its forms were totally disregarded, and this too, before an array of persons banded together in contravention of law, and from whose mandate of execution there was no appeal. However, I took the opportunity thus offered to declare fully my sentiments on the subject of slavery. While I told them I believed slaveholding to be inconsistent with the gospel, and a constant transgression of God's law, I yet said, that in bringing about emancipation the interests of the master were to be consulted as well as those of the slave. And that the whole scheme of emancipation contemplated this result, that the slave should be put in possession of rights which we have declared to be inalienable from him as a man; that he should be considered as an immortal fellow being, entrusted by his master with the custody of his own happiness, and accountable to him for the exercise of his powers; that he should be treated as our neighbor and our brother.

In reference to my demeanor towards the slave, that in the few instances in which I had casually conversed with them, I had recommended quietness, patience, submission; teaching them to "render good for evil," and discountenancing every scheme of emancipation which did not, during its process, look for its success in the good conduct of the slaves while they remain such, and to the influence of argument and persuasion addressed to the understandings and consciences of slaveholders, exhorting them to obey God in doing justice and showing mercy to their fellow men.

After my remarks were ended, the crowd was requested to withdraw while the committee deliberated on the case. In company with a friend or two, I was directed to a private room near at hand, to await their decision. Up to this period, during the whole proceedings, my mind was composed, my spirits calm and unruffled; nor did I entertain the most distant apprehension there would be so flagrant a violation of my rights as an American citizen, and so deliberate an attempt to dishonor me as a man.

In this confidence I was strengthened by the consideration of all the circumstances of the case. What I had done, I had done openly. There was no law forbidding what I had done. I had contracted no guilt that the law considered such—my intentions had been those of kindness to all—I had no secret feelings of guilt, arraigning me before the bar of my conscience, for any mean of clandestine movement. In addition to this, too, among my triers, there was a great portion of the respectability of Nashville. Nearly half of the whole number, professors of Christianity, the reputed stay of the church, supporters of the cause of benevolence in the form of Tracts and Missionary Societies and Sabbath Schools, several members, and most of the elders of the Presbyterian Church, from whose hands, but a few days before, I had received the emblems of the broken body and shed blood of our blessed Saviour.

My expectations, however, were soon shaken, by Mr. Braughton's saying, on entering the room where I was, that he feared it would go hard with me—that, while some of the committee were in favor of thirty-nine, others were for inflicting one hundred lashes, while others still thought me worthy of death. My suspence was at length terminated on being summoned to hear the decision; it was prefaced by a few remarks of this kind by the chairman, "that they had acted with great caution and deliberation, and however unsatisfactory their conclusions might be to me, they had acted conscientiously, with a full recognition of their duty to their God."—that they had found me guilty, "1ˢᵗ of being a member of an Anti-Slavery Society in Ohio;" 2ⁿᵈ, "of having in my possession periodicals published by the American Anti-Slavery Society:" and 3d, "they BELIEVED I had circulated these periodicals and advocated in the community the principles they inculcated." He then pronounced that I was condemned to receive twenty lashes on my bare back, and ordered to leave the place in 24 hours. (This was not an hour previous to the commencement of the Sabbath.)

The doors were then thrown open, and the crowd admitted. To them it was again remarked, that "the committee had been actuated by conscientious motives; and to those who thought the punishment too severe, they would only say, that they had done what they, after mature deliberation, thought to be right; and to those who thought it too light, they must say, that in coming to their decision, the committee had regarded not so much of the number of stripes as the disgrace and infamy of being publicly whipped.

The sentence being again repeated, it was received with great applause, accompanied by stamping of feet and clapping of hands. The chairman then called for the sentiments of the spectators in reference to their approbation of the decision of the committee, desiring all who were satisfied with it, and would pledge themselves that I should receive no injury after the execution of the sentence, to signify it in the usual way. There was no dissenting voice.

The chairman then expressed in terms bordering on the extravagant, his high gratification of the sense of propriety that had been manifested in the conduct of the meeting, and that so much confidence was placed in the committee. The crowd was now ordered to proceed to the public square, and form a ring.

I had been assured that my trunk, with all its contents, as they were taken out, should be returned to me. But whilst the crowd were leaving the house, Mr. Hunt, editor of the Banner, as I am informed an emigrant from New England where he was born, set himself busily to work to secure in his own hands my journal, sketch book, business and private letters, &c.

By no one concerned in the whole proceeding was there so much exasperated feeling shown, as by Mr. H. It was now displayed in the pale death-like countenance, the agitated frame, the hurried furious air with which he seized the papers and tied them up in his handkerchief, clinching them in his hands and at the same time eyeing me with an intense yet vacant gaze, bespeaking not only rage, but a consciousness of doing wrong. Of my papers I have heard nothing since Mr. H. took them into his custody.

I entered the ring that had been formed, the chairman (accompanied by the committee) again called for an expression of sentiment in relation to the sentence passed upon me; again the vote was unanimous in approval of it and again did he express his ratification at the good order by which the whole proceeding had been characterized. While some of the company were engaged in stripping of my garments, a motion was made and seconded that I should be exonerated altogether from the punishment. This brought many and furious imprecations on the mover's head, and created a commotion which was appeased only by the sound of the instrument of torture and disgrace upon my naked body.

I knelt to receive the punishment, which was inflicted by Mr. Braughton, the city officer, with a heavy cowskin. When the infliction ceased, an involuntary feeling of thanksgiving to God for the fortitude with which I had been enabled to endure it, arose in my soul, to which I began aloud to give utterance. The death-like silence that prevailed for a moment, was suddenly broken with loud exclamation, "G—d d——n him, stop his praying." I was raised to my feet by Mr. Braughton, and conducted by him to my lodging, where it was thought safe for me to remain but a few moments.

And though most of my friends were at the camp-ground, I was introduced into a family of entire strangers, from whom I received a warm reception, and the most kind and tender treatment. They will ever be remembered with grateful emotions.

On the ensuing morning, owing to the great excitement that was still prevailing, I found it necessary to leave the place in disguise, with only what clothing I had about my person; leaving unsold property to the amount of nearly three hundred dollars, and sacrificing at least two hundred on my barouche, horse, &c. which I was obliged to sell. Of my effects at Nashville, I have heard nothing since my return, though I have frequently written to my friends concerning them.

AMOS DRESSER. Cincinnati, Aug. 25, 1835.

In response, the New York newspaper *The Anti-Slavery Record* published the following:

Perhaps some of Mr. Dresser's self-styled judges may justify themselves by saying that had they voted to exonerate him from punishment, he would have been put to death by an infuriated mob. This is very probable, but what does such a probability prove of slavery? What sort of an institution is that which cannot bear to be spoken of in the language of truth? Which drives the most respectable members of a community into a disgraceful and unlawful outrage upon the rights of an American citizen, to save the perpetration of a crime in its defence still more diabolical? Is there any longer a doubt that such an institution is dangerous to the country—nay, to the weal of the whole human race?

That summer of 1835, the American Anti-Slavery Society declared an information war on the South by sending more than one million copies of antislavery publications, including Rankin's letters, out of New York into Alabama, Tennessee, South Carolina, North Carolina, Virginia, and Georgia via the mails and via human messengers. "The American Anti-Slavery Society aims to overthrow slavery by revolutionizing the public sentiment of the country," the society's annual report that year stated, and information was one of its weapons.

The "great pamphlet campaign of 1835" provoked mobs in Charleston in July that seized mailbags and burned them at the post office. In the autumn, a grand jury in Virginia called for the extradition of the society's executive committee, ordering them to stand trial. In his message to Congress in December that year, President Andrew Jackson called for the passage of a bill that would exclude the distribution of "incendiary publications intended to instigate the slaves to insurrection." Jackson beseeched the Northern states to outlaw the activities of all abolitionists. On December 18, Congressman James Hammond of South Carolina implored the House of Representatives to stop the receipt of all antislavery petitions to Congress. Soon John C. Calhoun, the strident senator from South Carolina, would bring the petition issue to the Senate. If the South had the right to hold slaves, which Calhoun believed it did, then, he reasoned, it had a right to hold them in peace and quiet. If Congress continued to accept the deluge of antislavery petitions, then it was waiving a right to determine what to accept or reject, and by doing this it would then become the receptacle of all that was "frivolous, absurd, unconstitutional, immoral, and impious," said Calhoun. And if the antislavery petitions to Congress were never read, if the abolitionist publications were banned in the South, and if activities such as Dresser's in the South and Rankin's in the North were outlawed, then, it was the hope of Southern sympathizers, abolitionism would be silenced and the crusade crushed.

In response, antislavery societies across the North were proliferating as quickly as Southerners were burning their publications and flogging their messengers. In Ohio alone, the number of antislavery societies increased from twenty-five in 1835 to 120 in 1836. And antislavery chronicles were proliferating across the nation.

In April 1835, Theodore Weld, John Rankin, John B. Mahan, James G. Birney; Lane Rebels William T. Allan, James A. Thome, Horace Bushnell, Augustus Wattles, and Henry B. Stanton; a number of Quakers; and 110 delegates from antislavery societies in twenty-five Ohio counties gathered in Zanesville to form the Ohio Anti-Slavery Society and to launch its newspaper, *The Anti-Slavery Bugle*. Weld was the first to arrive; Zanesville was the climax of his statewide campaign. His task was to lecture to the citizenry to inspire them to attend the convention. Birney came by stagecoach with the Hamilton County delegation; later, he wrote that Rankin was "the most noted abolitionist at the Zanesville convention" and that it was not uncommon then to call him "the Martin Luther" of the cause.

Zanesville was Rankin's first exposure to mob behavior—a rehearsal for what he soon would be facing rather frequently. One evening when he was on the way to the house of a friend, several men showered Rankin with rotten eggs. And on his trip home from Zanesville, he stopped and preached to two black congregations in Chillicothe, where people hurled stones through windows, injuring some members of the congregation. The mob, he later learned, had been told that Rankin and all of the abolitionists believed in the intermarriage of poor whites and blacks as a way to provide for more servants in the North. After the church gathering, he walked to the home of a friend, where a messenger had come to inform him that a mob was planning to attack him. His host's wife was ill, so Rankin went to the house of another friend. That friend's wife told him that he ought to "let the niggers alone." Still, the couple took him in, the mob did not find him, and he safely rode home the next day.

That spring in the Ohio Valley there was more than the threat of mobs to provoke an atmosphere of fear. The season had been unusually cold, with one of the hardest rains in memory. Although the river didn't flood, for days the sun rarely shone through the cover of clouds. At a time when weather was thought to be one of the causes of cholera, this was indeed ominous. The disease, it was thought, might somehow originate in the darkest of clouds or be brought by the wind or showered upon the earth by the rain. More than one person observed that the spring birds came as usual but the martins left before the summer—another sign, some people believed, that cholera might strike again. In July, just over the Brown County border in Adams County, a lawyer in West Union wrote to a local paper saying that he had noticed one ominous black cloud and remarked to his wife that he thought the cholera was coming. Two weeks later, the same paper reported, he was dead. West Union was hit the hardest. The scourge began in late June, and by the beginning of August it had passed through the Ripley area, where Rankin and his wife tended to the sick, as they had in previous outbreaks.

The cholera outbreak disrupted efforts in Ripley to launch a local anti-slavery society. It was not until the late autumn that Rankin and others were able to focus again on the antislavery cause. Then, on the night of November 25, 1835, Rankin, Alexander Campbell, James Gilliland, Thomas and Theodore Collins, and others met at the church in Red Oak to organize the Ripley Anti-Slavery Society. Rankin was appointed secretary, Campbell president, and Gilliland vice president. There were 337 charter members, who agreed to seven resolutions. Among them: "Resolved that this whole nation is involved in the guilt of slave holding and in the degradation of the people of colour: and no citizen can absolve himself from this guilt but by protesting against the sin; and using all lawful and righteous means in his power for its removal." The society's constitution called for an annual meeting to be held on December 25 and pledged its members to "convince their fellow citizens that slaveholding is a heinous sin in the sight of God," to "influence Congress to abolish Slavery, and to prevent its extention to any State that may be hereafter admitted into the

Union," and to "aim at the elevation of the character and condition of the people of colour by encouraging their intellectual, moral, and religious improvement and by removing publick prejudice, that thus they may according to their intellectual and moral worth share an equality with the whites in civil and religious privileges but this Society will never in any way countenance the oppressed in vindicating their rights by resorting to physical force."

At the society's next meeting, on April 13, 1836, members unanimously voted to send Rankin as their delegate to the Ohio Anti-Slavery Society's first anniversary convention in two weeks. The meeting was to be held in Granville, Ohio, approximately 135 miles north of Ripley.

Believing that the abolition movement was gaining momentum, Rankin felt compelled, more than ever perhaps, to write articles, newspaper commentaries, and pamphlets against slavery; to fight for schools that opened their doors to black students; to persuade his congregation at Ripley and his superiors at the Chillicothe Presbytery that immediate emancipation was the only solution to slavery; and to sustain his work in the local underground. He also had to run his church and the college. His wife had just given birth to their eighth son, whom they named Arthur Tappan, in honor of the New York abolitionist. And he was sensitive to the fact that some of his parishioners had begun to complain about the time he was spending away from the church doing his antislavery work. Worse still, he was beginning to feel the strain on his health from the intensity of his schedule. But sensing that the solidarity and proliferation of antislavery societies was critical to the growth of the movement, he was unable, as always, to resist the call of duty. No matter how impractical, stressful, inconvenient, or dangerous attending the Granville meeting might be, he agreed to go.

CHAPTER ELEVEN

MOBOCRACY

One hundred ninety-two delegates from antislavery societies throughout the state of Ohio journeyed to the village of Granville on April 25 and 26, 1836. Most entered the town on the very wide road known as Broadway. Past the dogwood trees that had just begun to display their pink-and-white splendor up and down Granville's main streets; past the stately houses where women and children stood in their yards to watch the reputed troublemakers, as if the ragtag troops from some distant army had invaded the town; and past the dozens of strangers from neighboring towns leaning against buildings and hitching posts, malingering and scheming, drinking and waiting. Many had never ventured farther than twenty-five miles from home, and now, in dedication to the cause they risked their lives to advance, they had traveled a hundred miles and more to this seemingly peaceful and innocent town.

Nestled among the ridges, spurs, and hollows of the hills rising above Raccoon Creek, the middle fork of the Licking River, Granville was situated at nearly the center of the state of Ohio: hence the choice of the town for this meeting of delegates from all parts of the state. By the spring of 1836, Granville was largely an antislavery town surrounded by small, intense enclaves of proslavery zealots. It was the home of two schools, the Granville Literary and Theological Institution for men, and, for women, the Granville Female Seminary. And there were several safe houses for fugitives, well known among those who worked in the underground movement. Passions had been aroused the year before, in both the academic and residential communities, when Theodore Weld passed through Granville on his statewide tour. Speaking for three nights in a row, he barbed the conscience of the town as he dodged a steady stream of rotten eggs. One of the nights, he spoke near an open window and was repeatedly covered with eggs. Each time, he would wipe the slush from his face and clothing and barely miss a beat.

Granville's roster of antislavery advocates expanded after Weld's tour, but most of the peace-loving citizens of this quiet village considered themselves to be antiabolitionists and wanted nothing to do with what they believed to be a fanatical movement. Although they did not condone slavery—and, indeed, considered themselves antislavers—they also did not know how to end it. Many favored gradual emancipation, and many more were advocates of colonization. And so, in November 1835, during the very same days when Rankin, Campbell, Gilliland, and others in Ripley were discussing how to shape their convictions into the context of a constitution for their new antislavery society, another group of men with a different set of values was meeting in Granville.

There, at the Methodist church, twenty-six leaders of the community, all considered men of conscience as well as property, discussed what they could do to discourage the now-imminent invasion of their town by hundreds of abolitionists. They compiled nine resolutions. And after reassuring each other that they ardently believed in freedom of speech, they wrote: "We consider discussions [that] from their nature tend to inflame the public mind—to introduce discord and contention into neighborhoods, churches, and literary institutions, and put in jeopardy the lives and property of our fellow citizens—to be at varience with all rules of moral duty and every suggestion of humanity." Although they condemned slavery as a menacing evil, they were critical of the abolitionists for scaring slaveholders into strengthening their opposition to emancipation. The measures of the abolitionists, they said, dangerously "strengthen and rivet the chains of the slaves and perpetuate their bondage."

Worse still, they agreed, the abolitionists should not use strident language such as "man stealers," nor should they suggest that Negroes could be educated and one day achieve a place of equality. Such beliefs were "utterly vain and delusive."

They praised the efforts of the American Colonization Society and approved its plans to transport free blacks from the U.S. to Africa, saying that "the unwillingness of the blacks of this country to emigrate to Africa is one of the strongest evidences of that degradation and imbecility which naturally results from their condition while resident among the whites." And on March 31, 1836, the *Gazette* of Newark, Ohio, published a proclamation signed by the mayor, village clerk, council members, and sixty-nine other citizens of Granville urging against the upcoming abolition convention.

By the morning of April 27, men from the towns and hamlets around Granville began to gather in the taverns, back alleys, and tree-lined streets of the town while the big barn north of town owned by Ashley Bancroft and dubbed by the abolitionists as the "Hall of Freedom" was coming alive with the spirit and sounds of solidarity. That the energy and passions of both groups would eventually collide seemed inevitable.

It was after the townsfolk had rejected all requests for space for the meeting that Bancroft, a thirty-seven-year-old carpenter and one of the leading abolitionists in the region, volunteered his barn, and even built a temporary addition to accommodate the expected masses. The barn was outside the jurisdiction of the mayor and village council, which meant that the delegates meeting there were not entitled to the privilege of police protection on their way to the assemblage, during it, or after it. Still, the delegation of so-called fanatics filed through the big double doors and side doors of the barn, one after another, tipping hats, shaking hands, putting faces to names. They came by the dozens, from as far as Cincinnati and Toledo, as close as Alexandria and Columbus. There were now 120 antislavery societies in Ohio, with the largest having a roster of 942 members in the town of Paint Valley, in Ross County, near Cleveland. The total enrollment of the state societies by the spring of 1836 was approximately ten thousand, out of a population of roughly 1.2 million people.

The list of delegates—most, if not all, active in the Underground Railroad in their regions—included: James Birney, the abolitionist editor and close friend of Rankin's who, on January 1, had issued the first edition of his new antislavery newspaper, *The Philanthropist,* out of New Richmond, Ohio, near Ripley; Rankin; John Isaac Mahan; Dr. Beck; Asa Mahan, formerly a Lane board member and now the president of Oberlin College; twenty-five others from that college and the town of Oberlin, including Lane Rebels Amos Dresser, Augustus Wattles, and James A. Thome; two students from the Granville Literary and Theological Institution who had become notorious for their oratorical speeches against slavery; and nine-teen women, some of whom were students from the local women's acad-emy and some delegates from antislavery societies.

On the first day of the convention, April 27, the delegates crowded the barn, finding space to sit in the hay mows, on high ladders, even on the rafters. More than one hundred spectators entered the barn, carefully watched by men assigned to guard the delegates, standing sentry at the doors of free speech and free assembly. For security, Bancroft placed a big chain across the large gate at the head of the trail leading to the barn from the road; this would require all members of the mob gathering in town to climb the fence, slowing them down and thus preventing a surprise attack on the barn. Others brought dozens of hoop poles from a local cooper's shop. By cutting each one in half, the group had an ample supply of sturdy cudgels, if necessary for self-defense. The poles were piled in a corner of the barn for all to see, and to serve as a reminder that the threat of interruptions and antiabolitionist violence was ever present.

The day commenced with a resolution from Birney "that in order to perpetuate our free institutions the subject of slavery ought to be fully dis-cussed by the non-slaveholding states." James A. Thome delivered a speech titled "Appeal to the Females of Ohio" in which he beseeched women to stand equally with men in fighting for the rights of the oppressed and to break away from "that odious sentiment" that can shape a woman into nothing more than "a painted puppet or a gilded butterfly." James Dickey, who worked the underground with Rankin out of Greenfield, Ohio, pro-posed several resolutions, all of which passed.

The next morning began with the election of officers for the coming year. Alexander Campbell and James Gilliland were voted in as vice presidents; John B. Mahan and John Rankin were appointed the society's managers for Brown County. Birney and two other delegates recom-mended that $5,000 be raised over the next year, and as $10, $20, and $50 bills passed over heads in the crowd to the platform where Birney stood, a cry for more, for a goal of $10,000, replaced the $5,000 figure. Within minutes, the crowd raised $4,500. After the amount was announced, hun-dreds of men and women sang until the timbers shook, "Praise God from whom all blessings flow."

A series of resolutions followed. Then Rankin walked up the three steps to the wooden platform at the center of the barn. A light must have kindled in the depths of his eyes as he looked out onto the throng of hundreds of people united in a cause far larger than themselves. His speech focused on the obligation of the church to take a stand against slavery and began with a denunciation of every Biblical justification for slavery. From Exodus to Deuteronomy to James, he explained, the so-called slaves, which Southern-sympathizers and slaveholders were constantly noting in the Bible, were, in truth, servants. And the difference between slaves and servants was that the natural rights of servants are protected by law, whereas slaves have no such rights to be protected. The servitude in Israel was similar to apprenticeships in America, he said. It was voluntary; the servants were paid for their services; they could be held for no longer than their term of contract permitted; and they had a right to hold property. Slavery in America, he went on to say, was the essence of human oppression. And the spirit, genius, and intention of the Bible were utterly hostile to human oppression.

"The Scriptures represent all men as having sprung from one common parent—all as 'made of one blood,' " said Rankin. "Consequently all are created equally free. Whatever rights the first man had, all his children must have. God created no slaves. He gave to all men the same original rights."

Those who uphold slavery, he said, are therefore committing a sin, and the church should take a strong position against it. And those churchgoers who hold slaves and advocate slavery, justifying their actions and beliefs with twisted interpretations of the Bible, should be excommunicated from the church and at the very least forbidden to take communion. It is the duty of the church to take a stand, he said, as applause filled the "Hall of Freedom."

Raising his voice to be heard above the din, he concluded, "Let the church universal as the army of the living God, come up to the help of the Lord against the mighty; let her voice be heard as the voice of many waters, proclaiming liberty to the captive, and the opening of the prison to them that are bound—and the poisonous fountains of death shall be dried up, the rivers of anguish shall cease to flow, and sorrow and sighing shall flee away. Union in this great work will prepare the church for the rising of millenial glory, when liberty shall be universal, and the song of redeeming love shall ascend from every tongue."

In unison, the crowd joined Rankin in saying: "Glory to God in the highest, and on earth, peace, good will toward men."

There was then a vote to furnish every minister in the state with a copy of Rankin's speech. Solidarity in the churches was essential, they all agreed. Asa Mahan announced a resolution "that the time has now come when it is the duty of the church to debar from her privileges all who persist in the sin of holding their fellow-men in the bondage of slavery." It was seconded, and the crowd cheered again. Jesse Holmes, of New Lisbon, Ohio, suggested that all antislavery advocates boycott the purchase of any items produced by slave labor. A cheer went up as someone seconded it. E. Judson of Milan, Ohio, shouted, "Resolved that slavery in its nature tends to dissolve the Union, corrupt public morals and destroy that sense of right and wrong, without which liberty soon degenerates into licentiousness." Cheers again. And then the meeting ended with a vote to forgive "the unkindness of that portion of our fellow-citizens which rendered it necessary to hold our meeting in so unusual a place."

Outside the barn and back in town, there was also an air of excitement, fueled by a barrel of local whiskey consumed by many of the men who had congregated on Granville's main streets, in loud anticipation of the moment when the Bancroft barn doors would open. These were mostly men trained in the local and regional militias, and so, though drunk for the most part, they began to march up and down Broadway, between Prospect and Green streets, moving their feet in response to the music of a fiddle. The music and the whiskey kept the crowd moving through town, sharpening the rough edges of their impatience as they waited for the Hall of Freedom "fanatics" to arrive.

Shortly after noon, the sentinels who stood strategically on the hills surrounding Granville, overlooking the town and the Bancroft barn, sent word down the hills and through the streets to leaders among the rabble, who then sent word to their cohorts that the barn doors had opened and soon the abolitionists would be moving through town. Among the crowd on foot, walking from the barn into town, were more than fifty women—the nineteen delegates and at least thirty others from the local female academy. The boarding house where most of these women lived was on the other side of town from the Bancroft barn, so that they had to walk through the center of town. As the abolitionists moved closer to town, their own scouts reported that a mob had gathered. Knowing this, the crowd organized into a column four people wide, to place the women in the interior two columns. Burly men were at the rear and in the front of the column, and men ready to fight walked in the exterior columns. Also at the rear was a procession of men on horseback and in wagons and carriages. Many of the horses no longer had tails or manes, "bobbed" by members of the mob during the convention session that day.

As they walked in their column of fours, they were suddenly hit by a noisome barrage of rotten eggs: the mob's first act of aggression against them. Fetid eggs came hurtling out of the throng, landing on a dozen or more men and women, who neither slowed their pace nor appeared to be scared. Amid the hoots and curses of the egg-throwers, the abolitionists walked ever closer together as they proceeded through the town. The leaders of the column tried to steer the group away from the middle of the street and onto the boardwalk, near the storefronts. But then the mob began to close in around and behind the column, cutting off the men on horseback and in vehicles. Suddenly someone shouted, "Let's egg the squaws." A few of the women burst through the column of people and rushed into the stores, arms covering their eyes and heads as eggs fell upon them. Seconds later, a college student named Cone and a young lady whom he was escorting were pushed into a muddy ditch. Cone grabbed the woman and pushed her into the protective arms of a colleague. That done, he sought out his attacker and with one blow knocked him to the ground. Some witnesses said later that Cone had a stone in his hand to give the punch more power. The gates of violence now wide open, the vanguard of the column and a large portion of the mob dived into each other, swinging and punching, screaming and cursing. At one point, two from the rabble, reeking of whiskey, laid hands on two of the women. A workman nearby witnessed this and, dropping his tools, picked up several stones and began throwing them at the two men. He was joined by others, who disabled one of the men by hitting him hard in the shin. Soon the men released the women.

The column wound through town, safely delivering most of the women to their boarding house and returning to join the free-for-all. One abolitionist student from Oberlin, John Lewis, sought refuge in a nearby home as he was being chased by a man with a club. But when he ran up to an open door, just upon entry, the door shut in his face. He then collapsed on the steps. His attacker took advantage and pummeled him. Another member of the mob pulled the man off the young student, though by that time the boy was covered with blood. The mayor was conveniently out of town that day. When the village constable arrived to establish some sort of order, he was pulled off his horse, and then ran through the town seeking shelter. Chaos and violence were the order of the day.

The horsemen at the end of the procession dismounted in front of the home of Ashley Bancroft's brother, planning to help wherever they could. Among them was James G. Birney, whom a town administrator sought out and asked to leave town. Birney told him that the meeting had adjourned and everyone just wanted to go home. The citizen cursed a time or two and said, "You have periled the peace of our village long enough." Birney remounted his newly bobbed horse. The other horsemen quickly mounted their steeds, gave the horses' flanks swift kicks, moved ahead of Birney, and then galloped away without looking back. Birney, meanwhile, sat on his horse and walked him through the center of town, the horse snorting loudly as it tried to resist Birney's tugging on the reins, wanting to catch up with the other horses, letting loose with a loud whinny every few steps, expressing Birney's own defiance through a prideful prance. High above the throng, Birney entered the flood tide of chaos without a hint of fear, never picking up speed, moving solidly, forcibly ahead, as the rabble-rousers moved to each side of his horse, as if he were parting the waters of the Red Sea. Eggs and stones hurtled through the air around him, though none hit him or his horse. He held the horse back and refused to let him go until he had reached a turn in the road at the very end of town; then he loosened the reins and gave the animal's flanks a swift kick.

Thome later wrote to Theodore Weld, "When I saw Birney egged out of town by a mob and no man or Christian or magistrate to punish the indignity, I could stand no more. I wept."

No firearms were used, and no one was critically injured, though one member of the mob, the Newark paper reported, suffered a knife wound. The "hen's argument against emancipation," better known as egg-throwing—and many of them were rotten in this case—was the worst part of the riot; thousands of eggs flew through the air that day like a meteorite shower upon the little Ohio town. The next day, abolitionists in the Granville area met at a stone schoolhouse in the Welsh Hills. There were no interruptions, but there were new recruits. In the days ahead, shame filled the town, and those who had never considered abolitionism found themselves espousing it, some with images branded upon their memories of Birney riding alone through the angry masses. There were also new additions to the Underground Railroad, and the town soon became a busy stop branching out in two directions going north.

On the long three-day trip back to Ripley, Rankin rode with fellow abolitionists from Brown County but said very little. His thoughts drifted to his newborn son and his eagerness for the miles to be fewer and the distance shorter. He must have thought about the recent rains, torrential in nature, and whether the river was rising too high. Were the creeks flooding yet? Would the fields be too wet to plant the corn next month? And was there enough money to buy cattle to fatten over the summer and sell in the fall? He surely thought too about his congregation, some of whom, he sensed, might be turning against him for his ardent views and for his time away from the church. And he likely began to think about the mobs and to worry. His devotion to God and his wife's devotion to him would never allow him to abandon the cause. It was he, among other early abolitionists, who had helped to stir the air that was bringing this storm. But should he now, for the sake of his family and his own health, try to avoid its fury? A rhetorical question, he knew, but one that had occurred to him more frequently in recent days, as if he sensed that, in the months ahead, his life, his health, and the lives of his friends and his family would be seriously threatened. The birth of the "mobocracy," those people nationwide who were rising up against abolitionists, was exposing the harsh reality of the slavery conflict. That the abolition movement had become powerful enough to threaten the slavocracy to take action of a violent nature was both a good and a bad sign. That some of its advocates might not survive the battle ahead was a thought that most, like Rankin, tried not to contemplate. Slavery was a sin and must be destroyed, whatever the cost. Nothing would stop him, or Birney, or Gilliland, or Weld, or his son Lowry, or the others who were now marching forward.

On May 14, Garrison's *Liberator* ran the following report from Augustus Wattles: "Granville, Ohio, April 28, 1836. Dear Brother Garrison, I seize a moment amidst the bustle of adjournment to inform you of the result of our Anniversary. We met in a barn, about half a mile out of the village, which had been fitted up for the occasion. One hundred and twenty Societies were reported. Two hundred delegates present. A resolution passed to raise ten thousand dollars this year for Anti-Slavery purposes, four thousand five hundred of which were pledged on the spot. The Executive Committee are located in Cincinnati. What will be effected this year remains to be seen."

Roughly two months later, the mobocracy struck at the heart of the abolitionist community in Cincinnati, James G. Birney's press. A few weeks before the Granville convention, Birney had moved the presses of *The Philanthropist* to Cincinnati, a town of forty thousand people. The town officials were habitually worried about the spread of "fanatics" like Birney; if Cincinnati became known as an abolitionist center, then its Southern trade and its plans for improvements such as a new railroad to Charleston would suffer. An antislavery newspaper, if allowed to profit and grow, might attract more abolitionists to the town and even convert the citizenry. Birney was viewed as a menace, and his press as an evil force that must be eliminated. Shortly after Birney moved the press into town, there was a riot in which a mob burned down a tenement building occupied by African Americans. The flames attracted a huge crowd, and the threat of more violence seemed imminent.

The humidity was high on the night of July 12 in Cincinnati, and so were tempers. Twenty men, carrying a plank and a ladder, met at the door of Birney's printer, a man named Achilles Pugh. The leaders of the group—a trustee of Lane Seminary; a steamboat builder from New York; the owner of a large and prosperous paper mill; the owner of a hat-and-cap store; and the son of one of the city fathers—climbed through a window on the roof of the building, shredded what had been put together for the next issue of *The Philanthropist,* tore the press apart, and carried parts of it out of the building. The next day, they circulated a leaflet throughout town that said that the destruction of the press the night before was merely a warning. But Birney and the Cincinnati Anti-Slavery Society were unstoppable. Pugh was given $2,000 to repair his press, and three days later, he resumed printing.

The next edition of *The Philanthropist* was issued on July 15. Two days later, a handbill signed "Old Kentucky" hit the streets; it offered $100 for the "fugitive of justice James G. Birney." On the 23rd, a public meeting was called to decide whether the city could permit the publication of the paper. At least a thousand citizens attended. Among the resolutions passed was one stating that nothing would prevent violence except the discontinuation of *The Philanthropist.* This was the antiabolitionist strategy of blaming the abolitionists for instigating the violence of the proslavery masses. Citizens at the gathering appointed a committee to inform the abolitionists about the public sentiment of the town. And on July 30, the committee reported that it had failed to persuade the abolitionists to surrender. That evening, the mob assembled, led by some of the same citizens who had broken into Pugh's offices a few weeks prior. Their plan was to destroy the press, and their support came from editors of mainstream presses, civic leaders, officials of the state, wealthy merchants, and other members of the property-owning class. At midnight, they broke into Pugh's shop, dismantled the press, threw the type into the street, and then proceeded to Pugh's home, the home of another abolitionist, and finally to Birney's, where they found only his son. After stopping at the office of a doctor, who was an abolitionist, to dump the contents of his office into the street, they returned to Pugh's office and dragged all the press equipment out into the street, down to the banks of the river, and into the water. Pausing at a hotel for something to drink, they continued their rampage, despite pleas from the mayor to stop. They moved into the black community and shattered windows, chopped up furniture, and scared the residents out of their beds at 3 A.M. Mob actions continued for the next two nights, threatening and terrifying every black person and anyone who had shown sympathy to the antislavery cause. In the aftermath, the abolitionists were blamed for inciting such violence by their very presence in the town.

On August 11, the Ripley Anti-Slavery Society met at Red Oak Church to "take into consideration the alarming state of things occasioned by the spirit of mobocracy that is abroad in the land and especially the late proceedings of the mob at Cincinnati."

The group voted on several resolutions. Among them:

> Resolved that we view the origin of this disgraceful affair to have had its rise in the nature and system of slavery. As slavery was first established by violence and continued by force, mobocracy is only one of the ways in which it exhibits its legitimate results and develops its true character. . . .
>
> Resolved that we do not view the getting up of the late mob in Cincinnati to be the act and doing of the honest industrious, and labouring class of our fellow citizens; but the deliberate working of a few wealthy aristocrats combined with a few Orlean traders and principle mechanicks who are interested in trade with slaveholders. A few of those two classes appear to have been the prime movers and instigaters of the mob, the former appear to be tired of our institutions and wish a change, the latter it seems are willing to barter their birth right freedom of speech and of the press; and become the service minions of the Southern slaveholder for money.

They then resolved that the mayor and civil authorities in Cincinnati had behaved passively, which was a "dereliction of official duty." They pledged themselves to aid in the re-establishment of *The Philanthropist*. And they called on citizens of Ohio who valued their Constitution and the laws of their nation to crush the mobocracy and all of its supporters "be they high or low, rich or poor."

After the unanimous adoption of the resolutions and agreement to send them to several newspapers to make the public aware, pledges were taken to send money to re-establish the press, raising $156.50 immediately. Gilliland and Campbell led the meeting. Rankin was on the road.

CHAPTER TWELVE

THE SEVENTY

The American Anti-Slavery Society called them "the Seventy." Their teacher was Theodore Weld; their style was modeled after the evangelistic agitation of the Great Revival; their goal was to convert the congregations of the North to take a stand against slavery. Named after the seventy men sent out by the apostles to convert the world to Christianity, this "Seventy" consisted of agents of the Anti-Slavery Society traveling to rural communities of the North and using the methods of religious revivalism to persuade the masses to support immediate emancipation and to launch antislavery societies. The society appointed Weld to select the members of this elite group. Henry B. Stanton, a fellow Lane Rebel, and John Greenleaf Whittier, the poet and abolitionist, assisted him. Many of the anointed agents were students from various seminaries. Several were experienced ministers, including John Rankin, who was invited to join on July 6, 1836.

In the Seventy, the antislavery agitation was manifesting its religious roots. Rankin, having preached antislavery reform only through the church for the past twenty years, was eager to serve. But his congregation was skeptical. The appointment would take him away from his church for one year. And already his speaking engagements and duties at Ripley College had stolen Rankin from his church for weeks at a time. Members expressed concern that his absence might cause a division within the church between those who supported him and those who did not. They worried too about the dangers he might encounter at a time when the mob spirit raged so fiercely. Stories abounded about violence inflicted on antislavery speakers in recent months. One Lane Rebel was driven from a town by farmers with buggy whips. Another was dragged from his bed, stripped naked, tarred, feathered, and dumped ten miles outside a town where he had spoken the night before. Stones, eggs, even shards of glass were thrown in the faces of touring abolitionists. Some in Rankin's congregation feared he would be maimed or even killed. In the end, after much debate, they voted unanimously to allow Rankin "to labor in behalf of the poor slave" for one year. And so, in August, at a time when mobs were still running roughshod over Cincinnati, he took to the road.

The society paid him $500 for the year plus travel expenses. It gave him total freedom to choose where he went within the boundaries of the state of Ohio, though it advised that agents confer with local abolitionists before making any decisions about how to proceed locally. It asked him to send donations to the society's treasurer in New York as soon as he collected them. If he formed a new antislavery society, he was to send the list of members and officers immediately to the secretary of the national society. The society required that he write reports about his experiences and progress in organizing new societies, all to be published in their organ, *The Emancipator,* and republished in other newspapers nationwide. And it asked that he seek an exchange between local editors and *The Emancipator.*

"Rankin began his agency particularly desirous to obtain collections for the anti-slavery cause," *The Emancipator* wrote on September 29. "Even before leaving home, he gathered $22.50 at Ripley on August 1 to be used for the replacement of Birney's *Philanthropist* press. At his initial stop in Sardinia, he lectured for several days and received $221 in payments and pledges. . . ."

At nearly every stop, Rankin heightened the passions of both the friends and foes of slavery. Though a lean man of average height with narrow shoulders and a delicate structure, and though plagued for years with insecurities about his public speaking, he was now a powerhouse. After his lectures at Grassyrun, at Yankee Settlement, at Beech Grove—all small Ohio towns—he inspired dozens of people to sit down on the very day of his talk to organize their new antislavery societies. At Winchester and West Union, both in Adams County, he encountered formidable mobs, though he enlisted forty-eight new members to existing societies. At West Union, many of the horses outside the church were bobbed while Rankin was speaking.

Having had more than one horse sheared of its mane and tail, Rankin had locked his own horse in a stable at the other end of town. At Winchester, a man sodden with whiskey pushed his way to the front of the audience and tried to strike Rankin with a club. And as Rankin left the town, he was deluged with eggs from equally drunken proslavers.

In Clermont County, Rankin discovered many fans of his letters. The "mobocrats have as yet been unable to get up a mob in this county," Rankin wrote in *The Emancipator*. However, in Batavia, the Clermont County seat, a small gang of young men had thrown eggs and rocks at him through a window as he lectured. He never skipped a word of his talk, but the audience fled before he completed it. At Felicity, in the same county, the elders of the Cincinnati Presbytery, which was coincidentally meeting there at the same time, prohibited Rankin from preaching at the local Presbyterian church. This was particularly upsetting because his brother Alexander was the pastor of the church. Rankin had even helped to build it. Upon hearing that the leadership of the church had turned one of their own preachers away, the elders of the local Methodist church voted unanimously to open their doors to him. And on the night of his lecture, there was standing room only as the entire Methodist congregation and some members of the Presbyterian church attended. An antislavery society was formed that night with a beginning roster of sixty members.

At Williamsburg, also in Clermont County, the local Presbyterian minister preceded Rankin's talk with a proclamation that Rankin's views would lead to war and bloodshed. The audience was silent as Rankin walked up the aisle of the crowded church to the pulpit. Throughout the lecture and afterward, there was barely a nod of the head, and Rankin couldn't judge the response except to believe it was a total rejection. Later, on the road from the church to the house where Rankin was staying, a man came out of the bushes and struck him with a club, hitting him hard in the neck. It was unseasonably cold that night, and Rankin had worn layers of clothes that protected his neck enough so that bruises and soreness were the worst of his injuries. After leaving the town, he learned that not only had the lecture been a success but a few of the townsfolk were planning to start a society. And soon there were safe houses for the Underground Railroad in the town of Williamsburg.

His worst threat in Clermont County occurred in the town of Withamsville, where two rowdy young men followed him after his lecture at a school and threw firebrands at him from the school stove. He was struck on the shoulder but not seriously injured. Shortly after that, in a letter to one of his sons, he confessed that at times on his tour he was tempted to believe that there were men of his own race who "did not seem fit to be free."

By early September, Rankin had delivered twenty-six lectures and was pleased with the response he was getting; at one point in the tour, he formed three new societies on three consecutive days. His audiences were larger than he had ever experienced, and he felt that they were more deeply interested in the subject than ever before. "I have reason to believe that I have succeeded in bringing the larger part of all who have heard me to favor our views," he wrote on September 6 in the antislavery newspaper *The Advocate of Freedom,* out of Augusta, Maine. "The larger part of opposition is occasioned by the slanders circulated about us," he went on to say.

When the people come to hear for themselves, they readily embrace the truth. I have as yet delivered but two lectures in a place. I first discuss the question "What business have the people of the free states to interfere with slavery?" and answer the common objections of opposers. I next present the Bible view of the subject and bring divine truth to bear upon the conscience. This produces a most powerful effect. I have seldom seen audiences as much moved under any other subject. It is common for opposers to renounce immediately. The system of slavery was founded and it now stands upon a false interpretation of the scriptures and the blood of it lies peculiarly upon the gospel ministry. Let the foul strain be washed from the sacred page, and let the effulgence of divine truth be poured upon all the churches, and the bands of wickedness shall be broken, and the oppressed shall go free.

If he knew in advance that his audience consisted of more than the usual numbers of Southern sympathizers, he sometimes began with a slightly different approach: proclaiming his belief in the Declaration of Independence and reiterating its opening passages. This, as he well knew, was not a point of contention for anyone in his audiences. Then he stated that God created all men of one blood, which also brought little or no disagreement, a point usually acceptable on Biblical grounds. Then he made the point that men should either do their own work or pay someone else to do it. No one disagreed. By this time, his audience was held in suspense: the antislavers wondering what his point would be, and the Southern-sympathizers waiting and waiting for the fanaticism to kick in. He concluded his introduction by making the point that these three principles were the cornerstones of the abolitionist belief that all men, regardless of color, held the same God-given rights. And then he launched into the evils of slavery.

On the first Monday of October, Rankin returned home to accompany Lowry to Lane Seminary and help him settle in. Lowry had intended to enter a seminary in Andover, Massachusetts, but the Rankins' financial situation was unstable that year, Lane was far less expensive, and Lowry had been promised a job doing carpentry to pay his board. Rankin stayed at the home of a friend who was the editor of the *Cincinnati Journal* while Lowry went on to the school to enroll and to find a room. The next day, he and Lowry met with Calvin Stowe, a Lane professor and husband of Harriet Beecher Stowe, and Lyman Beecher to discuss Lowry's course of study. Though he was only twenty years old, Lowry's studies and preparatory work allowed him to enter the junior class. Benjamin Templeton, the black man Rankin had tutored in his home, had just finished his studies at Hanover College and was enrolling as a Lane senior at the same time. Rankin asked his son to look after Templeton; his anticipated presence had already disturbed at least one faculty member and the head custodian of the school, who told Lowry, "I am not here to wait on a nigger." Templeton, who would come a few weeks later, would take the room across the hall from Lowry. Satisfied that his son was off to a good start, Rankin resumed his tour.

Within a month of his father's departure, Lowry received a note from a messenger asking that he report as soon as possible to the antislavery office in Cincinnati. His first thought was that something violent might have happened to his father on the tour, and so he sprinted the full two miles from his room to the office. On arriving, he was informed that there was a runaway slave hidden in the town's free black community and that a reward of $500 had been offered for his capture. Several parties were hunting him down, and it was no longer safe to keep him in the city. He must be moved as soon as possible to the home of a Quaker, William Butterworth, twenty-five miles from the city. The people who ran the local antislavery society assumed Lowry had experience with such risk-taking ventures. Would he be willing to go? Lowry agreed as long as they furnished him with the horses and detailed directions. He left at eight that October evening, and after delivering the fugitive safely into the hands of Mr. Butterworth, he returned the horses, walked the two miles back to the seminary, and was in bed just before dawn. No one, not even Templeton, knew of his absence that night.

Throughout his years at Lane, Lowry would continue to answer the calls of the antislavery society, spending a night and sometimes a day and a night escorting a runaway slave to a safe haven somewhere to the North. If Mr. Butterworth was not the host, it was Thomas Hibbin in the town of Wilmington, sixty or so miles away, or Abram Allen, whose home was five miles farther than Hibbin's. Usually Lowry could steal away for the night and not be seen, though the trips to Wilmington and beyond required more than a day there and back, in addition to frequent alibis and coverups.

Over time, Lane's professor of pastoral theology, Reverend Baxter Dickinson, grew suspicious of Lowry's absences and began to record them. Dickinson, a known proslavery man, had formed a bias against Lowry from the moment they had met, simply because he was John Rankin's son. Dickinson often reviewed the reports of the class monitor, who noted the comings and goings of students and knew when Lowry was gone. Sometimes he would quiz Lowry, who would say casually that he had been "tending to important business that simply couldn't be postponed." Lowry knew that Dr. Stowe and his wife, Harriet Beecher, were both well aware of the work he was doing, and he was confident that, if necessary, the Stowes would make up an excuse for his behavior.

At one point, Dickinson arranged for Lowry himself to be assigned to the post of class monitor. Dickinson handed Lowry the forms that every monitor used to chart the comings and goings of the students, but the following week, Lowry returned the forms without any absentees marked. The professor looked at them and returned them to Lowry saying, "As Brother Rankin has done so well, not a student has presumed to be absent while he is monitor, he will act for another week." At the end of the next week, Lowry, who was following in his father's rebellious footsteps in ways beyond his underground work, returned the sheets again without a mark.

"How is this?" asked a stunned Dickinson. Turning to a student, he asked, "Were you not absent Sabbath morning?"

"Yes," the student replied.

Then, turning to Lowry, he said, "Why did you not mark him absent?"

Lowry said, "For the reason that I was myself absent."

"Were you absent from prayers also?" he asked.

"I was not," Lowry said.

"Were there no absentees?" he demanded.

"I presume there were," Lowry said.

"And you refuse to mark their absences? Now will you tell me, sir, why you refuse to do your duty as a monitor?" the professor asked.

"I did not attempt to keep an account of the presence of the students at any of the exercises for these reasons," Lowry said. "I dislike very much to assume the position of watching the deportment of my fellows. To my way of thinking it is espionage that is not in keeping with Christian manliness. The second reason is that every member of the institution was supposed to be a Christian gentleman and the very fact that they are here because they are looking forward to the ministry presupposes that their deportment would not dishonor so sacred a calling. I respectfully decline to have anything to do with the monitor system."

Expecting a fight over the principle of the system, Lowry was surprised when, weeks later, the faculty voted to dispense with student monitors, which gave Lowry the freedom to work on the Underground Railroad anytime he could in his hectic schedule. By then, in addition to his classes, he was working in a broom factory—the carpentry job had been given to another student—for 45 cents a day. But he learned somehow to juggle his job, studies, and the underground. Dickinson never did find the proof of his involvement, but he continued to watch Lowry's every move. Lowry, who operated alone out of Lane, though in conjunction with the Cincinnati Anti-Slavery Society and the free black community, was never certain whom he could trust at the school. Because of the recent mob activity, most people feared associating with anyone who was helping blacks, and especially assisting in the escape of slaves. Only a few students at Lane were openly avowed abolitionists. Lowry assumed that any number of people suspected and some even knew of the undercover operation he was running, such as Calvin Stowe. But he was never certain about Stowe until one night in the early months of 1837.

Some free blacks Lowry had on several occasions worked with sent a runaway slave to him early one evening. Lowry had no team of horses, and he felt a fever coming on. Worse still, he knew that the temperatures outside were dropping. He could not hide the fugitive until he was well enough to travel, and in his near desperation about what to do, he confided in Professor Stowe. It was the first time he had said openly what he was doing, though he assumed that the Stowes, both close friends of his father's and frequent visitors to Ripley, had known all along.

"Brother Rankin," Stowe said after hearing of the dilemma, "you ought not to be out in the night air, it is too damp for a man as unwell as you are. It is equally true that you cannot keep the poor fellow in safety this close to the city."

"What can I do," Lowry asked, "but venture the going afoot. The risk would be less. I might not be disturbed so early tomorrow morning if I kept to the wood. The Miami River we will have to wade."

Stowe replied, "No, you must not do that. I see no other way out of the difficulty but for me to take my horse and carriage and go myself. If you will give me specific directions as to the way I will try and make the trip."

Lowry went to bed with a raging fever and a sense of satisfaction, knowing now that Stowe could be trusted and could be depended upon if such an emergency ever again occurred. Stowe and the black man hiding in Lowry's room set out for Butterworth's. For Stowe, who had never before done this, it was a challenge. In the early morning, Lowry awakened with a rush of anxiety about Stowe. From his window he could see Stowe's barnyard, and so he slept fitfully, now and again jolting awake and looking out his window. At first light, he saw Stowe drive his carriage into the yard; his clothes were wet, as were the horse and the carriage. Lowry met him in the yard to brush down his horse for him. "If it had not been for the efficient assistance of your colored friend, Lane Seminary would have had one professor less today young man," Stowe began. "Just think of you being the occasion of my death. And think how this community would be horrified when it learned a professor in Lane Theological Seminary was drowned while 'stealing niggers.' Just think of the scandal you would have brought on me, and the institution I represent. Do you think the city rabble would in the present temper of the popular feeling have left one of the seminary buildings standing? Well, I am glad I only got a good ducking. Also that I got the fellow safely to your station."

Each month more fugitives would be sent Lowry's way. In his two years at Lane, he would assist at least three hundred runaway slaves on the Underground Railroad, taking them to safe houses north of Cincinnati, to Lebanon, to Springboro, and sometimes east to his father's house at Ripley. Now and again Stowe would ask him about "operations" and how they were going, but Lowry never called upon Stowe again to make a run. Operating alone was the best policy during his years at Lane, Lowry came to believe, though on many nights he longed for the security of an armed partner. Everyone in Cincinnati knew that the runaway-slave traffic across the river was increasing, and that the abolitionists were determined. And so the movement to stop them was escalating too.

On that day in the autumn of 1836 when Rankin left Lowry at Lane, he had no idea that his son would be pulled into the local Underground Railroad, but, considering his own ties to the Cincinnati network, he must have sensed it would happen. With the peace of mind that his oldest son was finally on the way to becoming a minister, Rankin continued his tour for several more months, in Warren, Butler, Highland, and Preble counties. After several lectures in Hamilton County, a citizen of Springfield wrote, "After hearing the addresses of Mr. Rankin, every one seemed to think, who could mob such a man and who could disturb a society formed to advance principles so noble and elevating in their nature and calculated to bless and save our nation. The fact was clearly seen that the community generally have incorrect views of anti-slavery principles and that when they are clearly presented, they commend themselves to every man's conscience. It is manifest that the opposition of a community to those principles is generally to be attributed to want of correct information on the subject. . . ."

During the second half of his tour, he delivered sixty-three lectures and formed ten new antislavery societies before he had to return home because of extreme exhaustion, a severe cough, and congestion of the lungs. There were rumors throughout the border counties that Rankin was not expected to recover, though he was quoted in *The Emancipator* as saying, "I am much pleased with my work. Were it not for the state of my family and congregation, I should be glad to pursue it until there should not be a slave in the land. I never grow weary of my theme. I dwell upon it day after day, with increasing interest. It is universal benevolence to man. Every lecture is calculated to better one's own heart. . . ."

He did recover, and his congregation hailed him as a hero. In the weeks after his homecoming, the church brought in forty-eight new members, and the Ripley Anti-Slavery Society welcomed thirty-two newcomers to its already burgeoning roster. Because of the newspaper coverage of his "agency," his audience once again widened as it had four years before, when Garrison first published his letters. At an upcoming anniversary of the American Anti-Slavery Society, he would be one of the principal speakers, and as Garrison wrote in *The Liberator* after the meeting, "He was to us an object of special interest in consequence of his early labors in behalf of the oppressed. Who among abolitionists has not yet read the Letters of this excellent man?"

By the start of 1837, the number of antislavery societies in the state of Ohio was nearly 150—up from 120 the year before and thirty-five the year before that; runaways were routinely moving through Ripley and other river towns, aided, if necessary, by black and white conductors of the Underground Railroad; antislavery petitions inundated the offices of federal and state legislators; and Southern legislators pushed harder than ever before to stop the education of blacks, the loss of their "property," and the mere discussion of their peculiar institution.

On February 6, 1837, Senator John C. Calhoun delivered his impassioned "Speech on the Reception of Abolition Petitions" just as the antislavery petitions to Congress, like a mighty flood of anger, had reached an unprecedented volume. The gag rule of May 1836 automatically tabled antislavery petitions to Congress without discussion. The rule meant that neither the House nor the Senate would ever act upon them, but it did not stem the flow of petitions. Instead, it stimulated the flood. More petitions, with longer lists of names, deluged the state legislatures, the U.S. Senate, and the House. The session of Congress for 1834–35 had received—and rejected—thirty-four thousand citizens petitioning Congress on the subject of slavery; the session of 1835–36, 110,000; and the session of 1837–38, three hundred thousand. Among the petitioners were Rankin, William and John B. Mahan, Gilliland, and each of their wives.

In his speech, Calhoun said:

We of the South will not, cannot surrender our institutions. To maintain the existing relations between the two races inhabiting that section of the Union is indispensable to the peace and happiness of both. It cannot be subverted without drenching the country in blood, and extirpating one or the other of the races. Be it good or bad, [slavery] has grown up with our society and institutions, and is so interwoven with them that to destroy it would be to destroy us as a people. But let me not be understood as admitting, even by implication, that the existing relations between the two races in the slaveholding states is an evil: far otherwise; I hold it to be a good, as it has thus far proved itself to be to both, and will continue to prove so if not disturbed by the fell spirit of abolition. I appeal to facts. Never before has the black race of Central Africa, from the dawn of history to the present day, attained a condition so civilized and so improved, not only physically, but morally and intellectually. It came among us in a low, degraded, and savage condition, and in the course of a few generations it has grown up under the fostering care of our institutions, reviled as they have been, to its present comparatively civilized condition. This, with the rapid increase of numbers, is conclusive proof of the general happiness of the race, in spite of all the exaggerated tales to the contrary. . . .

CHAPTER THIRTEEN

TWO ABDUCTIONS AND A MURDER

By the time her neighbors discovered the source of the screams rippling through the woods north of town, Eliza Jane Johnson had been whipped into submission and thrown upon a horse behind James Fox, a slaveholder from Kentucky.

The dust stirred up by the hooves of Fox's horse and three others had not yet settled when six horsemen from Sardinia, including John B. Mahan and James Huggins, appeared at the cottage that Eliza shared with Gabriel Johnson and their five children. The men instantly realized what had happened. They dug their heels into the flanks of their horses and took off for the river. Their plan was to ride as fast as their horses could carry them to Red Oak, where they would get fresh horses and enlist the help of the Gilliland boys and the Hopkins family. They hoped to ride to the river-bank fast enough to cut off the kidnappers and stop them from crossing. On the way, one of the men would stop in Ripley to obtain a writ of authority for the arrest of Fox and his men. From the route the kidnappers took, it appeared they would try to cross at Levanna, a village of a dozen or so houses two miles west of Ripley.

The man at the head of the team of rescuers, William G. Kephart, was the first of the ten men—four kidnappers and six rescuers—to reach the banks of the river. He took a shortcut down a steep portion of the bank, and in the process his horse's foot caught on a protruding tree root. The horse stumbled and rolled, and Kephart fell over the horse's head and struck the hard, stony beach on his face. Witnessing the accident as they approached the bank, one of the kidnappers shouted "Hoorah!" and grabbed the arm of the black woman. He hoisted her into a small boat while another of the four men pushed the boat into the current.

Two of the men were left standing on the bank—one from Brown County and one from Highland County, farther north—and both drew their pistols as one of the rescuers attempted to arrest them. The remaining rescuers, including Adam Lowry Rankin, who had stopped to help Kephart, arrived on the scene, and the two remaining kidnappers surrendered. While Lowry took Kephart in a wagon to his home, several miles north, the other men accompanied the kidnappers into Ripley for a preliminary trial. Lowry then walked back to Ripley to witness the trial. On the way, he was approached by half a dozen men who he remembered had ridden at a distance behind the kidnappers.

"She was a runaway nigger," one shouted to Lowry.

"Oh, yes," said Lowry, "that only makes the meanness the more apparent. There is a legal way to return runaway slaves that you knew would not be successful so you would steal a poor, helpless woman and sell her. All women thieves are cowards."

One of the men rushed up to Lowry as if to strike him but was interrupted by friends of Lowry who had come to offer him a ride to the trial. The kidnappers were sent to county jail in Georgetown for one night.

In Kentucky that night, September 22, 1837, Eliza Jane Johnson, the thirty-two-year-old woman, who had lived in the free state of Ohio for at least three years and was a proud member of the Ripley Anti-Slavery Society, slept on the dirt floor of a basement jail cell in Washington, inland from Maysville; James Fox, meanwhile, claimed that he had recovered the runaway slave of his father, Arthur Fox, the sheriff of Mason County.

"This outrage on humanity," wrote the editors of the *Cincinnati Journal and Luminary* on September 30, "has occasioned no little distress on the neighborhood of Ripley. It produced an intensity of feeling that cannot be described. The innocent and helpless wife is torn from her husband and shut up in a dungeon! Not permitted so much as to fall upon the neck of her bereaved husband and mingle for the last time their parting tears! Oh slavery, thou fiend of hell, when shall thy ravages cease? Will not the humanity of the citizens of our sister State induce them to return this poor woman to her husband? Can friendship between the States be maintained, while such outrages are perpetrated by private citizens, and then sustained by the civil authorities? She must be replaced under the jurisdiction of Ohio, before any court can entertain jurisdiction of the question of free-dom and slavery, unless a jurisdiction can be acquired by such an act of vi-olence, which no man in his reason would pretend. And further, unless a border warfare between the two States is to be encouraged, these offenders against our laws must be made to feel the full penalty attached to one of the highest crimes in our penal code." The judge in Kentucky would not agree.

On the morning following Johnson's capture, as two of her captors were freed on bail in Ohio—and immediately fled the state—Arthur Fox came to her cell, looked her up and down, and shook his head from side to side. This was not the female slave who had fled his house four years before and who, he had been told, was assisted to her freedom by persons in Ripley. "I never saw two Negroes more alike in my life," he said, as he looked at her. "At the first glance I was sure she was mine."

His son, James, defended the blunder by saying that he had not seen his father's former slave for four years. He and his three sidekicks had made a mistake, a grave one for Johnson and her husband. But for the sheriff and other jail officials, it was a mere technicality—and one that indeed could make them some money. She must be someone's slave, they thought, be-cause she was, after all, a woman of color. Under Kentucky laws, Eliza Johnson, by color alone, was considered a runaway slave, and as such she must remain in jail for two months, while an ad describing her was posted on the door of the courthouse. If no one claimed her within this period, then the sheriff could run ads in newspapers in search of her owner for three more months. At the same time, he could employ her at the jail or elsewhere. By the end of one year, if no owner had appeared, then the sher-iff could sell her, and was required by law to put the proceeds into an ac-count in the event that the owner might come to claim her; typically, the funds were used to cover the costs of the incarceration. Eliza Jane feared she would never again see her family or freedom.

In the days that followed, men from Ripley and Sardinia—including John Rankin—rode to Washington to demand a habeas-corpus hearing for Eliza Jane Johnson. They challenged her detention, claiming that she was born free and was a citizen of a free state. The hearing was granted and held before Judge Walker Reid in Mason County on October 1, 1837. The men whom Rankin and his colleagues now sought to defeat, and whose princi-ples they attacked, would not forget who was there that day to "steal" their property and to take "their" slave woman back across the river.

Eliza Jane, witnesses swore before the judge, had confessed to having once been the slave of a Mrs. John in New Orleans. Three or four years ago, they said, she escaped by hiding on the *Tuscarora,* a steamboat leaving New Orleans bound for Cincinnati; when it docked at the Ohio port, she made her final escape. In Cincinnati, the story went, a Mr. Thompson furnished her with free papers. Her defenders claimed never to have heard such a story and worried she had been beaten into such a confession, if she had said this at all. Whatever her past, they argued, she had lived as a free woman for at least three years, and as a citizen of Ohio she should not be subjected to the laws of Kentucky.

After listening to various testimonies, Judge Reid issued his judgment:

> My duty in the present case would end were it not that the slave in question was forcibly brought from the state of Ohio, and now claims her freedom in consequence of her having lived there for three years or more as a free woman. With due respect for the laws of [Ohio] which compel the master to prove his slave before he has a right to apprehend him, and makes it [illegal] to bring a black man away without that, I am bound to consider every person of colour especially of the African race of negroes a slave until the contrary is proved.
>
> In the case of a person visibly appearing to be a negro the presumption is in this state that he is a slave and it is incumbent on him to make out his right to freedom. But in the case of a person visibly appearing to be a white man or an Indian the presumption is that he is free and it is necessary for his adversary to show that he is a slave.
>
> How must a judge act in such a case? I answer that he must judge from his own view. He must discharge the white person and the Indian out of custody, taking security they should not depart the state. And he must redeliver the black or mulatto with a flat nose and woolly hair to the person claiming him or her as a slave: this is all I can do at present.
>
> For the present, Eliza Jane Johnson is remanded to jail as a runaway slave. The law will not justify me in discharging her.

The men from Ripley and Sardinia left the courtroom discouraged and concerned. They vowed to keep fighting for Johnson's freedom. Next they would lobby the Ohio legislators and the governor to exert pressure on the state of Kentucky. They commented on how the case had not resulted in any violence, and they talked of heading for the river and home, some deciding to leave before the others. On the way to the river, somewhere between Washington and the ferry landing at Maysville, one of those who left ahead of the others, James Huggins, was attacked by riders who pulled his horse into a thicket of trees. There they dragged him onto the ground, stripped him, tied him to a tree, and whipped him, severely. By some accounts, a few tried to lynch him, but others lobbied for his release. His friends later found him unconscious in the woods.

A week later, the *Maysville Eagle* published a lengthy letter from a citizen of Dover, Kentucky, signed "Justice." Defending the judge and the case, "Justice" wrote: "In order to properly understand this case abroad, it should be remembered that Kentucky has lost millions of dollars in slaves; that her citizens have been most outrageously abused in Ohio when in pursuit of them, that there is a certain class of fellows there who make a business of stealing our negroes or aiding and abetting in getting them off. Hundreds of our citizens while peaceably and legally pursuing their property have been taken up, insulted and whipped while others who have really gone before a magistrate and proved their property and received written authority to bring them home, have been seized, beaten and abused, their negroes taken from them and set at liberty. Kentucky is as much opposed to slavery as Ohio, but she cannot all at once get clear of it, with safety to herself or justice to the other members of the confederation; it is an evil entailed upon her by her fathers, engrafted upon her constitution."

Three weeks after Judge Reid's decision, U.S. Senator Thomas Morris was returning to his home in Bethel, Ohio, from Washington, Kentucky, and stopped in Ripley for dinner with Alexander Campbell. There the two men discussed the Johnson case. Morris had just learned of Reid's decision and was enraged that Johnson was still in jail. A Kentuckian overheard the conversation and talked about it with fellow citizens of Maysville, one of whom attacked Morris's views in a letter to the *Eagle*. The so-called "Citizen of Kentucky," who wrote the letter, claimed that Morris had exclaimed to Campbell that "war ought to be immediately declared against Kentucky and that every Kentuckian should be shot down so soon as he set his foot on the Ohio side." And he beseeched Morris to apologize to the citizens of the state.

After Morris returned home, he wrote a formal letter to Campbell expressing his views about the eavesdropper, the gossip, and the case. He sent a copy to *The Philanthropist*, which published it. Morris called the Fugitive Slave Act of 1793 "unconstitutional and well calculated to produce collision between the states." And he revealed part of his conversation to

Campbell that night, reconfirming his views of Reid's decision. "Reflection," he wrote, "has confirmed my belief that a state which is unable to protect the person of individuals when found within its borders, from violence, has lost its sovereignty and is unworthy of the name of a free and independent state and that between sovereign and independent nations the very act which took place near your town of Ripley, though beginning in mere individual crime [sic]. Yet if that crime was begun in one country and consummated in another, whose government should justify the act or make it her own, it would by the nation whose sovereignty was thus violated be considered just cause of WAR and I am well convinced that if the scene in Ripley is to be enacted over again, and those who are engaged in it find countenance and protection in another state it would eventually lead to a nonintercourse between the states, and this in my opinion will be the most gentle and mild form it will assume; for if reports which have reached me since I was there be true, the peaceful and quiet village of Ripley is converted into a war-like town; the citizens having armed themselves to protect their persons from violence."

A week later, yet another of Ohio's free blacks—this time, downriver from Ripley—was subjected to violence in an attempt to capture and sell him. It happened in Evansville, Indiana, a port town along the Ohio. The local paper, the *Evansville Journal,* remarked that the incident "ought forever to damn every thing pertaining to the [river] boat in public estimation."

In the free states along the river, the steamboats that traveled between Pittsburgh and New Orleans were viewed suspiciously, their skippers seen as potential collaborators with money-hungry slave traders. At the same time, in the states south of the river, there was the fear that runaway slaves commonly used the boats as a means to escape, and that skippers sometimes profited from both. The Evansville incident occurred one Friday afternoon when the steamboat *Marmion* pulled into the port. A black man who worked for a local hotel had just delivered a trunk owned by a hotel guest, who was now boarding the boat. As the man began to step onto the shore from the boat's plank, an engineer from the *Marmion* came rushing onto the plank and, when the man's foot was inches from the ground, shoved him nearly into the river. The engineer then struck the black man again, at which time the man returned the blow, which caused a violent response on board the boat. A rush of men, fifteen or twenty, throwing stones and brickbats, pursued the black man as he ran away from the boat. They eventually cornered him in a steam mill where he attempted to hide.

They beat him and brought him back to the boat, walking slowly, one man holding a gun to the black man's head as two others held on to his hands and arms. There a cadre of men awaited him, knives and pistols drawn. Five men, dressed in the genteel fashion of the propertied class, drew their guns and threatened to shoot anyone who dared to rescue the black man.

The walk onto the boat was slowed by the man's insistent struggles and the counterblows inflicted by his foes. Then, just as his energy was starting to ebb and his struggle seemed hopeless, at least twenty men rushed noisily down the riverbank, leapt onto the plank, and stormed the boat deck. Though unarmed, their numbers and their seemingly unstoppable march terrorized the black man's persecutors. In the brawl that ensued, the black man slipped out of his enemies' grip and threw himself into the river, followed quickly by one of the crew members, who carried with him a rope tied in a noose. When the black man ran onto the shore and the noose was just about to hit its target, a man who said he was a magistrate caught the rope in the air, thrust it into the water, and helped the black man onto solid ground. Then, without a moment to catch a breath, they were both greeted by another gang of thugs, wielding clubs and slats of wood. At the same time, men from the boat hurled champagne bottles, rocks, and pieces of wood at the black man, all the while screaming oaths of anger and disgust and shouting at the local citizens, cursing them for not assisting in the kidnapping. The boat pulled away, amid a chorus of swearing coming from both the shore and the boat, and the black man returned to his job with a stream of blood trickling down the side of his face.

The editors of the *Evansville Journal* wrote that the black man was known to be "remarkable as an orderly, peaceable, and modest servant. We have frequently heard that there are steamboats that make a practice, particularly at wood yards, of raising quarrels with negroes and kidnapping them for the southern market; and this is the reason why we have been thus particular in describing this affray."

Two weeks later, in the Mississippi River town of Alton, Illinois, mob violence struck again when the abolitionist Elijah P. Lovejoy was shot and killed while trying to prevent the destruction of his printing press. A Presbyterian minister originally from Maine, Lovejoy had been the editor of the *Observer*, a newspaper in St. Louis, until his antislavery editorials provoked several mob attacks, one finally ruining his press. On July 21, 1836, Lovejoy brought his new printing press to the docks of Alton, Illinois, twenty or so miles north of St. Louis, at the junction of the Missouri and Mississippi rivers. It was the Sabbath, so Lovejoy chose to leave the heavy, cumbersome press on the dock until the following morning. By dawn, the press had been shattered into many little pieces, so small that many of them were floating down the Mississippi. That was only the beginning. Until then, Lovejoy's antislavery publications had promoted gradual emancipation. By the fall of 1836, he had become an advocate of immediate emancipation. The violence of the antiabolitionists and an increasing awareness of his responsibility as a clergyman had caused his conversion to an ardent abolitionist stand, and that in turn put dynamite under the seats of his enemies. The presses of the *Observer*—dubbed the "minister of mischief" by a proslavery newspaper, the *Republican* of Missouri—were destroyed three times before the night of November 7, 1837. Lovejoy, who was pushing hard for the formation of an antislavery society in the state of Illinois, had just received his fifth press two days before and had stored it in a warehouse known to be the biggest and strongest in town. That night, he and a militia that had recently been organized on his behalf, under legal authority, were inside protecting the press when a mob began throwing bricks at the building and firing shots. Lovejoy ran out of the warehouse in an attempt to stop a man who was climbing a ladder and trying to set the building on fire. Instead, five bullets stopped Lovejoy. He fell back into the warehouse and died. Two days before his thirty-fifth birthday, Lovejoy became the first white abolitionist martyr.

Indignation over Lovejoy's death provoked thousands of people to join the abolitionist ranks. The slave power had overestimated its ability to repress the movement. William Herndon, Abraham Lincoln's law partner, who urged Lincoln to change his point of view of gradual emancipation, was stimulated to become an abolitionist by the murder of Lovejoy. John Brown dedicated his life to ending slavery after hearing of the Lovejoy murder. And Lovejoy was the antislavery inspiration for the Massachusetts orator Wendell Phillips. "How prudently most men creep into nameless graves while now and then one or two forget themselves into immortality," said Phillips, of Lovejoy's death.

Several weeks later, on Christmas Day, in Ripley, the resounding voices of the Presbyterian church choir sang hymns in the late morning—not as part of religious services, for it was not the Sabbath, but, rather, for the celebration of the holiday and for the annual meeting of the Ripley Anti-Slavery Society. After the singing, Rankin offered a prayer. The society's president, Alexander Campbell, then called the meeting to order and introduced a multitude of resolutions reflecting the intensity of the past several months in the Ohio Valley. Each one was unanimously adopted.

Resolved that the liberty of the press and of speech is the inalienable right of all classes of human beings, and that all who attempt to abolish it are enemies to their country, and unworthy of a residence in a free government.

Resolved that slavery has abolished both the liberty of speech and of the press in the slave states, and is attempting to do the same in the free states.

Resolved that it was slave holding influence that procured the murder of the Rev. Elijah P. Lovejoy at Alton. Resolved that the City of Alton is a disgrace to the nation and deserves the execration of all good men, and must ever stand chargeable with the martyrdom of a faithful minister of Jesus Christ.

Resolved that Lovejoy was fully justifiable in defending his life and press and that he died a Martyr to liberty and righteousness and deserves a place on the brightest page of history.

Resolved that we highly commend the noble few who stood by the side of the faithful martyr when he fell and bravely hazarded their lives in defence of humanity and justice.

Resolved that we deeply sympathize with the widow and fatherless children of Lovejoy, and that we will contribute to their support whenever necessary.

Resolved that we recommend the establishment of the press at Alton so soon as a press and editor can be obtained.

Resolved that slaveholding influence is the prominent source of mobs and that nothing but its total abolition can save the Country from ruin.

Resolved that the blood of the martyred Lovejoy cried from the ground for the immediate abolition of slavery and that in view of his death we solemnly pledge ourselves to renewed exertions in the cause of liberty. . . .

Additional motions urged that the resolutions be printed in various newspapers, and that further legal efforts be made to regain Eliza Jane Johnson's freedom. The meeting closed with the choir singing another hymn. But as Campbell, Gilliland, and others prepared to leave, Rankin suddenly called for their attention once again. As if whispers of the real world had penetrated his mind, Rankin called on God to bring strength and courage to those convening that day in his church, those who were fighting against human oppression.

Outside the church, temperatures were dropping as strong winds from

Canada brought a surge of frigid air through the Ohio Valley. A stark white veneer of ice and snow covered the branches, logs, and debris that clung to both the Kentucky and Ohio shorelines. The green Kentucky hills had turned to bleak browns and grays against a white sky. And the shallow waters closest to both shores were slowly thickening to ice.

The year 1838 would bring with it danger and conflict, and reason to be wary of shadows in the alleys off Front Street.

PART II

1838

My dear children, I want you to know that I am wholly innocent of all the things for which I stand indicted. Give yourselves no concern about that. I am in irons for no fault. I have neither sinned against God nor the laws of men. I hope to see you all soon and find you happy. Learn to be pleasant without being foolish. Learn to be serious without being melancholy. Learn to be firm, without being self-willed. Learn obedience without servility. Learn patience without stupidity. Learn to unlearn all your errors and finally cease to do evil, learn to do well. Your ever-loving Father, J. B. Mahan.

—From a jail cell in Washington, Kentucky, October 1838

As I marked the steamer cleaving the waters of the Ohio and watched the waves rolling in opposite courses until seemingly they kissed either shore in token of love, I felt as if the very voice of nature murmured forth its eloquent sympathy in defence of perpetual Union. I hope this may be so, and that as long as these waves shall roll that Union may last; firm of policy and interest; but firmer, and more enduring yet, through principle and affection. If Mahan is doomed as a felon, a taint will be upon the escutcheon of Kentucky which no time or change can efface.

—J. C. Vaughan, defense attorney for John B. Mahan, closing arguments, November 1838

CHAPTER FOURTEEN

WAVES BREAK ON EITHER SHORE

On a blustery night in late February 1838, somewhere across the river from Ripley, the ice was breaking under the weight of an animal's body. Or was it the body of a human? The man standing on the banks of the Ohio side, near the mouth of Red Oak Creek, wasn't exactly sure what was causing the sounds he heard. His gun at his side, his ears primed to every discernible sound, his body wrapped in several coats to brace against the chill of the river winds, Chancey Shaw had roamed these banks nearly every night since the river froze on February 22, waiting, hoping, and listening for the sounds he was now hearing, the telltale sounds of the struggle of a slave escaping across the river. Slave catchers like Shaw knew that when the river froze the temptation for slaves to cross the icy "road" to freedom was sometimes too great to resist. Like the buzzards crisscrossing the sky above the river, the man hunters scouted the banks at night, watching the spots where skiffs had landed runaway slaves in the past, and waiting, waiting, waiting.

Skilled in the treachery of slave catching, Shaw was confident that patience would be rewarded—up to $500 for a fugitive slave captured on the Ohio side. But on this night, the ice had begun to thaw; he knew the odds were slim that his waiting would earn him any reward. "All the boys in town had been down on the slow ice that very afternoon, knew the ice was rotten, with air holes and cracks extending almost across the river," John Rankin, Jr., wrote later, of that night. What slave would be desperate enough to try to cross on a night like this?

Still, the cracking and splashing echoed back and forth against the snow-encrusted hills of both shores, and the sounds grew louder. Then came the baying of the hounds, the voices of men in pursuit, the desperate crying out of a woman. This was it, Shaw knew: the long-awaited catch. His pace quickened to nearly a run as he moved along the bank tracking the sounds, in an effort to target the exact place the slave might land.

Crossing the river from the other shore was a slave woman who belonged to a farmer a few miles south of Dover, Kentucky, on the river, just five or so miles from Ripley. She had fled upon learning that a slave dealer had been meeting with her master about the sale of his slaves—including her two-year-old child. From that moment, freedom seemed as necessary as drawing breath; there was no going back. She knew two facts: that the river had been frozen for at least a week, and that a white man who lived on a hill back of Ripley was known to help fugitives. The next night, she left her home with her child and ran north through the woods to a place called Stony Point. There an old white man took her into his cabin and fed her. She told the man of her plan to cross the river to freedom. No one, he told her, had been on the ice for the past few days, as far as he had been able to see. The river had thawed for at least the first eight feet from the shore, and the strength of the ice in the middle was doubtful. If she did not drown, she would freeze to death, he warned, and her baby would die with her. She listened, until the faint sound of dogs barking sent an all-knowing look between the two of them. Sensing that she was unstoppable, the man quickly wrapped her baby in a woolen shawl, rushed them outside, and tore a rail from his fence for her to use as support if she broke through the ice. Then, as the barking grew louder, he took the mother and child to a path that led to the river.

She followed the path and plunged down the bank just as the dogs broke from the woods nearby. With panic as her only guide, she ignored what the old man had told her, stepped upon a patch of rotten ice several feet into the river, and quickly stumbled into the icy water, up to the tops of her ankle-high shoes. For seconds, the freezing water seemed to paralyze her resolve. Then she heard the voices of her pursuers and the din of barking dogs grow louder and louder. Before her lay the freezing water and the darkness of the unknown. Holding the rail in one hand and her child in the other, she moved forward in the shallow water until she hit upon the ice, which for several feet grew firmer as she walked. The dogs and the men were searching the banks for her, still unaware that she was daring them to cross the river. She moved quickly and silently. Then the ice broke through with a loud popping sound—the sound that Shaw undoubtedly heard. So did the men behind her. As she fell into the now-deep waters, she threw the child onto the ice ahead and used the rail for support. Working her way to the firm ice again, she found her baby still partially wrapped in the blanket, which was now wet with the soft slush of melting ice. She scrambled to her feet again and pushed forward. Running across the ice, still ahead of her pursuers, she sensed that the other side was near, but it never seemed to come. A third time she fell and, saved by the rail, climbed back out. So cold and exhausted was she now that she let go of the rail that three times had saved her.

She was only feet from the shore. When she came upon the land, she collapsed onto the frozen ground, and just as she was beginning to stand again, a hand emerged from the darkness and seized her arm. With her child clinging to her, she sank helplessly to the ground, a feeling of defeat washing over her as if drowning in the anxiety of her entire race. Courage gone, with fear seeping through her like the water saturating her clothes, she lay on the ground and groaned in despair. As if responding, the child cried. And at that moment, the hand released her and a voice out of the darkness said, "Any woman who crossed that river carrying her baby has won her freedom."

After hours of patrolling the Ohio shore hunting for runaways in the discomforting chill of winter, Shaw had found his catch. Arrested for assault at least twice, and known to drink too much too often, Shaw was not given to expressions of kindness and compassion. But this night he showed another side: He forsook the master's gold that awaited him. He helped the woman to her feet, picked up the baby, threw the wet, cold shawl upon the ground, and took the woman by the hand. Rushing through the streets and alleys of Ripley, he watched for shadows, worrying he might collide with one of the men he knew so well, the men with whom he swapped stories of "coon hunting" on both sides of the river. Listening for sounds in a way he had never done before, he took her to the edge of the village, to the bottom of the steep hill, and then pointed up, telling her that the man who lived at the top of the hill would help her. The doors to the red brick house would be unlocked, he told her, and the man's dogs were trained not to bark at "niggers." "No nigger was ever caught that got to his house," Shaw told her.

It was late in the night when she arrived at the Rankin home. The door was unlocked, as Shaw had said, and a fire was in the hearth. Within minutes, she was poking the fire as she watched Jean Rankin sorting through a pile of clothes in search of flannel underwear she had made herself, a plaid dress that was her own, and a pair of home-knit socks. John Rankin entered the room, called two of his boys downstairs, and then commenced to listen to the woman's story of crossing the ice. John Rankin, Jr., later recalled the night:

I was aroused by father calling up the stairs for Calvin and myself. I had answered that night call too many times not to know what it meant. Fugitive slaves were downstairs. Ahead of us was a long walk across the hills in the dead of night under a cold winter's sky followed by the long cold walk back home which must be made before daybreak. So we were in no pleasant mood when we came downstairs. Seated before the fire was a mulatto woman, with her baby in her arms and a pile of wet woman's clothes on the hearth stones. Father who was standing on one side of the fireplace, said to us: "She's crossed the river on the ice!"

One of us exclaimed, "She couldn't!"

"But she did!" he continued.

There was mother, father, Calvin and myself looking down at the woman and her baby as she sat in the glowing light of the fire. She seemed so simple and yet how little did we know that this courageous mother who though now unknown was to stir the hearts of a nation. While she was safe enough for the moment, as a matter of fact, danger was imminent as long as she remained with us. So when the mother and baby were warm, well fed, and somewhat rested we prepared to resume the flight to Canada. Long before daylight she must be hidden safely away farther back from the river.

As Calvin was older it fell to his lot to carry the baby while the mother and I fell in behind. Our trail led over the hills way down the bank of Red Oak Creek which we waded and then came to the unlocked door of Rev. James Gilliland, the Scotch Presbyterian minister of Red Oak Chapel, which still stands; likewise the manse into which we now entered without knocking. The light, fire and food was there waiting. Here we turned over our fugitives. That we acted wisely in cautiously guiding our charges across the hills was forcibly brought to our minds before we reached home. For as we were crossing a bridge on our way back, one of the white patrols stepped out from a deep shadow and spoke to us. We knew the man very well and knew what he was about; when we asked what he was doing out so late he characteristically answered: "jes coon huntin'." At home we found father and mother both up. Father was deeply wrought over the affair exclaiming: "I hope she gets away, hope she gets away."

The woman and her child spent the following day sequestered in the Gilliland home. That night, one of his sons took her to the home of Dr. Greenleaf Norton in Decatur; from there she was taken to a Quaker home near Sardinia, and then, to confuse and avert her pursuers, who were still hunting her down, she was guided all the way to the home of the Quaker "conductor" Levi Coffin in Newport, Indiana, six miles west of the Ohio border. Eventually, she and her child would arrive in Chatham, Ontario. And one day she would return to Rankin's home on a quest to bring the rest of her family out of Kentucky.

A year or so later, as John Rankin, Jr., recounted, his father was visiting one of his brothers, who was a student at Lane.

One Sunday afternoon, father called upon Prof. Stowe, there in the presence of Harriet Beecher Stowe, father told of the flight of the slave mother and her child crossing the Ohio River on the ice. She was greatly moved by the narrative, exclaiming from time to time, "Terrible! How terrible!"

So moved was Stowe that she would later use the slave woman's story to model the character Eliza in her book *Uncle Tom's Cabin.*

So far as we were concerned it was only another incident of many of a similar character. Strange how this unknown fugitive mother figured into the history of this country. She had no name, no monument erected to her. We two boys had helped to make history and were deaf, dumb and blind to its magnificence.

CHAPTER FIFTEEN

"Mercy Enough?"

Eighteen hundred and thirty-eight was the year of the great escape of the Maryland slave Frederick Augustus Bailey, who, dressed as a sailor back from duty at sea, fled on a train to New York, where he changed his surname to Douglass after a character in the poem *The Lady of the Lake* by Sir Walter Scott. It was the year when Pennsylvania Hall, a large new building in Philadelphia erected for the cause of free speech, including abolitionism, opened with an assemblage of thousands, including William Lloyd Garrison—and closed four days later, after a mob burned it to the ground. And it was the year when the government forced the Cherokee, Choctaw, Chickasaw, and Seminole to march a thousand miles along a "trail of tears" out of their indigenous Southeastern U.S. to land west of the Mississippi.

That year, the state of Kentucky passed a law prohibiting slaves from riding as passengers on stagecoaches, fining stagecoach drivers $100 for transporting a slave, and charging drivers the full value of any slaves who successfully escaped in their coaches. The American Anti-Slavery Society published the fifth edition of Rankin's *Letters on Slavery*. Alexander Campbell, Ohio's first abolitionist, became the sixth mayor of Ripley. And a school in Red Oak that admitted black children became the latest casualty of arsonists making a statement against abolition and racial equality.

On February 26, after months of receiving letters and resolutions from antislavery societies throughout the state and from abolitionists such as Mahan, Beck, Rankin, and Campbell, Ohio's House of Representatives opened the floor to discussions of the case of Eliza Jane Johnson. Before them was the following resolution:

Whereas It is represented to this General Assembly that Eliza Jane Johnson, a free woman of color, was lately carried by force and without legal authority from her home in Brown County, Ohio into Mason County Kentucky on the pretence of being a slave of Arthur Fox, of said county of Mason, and though the said Arthur Fox disclaims any title to said Eliza, she is still detained in confinement in the jail of said county. Therefore, Resolved that: His Excellency the Governor be, and he is hereby requested to open a correspondence with the Governor of Kentucky, in relation to the illegal seizure and forcible removal of said Eliza Jane Johnson from Brown County, Ohio to Mason County, Kentucky where she is detained in prison and that he respectfully insists on the restoration of said Eliza Jane Johnson to the enjoyment of freedom and friends.

A. J. Foote of Cuyahoga County, a member of the Ohio Anti-Slavery Society, pled for the rights of Johnson.

Must I be taunted with the accusation that I do it for political effect? Is it not enough that when this people are charged with being slaves they can be carried off without the benefit of a jury trial that this public barrier of protection be broken down and every colored person placed entirely beyond the protection of our laws? A regard for the character and the violated sovereignty of Ohio, as well as sympathy for the oppressed, equally forbid it. You sir (the Speaker) might be taken from your elevated seat and I might be hurried from my place and subjected to the operation of the laws of another jurisdiction with the same propriety that this woman could be thus snatched from home and incarcerated in Kentucky. The only protection left us is the color of our skins.

Yes Sir, justice instead of longer being represented as blind must now open her eyes to ascertain the mere question of color and how long this quality will be a protection to us after we permit state sovereignty and individual security to be violated, no human mind could predict.

In the present instance none of the forms of law had been complied with; the sovereignty of the state had been invaded; one of its inhabitants

141

had been forcibly abducted in the face and violation of the laws. An act had been committed, which, between independent nations, was cause for war.

Unless they were for war with Kentucky, Foote went on, they should vote for the resolution that in effect was an invitation to Kentucky to negotiate. The case, he said, was not just about a woman wrongfully detained in Kentucky: It was about the future security of every citizen of the state of Ohio.

Other members of the House of Representatives stood up and spoke for the resolution. Then a vote was taken. The preamble and resolution passed, thirty-seven to twenty-three. In the *Cincinnati Gazette* the next day, an editor wrote:

This case has some attendant circumstances of most aggravated character. One of them is that the woman sought a hearing before a judge in Washington, Kentucky which was granted and a number of persons from Brown County were prevailed upon to attend as witnesses. One of them, on his return home, was waylaid, seized, stripped, tied and most brutally whipped. Another is that after Mr. Fox disclaimed ownership, the woman was retained upon the claim of an alleged owner in New Orleans—which detainer may ultimately subject her to be sold into slavery for her jail fees!!

On March 12, the day after the thaw on the Ohio River was complete and boat traffic was flowing once again, the Mason County circuit court issued the following order: "Upon the motion of the attorney for the county to hire out the Negro named Eliza Jane Johnston [sic] who was committed to the jail of Mason County on the twenty-second day of September 1837, it is now considered by the court that there being no just grounds that the said Eliza Jane Johnston is a slave, It is ordered that she be released and discharged from the custody of the jailer of Mason County."

The next day, Eliza Jane Johnson stepped off the ferry from Kentucky and onto the banks of Ripley. Her husband and a small gathering of teary-eyed bystanders watched as she stood in the sun of freedom for the first time in more than five months.

And the day after that, John Rankin wrote a letter to *The Philanthropist*, which was reprinted in local mainstream papers. Rankin shared in the excitement of Johnson's release from prison, but he also understood that this was no time to relax on the laurels of the victory. It was clear to Rankin that such victories, arousing the wrath of their neighbors to the south, only created greater challenges for people fighting against the injustices of slavery. It was fine to celebrate Johnson's homecoming, but the very same thing could happen again the next day, and the next day, and the next. And so he continued, through his writings and sermons, to try to draw attention to the injustices of her abduction and her months of incarceration for the crime of having a skin a different color from that of her abductors.

> Had the Mason court paid her reasonable damages, and discharged her before her case came before the legislature of Ohio we should have had a higher sense both of their justice and humanity. Ought not the state of Ohio, through the executive, to demand full justice? Can the people of Mason County sustain a character for honesty, if they refuse to pay reasonable damages? The court has, by her discharge, acknowledged that she was unjustly imprisoned.

Rankin's call for compensation from the state of Kentucky was answered by a call of a different sort. By April, notices were posted in the villages and towns of northern Kentucky—on the pillars of courthouses, on saloon doors, and on the trunks of sycamores and oaks—announcing the offer of rewards up to $2,500 for the abduction or assassination of Alexander Campbell, John Rankin, Dr. Isaac Beck, and John B. Mahan.

The war between Ohio and Kentucky forged ahead on three fronts: on the river, in the courthouses of both states, and on the free soil of Ohio, where no free black man, woman, or child could feel secure—and where soon white men too would feel the stunning grip of slavery's force.

CHAPTER SIXTEEN

THE TRAP

The summer of 1838 was hotter than usual in the towns on the Ripley line, especially inland from the river. On weekends, families flocked to the shores of the river, where temperatures were a few degrees cooler. Children crowded the sandbars, splashing and screaming as they escaped from the wretched air into the lukewarm water. Ladies conversed over the fluttering of their fans in parlors darkened by shades and drapes pulled tightly closed to shut out the sun. Porch-sitters swatted mosquitoes, and horses flicked flies with their tails. Days were longer than nights, though little was accomplished, since the pace of life was so slow that even the box turtles moving through gardens and across roads seemed to move faster than most people. The horsemen who came over from Kentucky seemed all the more conspicuous that summer as they frantically ran their horses, with coats matted down in sweat and hooves sending up clouds of dust, through the quiet, sluggish town into the hills, where they gathered posses of like-minded men and hunted humans as if they were deer.

From June 10 through Friday evening, June 15, heavy storms pummeled the valley every day. The river rose, and temperatures temporarily fell. Flash floods out of the creeks killed one man on the road between Ripley and Cincinnati. On the 11th, a few hours before midnight, the citizens

A nineteenth-century woodcut of Ripley, Ohio, from the Kentucky side of the river. Rankin's house can be seen atop the hill overlooking Ripley. The woodcut was originally published in 1847.

The Ripley shoreline in 1999, with the Rankin house just barely visible. (*Author photograph*)

John Rankin (1793–1886), abolitionist, Presbyterian minister, speaker, writer, and leader of the Ripley line of the Underground Railroad in Ohio (date unknown).

Rankin and his wife, Jean (1795–1878), on their fiftieth wedding anniversary, January 2, 1866. During their marriage they raised at least twenty-two children and helped thousands of slaves escape to freedom.

The oldest known photograph of Rankin's house on the hill above Ripley, taken around 1870, shortly after the Rankins had moved away.

Wooden stairs leading to Rankin's house. They were a continuation of stone steps that Rankin put in place during the 1830s. Many of the original stone steps remain; these wooden stairs were rebuilt by the citizens of Ripley in 1995.

The view across the Ohio River into Kentucky from the living room of Rankin's house, as photographed by the author in 1999.

The house of Nathaniel Collins, Ripley's first mayor and an ally of Rankin's on the Underground Railroad. Collins's sons Thomas and Theodore also worked with Rankin. Thomas, a carpenter, sometimes hid runaway slaves in the coffins he made in his workshop behind the house.

Broadway, the main street of Granville, Ohio, in 1842, six years after it was the scene of the clash between abolitionist and proslavery forces following the first convention of antislavery groups of Ohio. (Courtesy Granville, Ohio, Historical Society)

During an antislavery convention in Cincinnati in the spring of 1853, at which William Lloyd Garrison and John Rankin were speakers, Garrison presented Rankin with an inscribed copy of his writings and speeches.

Rev. John Rankin.

With the profound regards and loving veneration of his antislavery disciple and humble co-worker in the cause of emancipation, Wm. Lloyd Garrison.

Cincinnati, April 20, 1853.

An 1872 Rankin family portrait. *Seated, l. to r.,* daughters Mary Eliza, Julia, Rev. John Rankin and his wife, Jean, daughter Isabella. *Standing, l. to r.,* sons Thomas Lovejoy, William Alexander, Andrew Campbell, John Thompson (John Jr.), Samuel Gardner Wilson, Richard Calvin, and Arthur Tappan. Absent was son Adam Lowry. (Son David Wilmot died in 1847 and daughter Lucinda in 1856.)

The only known photograph of John Bennington Mahan (1801–1844), a conductor on the Ripley line who was arrested in 1838 for assisting fugitive slaves. His tombstone in Sardinia, Ohio, where he lived, reads, "Victim of the Slave Power." *(Courtesy of Rick and Elizabeth Franklin)*

(Below) The house of John Parker (1827–1900), an African American born into slavery, who, after gaining his own freedom, moved to Ripley and for nearly twenty years risked his life hundreds of times rowing across the Ohio River at night to Kentucky to bring slaves to freedom. No photographs of Parker are known to exist.

(Left) A portrait of Rankin's oldest son, Adam Lowry (1816–1895), who was active in the Underground Railroad from his youth in Ripley, and especially during his student years at Lane Theological Seminary in Cincinnati, where he assisted at least 300 fugitive slaves in the late 1830s. He remained active through the Civil War.

In his younger days, Billy Marshall, a free black, was a conductor for the Underground Railroad in Ripley.

Polly Ann Jackson Caldwell, shown here in 1910, was a free black citizen of Ripley who was known during the antebellum years for aiding fugitive slaves and attacking slave catchers with a butcher knife.

of Ripley and other Ohio Valley towns felt the quivering effects of an earthquake whose epicenter was somewhere around St. Louis. The aftershocks as far to the east as Ripley were only identified as such after the local papers reported the phenomenon. By the weekend, all worries had turned once again to the soaring temperature, which rose as high as ninety-five on some days, with humidity even higher.

Despite the climatic challenges that summer, slaves continued to cross the river, often arriving by their own willpower at Rankin's door, wet with sweat, throats parched after climbing the steep hill. And the slave-hunting riders seemed to increase as the summer progressed. "Our neighborhood has been unusually infested with Negro-hunters who have in several instances and in various ways displayed the demoralizing influences of slavery," said a citizen of Sardinia at a meeting called to discuss the problem. In one instance in June, the citizen went on to say, a Kentuckian and a hired gun from Ohio rode to a house in Sardinia on the afternoon of the Sabbath and inquired about a stray horse. The Kentuckian pretended to be an abolitionist, but the man in the house knew that abolitionists were not in the habit of hunting horses on the Sabbath. He surmised they were slave hunters and thus asked them to leave his property. The mercenary agreed to leave, but the Kentuckian declined the offer. The homeowner grabbed his ax and repeated the order. The Kentuckian drew a pistol. The man advanced with his ax, and the Kentuckian retreated. But as he left, he suddenly turned around and shot his pistol twice, missing the man both times. Then he walked away.

On June 20, several days after the storms had passed and temperatures had returned to the nineties, one of the Beasleys down on Front Street brought a tall, heavyset black man up to Rankin's house. A runaway slave between thirty-five and forty years old and weighing about 185 pounds, the man had been hiding in the Beasleys' barn since the early-morning hours. Lowry, who was at home for the summer, took the man to the cellar beneath the barn, then went into town to get a sense of whether or not the slave's master was in close pursuit. Lowry learned quickly that the slave belonged to a man by the name of William Greathouse who lived in Mason County, Kentucky; that he had run away the day before; that Greathouse valued him at $1,500; that Greathouse was indeed in town with a number of men; that he was absolutely certain that his slave was hidden somewhere in the town of Ripley; and that he and his men intended to watch all the roads that day and night in search of their runaway. Lowry, who knew of

Greathouse and had heard that he was a "hard customer to deal with," was certain now that the man in his father's barn was the same man Greathouse was boasting he would kill for.

The other Rankin brothers with experience on the underground were in Sardinia for three days at a music festival. Lowry's parents and the other children were out of town for the day, to return in the early evening. To continue harboring a sought-after fugitive much after dusk was unwise. But to take him alone when such a vigilant posse followed was unnerving to Lowry. And so he recruited the help of James Gilliland's son Alexander, who had chosen not to attend the festival. Together they made a plan to leave as soon as the sun had set, and to reach the deepest woods as soon as possible.

It was a cloudy, windy night, and between the house and the woods was a vast cornfield through which the three men must walk their horses. But as soon as they were fifty feet into the field, Lowry stopped. He was sure he heard voices. As the wind rustled the corn, it carried with it the indistinct sound of suppressed conversation. He changed their course to move with the wind, so that their own sounds would not be carried back to the people hidden somewhere in the field. Near the center of the field was an old black-walnut tree. When they reached it, Lowry dismounted and asked the other two men to wait for him while he inspected the field to find the source of the voices. On the edge near one of the roads out of town, he was able to spot five men watching the road. They were near enough to Rankin's house that Lowry felt he should warn his family, who he was certain had returned home. So he went back to the house, to which his family had indeed just returned. There he and his father agreed that the younger brothers would carry a lantern back and forth between the house and the barn for at least the next hour to distract the men in the field and hold their attention, while Lowry, Alexander, and the slave, whose name was John, led their horses through the rest of the field, past the rail fence, and into a densely wooded area. The scheme worked, and the three men, safely through one ring of fire, rushed their horses down a deep ravine and up again on the other side—"as fast as the uneven nature of the ground would permit our horses to travel," Lowry later recalled. Through another of Rankin's cornfields, along the edge of a long, densely timbered tract of several miles that skirted Red Oak Creek, then halfway up a hillside, they rode single-file, with Gilliland in front, John in the middle, and Lowry at the rear. After several hours of riding, a heavy rain began, and continued most of the rest of their journey. About an hour before dawn, they arrived at their destination: the tavern of John B. Mahan in Sardinia.

By then, Mahan—once described by James G. Birney as "muscular, raw-boned and stalwart"—had been working with Levi Coffin in Indiana and with Rankin in Ohio for nearly a decade. Often the fugitives moved from Rankin's to Alexander McCoy's house on Eagle Creek and on to Mahan's, though the routes differed depending on the weather and the location of the men in pursuit of the slave. Lowry and Alexander warned Mahan that Greathouse was in the county and was determined to round up his slave. Lowry suggested sending John on to Highland County and points north that very day. But Mahan thought it was better to keep him until it was clear that the slave master and his posse had left the county. And so Lowry joined his brothers at the music festival in the same town, and John the slave remained with Mahan.

In the days ahead, John told Mahan that for most of his life he had been the property of a man named Allen, also in Mason County, but one day Allen's daughter claimed she was attacked by a black man. John was the chief suspect. Allen felt he must sell John, despite John's claims that he had nothing to do with the assault. Around that time, Greathouse had made it known that he wanted another slave. And so Allen sold John to Greathouse, with the stipulation that if it was ever proven that John was guilty of assaulting Allen's daughter then Greathouse promised he would sell the slave to the Southern traders and send him downriver. Because John feared such a fate, from the moment he began working for Greathouse he also began plotting his escape. He fled Kentucky on the night of June 19.

During his days in Sardinia, John divided his time among Mahan's tavern and garden, and Mahan's store, which was across the street from the tavern. And he attended an abolition meeting at the Presbyterian church. Some in the town felt that Mahan should keep John behind closed doors. But after a few days without the appearance of any slave catchers, Mahan felt it was safe to allow him to be outside and to relax in preparation for the next leg of his journey north. For Mahan, taking in the slave, feeding him, providing a change of clothes for him, and supplying him with spiritual nourishment was an act of God. For Greathouse, it was closer to an act of war.

On June 24, word came out of the countryside that Greathouse was still in the county and, worse, riding toward Sardinia. Mahan and his network responded quickly. Just after sunset, Lewis and Abraham Pettijohn rode into Sardinia and took John to Lewis's farm, several miles north of town. The next night, just after sundown, Jackson Myers, a man who often rode for the underground, took John to the farm of Mahan's brother, William, in Highland County. From there, on the 26th, Myers and John took William Mahan's horses and traveled north; by most accounts, Myers took John all the way to Canada.

Though a gentleman of property and standing in Mason County, with nearly 800 acres valued at $22,800 and thirteen slaves worth a total of $3,300, Greathouse also had a criminal record. An 1831 indictment for fraud described him as "a wicked and depraved person seeking to obtain his living by various subtle fraudulent and dishonest practices." Now he was fuming like a steamboat fighting the river current. His slave had disappeared somewhere on this land beyond the river, and no one would tell him where the man was. Greathouse knew his slave had been in Ripley. He knew he had been in Sardinia. But where was he now?

On the 25th of June, Mahan's wife watched out an upper-story window as Greathouse and a small band of ruffians appeared at the Mahans' front door. She listened while her husband calmly told Greathouse that he could search the premises if he wished but that no black man resided within those walls. Then she saw something that made her heart beat so loudly she feared Greathouse might hear it: Hanging from the window directly above Greathouse's head was a shirt (described later as a "dickey") that the slave had worn when he first arrived in Sardinia. Mahan too remembered the shirt, its arms nearly touching his head, and he watched the slave master's eyes closely to see where they were focusing. Filled with impatience and disgust, Greathouse's eyes stared fiercely into Mahan's, hoping to scare the preacher into telling the truth. Greathouse could have identified the shirt his slave had worn the night he disappeared from the Kentucky farm, but the slave owner's obsessive focus on Mahan kept him from closely observing anything else.

One of the Huggins brothers wrote later, "After searching through the country for some time, [Greathouse] concluded that his slave was at the house of Lewis Pettijohn. He and his mercenaries traversed the country for five or six miles around Sardinia, and having succeeded in collecting a mob of twenty or thirty persons, of the filth and offscouring of society within that bounds, marched to the house of Mr. Pettijohn."

At 11 P.M. on June 25, Lewis Pettijohn responded to heavy rapping at his door and found Greathouse standing a few steps in front of a rabble of at least twenty men smelling of whiskey.

"I want my black man," Greathouse said.

"I have no black man," Pettijohn said. He then demanded the men's names, which they refused to give.

Greathouse fired back a demand to enter the house to search. Pettijohn refused permission. Greathouse said he had a warrant, and as Pettijohn leaned his candle toward a piece of paper to read it, a man rushed in, grabbed the candle, and pressed a pistol to Pettijohn's chest.

"Damn your abolition soul," Greathouse said, as he motioned the other men into the house. "And if you open your mouth, you will be dead."

They searched the house and found no black man. Greathouse then told Pettijohn that if he did not reveal whose house the man was hiding in he would receive five hundred lashes with a cowhide. Another man struck Pettijohn twice with a club, while still another stripped the nightclothes off his wife. Greathouse gave him a choice: $50 if he told them where the man was, or death to himself and his family if he did not. Pettijohn told them the escaping slave was at the Campbell house, several miles away. And so the horsemen left, without, of course, giving Pettijohn the $50, leaving the warning that if they had been misled they would return and fulfill their threat. No one was home at the Campbells', as Pettijohn well knew: no Campbells and no fugitive slave. Upon their return to the Pettijohns', the mob, now nearly thirty horsemen strong, found an empty house. An incensed Greathouse swore he would soon return with two hundred men from Kentucky.

Greathouse left Ohio later that night in a torrent of dust, heat, and anger, swearing and vowing to all he met on the way to the ferry that he would return one day to seek amends somehow for the loss of his slave— property that he claimed had a value of $800. The horsemen in his posse, most of whom were from Brown County, rode home. One from Sardinia, who may have been drinking later that night, stood in the street outside of Mahan's tavern and cursed at him, screaming that there was a $2,500 reward for his head.

A week later, in the early hours of July 1, a two-story, thirty-by-twenty-six-foot house burst into flames in Red Oak. It was the home of an interracial school that had been proposed at a meeting late in 1836 at the home of a local farmer and antislavery advocate John Shepherd. The school had opened in May 1838. Tuition was $4 a session. Shepherd, Gordon Hopkins, and Isaac Sutherland—all members of the Ripley Anti-Slavery Society—were its administrators. Boarding had been arranged in the neighborhoods of Red Oak and Ripley. Now the dream of several years was in ashes. No one knew who had done it, but many people suspected it was the work of Greathouse's cronies in Brown County.

On July 22, shortly after the wheat harvest, another Greathouse runaway, a man named Nelson, escaped through Brown County. He came with a black man named Benjamin Veiny, who lived in Georgetown, had received Nelson through one of the Rankin sons, and now was guiding him to the next safe house. No slave catchers were in pursuit; Greathouse was not aware yet that Nelson was gone. They did not stop at Mahan's but went on past Sardinia to the Huggins farm, where Nelson stayed for some time and actually worked on the land to earn some money before proceeding north.

No one on the "line" thought much about Greathouse and his slaves for the rest of the month, though everyone seemed to feel an indescribable tension building all along the river. In early August, farther east, the *Parkersburg Gazette* in Virginia expressed the sentiments of many people who lived south of the river:

In the last three months slaves valued at from fifteen to twenty thousand dollars have run away from a small section of this county and state; and although immediate pursuit has been made and large rewards offered in every instance not one has been apprehended and there is reason to believe that most of them are now beyond the limits of the U.S. To chronicle these facts is superfluous labor so far as this community is concerned but we wish it to be known as widely as possible that an organized band [is] residing in Ohio who are constantly guilty of inducing, abetting, and aiding these escapes. Whether they are in the pay of the abolition societies may be conjectured; but there is no doubt that facilities are furnished the runaways, which require the expenditure of larger sums of money than it is in the power of slaves to procure. Women and children of all ages have gone among the rest; and yet their pursuers, although frequently on their trail, have been uniformly baffled in their endeavors to reclaim them. The runaways are forwarded by night in covered wagons or are furnished with guides and led through the most unfrequented roads and by paths and are encamped in the woods or concealed in the towns. Their pursuers are misled by false information; obstacles are thrown in their way and signals are made in their presence and when answered they are deceptively told they are welcome to search. Such are the facts.

Then, on August 3, what seemed a routine act on the underground, just as the Parkersburg newspaper described, occurred in Sardinia. What was really happening was far from routine. A large, puffy-looking white man who called himself Mr. Rock came to Sardinia late that night, accompanied by a black woman, and determined to talk to Mahan. It was late, but Mahan, in his nightshirt with a rifle at his side, answered the loud knocking at his door. Standing outside, still holding his rifle, he listened carefully to the man's story. Unknown to Mahan, the man was really James Rock Perrigo, who lived at that time in Mason County, Kentucky, on the property of William Greathouse.

Rock told Mahan that he lived near the river on the Ohio side, and that the "Negro woman" had come to his house in search of her husband, a slave named John who had belonged to Greathouse. Did Mahan know anything about such a man, who might have come through Brown County in June?

Mahan told Rock that he knew of two runaways by the name of John who had passed through the area that summer, and one did say he was a Greathouse slave. Where was the slave? asked Rock. Mahan told him that John was probably in Canada by now. Could Mahan take care of the slave woman from this point forward? Mahan said he could guide her to her husband but asked if Rock could take her. If he did, Mahan would pay him $3. Rock agreed to do that and then asked Mahan to write a letter that would facilitate such a journey for both Rock and the woman. Mahan agreed to do so, and that very night, by the light of the full moon, wrote a note for Rock to take with him to the next stop on the Underground Railroad:

Dear Sir:
You will take care of the oppressed for the Lord's sake. Send her to Mr. Johnson's, brother of the Rev. Hezekiah Johnson, ten miles north of Hillsborough, or to Thomas Hibbens, at Wilmington. The Lord bless you.
     Two o'clock in the morning, by moonshine in the street.
                                        Yours,
                                        JOHN B. MAHAN

After receiving the $3 and the letter, Rock and the woman left Mahan, who assumed they were on their way to Highland County. In truth, they returned to their horses and met up with William Greathouse, who was waiting for them at a concealed location.

On August 14, a grand jury convened in Mason County, Kentucky, to consider the possibility of indicting John Bennington Mahan for stealing William Greathouse's slaves. The hope among Greathouse and his slaveholder friends was to identify all the links in the chain that extended from Kentucky to Canada. Mahan was one link that would eventually lead to the others. In this mission, the slaveholders believed, anything was justified.

"What have we to do with slavery?" Northerners often asked. In September 1838, some of them would find out.

CHAPTER SEVENTEEN

"The Matter Is
Highly Mysterious"

On Monday, September 17, 1838, Greathouse returned to Ripley with a band of horsemen who gathered on the bank of the river like an ominous force moving swiftly toward destruction. With the midmorning sun warm upon their backs, they rode up Ferry Street, spurring their steeds to a gallop in a menacing mass of hooves and dust, of whips, sweat, and fury. Sharp and fast like spears of sunlight shooting through the trees, they moved out of Ripley, up the steep hill where the Rankins lived, over the ridges, across the ravines, thundering through the town of Red Oak, through Russellville, through Georgetown, where more horsemen joined them, crowding up and down forested trails, dead branches breaking as shoulders and thighs pushed through shadowy thickets.

It was early afternoon when they reached Sardinia. The air was charged with the sound of pursuit: an unbroken roar of approaching horsemen that grew louder and louder, causing the ground to tremble as they neared the town. Flanks white with sweat, the horses ran unrestrained into the main street of the town, clouds of dust billowing behind them, their riders hardly visible. And then they skidded to a halt, snorting and stomping as they scattered sand and stones, their riders slowly emerging from the haze.

The men brought with them an arrest warrant, approved by the governor of Ohio, allowing the sheriff of Mason County, Kentucky, to arrest and extradite John B. Mahan. The charge was "aiding and assisting certain slaves, the property of William Greathouse, to make their escape from the possession of the said William Greathouse, out of and beyond the state of Kentucky." Mahan was accused of violating the laws of the state of Kentucky. His wife, Polly, saw him from a distance as he was hoisted onto the back of a horse.

An hour or so later, Polly Mahan sat on the stoop of the white frame house that she shared with John and their eight children. Clutching Alexander, their fifteen-month-old baby, in one arm, and embracing two toddler sons with the other, she spoke quickly, her body shivering with anxiety, as she told Eli Huggins about the men who had just come from Kentucky and taken her husband away. Someone, she said, had an arrest warrant. But what had her husband done? Three other children—eight-year-old Isaac, ten-year-old John Wesley, and twelve-year-old Anne Elizabeth—interrupted their mother as they tugged on Huggins's shirtsleeve and cried, "Papa is gone! Papa is gone!"

"Before he left I took his hand," Mahan's wife said, "and I told him to stand by the truth, that it's better to die on the right side than to live on the wrong."

September 17 was nearly one year to the day after the abduction of Eliza Jane Johnson, and now tragedy had again struck the Ripley line. Polly was frightened, and Huggins, with bitter memories of the Johnson case and the near lynching of his brother James, tried to hold back his own fears. Both knew that for the past year Mahan, along with Rankin, Beck, and others, had been targets of malicious gossip and rancorous threats from Kentuckians passing through Brown County and from antiabolitionist locals. They knew about the rewards of up to $2,500 for Mahan's capture or murder. Around September 12, Huggins remembered, Joseph and Zachariah Pettijohn had told him that they were approached by a man who said he would pay "$500 to any responsible man or set of men who would obligate themselves to deliver John B. Mahan" to him.

Everyone along the line had felt the escalating tensions that summer, but neither Mahan's wife nor his friends ever expected anything like this to happen. Now they were thinking that perhaps the man who came for the reward a week ago had known of the indictment and wanted to snatch Mahan before the Kentucky sheriff got to him, hoping, of course, to collect the reward money.

Before Huggins's arrival at the Mahans', one of Huggins's brothers, one of the Pettijohns, Dr. Beck, and others had caught up with the Kentucky men and Vincent Crabb, the deputy sheriff of Brown County, who—instructed by the Ohio governor's office—had delivered the arrest warrant to Mahan. Dr. Beck informed Crabb that Mahan had the right to obtain a writ of habeas corpus to challenge the arrest, and insisted that the men ride into Georgetown to obtain it, which they all did. Mrs. Mahan told Huggins that all she knew was that they had ridden into Georgetown; Huggins then left to find them. In Georgetown, he quickly learned that his friends and Mahan were at the office of Thomas L. Hamer, a well-known Georgetown attorney. Hamer had been practicing law in Ohio since 1821. He had also been the protégé of Thomas Morris, the antislavery U.S. senator from Clermont County, and had served in Congress for three terms. Having fallen out with his longtime mentor, on the issue of slavery, Hamer was now an antiabolitionist. And on this day, Hamer would make it clear that he was now loyal to the Southern cause. When asked to issue a writ of habeas corpus that might save Mahan from being forced out of his own state and that would indeed rightfully question the details of the indictments that allegedly warranted his arrest, Hamer said no. He was opposed to abolitionists, and if there was an arrest warrant for Mahan, it should be served. A writ of habeas corpus would have been a routine act for Hamer, simply allowing a citizen of Ohio to question his removal to another state. But he refused to oblige. Mahan's Kentucky guards pulled him out of the meeting, asked him to mount a horse, and then proceeded en masse to the Ohio River. In the minds of the Kentucky men, the visit to Hamer's office had been the one chance that Mahan and his cohorts had to obtain such a writ. Now the captors had the right to return home with their catch. The Ohio governor, after all, had approved the Mahan extradition. Mahan's friends, furious at Hamer for what they felt was a betrayal of his duty as a lawyer and as a citizen of a free state, were in a panic; they must obtain the writ before Mahan was taken across the river and thus out of the state. They ran their sweaty horses back to Sardinia, found a young lawyer who would issue a writ, and dispatched Josiah Moore to serve the writ.

Moore, a furniture maker who was one of the founders of Sardinia, knew well all the back roads and shortcuts through Brown County. He was married to one of the daughters of James Gilliland; his sisters were married to Hugginses and Pettijohns; and he and Dr. Beck had been working together in the Underground Railroad for nearly a decade. Riding as fast as his horse could take him on that hot September day, he finally caught up with Mahan and the Kentuckians just as they rode into Ripley. Moore saw the hope glinting in Mahan's eyes as he proudly served the writ to a man who called himself Sheriff Wood. Wood was in charge of the expedition and was acting as an agent for Mason County's Sheriff Arthur Fox—now notorious for the abduction of Eliza Jane Johnson. He rode his horse close to Mahan's at all times and kept his hand just as close to his gun. Moore quickly read the writ out loud to Wood, who shook his head and then jerked his horse to face the direction of the river. Mahan could not be taken back on the strength of this writ, declared Wood. The writ was from Sheriff Blair of Brown County, and in order to be valid and useful to the men of Ohio it must come from the sheriff of Mason County, Kentucky, said Wood, because the prisoner had been delivered into the custody of that sheriff's agent by the action of the Ohio governor. Nothing anyone did in Ohio, said Wood, could override the decision of that state's highest official. Moore was certain that Wood was either wrong or lying, or both. And just as he was thinking that it must not be true, the horses' hooves were hitting the shallow waters and rocks near the river's edge.

By nightfall, Mahan, his ankles and wrists in irons, was struggling to sleep in the dank basement cell that Eliza Jane Johnson had occupied in Washington, Kentucky, only seven months before. So distracted was he by the question of why he was there.

At this time, he was unaware that a grand jury in Mason County had actually issued two indictments against him. The first charged that on June 19, 1838, he had assisted "a certain slave named John, the property of one William Greathouse, then and there in the said county of Mason to make his escape from the possession of Greathouse and to escape to the state of Ohio and out of and beyond the state of Kentucky." The second indictment charged him with the same offenses regarding the slave named Nelson, who had escaped from Greathouse on July 21, 1838.

In order to apprehend Mahan legally in the state of Ohio and bring him back to the state of Kentucky to stand trial, the prosecuting attorneys from Kentucky had to establish to the grand jury that Mahan was a fugitive from Kentucky justice. Greathouse and his cohorts in Mason County knew this, and so they perjured themselves by testifying before the grand jury in August that Mahan had come to the state of Kentucky to assist Greathouse's slave in escaping. After the grand jury issued the indictments stating that a citizen of Ohio had come to Kentucky to commit a crime, James Clark, the governor of Kentucky, sent a letter to Governor Robert Vance of Ohio asking him to deliver Mahan to Kentucky authorities. This he must do by requesting that an arrest warrant be issued out of the Brown County sheriff's office.

The demand from the Kentucky governor's office, "To His Excellency the Governor of the State of Ohio," read:

> Whereas it has been represented by the affidavit of William Greathouse that John B. Mahan stands charged by two indictments in the Mason circuit court of this State in aiding and assisting certain slaves, the property of the said William Greathouse, to make their escape from the possession of him, the said William Greathouse, out of and beyond the state of Kentucky. And whereas information has been received at the Executive Department of this State, that the said John B. Mahan HAS FLED FROM JUSTICE AND IS NOW GOING AT LARGE IN THE STATE OF OHIO; and it being important and highly necessary for the good of society that the perpetrators of such offences should be brought to justice: Now, therefore, I, James Clark, Governor of the Commonwealth of Kentucky, by virtue of the authority vested in me by the constitution and laws of the United States, do by these present, DEMAND THE SAID JOHN B. MAHAN, AS A FUGITIVE FROM THE JUSTICE OF THE LAWS OF THIS STATE, and make known to your excellency that I have appointed David Wood my agent to receive said fugitive and bring him to this State, having jurisdiction of the said offence, that he may abide his trial for the crime with which he stands charged.

Enclosed were copies of the two indictments.

Vance agreed to give up the "fugitive" Mahan to Kentucky authorities. No questions asked. No questions such as whether Mahan had even been in the state of Kentucky that summer. Mahan, in fact, had not been in Kentucky for nineteen years. This would be his principal defense. In the Johnson case, Mahan had decided not to go to Washington, Kentucky, to the habeas-corpus hearing, as some of his closest friends and cohorts on the underground had done—a choice he now felt blessed to have made. Still, because Vance did not investigate the case before surrendering his citizen to another state, Mahan was in jail.

Mahan was also unaware that the crusade for his freedom had already begun. After the men from Sardinia watched Mahan being taken out of the state, they rode directly up the hill behind Ripley to Rankin's house to tell him what had transpired. Should they proceed as they had in the Eliza Jane Johnson case? No, someone said, such a plan was futile, because the Ohio governor had already handed over Mahan, legally, to another state. No writ of habeas corpus or any other judicial procedure could save him, because the governor's act in asking for a warrant overrode all other legal options. Mahan's only hope was to disprove the charges in the indictment, to show that there was no reason to hand him over, and to expose what these men suspected was a plot to deceive authorities and to entrap Mahan. Rankin said he would begin the task of raising money for Mahan's defense, and everyone pledged to spread the news about what had happened.

That night, Rankin wrote a letter to the editor of *The Philanthropist* describing what had happened. "This is more alarming than even the case of Eliza Jane Johnson," he wrote. "It has occasioned no little excitement among the citizens of Brown County. They begin to feel that no one is safe any farther than he may have physical force to defend himself. What shall the end be? What will not the protection of slavery lead men to do!!"

Recognizing immediately the political significance and powder-keg potential of the incident, and having recently been lambasted by the mainstream press for supposedly embellishing the exploits of antiabolitionists, *The Philanthropist* held Rankin's letter for several days—in fact, they held it long enough that he fired off another to remind them of the importance of the case and the urgency to stir up public opinion on behalf of Mahan. Despite the editors' respect for Rankin, they wanted to gather more information before publishing his letter. Toward this end, they talked with two men who had witnessed the events in Sardinia; they solicited a letter from the editor of the *Political Examiner* in Georgetown, an antiabolitionist paper; and they read the affidavits from men in Sardinia who swore that Mahan had been in Ohio on June 19 and on July 21, the days when he was accused of helping the slaves to escape in Kentucky. Believing that Mahan had been framed, that Vance had been careless, and that Greathouse had committed perjury, *The Philanthropist* moved forward. A week after Mahan's arrest, the newspaper revealed the drama to a national audience in the publication of an "extra" devoted to the Mahan outrage. The headline read: "A Citizen of the State of Ohio delivered up as a fugitive from justice, to be tried by Kentucky laws."

A circumstance has quite recently occurred in this State, which is well calculated to make every man unwilling to bow the knee to Slavery, tremble from his liberty. On Monday, the 17th of September, John B. Mahan, a respectable citizen of Sardinia, a local minister in the Methodist Episcopal Church, was arrested by an order of the governor of this

State, and delivered over to the Executive of Kentucky, as a Fugitive From Justice. The information is contained in the following letter from a well-known clergyman in Ripley.

After Rankin's letter, the paper continued:

Mr. Mahan is an Abolitionist, and his zeal as such has rendered him peculiarly obnoxious to slaveholders. Highly respected by the community in which he lived, even his enemies do not believe him guilty of the acts charged upon him. "Mr. M.," says the Georgetown 'Examiner' (a Whig paper opposed to him in politics, and untinctured with abolitionism) "is known here as a strenuous Abolitionist, yet, we presume there are but few who believe the story of his having carried the war regarding slaves into the state of Kentucky." It will be perceived, that, according to our correspondent, a Kentucky Grand Jury designate him as John Mahan "late of Mason County, Kentucky" when the fact is well known to hundreds, probably thousands in Ohio, that he is an old resident in this State. We are informed by Senator Morris that he has known [Mahan] as a citizen of Ohio since the time he was a boy. We have just conversed with two gentlemen from the neighborhood where the transaction took place. They say that the excitement produced by it is intense; the people are both alarmed and irritated. They tell us that on the very days on which, in the indictments, Mr. Mahan is charged with having committed the acts referred to, he was at home, attending to his business—a fact to which several persons in Sardinia were willing to testify.

Within the next few days, newspapers nationwide carried the reports from *The Philanthropist,* including Garrison's *The Liberator,* which ran the accounts with the preface: "An extra from the office of the Cincinnati Philanthropist brings us the following intelligence, respecting a transaction which is even more alarming than the assassination of Lovejoy."

Two weeks later, *The Liberator* wrote:

MAHAN IN IRONS. What will the people of Ohio think when they are told that the unfortunate Mahan is in irons! A minister [Rankin] went over the other day to visit him and found him with a chain round each ankle and another connecting them. Irons on a citizen of Ohio, the victim of perjury! What say our fellow citizens? Have they any regard for the sovereignty of their State? Mahan is in irons just because he chose to obey the dictates of common humanity. When the poor crushed slave, striving peaceably for liberty, stopped at his door, he gave him food, raiment and counsel. For this he is now immured in a Kentucky jail. No one believes that he is guilty of the offences charged on him in the indictments by which two governors have been hoaxed. Mahan is the victim of Slavery.

Day by day, newspapers nationwide picked up the Mahan story. "DISGRACEFUL SURRENDER OF A CITIZEN OF OHIO TO SLAVEHOLDERS!" read the headline in the *Pennsylvania Freeman*, whose editors wrote:

On our last page will be found an account of one of the most disgraceful transactions ever recorded in the history of the United States—the delivery of a citizen of Ohio over to the authorities of slaveholding Kentucky on the charge of assisting fugitives from Slavery, on their way to Freedom! A minister of the gospel has been torn from his family and friends and delivered up to the tender mercies of a slaveholding jury exasperated and maddened by the loss of their property in human beings. And all this to propitiate the unappeasable spirit of slavery! Let the Free Pennsylvanian read this article and ask himself how long it will be if these things are tolerated before his own household hearth will cease to be a sanctuary from the encroaching and inexorable despotism of slavery. The crisis is fast approaching when Liberty for the slave, or Slavery for the freeman, will be the alternative presented to the Northern citizen. Let him be wise in time and by effecting the liberation of the slave, secure and perpetuate his own liberties.

From the *Morning Star* in New Hampshire:

This is the greatest outrage the opponents of liberty have yet committed excepting the murder of Lovejoy and inasmuch as this is done under the pretence of law it is a more alarming outrage upon the rights of American freemen than that even. It is time for the freemen of the North to awake. Our own liberties, our own persons are in jeopardy. If slaveholders can go into Ohio and carry off its citizens and try them for crimes falsely charged against them under their own unjust and unrighteous laws they can come into New Hampshire, Maine or any other free state and do the same. Shall we submit to those things?

"WHAT HAVE WE TO DO WITH SLAVERY?" read the headline of the *Christian Witness,* whose editors wrote:

> Abolish it—or it will abolish us and our liberties with us. Every day is making more and more evident the fact that slavery of a part endangers the freedom of the whole. There is no safety for us but in the destruction of the system that makes man the property of his fellow man. The principle lying at the bottom of this system must be destroyed or it will destroy us. Humanity is throttled by the bloody hand of despotism and unless rescued will die of strangulation.

The *Cincinnati Gazette* was one of the few papers that quickly grasped the nationwide significance of the case. Its editor wrote:

> We have taken pains to investigate the grounds upon which the prosecution against Mahan was commenced in Kentucky. The indictments were found by the Grand Jury under the conviction that Mahan had been personally in Kentucky, engaged in assisting the black men named as abstracted to escape from their masters. Mahan avers that this is an unfounded allegation. But I understand that an effort will be made to sustain the prosecution on another ground. This ground is proof that the slaves were assisted in Kentucky by a person engaged for that purpose by Mahan. This mode of reaching citizens of free states has been looked to for some time by the owners of slaves as one of vital importance to their security in slave property. It is not improbable that Mahan's may be made a test case. Its importance in aiding a political revolution in Ohio may turn out to be but a lesser influence upon the affairs of the nation.

A letter in the Georgetown paper warned, "No man who is known to be a prominent abolitionist will be secure in the enjoyment of his liberty hereafter."

In the days ahead, everything from the arrogance of slaveholders, the evils of slavery, and the civil rights of Ohio citizens, to conspiracy plots, Vance's behavior, and Mahan's character was debated in the editorial columns of newspapers, from the pulpits of churches, and in city-hall meeting rooms throughout the region. One Cincinnati newspaper accused *The Philanthropist* and its "abolitionist friends" of devising a plot to entrap Mahan as a way to discredit Governor Vance in the upcoming gubernatorial election. In response to the attack, *The Philanthropist* outlined in detail the steps it had gone through before publishing anything about the Mahan case—including holding Rankin's letter pending further investigation. Whether or not Vance had behaved responsibly by turning Mahan over to the Kentucky authorities was one of the more popular questions. Southern sympathizers believed that Vance's actions were impeccably astute. A Massachusetts paper called his decision to extradite Mahan "at once manly and worthy of every honest citizen of the Union." But the *Pennsylvania Freeman* regretted that "Gov. Vance upon such a demand had not been more on his guard. Examples of refusal to act were not wanting. The Governors of New York and of Maine, both refused to surrender citizens of those States under like circumstances. There was enough on the face of the papers to have excited suspicion."

Governor Vance tried to repair the gaping hole in his political ship. He wrote to the Kentucky governor on October 1 and said that since the arrest and delivery of Mahan there "has been put in my possession evidence that cannot be doubted, going to show, that Mahan has not for many years been in the state of Kentucky and under our constitution cannot be answerable to the penalties of her laws. The union of these states and the peace and harmony of society require that the obligations to the constitution and laws should be faithfully observed by its members and whilst the chief Executive officer of this State I trust I shall always be found to give force to these obligations by surrendering to the authorities of our sister states those who may have violated the sanctity of their laws and have taken refuge within our jurisdiction. Yet I cannot consent that a citizen of this state shall be taken to another state and tried for an offence that he (as it appears by the evidence before me) did not commit within her jurisdiction."

Vance then sent a deputized representative from his office to the office of the Kentucky governor to present the evidence that he had and to plead for Mahan's release. But Kentucky Governor Clark had no intention of giving up an indicted man without a trial.

The *Ohio Statesman* responded:

The Gov. pleads that he could not for a moment withhold his action when Mahan was demanded. He pleads that he holds no discretionary power. Most ridiculous conclusion! Why does the law require the demand to be made through him, if not to use discretionary power? We understand this to be the object. If not, why not go and take the man at once without going through these forms merely? But the Governor himself flies in the face of his own argument; for he has sent his private Secretary, Col. Doherty to Kentucky after Mahan to bring him back, we suppose! He had no discretion while Mahan was a citizen of Ohio; but after he has given up and in a foreign State and in the hands of his enemies, then the Governor sends his private Secretary, without shadow of law to BRING HIM BACK! Oh, for a Solon to administer our laws!

Vance had won his 1836 election, as Ohio's first Whig governor, by a majority of nearly six thousand votes. But in 1838, he lost the election to Wilson Shannon, a Democrat, by roughly five thousand votes.

By the time Vance lost, Mahan had been in prison for more than six weeks and had spent many hours writing letters to his family and friends. He even wrote to Vance, though his friends suspected he was being pressured to do so—it was either pressure or fear, they figured, and it was not like Mahan to be afraid. He was told from the beginning by his Ohio friends, who quickly became informed on all options, that he could apply to the Kentucky governor for a pardon. But he declined. This was a case he firmly believed must be seen through to its end; he must be acquitted to prevent future cases of a similar nature. He knew that to apply for a pardon was an admission of guilt. And so he spent his days talking to the jailer, with whom he became friends, reading his Bible, and writing letters— many, many letters.

"It is no small matter to be severed from a beloved family and a large circle of friends," he wrote to Vance a week or so after his incarceration, "carried out of my own State, thrown into a foreign jail, and loaded with irons, having committed no infraction of the laws of my own State nor of the State of Kentucky. . . ."

To a friend, he wrote: "I am, by the grace of God enabled to endure imprisonment much better than I expected. I brought with me a conscience void of offence touching all the matters for which I am indicted. In addition to which I have the Word of God, the grace of God, the light of heaven and the convictions of innocence. Excitement runs high and my attorney informs me that there is something to be dreaded from that. But it is impossible for me to tell what the issue will be. Whether I am restored to my friends and fellow-Christians or not; yet it is certain till death destroy my memory, I never can forget their love and friendship. If I am not permitted to return to my family and friends I have every confidence that every effort will be made by you and all other friends to keep my property together, sustain my family, and educate my children. I am in God's hands."

He wrote often to his wife.

On September 26: "My Beloved Wife: Although destitute of many comforts which my own home furnished me, still my prison is a tolerable place. The prison keeper and family are kind and humane. The Lord reward them. There are indeed strong stone walls and iron doors and grates that deprive me of my liberty; but there is no unquenchable fire, no undying worm, no interminable hell, no indescribable anguish, no frowning Judge, no guilty fears, no haunting midnight, frightful specter, to chase my soul to mad despair. Yours till death."

On October 2: "My Beloved Wife, Every day I look through the grates of my prison towards the Ohio. I desire to be with you; but I am admonished by my Master to be patient; God knows what is best for me and often times in my prison amidst the clanking of chains, I feel happy and am constrained to say it is enough, Lord. I think I feel reconciled to whatever may be the issue of my case. My hope and my trust is in the Lord. Your loving husband."

And to his children he wrote, on October 2: "My dear Children, I need not say I love you—you have had too many tokens of my love to doubt it. I need not say I feel the deepest interest in your happiness and an abiding solicitude for your everlasting salvation. I have spent years of toil and care and labor for your support and instruction and now I do most ardently solicit you by the mercies of Heaven and the atoning blood of a crucified Redeemer, that you avail yourselves of all the godly admonitions I have given you and all the efforts I have made to make you virtuous, respectable and happy. . . .

"My dear children, I want you to know that I am wholly innocent of all the things for which I stand indicted. Give yourselves no concern about that. I am in irons for no fault. I have neither sinned against God nor the laws of men. I hope to see you all soon and find you happy. . . . Your everloving Father, J. B. Mahan."

On his second day in jail, Mahan was told that Greathouse had commenced a civil suit against him claiming damages of $1,700 for the loss of his property, John and Nelson. A few days later, the jailer brought to Mahan an envelope containing a proposal for a compromise. In it, Greathouse offered to send the witness James Perrigo "out of the way"—he would not appear in court against Mahan—and to assure Mahan's acquittal and safe delivery to his side of the river if Mahan would have $1,400 deposited with a friend of Greathouse's in Ohio. The money would be turned over to Greathouse upon Mahan's return to his home. Mahan declined the offer. Several days later, another envelope arrived. This time Greathouse said he would accept $1,200. Mahan again refused.

After his first week in prison, amid a flurry of rumors about mobs plotting to break into the jail and lynch him, Mahan wrote up a will and sent it to his wife. Shortly after receiving it, Polly Mahan and her sister Cassandra, who was married to Mahan's brother William, traveled to Washington, Kentucky with William. At the jailhouse, the women went first. They walked down the narrow stairs to the dirt-floor cellar, stooped under a low-hanging doorframe, and entered Mahan's cell. Polly wept when she saw the cuts on her husband's wrists and ankles from the iron cuffs that had gripped them for months. She called to the jailer and asked if he could loosen the irons, which he did. Then she knelt at her husband's side and began to rip off strips of cloth from her underskirt. Cassandra did the same. They wiped the blood from the cuts and wrapped the areas where the irons had rubbed against his skin. When they left, Mahan slipped another letter into his wife's hand. The local excitement worried Mahan, his attorneys, and his family. Mobs had brutally beaten abolitionists in recent months, and everyone knew it could happen again. But on that day no word was spoken about the potential dangers that the Mahans and all whom they knew now faced.

On November 6, *The Philanthropist* ran this advertisement: "WHO WILL CONTRIBUTE? Our readers will be pleased to learn that our friends in Ripley and in this place have procured able counsel to appear in behalf of Mr. Mahan. The expense will be great; the burden has been assumed by a few. It is a case which appeals to the sympathies of every citizen of Ohio. It would be a disgrace to the freemen of this State to permit Mahan to suffer one jot or title from this most unwarrantable attack on his rights. They are all deeply concerned in the result of the case; they are all deeply interested in having it argued by able counsel for the defendant. Every chance should be afforded the victim of slavery, and all needful expenses should be borne by the people of Ohio. Who then will contribute for this purpose? Any who may feel so disposed will please forward their contributions to Mr. William Donaldson of Cincinnati, or Rev. John Rankin of Ripley, Brown County."

CHAPTER EIGHTEEN

Exposing the Chain

In late October, a posse of Mason County men came through Ripley and headed north, expanding their band as they rode. Their aim was to abduct a black man and his family who had made it on the underground as far as Delaware, Ohio, at least 130 miles from the river. The man had stayed in Ohio for more than a year, always with the intention of one day moving on to Canada. He was the former slave of someone in Kentucky, and a chain of informers had exposed his new life to his foes across the river. The abduction was a success, and the posse returned through Ripley, with its prey on the back of the lead rider's horse. A month later, the black man from Ohio was sold downriver in the South as punishment for his escape.

In response to the incident, *The Philanthropist* wrote, "When was Ohio free? Never: It is a mere race-ground between the slave states and Canada, between the land of violence and oppression and the land of liberty. And all its highways and by-ways are so many courses, entered and scoured and run over by the slaveholders and their hirelings to run down, seize and kidnap either bond or free black or white. . . ."

Ten days or so before the Mahan trial, northern-Kentucky farmers in the counties along the river collected their axes from woodpiles and their pitchforks and scythes from the fields and locked them in boxes and cellars. They cleaned their guns and piled up reserves of ammunition. They checked the strength of bars on doors and filled barrels with water in case of fires. They did anything they could think of to prepare for what they were told was about to happen: a slave insurrection in Boone County, directly across the river from Cincinnati. All the slaves between Florence and Covington were planning to leave, it was said. And this would happen on the night before the Mahan trial was set to begin, the rumors warned.

The plot was exposed a few days after the rumors started, in just enough time before the trial to assess the reasons for the terrible scare. The *Warsaw, Ky., Patriot*—like other local papers—blamed the insurrection on the abolitionists. "The wicked machinations of the abolitionists have in this instance been defeated, but this defeat will not discourage them—it will but stimulate them to renewed exertions and more desperate attempts. We would seriously advise all to be on their guard—to keep a sharp look-out and closely observe the movements of the negroes. If one of them gets across the river and reaches Cincinnati, it is impossible to recover him. The abolitionists there have every convenience for secreting him and for sending him to Canada."

The abolitionists in the region believed the alarm had been sounded to enhance tensions against the antislavery cause and its advocates in the days leading up to the big trial. The story, they believed, was fabricated. Whatever the truth may have been, the Mahan trial went forward on the morning of November 12, when twelve men of Mason County, mostly farmers and a few local merchants, took their seats in the Washington courthouse. Most of the jurors were farmers; some must have been among those collecting axes and bolting doors in the days preceding the trial. And now they listened to the words of Judge Walker Reid as he outlined the case before them and their task as jurors.

By 1838, Walker Reid, the fifty-three-year-old judge who had detained Eliza Jane Johnson the year before, was a prominent figure in northern Kentucky. Born in Virginia, Reid had come to Kentucky in the early part of the nineteenth century, had served as a state representative for the district four times between 1810 and 1817, and had been appointed to his current post as circuit judge in 1832. Notorious for his strident, brave, and often combative opinions, he was highly respected among lawyers and politicians in the state. Slaveholders especially were drawn to him, because he was known for his ardent soliloquies in defense of slavery. His precise and puritanical approach to the law was like that of a scientist. But when it came to slavery, he was a philosopher who could not see the lion that had swallowed him and his region. He told the Mahan jurors:

I cannot believe that any country, however enlightened by Christianity or philosophy, has done more to ameliorate the condition of its slaves than Kentucky.

They are indeed happy and if let alone would still remain so. Where "Ignorance is bliss, 'twere folly be wise." The efforts of their pretended friends to educate them and emancipate them among us in the present state of our laws and of public opinion, render their condition worse—they are rivetting the fetters which they feign believe are irksome and galling still stronger, and freedom, like the cup of Tantalus, though presented to the lip, is still withheld, and still further removed from fruition.

The relation of master and slave is so wrought up in our social and political existence, that it ought not to be tampered with by any and every political or religious empyric; the consequences of its sudden disruption are alarming to the real friends of freedom, to the philanthropist in every clime. It is a sacred relationship; it existed among the Jews and Gentiles, long before the coming of the Messiah, yet it is among his professed Disciples that we find many of those whose sympathies seem enlisted in favor of educating and emancipating slaves.

I am mistaken if they are not pursuing a course contrary to that marked out by their Savior, or his great Apostle to the Gentiles, all that twattle on the subject of equality, to the contrary notwithstanding. . . .

After noting that the Constitution recognized the right to hold slaves, Judge Reid continued:

When they talk about the truths which they maintain as self-evident, "That all men are born equally free, &c," we must point to the practice of our fathers ever since the adoption of the Constitution, to prove that slaves were not included in that expression.

Your duties in the presentation of crime extend only to the county of Mason. You must state the place where the crime was committed to enable the accused to make defence understandingly; it is essential, and without designation of the place where the crime was committed the indictment would be bad at common law much more under our constitution which secures the accused a right to trial in the county where he is charged to have committed the offence and by a jury of the vicinage. Do not, therefore, suffer yourselves, by an honest enthusiasm for the public safety, or because of the alarming magnitude of the offence, to be deluded into a belief that this court can take jurisdiction of any crime committed out of the State. Heaven and hearth may pass away sooner than one jot or tittle of the law shall be violated. And if you should inadvertently present, for crime committed out of the county of Mason, the humblest citizen shall have the law, when the evidence comes to be heard in court.

Two days later, on November 14, a dirge of hard rain fell upon the valley as the trial commenced in the courthouse in Washington. A two-story building made of native limestone with walls two feet thick, this was the same courthouse where Eliza Jane Johnson had feared for her life a year before. Behind it was a whipping post where the sheriff performed the court's decrees against disobedient slaves: often twenty lashes with a rawhide "well laid on" to the back of a naked slave whose up-stretched hands were tied to the post. In the front and to the side was a stockade where slaves were sold, the same auction ring where, five years earlier, Harriet Beecher Stowe had watched in horror as families of slaves were separated, mothers and fathers, sons and daughters traded like horses and cows. The courtroom was on the second floor. A small room no larger than 500 square feet, it was quickly overrun with spectators. The overflow retreated to the building's wide colonial porch with its eight massive stone pillars and to the lawn under the generous shade of two large locust trees. Under the advice of Mahan's attorneys, neither Polly nor Cassandra Mahan attended the trial. The fear of mob violence was greater than anticipated, in large part because of the Boone County scare in recent days. Atop the courthouse, a bell tolled eleven times as Judge Walker Reid took his seat and called the court to order. The room, despite the throng, was as silent as a held breath.

This was the second day on which Judge Reid had lowered his gavel and begun the proceedings for the Mahan trial. On November 13, the same people had gathered in the same places, but the lawyers for the commonwealth had urged the judge to postpone until two of their witnesses arrived. Greathouse had assured the lawyers that these two men, both neighbors of Mahan's in Sardinia, would swear to having seen him talking with the slave John, assuring the slave that none of the "many slaves" who reached his house was ever caught. But the two men had not yet appeared, and the lawyers told the judge that perhaps they should wait until the next court term—several weeks later—and try again. Mahan's lawyers objected vociferously. One said that his client had been in a jail cell, in irons, for nearly eight weeks. Mahan's health was not good, he said, and the trial must go forward. The judge gave the commonwealth one more day; the men from Sardinia never showed up. And so, on the morning of November 14, two men came to Mahan's cell, removed the chain from the manacles on his ankles, and led the tall, swarthy, bearded Ohioan, his eyes adjusting to the autumn sun, along the flagstone walk to the courthouse.

Mahan's defense team consisted of four attorneys whom Rankin had helped procure through his contacts in the region. They were the Honorable John Chambers, a native of New Jersey who lived in Washington, Kentucky, and who had served as a Whig member of Congress since 1835; his son and law partner since July of 1838, Francis T. Chambers, who would one day gain fame for representing Margaret Garner, the slave out of Cincinnati who killed one of her children to prevent him from living in slavery; John C. Vaughan, a prominent Unitarian who worked at the Cincinnati law firm Vaughan and Cranch; and Ripley's own renowned and highly regarded attorney Chambers Baird. Thomas Y. Payne headed up the commonwealth team and was assisted by John A. McClung, John D. Taylor, and Henry Waller. Payne and Waller, partners in a Maysville firm since June 1838, solicited cases in Mason, Bracken, Lewis, Fleming, and Greenup counties; Payne had worked in the circuit courts of the First Judicial District since 1836. McClung was a Washington, Kentucky, attorney, and Taylor practiced in Maysville.

There were two indictments against Mahan, one regarding the slave named John and the other the slave Nelson, and they were to be judged in separate trials.

Attorney Payne began the proceedings of the first, concerning John, by calling William Greathouse to the stand. After eliciting some background testimony from Greathouse, Payne asked about Perrigo's encounter with Mahan and the letter Mahan allegedly wrote that night.

"On the night of the 4th of August, I was in hearing of Mahan and Perrigo, the same night this letter was written; this is the same letter Perrigo handed me. Perrigo had with him a negro woman, who Perrigo said to Mahan, was John's wife. Mahan came out with a rifle on his shoulder, and told Perrigo he must go to John Hudson's. Perrigo refused. Mahan insisted, and talked loud, Perrigo being deaf."

"Tell all from the beginning."

Mahan, said Greathouse, told Perrigo if he would go on to some place inaudible to Greathouse, some place to the north, he believed the woman would find her husband. He gave money and a letter to Perrigo who went on with the woman, and Greathouse claimed he followed them. He saw

Mahan writing the letter in the street that night, he testified. After answering a series of questions about how he knew Perrigo and the woman who accompanied Perrigo to Mahan's, Greathouse stepped down.

Perrigo was then called to testify. With his large evasive eyes and nervously quick manner of speaking, Perrigo informed the court that he had indeed gone to Mahan's in late July and had told Mahan that he lived near the river, on the Ohio side. He also told Mahan about a black woman who had come to his house, the wife of a black man named John. He testified that he asked Mahan if he had seen such a man and Mahan told him he had seen two black men by that name, one belonging to a Mr. Greathouse near Washington, Kentucky. Two of Greathouse's slaves had fled, he said, and Greathouse had nearly caught one. Perrigo then, according to his testimony, asked Mahan if the woman could find her husband, and Mahan allegedly said she could but only if Perrigo would bring her to Mahan's tavern. And so, six days later, at night, very late, Perrigo brought the woman to Mahan's tavern and stood outside, calling for Mahan. Mahan came out to the street, Perrigo testified, and Perrigo then asked him where he could find the woman's husband. Mahan said he didn't know but that he was likely in Canada by then. Mahan told Perrigo to take her on to "the next friend." Perrigo agreed, but, to facilitate his journey, he asked if Mahan would write a letter of introduction for him. Mahan went inside to get some paper, returned to the street, and by moonlight wrote the note to the next "friends" on the underground—the note that was now held in evidence at his trial.

Holding the letter, Payne asked Perrigo: "Is this the same letter that he gave you, and that you handed to William Greathouse?"

"Yes, Sir. Mahan then asked me, if any more came to my house to send them to him. He said there was a colored man in Maysville who sent him all he could and that he had helped along fifteen within a short time past."

"Did he say that Greathouse's negro had been there?"

"I understood him so."

"Did he say he would pay you for sending him negroes?"

"He did."

"Did he pay you for bringing the woman?"

"He paid me three dollars. . . . He said if it was any inducement, he would pay me if I would send him all that came to my house; that a colored man in Maysville, a barber, sent him all he could."

Mahan's lawyer Chambers then asked, "Was this during the first interview?"

"Yes, Sir."

Payne again: "Tell what he said about the connecting chain of friends from Kentucky, running all the way to Canada, of which he himself formed a part?"

"I object," said Chambers. "The question is calculated to incense the public mind unnecessarily, without having an effect to throw light upon the indictment."

Then Payne, "This will open the question as to the whole fact, whether the prisoner can be convicted through agency."

Chambers again: "The attorney for the Commonwealth had better withdraw the question and press at the conclusion, when the general question will be made. He was willing to open the debate and rest the whole upon this question, if the attorney for the Commonwealth pressed it, but he hoped he would not check the examination now."

The judge intervened; the lawyers presented arguments regarding the question about a "chain" to Canada. The judge adjourned the court until the afternoon, giving Chambers time to consult with his client. From the point of view of the judge, if the question about a band of men helping slaves to Canada were to be discussed, then the trial could diverge from the charges in the indictment. It was Payne's hope—and Greathouse's—to explore that tangential path. Judge Reid gave Chambers the right to decide whether or not the question could be asked, and he adjourned the court until the afternoon.

When they returned, Chambers permitted the question to be asked. And so Payne continued, "What did Mr. Mahan say about the connecting chain of which he himself was a part, extending from Kentucky all the way to Canada?"

"Mr. Mahan asked me if the negro had any money, and I told him not that I know of. Mahan then said there was a connection of friends who paid the passage of the negroes to Canada."

"How much were you paid for bringing the woman supposed by Mahan to be John's wife?"

"Three dollars."

"What did you do with the three dollars?"

"I kept it."

"Did you consider you had a right to it?"

"I didn't know."

"Where did you leave Greathouse when you went to talk with Mahan?"

"I left him with the horses."

"Did you expect him to follow you?"

"I did."

"Were you a tenant of Greathouse?"

"Not then, but I am now."

"For how long?"

"For three years. We cultivate the farm on the shares. I get one half of all I raise."

"Where did you reside before coming to Kentucky?"

"In Pennsylvania. Was raised in Washington County, New York."

"Did you ever live in Ohio?"

"Yes, sir, in Columbiana County."

"What was your calling in Pennsylvania?"

"Farming and other business."

While Perrigo was still on the witness stand, a juror fainted. During the necessary break, Perrigo left the courtroom for a short time. Outside, he conversed with Greathouse, then returned to the trial.

Payne continued: "Is there any arrangement to live with Mr. Greathouse longer than this winter?"

"No sir; but there is a verbal agreement to live there longer."

Chambers now: "Since you left the court-house a moment since, have you had any conversation with any person about your contract with Greathouse?"

"Yes, sir, with Mr. Greathouse."

"What is the contract between you and Greathouse?"

"A written agreement for the winter, and a verbal contract for three years."

At this point, the Commonwealth recalled Greathouse. Payne said, "Explain the circumstances of the contract."

"There is a written agreement for the winter, and a longer time spoken of. We spoke of breeding cattle, and making cheese, but having bought another farm, I have concluded not to keep him any longer. He considers it an agreement: I do not."

A lawyer who worked for the county then took the stand and Payne asked him if he believed the handwriting was Mahan's in the letter that Perrigo testified Mahan wrote for the slave to carry to the next stop. He said that it was. Chambers then asked, "Did you ever see him write?"

"No, I judge from comparison, having seen and read a good many letters written by Mahan, since he has been in jail, and which were handed me by the jailer to read."

John Hill, the jailer, was sworn in. Payne asked, "Is this letter Mr. Mahan's handwriting, and have you seen Mahan write?"

"I could not swear positively, but it is my impression that it is, having seen him write 20 or 30 letters since he has been in jail."

"Would you swear positively to your own hand writing?"

"No sir, not always."

Chambers then asked, "Did you read his letters?"

"I read all he received and wrote, in his presence, and at his request."

At this point in the trial, all attention was focused on this letter that Mahan allegedly wrote under the light of the August 4 moon. Payne and his team of lawyers wanted to read the letter to the jurors to enter it as evidence in the trial. Chambers objected, on the grounds that the letter was irrelevant to the government's charges. The letter, he argued, did not help to prove that Mahan had violated any laws in the state of Kentucky. The only motive in reading it could be to prejudice the minds of everyone in the courtroom against Mahan and all of his so-called links in Ohio. It was a ruse, just like all that had touched Mahan regarding this case—and just like the case itself.

But Payne was insistent. "It is relevant because it tends to corroborate the details given by Perrigo of his conversations with Mahan and because it is necessary to prove that Mahan was one link in the chain of friends extending from Kentucky to Canada, and for this reason, if for none other, it is strictly legitimate that the jury may infer his participation in the crime [by introducing the letter]."

Judge Reid ruled in favor of the Commonwealth. And the letter that supposedly proved the existence of a "chain of friends" between the Ohio River and Canada was entered into the public record then and for posterity.

In his closing argument, Chambers urged the judge to instruct the jury that, in the absence of any evidence to prove that Mahan had actually been personally present in Mason County at the time the offense was committed, he was not legally subject to conviction on the charges in this case, and that neither the court nor the jury had jurisdiction if the jurors were indeed satisfied that Mahan was a citizen of the state of Ohio and had not been in Kentucky until he was thrown in jail in September 1838.

His colleague J. C. Vaughan, the lawyer from Cincinnati, then rose and faced the jury.

All—all of us are full of anxiety. And why? Not because we sympathize with crime; not because one of our citizens is imprisoned; but because we believe that citizen cannot be convicted here and now, without violating the law and the Constitution. . . .

There is, it is supposed "a line formed, commencing at this place and extending through Ohio to Canada; the object of which is to further the escape of slaves. Now the men who belong to it in Ohio are as guilty as the men who remain in Kentucky. And are they to escape? Are they amenable to no law? While thus violating our rights and destroying our property, ought they not to be and are they not punishable by law?" This is put before us, Sir, and the case is a hard one, and it is well and strongly put. But I shall meet it and I tell the gentlemen plainly that by the laws of Kentucky they who thus act, bad as they are, shall not be touched. Better far would it be that the property of both States, and every living thing in both were annihilated than sacrifice this principle. No. The law of Kentucky does not and cannot operate in Ohio.

After much more discourse, he concluded: "If Mahan is doomed as a felon, a taint will be upon the escutcheon of Kentucky which no time or change can efface."

The jurors were then given a break, and when they returned, Henry Waller, a lawyer for the Commonwealth of Kentucky, delivered his speech.

I agree that the question upon which [this case] turns is one of deep and vital importance. . . . But it is a grand question of state jurisdiction and national right. It is a question which reaches the most sensitive principle incorporated in our institutions; on which is already agitating this entire Union to its farthest extremities and under the influence of which our Republic even now trembles to its deepest foundations.

I understand these facts to be in evidence before the court: That the accused stated to Perrigo, the principal witness, that during the preceding month, fifteen slaves had passed through his hands on their way from Kentucky to Canada and of that number two belonged to Mr. Greathouse (being the slaves named in the indictment)—that there was a line of posts, reaching from the friends in Kentucky to Canada, with the express view of forwarding fugitive slaves from this state—and that when they were once safely arrived at his house, they were secure from the danger of apprehension—accused at the same time made the proposition to the witness to embark in the same enterprise offering to pay him for his services, and when the witness hesitated, the accused assured him there was no danger, for that there was a colored barber in Maysville

175

who sent him all he could. Here sir, is proof of an attempt to hire an agent in Ohio for the purpose of aiding the escape of slaves. . . .

We are met by the question: Can a man actually be in one state and commit a crime in another? I answer broadly and unqualifiedly that he can. I refer to the principle that requires that the crime must be punished where it is committed. Take one instance, sir. A man standing on the Ohio shore fires across the river and kills a man on the Kentucky side. The crime is not committed in Ohio where the discharge takes place but in Kentucky where the ball takes effect—where the death happens—where the crime is consummated. The laws of Ohio cannot punish him because the laws have not been violated. But he is triable where the crime is committed—he is subject to the jurisdiction of Kentucky where soil was desecrated, where laws were infringed.

The crime does not exist in Ohio, nor as a consequence is it punishable there. The crime would go unpunished were it not punished in Kentucky. Sir, should it be decided that this court has no jurisdiction of this crime; should Kentucky law be found to be unequal to the protection of the rights and property of Kentucky citizens; should this dark and dangerous league against our enjoyment of property sacredly secured to us by the Constitution of the United States be pronounced beyond the avenging reach of our law; I ask you, sir, What is that Constitution worth?

Waller took his seat in the courtroom, and commonwealth attorney Payne took his turn before the jury. He began:

Can it be said that Ohio would take part with the writer of this disgusting and celebrated midnight letter that I now hold in my hand? Can it be said that Ohio takes part with those who at midnight at that lone and still hour when all whose hearts are honest are either in communion with their God or else buried in repose with their families—steal abroad and by themselves or their agents or their unaccountable minions pilfer and filch from their neighbors their property, which they obtained by the sweat of their brow and which is secured to them by the same sacred instrument as secures to every citizen the quiet of his own hearth?

The court adjourned until Saturday morning when defense counsel Chambers was the first to speak: "How long before civil war shall come? If I were permitted to judge from the tone of the gentlemen prosecutors I would say, not long." The present case, he said, had "created unusual excitement." And it should never have happened.

Paragraph after paragraph was elicited from the press on either side of the Ohio. It has even entered into the spirit of the elections. Mahan was demanded of the Governor of Ohio as a fugitive from justice, charged with having committed a crime within the county of Mason—a fact now conceded by all to be untrue. This was fraud. The prisoner is here in fraud of the Constitution of the United States. . . . That fifteen negroes had passed through the prisoner's hands within a month, that two belonged to Greathouse, it matters not. It matters not what number passed through, there was no obligation upon the prisoner to seize them and to send them back.

Chambers, Taylor, and others spoke into the early evening on Saturday, after which the court was finally adjourned until Monday. On that morning, November 19, Judge Reid offered his opinion to the court before ordering the jurors into deliberation. "The deep interest which a crowded house for the last five days bespeaks has influenced me to give the law according the best of my judgment in writing that it may not be represented or misunderstood," he began.

Perhaps no question was ever more ably discussed in this courthouse than the one now under consideration. An array of talent, a degree of eloquence, and a depth of research, highly creditable to the bar have been displayed and have aided me in coming to a conclusion, whether just or unjust this jury my countrymen and posterity must determine. It is: that the prisoner has not violated the law of Kentucky, unless "he aided and assisted the slave in making his escape from the owner and possessor here to another state or foreign country," personally. The crime must have been committed here, in Kentucky, to give this Court jurisdiction. It is so stated in the indictment and must be proved as stated. No after act will do. No aid and assistance given out of this State will do unless he was near enough at the time the escape was effected to receive information personally and aid in case of alarm by previous arrangement. But if near enough at the time the escape was effected here to aid in case of alarm or danger by agreement he might be said to aid and assist the slave to escape from his master in Kentucky, to another state. . . .

In slave stealing, or any other kind of larceny, the thief as well as the

177

accessory to the thief is moved and seduced by the love of gain. Can we say this of all whose mistaken zeal has inducted them to give their money and means to establish a chain of posts or houses of refuge from Kentucky to Canada—to send out proclaimers to infuse their doctrines along our frontier—or agents to give information of the ease with which slaves can make their way to Canada? Would we not thereby include many of our best, though I conceive deluded men from Massachusetts to Mississippi whose zeal proves the sincerity with which they endeavor to sustain what they believe to be "the holiest cause that tongue or sword of mortal ever lost or gained"—the freedom of all mankind? While I deprecate their course, and fear its consequences, I am not willing to call them felons; but to attribute it to a higher and nobler motive than sordid gain.

The result of the whole of my examination and deliberation is . . . that this court and jury have no jurisdiction of [Mahan's] case if from the evidence they are satisfied the prisoner is a citizen of the state of Ohio and had not been in the state of Kentucky until brought here by legal process to answer this prosecution. The jury have now heard the opinion of the court on the law of the case. They will apply that law to the facts if they choose and will find a verdict of guilty or not guilty as their own consciences may direct.

On Monday afternoon, jurors asked that the witness Perrigo be called again to the stand, because they could not agree on parts of his testimony. The judge then interrogated Perrigo, asking the questions the jurors had submitted to him. When they retired to the jury room, the courtroom thinned out in anticipation of a long deliberation. But as people were still leaving the building, the jurors returned. Their verdict: not guilty.

Judge Reid turned to Payne and asked if the Commonwealth wished to proceed with a trial of the second indictment, regarding Greathouse's slave named Nelson. Payne declined. Judge Reid then turned his attention to the prisoner. After nine weeks almost to the day since the arrest, the Kentucky judge dismissed all the charges against the preacher from Ohio. In that single moment, the proslavery judge from Kentucky and the abolitionist felon from Ohio came together for the cause of justice.

One newspaper commented on the long silence after the verdict. Mahan, they said, stood motionless and stared silently at the judge. And for minutes after the dismissal, the judge was silent, too, abandoning his usual style of uttering philosophically sweeping statements at the close of case. But perhaps what was most stunning about the verdict was the fact that, although acquitted, Mahan was still not free. He spent that night in the windowless cell where he had dwelled now for more than two months. Because of the civil suit that Greathouse had filed, Greathouse's lawyers insisted that Mahan remain in jail until he compensated Greathouse for the lost property: a total of $1,600. Despite donations, the Mahan family did not have enough money to pay such a penalty in addition to attorneys' fees.

On November 20, Mahan's lawyers were back in court. And Polly Mahan, in Sardinia, was packing her grip and arranging for a friend to take her children to her sister's home in Highland County. But before she left, a man who knew the Mahans well, William Dunlop, posted the security for Mahan's release. Dunlop was a wealthy farmer who had migrated from Fayette County, Kentucky, to Brown County, Ohio, in 1796, bringing a large number of slaves with him, then liberating them and giving them land north of Ripley. If Greathouse lost the civil suit, Dunlop would owe nothing; if Greathouse won, Dunlop would have to pay the $1,600. In that case, Dunlop stipulated, Mahan would be obligated to give Dunlop all of his real-estate properties in Brown County. As long as Mahan was alive, however, he and his family could live on the property, even if it were forfeited to Dunlop.

CHAPTER NINETEEN

"These Men Are Dangerous"

The trial was over, and violence had been averted. But the undeclared war between Ohio and Kentucky had only intensified. Mahan's acquittal provoked months of discussion in the nation's newspapers over the property rights of slaveholders, the personal liberties of individuals who assisted runaways, and the obligations of free states regarding both. The debate between slavery's friends and foes seemed angrier and louder than ever.

Soon after the acquittal, Kentucky legislators passed a resolution providing for the appointment of two commissioners to go to Columbus, Ohio, to urge Ohio legislators to pass a law to crack down on citizens who "interfere with the relations of master and slave in the State of Kentucky." The resolution referred to a subject of "vast importance to the citizens of Kentucky." The *Maysville Monitor* wrote: "Developments in the case of Mahan have shown conclusively that the interference of the abolitionists of Ohio with the slaves of this State is carried to an alarming extent and lest they should become emboldened by his acquittal, the State of Ohio owes it to Kentucky to adopt some speedy restrictive measures. We have no doubt that her sense of justice will prompt her to grant all that in reason our Legislature can ask."

The editor of the *Cincinnati Gazette* concurred. He suggested that Ohio's laws regarding aid to runaways be aligned with Kentucky's laws, which meant a jail term of two to twenty years for anyone caught and convicted of assisting a slave in escaping to another state. *The Philanthropist* responded to the *Gazette* editor (both exchanges were later published in Garrison's Liberator):

[In the Mahan case] Kentucky has graciously condescended to limit her jurisdiction to her own territory to give up all claim to punish citizens of Ohio for acts, done within her own state and now forsooth, to show our gratitude for so stupendous a favor, we are called on to make it a penitentiary offence, to act like a Christian; to subject a man or woman to confinement in the penitentiary two or 20 years for giving a blanket or loaf of bread or lending a horse to an unfortunate human being who after spending his best days in the service of one who never paid him wages is striving to reach a land where he may be able by hard labor to earn a small pittance for himself. Just take a single example of the working of such a law. The farmer, returning from market, who should take up a poor, leg-weary runaway and give him a ride of five miles on his way would subject himself to the risk of lying twenty years, perhaps his whole life in the penitentiary!

In December, Kentucky's Governor Clark publicly bemoaned the outcome of the Mahan case as a signal failure of slaveholders to win Ohio's cooperation in stopping the flight of their slaves. So deep was his abhorrence of abolitionists that he advocated death as a punishment for the crime of aiding runaway slaves. His message was published nationwide:

. . . There is a spirit of Abolition now abroad in the land that threatens fearfully the overthrow of all social intercourse between neighboring States and is ominous of consequences appalling to every true lover of his country. It is a fact no longer to be disguised that the conduct of the Abolitionist is at war with the acknowledged and legal rights of the citizen that he tramples under his feet laws that hold sacred the property of others, and feels no scruple in the commission of a crime to advance that cause in which he has embarked with such reckless desperation. Kentucky has already exercised too much forbearance on this subject and the advocates of these doctrines have been emboldened to progress from that which may be considered speculative to practical Abolitionism, or in other words, from the use of absurd and fanatical arguments to the actual abduction of our slaves for the purpose of emancipation. These men are dangerous, not from their numbers, but from the principles by which they are actuated and which influence them to action in defiance of all law, regardless of all consequences, under a feeling of desperation and recklessness that usually characterizes the misguided and the fanatic. . . .

On January 26, 1839, the two men whom the Kentucky legislature had sent to Ohio to plead their cause of protecting their slave property from the thieving abolitionists of Ohio sent a letter from their quarters at the National Hotel in Columbus to Ohio Governor Wilson Shannon, urging him to make it illegal in Ohio to assist runaway slaves. The governor sent a copy of the letter to the Ohio legislators appended to a message in which he urged the legislators to pass legislation to assist slaveowners (or their agents) to recapture slaves who had crossed into Ohio.

On February 26, Ohio had a new law, "The Ohio Fugitive Slave Law," that called for, among other things, a maximum penalty of sixty days in the county jail and a $500 fine for anyone who prevented a sheriff or constable from arresting a runaway slave; anyone who aided in the rescue of a fugitive from the sheriff, constable, claimant, agent, or attorney; two or more persons who assembled with the intent to obstruct, hinder, or interrupt the removal of a fugitive to the state from which he or she had fled; and anyone who enticed a person bound by labor in one state to "leave, abandon, abscond or escape from the person or persons to whom such labor or service, by the laws of another state, is or may be due or shall furnish money or conveyance of any kind or any other facility with intent and for the purpose of enabling such person to escape."

Ohioans were largely indifferent to the law because it did not affect them. Few, after all, were engaged in the business of transporting runaway slaves through the state. Those who were saw the new law as weak, ineffectual, and little more than a business transaction between Ohio and Kentucky. It was designed to pacify their sister state along the river, and intended solely for political effect. In response to the announcement of the new bill, the newspaper *Christian Witness* wrote, "The slaves run away in greater numbers than before and the Ohio abolitionists—God bless them!—are more active than ever in aiding them to the land of freedom."

While politicians and pundits continued to dissect the meaning of the Mahan trial well into 1839, and to twist the event to serve their own purposes, the people on the front lines in Maysville, Ripley, Sardinia, and the nearby free black settlements had no doubts about the meaning of Mahan's ordeal. The Ripley line of the Underground Railroad was now exposed, which meant that anyone who dared to continue working with Rankin or Mahan, with Beck, McCoy, or Gilliland, with the free blacks in northern Kentucky, including the barber in Maysville, was increasingly at risk. It meant that Greathouse could use his knowledge of the underground to try to intimidate and harass Mahan and others with his night riders and with the legal device of yet another case, the Mahan civil suit, to drain, distract, and disturb the line. And it meant that more slave catchers and bounty hunters were gathering in the woods and hills of Brown County with names, maps, and descriptions of houses and people written on slips of paper folded together with reward notices torn off tree trunks and stuffed into their pockets. Hunting "niggers and nigger lovers" in Brown County had become a favored sport for men like Greathouse and the ruffians on both sides of the river who were eager to ride with him.

"Brown County is becoming quite celebrated for its slave catchers. We should suppose that the slaveholders of the far South might select some of the finest specimens of Negro-drivers from a certain class of population resident in that county," wrote the editors of *The Philanthropist* in March 1839. They were eerily close to the truth.

CHAPTER TWENTY

The Unappeasable Spirit

Spring came early to the Ohio Valley in 1839, and with it a storm of violence that was far worse than any of the seasonal clashes of warm and cold fronts. In Ripley, the storm began with the beating of a free black man in late March.

A Ripley woman who was once a slave had borrowed $500 from various Ripley residents back in December to pay for the purchase of her son-in-law's freedom. He had lived in slavery in northern Kentucky for all of his life, and his wife and children had come to Ripley the year before. After his arrival, he immediately found housing on the edge of town for his wife and his four children, and he secured a job with a local merchant. Intelligent, with a drive to succeed, the young man quickly earned a reputation as reliable, honest, and competent. But his very success, like that of Benjamin Templeton, provoked resentment among Ripley's Southern-sympathizers. Like the irrepressible streams in spring, these men gushed hatred.

On the last night of March, two such men agreed that when they saw the man passing along Second Street one would push the other against him to create a scene that would give them an excuse to beat him. One of the men carried a brick in his hand, and when the beating began, he hit the black man in the head with the brick—again and again. The next day, "A Citizen of Ripley" who, living on Front Street, had heard the sounds of the beating during the previous night and had rushed to the scene, perhaps curtailing the incident, wrote to local papers and to *The Philanthropist* about what he had seen. The man, he said, would likely recover, though no one was certain yet. And the town, for the most part, was sympathetic, though the culprits had not been punished. "These hateful and groveling wretches but carried into practice the spirit of hatred to colored people so prevalent among many of the better class of society," he wrote, "and they are but a looking glass in which many respectable people may see a picture of their own hearts."

On April 7, in a series of events that would once again pull Mahan into the public eye, Thomas Fox, a free black man living in the free black settlement near Sardinia, nearly met the same fate. Fox was a respectable cooper who had lived in the "camps" for nearly four years. On that Sabbath day, he was approached by five men from the neighborhood of Georgetown. They wanted to talk to him about some work, they told him. Would he come with them into the woods nearby, for some privacy, away from the people in the settlement? Once there, they asked Fox for some tobacco, and as he reached into his pocket to accommodate their wishes, they accused him of reaching for a gun and seized him. They threatened him with death if he screamed, then fetched chains and collars from their saddlebags and secured him against a tree. Fox ignored the warning, and as they threw him against the trunk of a sycamore he belted out a scream. Before the collar was secured on Fox's neck and the chains wrapped around him and the tree, an old white woman who lived on the edge of the woods approached the men and told them to let Fox go. They ignored her. Suddenly the ground began to tremble from the pounding of horses' hooves. A posse of one white man and several black men arrived at the scene. What legal authority did they have to hold Fox captive? one member of the posse asked. Another man headed straight for the tree where the old woman was struggling to untangle the ropes and chains that now held Fox. Once released, Fox ran out of the woods. His rescuers again demanded to see proof of any legal authority for holding Fox. Few words were spoken as the abductors mounted horses, jerked reins, kicked flanks, and left.

Exactly one week later, they returned to the community, this time with nearly a dozen riders, in search of the people who had thwarted their plans the Sunday before. They went directly to the house of Moses Cumberland and, learning that he was at church, followed him to his place of worship, where they forced him from his pew. Valentine Carberry, a local constable, waved an arrest warrant in his face, charging him with assault against two of the men from the mob the week before. The warrant stated that "on or about the 7th day of April 1839 at the county of Brown . . . Andrew Newman [one of the mob that tried to beat up Fox] was violently assaulted and severely threatened and . . . Moses Cumberland, late of said county, is guilty of the fact charged."

As Cumberland struggled against his captors, others in the church began to pounce upon and punch the intruders. At the same time, another member of the congregation sneaked out a side door and rode into Sardinia with the news that some white men were trying to take Moses. Upon hearing this, John Mahan, Amos Pettijohn and his brother Joseph, and a dozen more men rode as quickly as their horses could carry them toward the church. About two miles from the church, on the way to Sardinia, at a place known as Ross's Mill, they spotted the posse that held Cumberland and the black men who were following the posse. What happened next would become a much-disputed matter.

Carberry and others claimed that the black men at the church had beaten them with clubs and that "the bloodhounds of abolition headed by the notorious John B. Mahan," whom they now had met on the trail, were armed—"every one of them"—with pistols. Amos Pettijohn came upon the group first, jumped off his horse, and pulled two pistols out of his pocket, said Carberry. Pettijohn told the black men following the posse to "fight till you die," that there were enough of them to whip each member of the gang and plenty more reinforcements were on the way.

Next came Joseph Pettijohn, who asked, "Where are those thieves that disturbed the large congregation at Sardinia?"

Amos then challenged a man named Grant Lindsey to a pistol duel in the woods. "Get down any of you right here and take it," Amos said, according to Carberry.

When Mahan arrived, he supposedly referred to the posse as "thieves, mobocrats, manstealers," and told the black men to pull the white men off of their horses and "whip them to death." And, said Carberry, Mahan cursed the men for being Democrats, saying, "Hell's doors should be darkened with such Democrats." Carberry testified later that he told Mahan that he wished to move on, uninterrupted, with his prisoner. Mahan, he said, told him that if any one of them took another step they would all die. Carberry claimed too that Dr. Beck was there, and that there were at least a hundred men in the group that confronted him, including thirty or forty blacks.

Carberry's conclusion was that Mahan and the Pettijohns were inciting a riot. Trying to wrest Cumberland from the grip of the posse, he would later testify, was a violent act. The men from Sardinia overwhelmed Carberry and his men, and although he did have legal authority to take Cumberland, he was forced by Mahan and his men to let Cumberland go.

Others, including William Ross, on whose land the incident took place, claimed that neither Mahan nor the Pettijohns were violent. Neither Amos nor Joseph wielded a pistol, Ross said. According to Ross, who was standing roughly two hundred yards from the scene, Mahan calmly asked Carberry if he had legal authority to take Cumberland, and if he did, Mahan said he would accompany them to the magistrate. He did not threaten Carberry, or even hint at committing any form of violence. Ross didn't hear Mahan ask the black men to dismount and commence whipping the white men, though he believed he had heard all of the exchange.

The next morning, Mahan, Amos, Joseph, and Isaac Pettijohn, Dr. Isaac Beck, and Robert Huggins were arrested for unlawfully and riotously assembling to disturb the peace of the state of Ohio and for assaulting, striking, wounding, and threatening Valentine Carberry and Grant Lindsey. Beck, Huggins, and Isaac Pettijohn proved they were not present at the so-called riot. Mahan and the other two Pettijohns were released under bond of $150. The trial was set for September 30.

On the following Sabbath, April 21, the same horsemen, plus some newcomers from New Hope and vicinity, visited the black settlement once again. Their goal was apparently to harass some of the men who had fought them in the Fox and Cumberland incidents. Marauding through the community, they could not find the men they sought, and so they left. Nine days later, on April 30, a gang of eighteen proslavery men, including some from the previous three expeditions, again arrived at the "camps" and arrested another of the men who had helped Fox gain his freedom. As they were serving the man, Jacob Cumberland, Moses's brother, with a warrant, a number of black people gathered round them to protect Jacob. In the group was Sally Hudson, a cousin of the Cumberlands and a sister of John Hudson, by then a major player on the Underground Railroad. Sally Hudson had allegedly struck at Grant Lindsey several times during his effort to take Moses Cumberland from the church on April 14. At one point she hit him hard on the nose. And he remembered that. He pointed her out to a few of his colleagues, one of whom jumped off his horse and began to beat her. In self-defense, she bit him in the arm. He let out a scream and dropped her. But just as she was running inside a nearby house, one of the men, James Kratzer, shot her in the back, shattering one of her vertebrae and severing her spinal cord. The moment Sally Hudson fell to the ground, the men dispersed. Those on horses galloped away, and the ones who had dismounted jumped onto the nearest horses in sight.

Dr. Beck tended to Sally almost immediately, but she lived for only two weeks after the shooting. Kratzer was arrested and retained Thomas Hamer who, Beck later wrote, "bulldozed the Justice who dismissed the murderer. We then succeeded in getting the case before the grand jury but Hamer prevailed on the Judge (John W. Price) to send the witnesses for the defence before the grand jury. No indictment was found and Kratzer was unpunished except for what Hamer inflicted: he got his farm for clearing him." This incident convinced Beck and others that, even if any of them were assassinated in broad daylight, their assassins would never be indicted.

That summer, Mahan worked out an arrangement with Ripley attorney Chambers Baird to use Baird's office on Second Street in Ripley to conduct depositions for his defense against Greathouse in the civil case. He also sent a petition to the Ohio legislature seeking a redress of grievances and remuneration for financial and emotional damage suffered as a result of his arrest and imprisonment in Mason County. The petition was immediately referred to the Judiciary Committee of the Senate that eventually rejected it. At the same time, Mahan wrote to Mason County officials and legislators in Kentucky offering them $10 for the purchase of the chains that had bound him in the Washington jail; they declined. He also spent considerable time working with his lawyers for his upcoming criminal trial in Brown County.

Mahan had achieved such notoriety that finding attorneys for the criminal case was easy. And his legal-defense team was stellar. First and foremost perhaps was the highly regarded U.S. senator from Clermont County, Thomas Morris. Morris was now nationally known for his recent incendiary and controversial abolitionist speech on the floor of the U.S. Senate. The speech was Morris's counterattack against Senator Calhoun's effort to stop the reading of antislavery petitions in Congress—and it would cost him the next election. Morris was also the father-in-law of Dr. Isaac Beck, and so he was very interested in the case.

Next on the team was John Joliffe, who would one day be widely known as an outstanding figure in the antislavery crusade. Joliffe, who was raised in a Quaker community in northern Virginia and weaned on antislavery views, completed his law degree in 1827 and came to Ohio to practice law with Thomas L. Hamer, before Hamer switched to the antiabolition side. Both Hamer and Joliffe became well known for their eloquence in the courtroom. In his youth, Ulysses S. Grant, who lived nearby, would sit in the back of court proceedings to listen to them both. In 1833, Hamer took a seat in Congress and Joliffe assumed the post of Clermont County prosecutor. Their ideological paths diverged, and by 1839, Joliffe was well established in the antislavery community nationwide. He was also on the verge of being ousted from his prosecutorial post, which was an elected position. Ohioans who did business with slaveholding Kentuckians had grown impatient with Joliffe's abolitionist ways; representing Mahan clearly did not help. But fighting slavery was far more important to Joliffe than any political post.

The third attorney on the Mahan team was Owen T. Fishback. Married to the daughter of one of the most active members of the Underground Railroad in Clermont County, Charles Huber, Fishback was a distinguished Clermont County attorney who had opened his practice in 1815.

On the other side of the courtroom, representing the county against Mahan and Pettijohn, was the prosecuting attorney David G. Devore and two local private attorneys appearing for the prosecution, W. C. Marshall and Thomas Hamer. Hamer was taking on his former partner, Joliffe, and his former mentor, Morris. The trial lasted only four days, but the sentiments that it provoked lingered for a long while. At least fifteen witnesses came to the stand. Those who were riding with Carberry told one version of the events of April 14 at Ross's Mill, and those riding with Mahan and the Pettijohns told another, as if two distinctly different plays had been performed simultaneously, yet with the same actors. On October 4, the jurors announced, "We find the defendants guilty in the manner and form as they stand indicted." The defense attorneys called for a new trial, claiming among other things that the evidence regarding one witness's previous convictions was not allowed to be entered into the court record, that there was no evidence that Valentine Carberry was ever wounded that day, and that the facts regarding events on the previous Sunday and the following Sunday were not permitted to be included on behalf of the defendants.

On October 11, the county sentenced John B. Mahan and Joseph Pettijohn to be imprisoned in the "dungeon of the jail of Brown County during the period of ten days and fed on bread and water only during that period; that they each pay a fine to the state of Ohio of fifty dollars and pay all the costs of this prosecution." Charges against the other defendants had been dismissed. After delivering the sentence, the judge looked directly at Mahan and reminded him that he was a minister of the gospel of peace, that the riot had taken place on the Sabbath, that instead of attending to the duties of his sacred calling he had been traversing the countryside on horseback in the company of armed men, violating the laws of his nation and resisting a ministerial officer who was trying to bring a criminal into custody. The judge advised him, "Your present situation should be a warning to you and you should not allow your excessive philanthropy to lead you into similar aggressions in the future."

Mahan never served his ten days on bread and water in the dungeon of the Brown County jailhouse. The sentence was reversed on appeal to the Ohio Supreme Court, which found an error relating to the empaneling of the jurors. But he continued to be burdened with legal responsibilities. From the summer of 1839 on, he spent much of his time on his ongoing civil battle with Greathouse. Without the funds for more legal assistance, he represented himself, which meant that he not only sought out witnesses from several states to disprove Greathouse's charges and to discredit Greathouse's witnesses, but also paid their travel costs and deposed them himself.

One of Mahan's strategies was to discredit Greathouse's key witness, the infamous James R. Perrigo, a.k.a. "Mr. Rock." To do this, Mahan deposed ten highly respected men and women who had known Perrigo in Huron County, Ohio. Among them were the county's head prosecuting attorney, the deputy clerk of the Court of Common Pleas, two magistrates, the county auditor, and the chief judge of the Court of Common Pleas. Perrigo, the ten men and women confirmed, was a notorious gambler, swindler, and horse-racer. In 1834, he and his associates had conducted a series of scams in Sandusky involving transactions on the building of the Milan Canal. In another scam, they defrauded several Huron County citizens of $20,000.

In all, Mahan deposed sixty men and women, both abolitionists and antiabolitionists, in 1839 and 1840.

During the same period, Greathouse hired a lawyer in Cairo, Illinois, to take the deposition of a Mrs. Ann Devore, who claimed that she was boarding at Mahan's tavern house and teaching school in the neighborhood at the time when the slaves John and Nelson came through town. Mahan had hidden them both upstairs in the tavern for eight or ten days, she said, and then he gave them a $5 bill and sent them off to Canada. She remembered, she said, many conversations at both the Mahan brothers' homes about the underground "road."

Then Greathouse's legal representative in Illinois asked: "Did you ever hear Mahan say anything about a line or route that runaway negroes were taking from Kentucky to Canada?"

Mrs. Devore: "I have heard [John Mahan] and Doctor Beck and others in conversation on that subject. I heard them say that the negroes crossed the Ohio River below Ripley and were taken to Rankins on the Hill above Ripley and then conveyed to the McCoys on Eagle Creek and from there to [John B.] Mahan's and sometimes to William Mahan's and then to Hillsborough to Col. Keys or Sam Hibbens and to Wilmington to an abolitionist whose name I do not now recollect. I have frequently heard them speak of an old Quaker near the lake who sent them over to Canada."

"Did Mahan assist Nelson any and if he did what did he do with him?"

"That Negro was fed and his clothes washed by Mahan's family. He was in a great hurry to get off as there had been so much noise made about John, the slave, and Mahan sent him the same route that John went and gave him a letter directed to persons who would assist him."

To discredit Mrs. Devore, Mahan deposed Cassandra Mahan, William Mahan, and Cassandra Beck (wife of Isaac Beck) in the Baird office several weeks later. They all revealed that she had lied about living at Mahan's tavern and teaching school in Sardinia. They referred to her as a "strolling woman."

Mahan: "What do you know about Ann A. Devore boarding at my house and teaching school in the neighborhood of Sardinia in the summer of 1838?"

Cassandra: "I know that she did not teach school in the neighborhood of Sardinia. She taught school in Highland County between three and four miles from Sardinia. She boarded at my house in Highland County. She was boarding at my house when John, the slave of William Greathouse of Mason County, Kentucky passed through Sardinia and when he passed through Highland County on his way to Canada."

Mahan: "Did you see the said John, the slave of William Greathouse?"

Cassandra: "Yes. I saw him at my house as he passed on his way to Canada about the latter part of June, 1838. Jackson Myers took the horses of William Mahan, my husband, and took the said slave John on his journey toward Canada."

Mahan: "Was Ann A. Devore at your house at that time?"

Cassandra: "She was and she conversed with the said John and wished him great success and that he might not be overtaken on his journey by his master or pursuers."

In some of the depositions—mainly the Mahans' and Hugginses'—the fact that the slave John was openly walking around the town came out as positive, supportive of Mahan, whereas it had been a whispered criticism in Rankin's circle. Some, including Rankin, questioned whether Mahan had been watchful enough. But now his casualness might be helpful because it proved that he was not concealing John, that he was not hiding a fugitive slave, that John may have been a fugitive slave at some point but by June 20 was a free black man of Ohio who was openly walking the streets of Sardinia. Lewis Pettijohn testified that he had invited John to go with him to his residence; he did not steal him away to his residence on some mysterious "underground road," as Greathouse so desperately wanted to prove. And his friend William Myers then decided to ride north with the man as he proceeded to Canada. There was nothing secretive about it, and nothing illegal, they testified. John was a free man in the state of Ohio. And John Mahan had nothing to do with facilitating any escape. This man was free, so why did he need help escaping?

As for Nelson, Mahan found the free black man Benjamin Veiny who said in a deposition that he met Nelson on a road near Georgetown and invited him to go to the house of his friend Amos Huggins. Here James Huggins, Amos's brother, took two horses and rode with Nelson to Wilmington, in Clinton County. Nelson never set foot in the town of Sardinia, the witnesses said. Mahan never even saw him.

From the choice of his witnesses and the choice of his lawyers' questions, it was clear that Greathouse was far more interested in continuing to expose every detail possible about the Ripley line of Underground Railroad conductors. Throughout 1840, he seemed particularly obsessed with proving that John Rankin owned a carriage that had been used frequently for the criminal activities of transporting slaves—"stolen property"—from one hiding place to another. And so that year, at the Baird office, Mahan deposed both Theodore W. Collins and Rankin, with a tight focus on the subject of Rankin's carriage.

Mahan to Collins: "How long have you been acquainted with John Rankin and please state what you know about runaway negroes having been conveyed from Ripley to Sardinia in Mr. Rankin's carriage."

Collins: "I have known John Rankin ever since he arrived in the vicinity of Ripley. I do not know that he ever owned one. I have been intimately acquainted with said Rankin for the last ten years and with his domestic concerns. If he had owned a carriage I should have known it. I have been a trustee of the Church of Ripley of which John Rankin is pastor for the most part of the last ten years. I have been the principal to collect his salary and settle with him and in that way I became acquainted with his domestic concerns."

And then, on the same day, Mahan deposed John Rankin.

Mahan to Rankin: "What do you know about conveying fugitive slaves from Ripley to Sardinia in your carriage?"

Rankin: "I have not owned any carriage since I have been a resident of this state, nor have slaves ever been conveyed to Sardinia or anywhere else in any carriage or other wheeled vehicle, either owned or in any way procured by me."

Greathouse could never prove that Rankin transported slaves in a carriage, and Rankin never lied about doing so. He usually instructed his sons to take their sturdiest horse, Old Sorrel, who was strong enough to carry a man, a woman, and a child into the night and onto the next stop. Still, the law, even in the inept hands of someone like Greathouse, proved to be a powerful weapon against the "thievery" beyond the river. The long battle with Greathouse, now approaching two years, drained Mahan financially and physically. From the moment he was taken across the river in September 1838, his life changed. And so did the lives of his co-conspirators. Whether or not Greathouse won the civil case, it was clear by now that both legal assaults against Mahan—the criminal and the civil—had damaged the Ripley line. Although neither case had legally proved the existence of "the chain" to Canada, both had exposed the identities of several of the chain's "links" and directed the devious attentions of more and more slave hunters and mercenaries to Ripley's shores. Curiosity about life on the high hill above Ripley had never been greater, and intruders never more common—such as the ones who appeared on Rankin's hill on February 17, 1840.

That morning, Jean Rankin, holding her year-old child, Thomas Lovejoy, stepped out of their hilltop house after hearing men's voices, she thought, coming from the direction of the barn. Another of her sons, seventeen-year-old Samuel, joined her on the front stoop and watched as five men and two bulldogs approached the house. At least one of the men carried a pistol. John Rankin was in Manchester that day, a town about twenty-five miles east of Ripley, and two of his older sons, twenty-two-year-old David and eighteen-year-old Richard Calvin, had ridden with a runaway slave the night before and not yet returned to Ripley.

As the men walked closer to the house, one cupped his hands and shouted that they were trying to find their way to the house of a neighbor of the Rankins: a Mr. Smith, they said. Before Mrs. Rankin could answer, though, another of the men, Amos Shrope, from Dover, Kentucky stopped the procession.

"Madam, to be plain with you we do not want to go to Mr. Smith's, but there was a store broken open in Dover," said Shrope. "A man took some goods, crossed the river in a skiff and we found that and we tracked him up the point, up the hill to some straw in your yard, by your barn, and we think he must be in your house. We want to look for the man and the stolen goods."

"Is the man black or white?" asked Mrs. Rankin. "And is he a slave?"

"Yes, ma'am, he is a slave."

"There is no slave here; we neither harbor thieves nor conceal stolen property and you are welcome to come to look through the house," Mrs. Rankin told the man.

But just as Shrope motioned the men to march forward, closer to the house, young Samuel Rankin stepped inside the house and grabbed the shotgun that hung on the wall above the front door. Standing next to his mother, who hadn't moved, he called out, "Halt! If you come one step farther I will kill you."

The men stopped. "We're all armed and we know you're alone," said one of them. He motioned for two more men, standing like sentinels at the top of the hill, to join him. "I reckon we'll search your house with or without your say so."

Samuel moved a step closer to the men, and he cocked his gun. The men, having taken only a few steps forward, stopped again. Silence fell over the scene, as if the men did not know exactly how to respond to a lone boy so stridently and bravely standing against them. Then the sound of horses and men coming through the thicket on the side hill distracted everyone. Samuel heard a familiar voice. "I'd stay just about right where you are now," said Richard Calvin. Riding up behind him were his brother David and eight or nine men from town, all bearing their revolvers, muskets, and squirrel rifles. Word had gone out in the town that slave catchers were headed for Rankin's house to retrieve their runaway slave and were as angry as a pack of rabid dogs because they had tried to get a warrant to search the house and the barn but no one within three towns complied.

So certain were these men that their prey was hidden somewhere on the Rankin property or that, at any moment, the runaway would arrive at Rankin's door, that they stubbornly remained on the land, even after

Rankin's sons returned with a small army of guards to protect Mrs. Rankin, the children, and the land. They snooped around the property. They poked at the hay mound in the barn. They watched. They waited.

Meanwhile, Richard Calvin, escaping their watchful eyes, hiked down the hill on one side of the house and, following a ravine through the woods, carefully pressed his shoes into the mushy soil to make clear footprints. He returned by a different path, and when he arrived back on the land between the barn and the house, he confessed to one of the hunters that he had found the steps of the slave and perhaps they would want to follow them. "This excited no little mirth," as one account later said. The men now believed that the slave had indeed been at the Rankins'. But they still did not leave, as Richard Calvin had hoped. Perhaps the fugitive would return, one of them said. Another surmised that the footprints could belong to anyone; perhaps even one of them.

In the next attempt to get rid of the intruders, one of Rankin's friends from town started a conversation with two of them whom he knew, and who he was certain knew the Rankins. He tried to persuade them that what they were doing was rude and wrong. They had bartered their souls to a brute master; how could they not see that slavery was evil and how it had tainted their lives—especially their behavior that very day?

"Is it a small matter for men armed as some if not all of you are, and some of you strangers too, to come to a man's house in his absence and demand of his helpless wife and children the liberty of searching it?" he said.

But the intruders still didn't leave. Then one of the men from Ripley, who was well acquainted with the Rankin family and whom Mrs. Rankin and the children might trust to enter their house, suggested that he search the house and show the intruders that there was no black man inside. This would be more decent; the young boy wouldn't have to put down his firearm; and Mrs. Rankin would feel more at ease. And so two men from Ripley did search the house and returned with the news that it was empty of slaves. Around this time, the owner of the slave in question arrived, and despite the recent search, he demanded permission to enter Rankin's house. It was clear now that the men who were "occupying" the Rankin land had been waiting for the man who was paying them—the slave owner—to arrive.

Mrs. Rankin appeared on the porch again and said he must not enter. The house had been searched, and she would not put the children through another intrusion. Samuel reappeared with his shotgun. The slaveholder then, with his voice and his temper raised, proclaimed that there was not a slave between the river and Lexington who did not know about the red house on the hill in Ripley, and that it must be "broken up."

Then, for the first time since the standoff had begun, Mrs. Rankin raised her own voice, with utter confidence and with enough steam to propel a riverboat. Slave catchers from Kentucky, she said, were "in the habit of lurking round" her house after nightfall and sometimes even forcing their way into the house when she and her husband were down the hill in town and the children were there alone. "I give you fair warning that if you do not hereafter keep away you will feel the force of powder and lead upon you and that if no one else would shoot you I would do it myself."

Seizing the spirit of the moment, two of her sons, both armed, escorted the slave master to his horse, helped him mount it, gave it a kick in the rear, and then marched toward the other men to repeat the procedure.

One of the men from Ripley who was there that February day on Rankin's hill sent his version of the episode to *The Philanthropist*:

Now the question is often asked, what have the people of the free states to do with slavery? We now see what slavery has to do with them. Women and children cannot any longer be safe in the absence of their husbands and fathers. The most serious consequences could result from a woman being assailed, as Mrs. Rankin was, by rude strangers, all armed. And Mr. Rankin's house must be broken up or destroyed because the slaves see it from the Kentucky hills and Mr. Rankin must be murdered if the threats made can be carried into execution. And even the town of Ripley must be burned. And why all this? Because the slaves will run to Canada, and Mr. Rankin and the people of Ripley will not catch them! Has Mr. Rankin ever gone to Kentucky to interfere with the slaves? Oh, no, that is not pretended. Can Kentuckians now say they have never interfered with Mr. Rankin's wife and children? But then Mr. Rankin is a propagator of Abolitionism. And has he not at least as much right to be an Abolitionist as the Kentuckians have to be slaveholders? Has Mr. Rankin done anything more than exercised his own rights? Never. Why then outrage his family, threaten to destroy his property, and murder himself? Why?

It is believed that Mr. Rankin and other of his friends help the slaves on their way to Canada. Of this they have not the slightest evidence, though they tried through legal cases to get it. The Kentuckians have no evidence that any of their slaves have ever passed through Ripley on their way to Canada. But suppose Mr. Rankin were to take in and lodge a poor fellow escaping from bondage and help him on his way to Canada. Would he in such case do anything but what humanity prompts and the Bible commands? The Bible plainly declares, "thou shalt not deliver unto the master the servant that is escaped from his master unto thee." "All things whatsoever ye would that men should do unto you, do ye even so to them." Mr. Rankin is bound by every principle of humanity and by the authority of God to help the fugitive slave. A minister of the Gospel that would not do it is worse than a devil! If Mr. Rankin had been represented as having helped so many white men out of bondage would not the nation have rung with his praises? Is he not bound by the laws of God to do just as much for a black person as for one that is white? I can assure my Kentucky neighbors that the case with respect to their slaves running away will never change while there is either religion or humanity in the state of Ohio.

The man who takes up a runaway slave is looked upon with abhorrence by all respectable people. There is a general impression throughout Ohio that it is both cruel and wicked to take up a runaway slave. I would remind my friends on the other side of the river that if they murder Mr. Rankin, destroy his property and even burn the town of Ripley they will never save one slave by it. And I would say to them while they are talking about taking lives and property and towns that they too have lives and property and towns as well as we do. And I will say that we are not to be deterred from our duty by any threats they can make. God has given us the right of exercising hospitality and we will never surrender it but with our lives.

A CITIZEN OF BROWN COUNTY, OHIO

PART III

Midnight Assassins

We feel the hand of oppression not only upon the slave, but upon ourselves. Where I live, my soul is harrowed continually with the cruelties committed in sight of my house, where slavery exists in its mildest form. I rejoice in the triumph of principles of immediate emancipation because I know, from long observation, that it is the only thing that can relieve both master and slave from inevitable ruin.

—John Rankin, speech at American Anti-Slavery Society
sixth anniversary meeting in New York, 1839

It evidently was the purpose to burn both the barn and the house. The house was brick; the barn, wood. The burning barn was expected to set the roof of the house on fire. And sentinels were placed to see all was right at the house. Their signal whistle that all was quiet at the house was what Calvin heard that night.

—Adam Lowry Rankin, from his unpublished autobiography

CHAPTER TWENTY-ONE

A New Season

By 1840, Ripley was a flourishing river town with five churches, three flour mills, twenty stores, and 1,245 inhabitants. Each year, eighty or more flatboats were built in its two boatyards, where steamers such as the *Fair Play,* the *Caledonia,* the *Joan of Arc,* the *Banner,* the *Ajax,* the *Shepardess,* the *Fox,* and the *Champion* had also been designed and constructed. The *Fair Play* left Maysville for Cincinnati every Monday, Wednesday, and Friday at 9 a.m. and reversed the trip every Tuesday, Thursday, and Saturday at 10 a.m., stopping at Ripley each way. Many more of the boats passing through Ripley were bound for Pittsburgh or New Orleans, for much of the town's prosperity depended on trade with the South. Ripley farmers sold sixty-three thousand pounds of tobacco each year, pressed it in hogsheads, and shipped it south to New Orleans. On many days, from four in the afternoon to noon the following day, massive quantities of pork were loaded onto southbound boats at the Ripley wharf. Even the wine that came out of the vineyards five miles from the town was shipped to Cincinnati and then to Southern ports.

The town's burgeoning business life affected the Ripley line in different ways. Underground men like Ripley's Front Street resident, the pork-packing mogul Thomas McCague, whose immense wealth came to him through the Southern markets, were now becoming, by an almost urgent necessity, more secretive and more cautious than ever before. So successful was McCague that he was called to Washington, D.C., to assist in resolving the nation's banking crisis during the Panic of 1837. There was no reward for McCague's head: Thus far, his double life, and that of his wife, were known to very few, even after the Mahan trial. But if caught with a fugitive slave in the garret of his riverfront home—or even if exposed for his association with a man like Rankin—he might lose his ability to continue his trade with Southern merchants.

On the other extreme was Rankin, who openly advocated boycotting the purchase of products grown or made by slaves, and who protested the shipping of Northern-made products to the South. He urged his Ohio friends and colleagues to grow sugar beets to obtain their sugar rather than purchase slave-harvested cane sugar. He and McCague, though dependent upon each other during many nights, showed little or no connection in public.

By the 1840s, Rankin had become more outspoken than ever before and was well known on both sides of the river for his work with runaway slaves. So unabashed was he, and so dedicated to aiding slaves, that he had even erected a thirty-foot pole at the top of his hill where he or one of the boys would hoist a lantern each night, making his mission ever more obvious.

By now the "never-failing fountain of the grossest immorality and one of the deepest sources of human misery," as Rankin described slavery in 1824, was drawing the public's attention in a way that for a quarter-century Rankin and the early abolitionists had so ardently worked for, prayed for, and risked their lives for. And certainly along the river the Underground Railroad had never been stronger or busier. But by 1840, the national antislavery movement, which consisted of many smaller organizations, was less unified than it had been in the 1830s. Two strong—and sometimes conflicting—points of view had emerged within the movement. The evangelical abolitionists, such as Rankin, believed that slavery would be defeated through a moral revolution in America. The political abolitionists, however, saw victory only through a larger coalition of interests represented by mainstream political parties. Whereas the evangelical abolitionists had brought Americans to a new consciousness about the evils of slavery, the political abolitionists, who comprised most of the movement's recent recruits, were more focused on the menace of the slave power. Having witnessed such events as the torching of Pennsylvania Hall, the murder of Elijah Lovejoy, the incarceration of John Mahan, and the South's campaign to stop abolition petitions to Congress (known as the gag law), they had awakened to the slave power's sinister disregard for what they believed to be every American's civil rights. They were well aware of the slave power's insatiable hunger for new territory. And they were beginning to link slavery to larger issues—for example, blaming the slave power for the Panic of 1837 and the continuing economic hardships.

As Rankin well knew, this broadening of the movement carried with it the danger of a dilution of the moral principles that had been its foundation, the most endangered ones being immediate emancipation and equal rights for all black people. It was becoming more and more evident that the solution to the national problem of slavery would be political, not ideological, as Rankin had envisioned it for so many years. He and other evangelical abolitionists, such as his friends James G. Birney and Theodore Weld, were alienated, disappointed, and discouraged. "In discussing the subject of slavery I have presented it preeminently as a moral question arresting the conscience of the nation," wrote Weld in a letter to a friend. "As a question of politics and national economy, I have passed it with scarce a look or a word, believing that the business of abolitionists is with the heart of the nation, rather than with its purse strings."

For several years, evangelical abolitionists had organized local societies, published materials, assisted runaways, and promoted "Come-outerism," which was the struggle to persuade church members to leave congregations, and congregations to leave national churches that would not condemn slavery. Despite a few individual successes in the campaign, the evangelical abolitionists now had to admit failure. Never before had opposition to slavery been "considered so much a matter of money policy—so little as a matter of religious duty," wrote Birney, in an 1842 letter to Salmon P. Chase, after the December 1841 Liberty Party convention in Ohio. Also in 1842, he wrote Lewis Tappan, "There is no reason for believing that the virtue of our own people would ever throw off slavery. Slavery has corrupted the whole nation."

As the movement began to re-form for the battles ahead, schisms erupted, causing chaos within it. Rankin felt the earth begin to tremble at the American Anti-Slavery Society's sixth annual meeting at the Broadway Tabernacle in New York in 1839. He was asked to give the opening address and was excited about the honor. But what he witnessed at the meeting was anything but exciting: sharp, bitter divisions and fighting between the factions of the membership. The conflicts revolved around the issues of uniting the antislavery cause with the growing movement for women's emancipation, and using mainstream politics to end slavery.

At the May 1840 meeting of the society, the issues came to a head when a woman was nominated to an executive post—and elected. Those who voted against her withdrew and formed their own society, the American and Foreign Anti-Slavery Society. By the summer of 1840, the momentum of abolitionism was clearly no longer in moral suasion but, rather, in political action. Evangelical abolitionism was not the prime motivation behind the movement, though it was still the movement's conscience. In explaining his attitude toward the emerging role of mainstream politics to end slavery, Garrison said, "I feel that great care is demanded of us in giving credit to whom credit is due and yet in no case ever seeming to be satisfied with it."

Rankin immediately took this torch of conscience to the political arena in the presidential election of 1840. Ardently critical of the Whig Party's weak antislavery stand, he nonetheless supported its candidate, William Henry Harrison, while agitating for the principles of full and immediate emancipation.

In Ripley, during the late-summer and early-autumn months that year, the debates and questions of presidential politics were the talk of the town. Harrison and his running mate, John Tyler, were so strongly supported that "Tippecanoe and Tyler Too" nearly achieved the status of a daily greeting. One autumn day, thirty steamboats came in and out of the Ripley docks, dropping off hundreds and hundreds of people from Ohio, Kentucky, and Virginia to attend the rally where Harrison and Henry Clay were the featured speakers. There was seating for thirty-eight thousand, but the last count revealed at least forty thousand people crowding onto a large expanse of land west of town, along the river, in a neighborhood known as Pomposity. Hard cider and coonskin caps were popular items; loaves of cornbread three feet in diameter baked in long iron kettles, and cattle roasted whole, could be seen along the perimeter of the immense gallery of backless wooden seats. Every house in Ripley opened its doors and offered buffet meals spread across plainly appointed dining-room tables. Rankin was one of the more prominent members of the audience.

But the same commitment to principle that Rankin expressed through support of Harrison drove other abolitionists to different loyalties. Rankin's son Adam Lowry, his friends Thomas Collins, Alexander Campbell, and William G. Kephart, and his brother-in-law William McNish made it a point not to attend the Whig rally. They favored the new Liberty Party, with its strong antislavery candidate for U.S. president, James G.

Birney, the Kentuckian, former slaveholder, and lawyer who had launched *The Philanthropist*—and who was a very close friend of Rankin's.

Mealtime at the Rankins' that autumn was an unusually stressful time. A family that, by the demands and dangers of their covert ventures, worked well together was shaken by the new allegiances of their rock-solid oldest son, Adam Lowry. Lowry firmly believed that the antislavery movement needed a political party of its own, that the Whig and Democratic parties did not—and would never—enact an effective antislavery platform. Harrison's running mate, Tyler, a slaveholder who was outspoken in his denouncement of the abolitionists, was brought to the ticket to carry Virginia. To Lowry, such a sellout was despicable and detrimental to the antislavery cause. Now was the time for antislavery men to drop their naïve hope for any antislavery action stemming from the mainstream parties, and to unite in strength to form a new, vibrant third party.

Rankin told his son that antislavery men must be the voice of conscience within the structure of the existing parties. A vote for Birney would be a vote for the Democratic candidate, Martin Van Buren, he argued. And Van Buren was a far worse choice for abolitionists than Harrison. Rankin was so passionate in his beliefs that he debated week after week in *The Philanthropist* with its editor (Birney's replacement), Dr. Gamaliel Bailey, who was equally zealous in his stand that the established parties were useless to the antislavery cause.

Lowry felt that Bailey's writings were more powerful than his father's, but he didn't dare say so. To choose from the lesser of two moral evils was against the writings of the Scripture. In the presence of his family during those months preceding the 1840 election, he felt like a "strange bird in a barnyard," he later wrote. If his voice rose at the dinner table in defense of the Liberty men, his mother glared at him and he felt that his father and siblings were "running fire" on him. In town it was no better. "Where two evils confront a man it is his duty to choose the least," the Whig supporters in town told Lowry, again and again.

In the end, there were only five Liberty men in Ripley that election year—Alexander Campbell, Thomas Collins, William McNish, William G. Kephart, and Lowry. Theodore Collins stood by Rankin, and so did the entire Ripley Anti-Slavery Society, which, at a special meeting in 1840, passed a resolution, suggested by Collins and then edited by one of Campbell's sons: "that while we recognize the duty of abolitionists to carry their principles to the polls we deem the formation of a distinct political party, in reference to the anti-slavery cause, inexpedient and uncalled for at the present time."

Harrison won. The Liberty ticket carried forty-eight thousand votes, which was only .29 percent of the popular vote. Though a bold step into the electoral arena, its one-plank platform—abolitionism—was not the kind of platform that could build a coalition of interests to carry the day. Nevertheless, Lowry would later be able to say that it represented the birth of Lincoln's Republican Party. For now, Lowry stopped challenging his father, even if he felt in his heart that he was right and that he would one day be proved right, perhaps the way Rankin had felt as a youth about his outspoken opposition to slavery and his own father's refusal to speak out publicly against it.

After the election, Rankin's dwindling funds forced everyone in his family to focus on financial survival. Ripley College, which the state had chartered but never endowed, had closed, though temporarily, and Rankin was now running a high school for about forty students, including several black children. This boosted his spirits because the school in Red Oak, which he had helped to start and which also admitted black children, had been torched twice now, and there was not enough support this time to rebuild it.

Rankin, who always dipped into his own shallow pockets to support his ideological ventures, had invested in both schools as well as four or five start-up churches in the region—most of which he launched himself. He and Jean had also taken in yet another child, in addition to the thirteen of their own. This was an orphaned niece whose father had died shortly before she was born and whose mother had died a few weeks after her birth. And they were raising a young black girl, whom they would support until she married at age twenty-five. Rankin donated money to many antislavery causes, such as the Mahan defense fund and the Ripley Anti-Slavery Society. He wrote dozens upon dozens of articles for newspapers without getting paid, including a lengthy antislavery series in 1839 and 1840 in *The Philanthropist*. Except on his tour as an agent of the American Anti-Slavery Society, in 1836, he typically paid all of his travel expenses, and his travels were extensive.

Lack of funds never stopped him from doing anything he believed he should do, but the strain on the family was sometimes overwhelming. The view from the Rankin hill was sometimes cloudy.

Part of the problem was that Rankin's job earned him a mere $350 a year. The income from farming his land varied dramatically from year to year, depending on weather, though the acres of timber consistently brought in cash during many of his hardest years. And, to be sure, he could always find a way out of a financial predicament, sometimes by selling tracts of his now-considerable land holdings at the top of the hill above Ripley, sometimes by devising barters connected to his land ownership, and sometimes by borrowing from banks.

This time, shortly after the 1840 election, he asked Lowry to take to the road on horseback for several months to peddle some of his published works, which were now many. *A Present to Families,* which instructed parents on how to raise their children and how to work together as a family unit, was the most recent. A more popular one was *An Antidote for Unitarianism.* In southern and central Ohio and in parts of Indiana, Lowry sold over a thousand copies of *A Present* and at least five hundred of *An Antidote.* The book sales and a loan from a member of Rankin's congregation put the Rankins on more solid ground again.

Lowry returned to Ripley in the spring of 1841, just in time to watch the seasons change and the valley transform from grays and browns to every imaginable shade of green. A new season had arrived, and as the red buds bloomed and the daffodils, irises, and azaleas lit up the landscape, a new crop of slave catchers appeared in the hills and valleys on the north side of the river.

CHAPTER TWENTY-TWO

Double or Nothing

On breezy days along the river, the sound of a farmer's ax hitting the trunk of a tree in Kentucky, or the prow of a skiff banging up against either shore, or even the barking of a lone dog could be heard on Rankin's hill, although the exact location could never be discerned. Likewise, a breeze through the valley could carry voices and activities to Kentucky from the hill above the river. And when the sounds of one shore landed on the other, there were always a few quick seconds during which the differences that so separated the worlds on either side of the river were easily forgotten, as if the familiar fascination of such a phenomenon of nature overcame all ideological divisions.

On Rankin's hill, there was always an acute awareness of sounds. The children were trained early in their lives to listen for the ominous rustling of tree branches in the thickets that flanked the house and the barn, the loud crunching of leaves breaking beneath the weight of boots and hooves in autumn, and the distant thumping of thousands of pounds of horseflesh that preceded the sudden appearance of a silhouette of strangers at the crest of the hill.

On one of those clear, breezy days in early July 1841, John Rankin was in the hilltop garden tending tomatoes and examining the corn, which was waist-high. Two of his sons were hoeing potatoes while their mother checked the progress of the pole beans—now almost to the top of the poles that were propped like tepees, one after the other, in four long rows. No one heard two people coming onto the land, though they must have made a stir when they climbed the garden gate. Perhaps the wind that day carried their stirrings to another place. Rankin was the first to see them and the only one without the immediate instinct to run into the house for a gun or to position the hoe as a weapon. For, despite a disguise, he recognized the petite, round individual dressed in a waistcoat and pants buttoned up the front. Not a man, he knew, nodding his head at the boys, who then knew not to worry. These were not the midnight assassins about which he had warned his family, nor were they the men who might approach in the day-time, as Isaac M. Beck had always feared, surprising them in the midst of daily chores. The person in the waistcoat was the woman who had escaped on the ice that night in February 1838 and who had told them all she would return one day to enlist their aid in bringing the rest of her family to freedom.

"What has brought you back?" Rankin asked.

"Oh, Mister Rankin, I want my daughter and her children. She belongs to Mr. Thomas Davis, over back of Dover. I've come back, just as I said."

Catching his protective scrutiny of the man who accompanied her, she added, "This gentleman here is a good boatman and farmer and wood-chopper and he will go over there and get them across the river and I will pay him well."

"As sure as you and that man go over there, they will catch you and they will sell you down the river, and they will hang him," said Rankin. "Now do not try it. Slavery will be your partner and death or the penitentiary will be his."

But to stand on that hill and look over the river at the Kentucky hills, and to know that her family was still there, was too much for her. Rankin understood as they walked toward the house that to persuade her to return north without her daughter and seven grandchildren—four boys and three girls—would be impossible. And so, that night after dinner, they spoke more about her plans, and Rankin offered a few of his own ideas. Jean sat in on the meeting because she would be asked to make clothes for both the man and the woman—the woman whom Harriet Beecher Stowe would use as the basis for her character Eliza in *Uncle Tom's Cabin*.

The plan was that the man, a French Canadian whom Eliza had met up with in Cleveland, would go to the Kentucky side, dressed in a common laborer's suit of clothing, and hire himself out to the owner of Eliza's daughter. The man had associated with so many Americans through his years of work as a sailor and fisherman that he spoke English without a foreign accent. And he would have no problem finding work because in Dover at that time landowners were clearing land to farm tobacco and hauling the wood to the Dover landing, where it would be used as fuel on steamboats. He would spend his free time at the taverns and learn about patrols along the river and the rhythm of their work. Eliza assured him he would be paid well when the job was done.

At the same time, Eliza, wearing a dress that Jean Rankin had made that would give her the appearance of having lived on farms in that region for many years, would go to work for the Archibald Hopkins family near Red Oak. There she would wait for the Canadian to communicate with her daughter and to set up the escape. The Canadian insisted that Eliza be part of all plans because she could keep the children calm while he focused on the logistics of the plot—and because she insisted on being there in Kentucky to help.

In Kentucky, the Canadian worked out a nearly perfect situation. He worked at the Davis farm, where Eliza's family lived. And he lived in Dover, where he could learn all about the habits of the people who would be chasing him someday soon. The men who patrolled the area, he found out, typically went home at about half past three or four in the morning, and were rarely sober. And he knew which of the farms on the way to the river had dogs that barked loudly if they saw people on their master's land. By the first Friday in August, the arrangements had all been made.

Upon getting word that the time had come to put the plans into motion, Samuel Rankin, eighteen years old, and John, Jr., fifteen, saddled up three horses, riding two and leading one out to the Hopkins house. There they found Eliza, dressed like a man in a brown brimmed hat and a vest, coat, and trousers donated for the occasion by Rankin's longtime friend William Humphrey, a local well-to-do merchant who was large and portly. Mr. Hopkins led the horse up to the two stone stairs—the upping block— so that Eliza could mount it. Eliza was about five feet four inches tall. She was a stout woman, but not as big around as Mr. Humphrey, and so, to fill out the costume, she wore her own clothes beneath his. John, Jr., found her a comical sight. Sam paid little attention, so focused was he on the task ahead: to get to the landing just below the Collins house on Front Street as soon as possible. Shunning the public road, they rode deep into the woods on a trail known as Bridle Path, with Samuel in the lead, then Eliza, and then John, Jr. It was a bright, starry night and Samuel could see the French

Canadian and Thomas Collins standing by a skiff as they approached the river. Collins said he would take the horses back up the hill to the Rankins' while the boys rowed the skiff across the river, dropped off Eliza and the Canadian, and brought the skiff back.

Eliza positioned herself at the back of the skiff. The French Canadian took the oars in the back. And each of the Rankin boys took an oar up front. John, Jr., remembered it as the smoothest of rides, "not a splash, not a ruffle," and when the Canadian came upon the shore he ran the prow of the boat into the bank with such a thrust that there was no need to tie it down. The boys then wished them well, took the oars, and headed back to Ripley. "No two boys ever put a skiff over that river in quicker and better style," John, Jr., later wrote. After chaining the skiff to a stake at the foot of the bank in front of the Collins place, the boys ran up the hill equally fast. That was Friday night. On Saturday night, Eliza, her daughter, and six of the grandchildren fled the plantation. The oldest girl was left behind in the main house.

The Canadian's plan was to return to Ripley that night, but there was one thing he had not counted on: two to three hundred pounds of possessions that Eliza's daughter insisted on bringing. The farm from which she was fleeing had been her home since birth, and there was much that she wanted to carry to her next home. The innumerable bags and the six children slowed their progress from the farm to the river's edge. Their journey was three and a half miles without a path or road through timbers and over hills. It was not long before the Canadian and Eliza reluctantly admitted that they both knew their caravan could not reach the river before daylight. And so their new destination became the heavily timbered hill back of the Sullivans' farm, on the shore, almost directly across the river from Ripley. The property was overgrown with bushes and trees, and there was a stream running through it. They would have plenty of shade and water to endure the sweltering August day.

Eliza stayed with the children while the Canadian unearthed a pair of oars from beneath a large tree stump along the shore. Then, taking the skiff of the farm owner, Mike Sullivan, a proslavery man, he rowed across the river, competing every second with the sun, which was threatening to rise. His idea was to fool Sullivan and the others into believing that the runaways had taken Sullivan's skiff to the other side. The slave catchers would then spend the day pestering the Rankins and others in Ripley and at the end of the day they would return, believing the woman and the children were well on their way north.

The Canadian rowed the skiff to a point on the shore directly in front of Thomas McCague's house on Front Street and then went to the Collins house, where he spent the day. He spoke to Collins about the challenges of the venture, how he had thought there were five children, not seven, and how they had to leave the oldest girl behind because she was a house servant and they had not found a way to inform her of the escape or to get her out.

On the other side of the river, the slave master and his cronies, as predicted, mounted their horses and headed to the river to scour the bank for missing skiffs. Finding Sullivan's skiff conspicuously gone, they asked him if he knew where his skiff might be.

"Tucked down under the bank," said Sullivan.

"No, it is not!" they said.

Sullivan walked to the edge of the bank and scanned the Ripley shoreline. "There she is, right in front of old Tommy McCague's. Them niggers are right over in that town; they sure are up in some of them holes they say John Rankin has to hide niggers in. I would know my skiff two miles off. Over there is just where you will find them, if ever you do. Niggers is mighty hard to find over there but that's where they are."

By the time Sunday school was over that day in Ripley, there were more than a dozen horsemen from Kentucky riding through the town, stopping to ask people if they had seen the slave mother and her "piccaninnies," and offering cash rewards of $400 to the man or woman who could point to the house where the runaways were hidden. When the Rankin family returned from church that day, they fully expected to find men ransacking their house in search of the seven runaways. It had happened before. But the men had already left. And as the Rankin family stood at the top of the hill and looked at the Kentucky shore, they knew that Eliza and her family were hiding in the thicket. "We had excitement and anxiety all along our young lives," wrote John, Jr., later, "but none to exceed this."

More men rode into town all the day long—from Dover, a few miles downriver from Ripley on the Kentucky side, and from surrounding towns in Ohio. These men were typically hired for 50 cents to a dollar a night or day to help round up a runaway and hold him or her until the master arrived. Whiskey flowed freely that day in Ripley, at 12.5 to 18.75 cents per gallon.

By midnight, most of the men were gone. Those who were not were drunk, or fast asleep, heads down on barroom tables. Some had passed out on the riverbank near the main part of town. At 3 a.m., everything was quiet, and the Canadian, Thomas Collins, and another man from town, Robert Patton, a deacon in the Associate Reform Church, went down to Collins's skiff, untied the rope, and threw in the oars. The Canadian rowed alone across the river while Collins and Patton settled into a secluded place beneath the bank and waited. Two hours later, the boat returned and the two men helped pull it ashore. Eliza gave the Canadian a small cloth pouch filled with gold pieces and thanked him for his help. He left immediately. Collins and Patton helped the family up the steep bank and over to McCague's house, which was enclosed within a seven-foot-high plank fence with a gate fastened on the inside. This morning, McCague had left the gate ever so slightly ajar so that the Canadian and the fugitives could slip through, enter the house, and climb the back stairs to a large open room on the third floor, where a tiny window gave them a view of the river. It was the best place on Front Street to hide, some would say, because no one in Kentucky suspected McCague or his wife, Catherine, who was known as Kitty, to be involved in Ripley's dirty little secret. McCague, after all, was one of the wealthiest men on the Ohio River, if not the wealthiest. He owned the largest flour mill, the largest pork-packing house, and the most profitable slaughter business along the river. Both Kitty and Thomas were from Kentucky and had many friends and relatives who owned slaves. Well known for their elegant parties and for their high-level political connections, they would surely not associate with the town's fanatical fringe. But they had worked with the Rankins and the Collinses since the late 1820s, and their role had recently become all the more important because they had not been exposed during the Mahan trial.

On Monday morning, Thomas McCague left his house at the usual hour to make the rounds of his businesses. A trusted man who worked for him was sent up the hill to tell Rankin that the family—Eliza, her daughter, four little boys, and two girls, one of whom was only sixteen months old—had arrived. Kitty took food and changes of clothing up through the narrow flights of back stairs to the third floor.

In the original plan, the whole crew was to be taken to the Hopkins farm, where a wagon, borrowed from a friend for that Sunday only, would take them north, into Highland County and onward. But the plan was botched, as now it was Monday and the wagon had been returned. Now they would have to walk across the fields, through the woods, along the hollows, and find their way to the Hopkins farm. The problem was what to do about the youngest child. At a meeting that morning at the McCague house, Kitty came up with an idea: She would dress the child in her own little daughter's clothing and carry the girl on her lap while she rode on her horse through town and out to the Hopkinses'.

Rankin appointed John, Jr., to guide the family from their house on to the Hopkinses' because he was well acquainted with the paths from farm to farm. Two other boys, Hugh Wiley and John Newton—friends from school whose parents also worked on the underground—would accompany him. The only problem now was how to get Eliza, her daughter, and the five children who could walk, out of McCague's garret and up to Rankin's house to begin the trip north. Because Davis, the slave owner, and his men were scattered throughout the town looking for their quarry, the family must begin its journey north as soon as possible; they could not wait until dark. Daniel B. Evans and his wife and Robert Poage, a son of Colonel James Poage, volunteered to escort the fugitives one at a time to an appointed place where they could connect with John, Jr., and his two friends and head up the hill. Soon they were all standing in the same room at the Rankin house, where John, Jr., and Sam had first seen Eliza three years before. They left by the back door and, carefully avoiding freshly plowed wheat fields that would reveal their path, they arrived at the Hopkins house, where Kitty McCague and the baby awaited them. There they piled into a wagon driven by an acquaintance of Hopkins, a traveling salesman, referred to as a "huckster." And on they went to the next stop, which was Hillsboro. The boys were home again before dawn, in time for an hour or so of sleep. "In the morning mother had us up to regular breakfast," John, Jr., later wrote, "and soon it was school time. We hustled ourselves down and were at school just as gay and lively as any other boys there and never whispered a word to each other. No one in that town except those who were personally involved ever knew a word of what had happened or how it was done any more than if Mr. McCague had pushed them down an underground road." And Eliza, her daughter, and the six children were on their way north, first to Cleveland and then to Canada.

By the early 1840s, there were approximately fifteen thousand former runaways living in Canada, operating farms and businesses and often prospering. In a sardonic note in a small local antislavery publication called the *Agitator,* the editor wrote in 1841: "It will no doubt give the humane and philanthropic slaveholders who have the good of the colored man so much at heart, pleasure to learn that the fugitives are comfortably situated in their Canadian homes."

CHAPTER TWENTY-THREE

By Fire and Sword

In the summer of 1841, in the civil case of *William Greathouse v. John B. Mahan,* a Mason County Circuit Court jury returned a verdict favoring the Kentucky slaveholder. After more than two years of harassing Mahan and other members of the Ripley line, Greathouse now had the legal right to claim the value of his runaway slaves John and Nelson. This was the $1,600 that abolitionist William Dunlop had pledged as security back in December 1838 to gain Mahan's release from the Washington, Kentucky, jail. The day after the verdict, Greathouse filed a new lawsuit to collect the secured funds from Dunlop. Despite his conviction that Greathouse was morally, ethically, and legally wrong, Dunlop paid him immediately. He wanted nothing to do with the man. The case was dismissed. And Greathouse finally disappeared from Brown County, though his spirit of revenge lingered in the valley like the smell of smoke after a fire.

That summer, tensions along the river were rising faster than temperatures. The free black communities, especially in the Cincinnati area, were crowded with slaves seeking refuge; the Underground Railroad had never been more taxed; and the prices on the heads of those who facilitated escapes had risen higher. The reward for John Rankin's had now gone up to $3,000—dead or alive.

In most of the nation, mob activities had been slowly diminishing since the height of the mobocracy in the mid-to-late 1830s, but in Cincinnati and other Ohio Valley towns, racial violence appeared to be intensifying. One reason was a June ruling from the Ohio Supreme Court that slaves who accompanied their masters over the river into Ohio, if only for a few hours of business in Cincinnati, Ripley, Marietta, or any town in Ohio, were free. The court ruled that "the bringing of slaves into this state even with the view of passing through it to settle in another slave state of itself made such colored persons free and any claim of right or attempt to carry them into a slave state in order to retain them as slaves was an offence against the laws of Ohio, which any citizen had a right to prevent even by such forces as were necessary to rescue them from such illegal custody of any person in whose possession they might be found."

In Cincinnati, the tide of runaway slaves that summer set off an alarm among white citizens much like the panic that caused the 1829 riot. On August 22 of 1829, several hundred white men had stormed Cincinnati's free black community, known as Bucktown. Buildings burned; men and women were dragged from their beds and beaten with sticks and clubs; houses were looted. The free black population had grown so quickly that white citizens felt threatened by it. By 1828, free blacks constituted nearly 10 percent of the population of Cincinnati, up from 4 percent four years before. At a time when Kentuckians were complaining about the loss of property into Ohio, white citizens of Cincinnati were equally threatened by the swelling ranks of blacks in their town. One suggested way to "correct the problem" was to enforce Ohio's Black Laws, which were passed in 1804 and, among other restrictions, required a $500 bond from all blacks entering Ohio as a guarantee for good behavior. The bond had never been rigidly enforced. But in July 1829, Cincinnati's top officials announced that the $500 bond would be required of every free black in the town who had not already paid it. The deadline for payment was thirty days. During the next few weeks, gangs of white thugs, who felt legally sanctioned by the local government's sentiment, launched an attack on the black neighborhoods. The rioting climaxed during the weekend of August 22. Out of sheer terror, black families began to flee the city, their wagons and carriages weighted down with their possessions and their grief. Within the next few months, roughly half of the free blacks of Cincinnati had fled—some to communities farther north, some to outlying towns such as Ripley, and many to Canada.

Now, once again, in the summer of 1841, there were simply too many free blacks in Cincinnati for the white citizens to feel comfortable. The

Ohio Supreme Court ruling, the white people feared, would intensify the problem. This time, the solution appeared to be mercenaries and slave catchers. "Our city is infested with kidnappers," wrote the editors of *The Philanthropist* that summer. "There are villains now prowling in our streets who are keener than bloodhounds on the track of the negro."

The inevitable soon occurred.

On August 31, a Tuesday night, on the corner of Cincinnati's Sixth Street and Broadway, a quarrel between several black men and several Irishmen ended in a skirmish in which two of each group were wounded. The next night, a mob of white men armed with knives and clubs attacked a free black boarding house on MacAlister Street, breaking windows, screaming racist remarks, and demanding that a fugitive harbored in the house be surrendered. The battle soon pulled in black neighbors, and several individuals of both races were wounded. In the neighborhood of Lower Market on Thursday night, some white boys threw stones at several blacks walking past. A knife fight ensued; one white boy suffered four knife wounds, and another was supposedly slashed so thoroughly that "his bowels fell out."

On Friday, at about 8 p.m., a white mob armed with clubs and stones met on Fifth Street and proceeded to walk, increasing its size and its arsenal of weapons as it moved forward, to Sixth and Broadway. Shouting racist insults and throwing stones, the mob attacked a confectionery owned by a free black family on Broadway, next to a synagogue. They broke down the doors and shattered the windows. By 9 p.m., the mayor had arrived on the scene and was attempting to calm the mob, which yelled at him, "Down with him! Run him off!" At this point, the white mob and the blacks in the neighborhood rushed toward each other; not even the sound of pistol shots could stop them. Many men were wounded, and some were killed. By midnight, it seemed that all of Cincinnati was at the mercy of the mob. The riot continued until at least 2 a.m. Saturday, when military troops, called for by the mayor, arrived. Several blocks of the city were now under martial law.

Later that morning, the mayor presided over a town meeting in which dozens of citizens passed resolutions calling for the arrest of the black boys who had knifed the two white boys on Thursday night; for the prompt return of all fugitive slaves to Kentucky; for the repudiation of abolitionism by all citizens of the town; and for the disarming of the city's black population. Out on the streets, the mob and its leaders continued to harass blacks without police intervention. The city council also met that Saturday morning. And at a church in the neighborhood most affected, dozens of free blacks gathered to pass their own resolutions. They thanked the mayor and several officers and gentlemen of the city for the efforts to save their property and their lives. They also assured the mayor that they would work to prevent any violent conduct from surfacing in their community. In the afternoon, numerous black men voluntarily went to jail for safety, with the hope that their action would mitigate the attacks, and with the promise that their wives and children would be protected. But the violence resumed that night. The mob, having gathered strength during the past day, widened its attack to the shops and homes of white abolitionists as well as free blacks. They broke into the offices of *The Philanthropist,* tore up the press, and carried it in pieces, amid savage yells, to the river. They then moved on to several houses owned and temporarily vacated by abolitionists and free blacks, where they destroyed the furniture and china; they even rampaged through a black church. They drove women and children out of their homes onto the ravaged streets. Police were able to stop them from destroying a bookstore owned by two white abolitionists. About 11 p.m., a bonfire started on the Kentucky side of the river across from Cincinnati, as if announcing a great victory. The next day, which was Sunday, the governor of Ohio arrived, the military presence doubled, and by nightfall, after six days of violence, the streets were finally quiet.

In Ripley, a week later, on September 12, around midnight, what Rankin family members had been warned about, and what Rankin had anticipated since the Mahan acquittal in 1838, finally happened: an attempt to destroy the safe haven on Ripley's highest hill.

CHAPTER TWENTY-FOUR

"Thus Have I Been Attacked"

On a Sabbath morning in September 1841, Richard Calvin Rankin, third oldest of the Rankin sons, thought he saw more than the usual number of young men from Kentucky loitering in town and eyeing him as if they had something in mind to do to him. After church he had even escorted a young lady who was worried about walking home alone. When he told his family of his instincts, they thought he might be overreacting to the general tension caused by the recent riots in Cincinnati. Still, Calvin, as he was called, couldn't shake the feeling that there might be trouble before the next sunrise. His cousin John P. Rankin, who lived with the family then, agreed with him, and so, when they went to bed that night, they decided to stay clothed so they could leave the house quickly, if necessary. They pulled off only coats, vests, shoes, and socks and slept lightly for three or more hours.

At half past two, Calvin heard a low whistle outside his bedroom window. He and his cousin slipped down the stairs and out the back door. Outside the house, Calvin and John separated to search for the source of the whistle. Both were carrying guns. Calvin turned toward the north end of the house, and John turned to the south. At the north corner, Calvin quickly came upon a man holding a gun. Nervously spewing out words, Calvin asked what the man was doing sneaking around his father's house.

The man did not reply; instead he shot at Calvin, grazing his shoulder. But so close were they that the powder from the pistol set Calvin's shirt on fire. Shocked, he fired back. The man yelled "Oh" and ran toward the woods.

Another man was awaiting John, at the south end of the house. And just as John turned the corner and their eyes met, the man fired his pistol at John. He missed, but, seeing the other man running, he ran too. As the two men climbed the fence that enclosed the Rankin yard, John fired at them and hit one in the shoulder blade. The man's scream brought other men out from the darkness. The shots and the scream awakened Lowry, who jerked on his boots and clothes and started for the door. Jean Rankin heard the noise, too, and by the time Lowry reached the front door, his mother was standing in her nightclothes with her back against the door, holding three keys in her hand; she had locked all three of the outside doors. Lowry and two other brothers pleaded with her to open the door. She wouldn't move. She feared that the shots she had heard might have killed Calvin and his cousin John, and that the killers were watching the doors, waiting for more Rankins to appear. "We can do the dead no good so our next duty is to preserve our own lives," she said. Rankin, the father, was meanwhile nailing windows shut.

While the other brothers continued the standoff with their mother, Lowry and his brother Samuel went into a back room, forced open a window their father had nailed shut, and jumped into the darkness. Walking around the house, they could see Calvin and John demanding the surrender of several men; they could also see the flickering of flames coming from the barn. Lowry picked up a pail full of water that was sitting on the cistern and ran to the barn. He threw the water onto a low blaze as Samuel frantically kicked the kindling away and stomped out errant flames with his boots. If they had come but three minutes later, the fire would have easily reached the unthrashed wheat stored in the barn, which would have exploded, taking their entire crop of wheat, oats, and hay. With a strong wind blowing toward the river that night, from the barn to the house, such a fire would have taken their house too, for flames would likely have blown onto the shingled roof.

Calvin and John lost most of the men they were trying to capture in a wheat field over the fence east of the house, because the stubble of the recently sown crop was too painful to cross in their bare feet. Still, they continued to shoot at the fleeing men, and just as they were giving up the chase, a cadre of men from town who had heard the gunfire took over the battle.

It was clear to everyone involved that the intention had been to burn down the Rankin house and barn that night. Rankin and others in his family surmised that the low whistle Calvin had heard was signaling that all was quiet and it was time to torch the barn. But a rain shower earlier that night had dampened the planks of the barn enough so that it did not explode into flames as quickly as the men had hoped. The man whom John P. shot, later died; he was a shoemaker from Ohio who had been working in a shop in Kentucky. Though Calvin suffered only a slight flesh wound, he had lost enough blood that two of his brothers had to carry him back to the house that night. Together Calvin, John P., Samuel, and Lowry recognized enough people that they were able to file a complaint against several men of Ohio and Kentucky for attempted arson and attempted murder.

On September 13, John Rankin described what had happened the night before in a passionate letter to the *Ripley Telegraph*. His letter was reprinted in several antislavery papers. He began:

As various false reports are in circulation respecting the recent attack made upon me and my family by midnight assassins, perhaps it may be interesting to the public to have a statement of the facts in the case, and such I shall now give. Soon after the resolutions passed against abolitionists and the colored people during the great mob in Cincinnati, reports reached me that the mobocrats of that city were threatening to come to Ripley and tear down my house. Similar threats were reported as having been made in different places in Kentucky and also in Ohio. Little danger was apprehended, yet it was thought prudent to provide the means of defence, and a number of fire arms were accordingly provided; and my family being very large, I had the means of using them if necessity required. Some degree of watchfulness was kept up. On Sabbath, the 12th instant . . . one of my sons heard a low whistle. . . .

After a detailed description of the incident, he concluded:

Thus have I been attacked at midnight with fire and weapons of death, and nothing but the good providence of God has preserved my property from flames and myself and family from violence and death. And why? Have I wronged anyone? No, but I am an ABOLITIONIST. I teach the doctrine that "all men are born equally free and independent, that we must love our neighbors as ourselves, that to buy, to sell and hold human beings as property is sin. I do not recognize the slaveholder's right to the

221

flesh and blood and souls of men and women. For this I must be proscribed, my property burnt, and my life put in jeopardy!! I am charged with feeding the hungry and clothing the naked; the poor man, white or black, has never been turned away empty from my door. And for this I must stand guard over my property and family while others sleep in safety.

Have I ever merited anything but good from the community in which I live? Can any person say that I have not labored to promote the best interests of all classes of men? Why then am I beset with armed men around my house at midnight? Because I am an ABOLITIONIST! These men came to sustain the slaveholders' claim to human beings as property. Such defence well becomes the dark system of slavery.

Now I desire all men to know that I am not to be deterred from what I believe to be my duty by fire and sword. I also wish all to know that I feel it my duty to defend my HOME to the very uttermost and that it is as much a duty to shoot the midnight assassin in his attacks as it is to pray.

I therefore forewarn all persons to beware lurking about my house and barn at night. When I am put upon the necessity of standing guard over my family and property, I shall not do it in vain.

JOHN RANKIN.

Ripley, Sept. 13, 1841.

Rankin's fury did not abate in the months ahead. As if fueled by the midnight assassins, he attacked his causes with renewed vigor. He was writing enough commentaries and editorial letters to fill a book easily—all in an effort to counteract an assault on the underground movement and a menacing surge in kidnapping incidents. Rankin, Isaac Beck, and others in their circle discovered that the slaveholders' defense strategies included developing what they perceived as the tools and weapons of the abolitionists: societies, agents, and newspapers.

In an effort, for example, to counteract the Ohio Anti-Slavery Society and *The Philanthropist,* Southern-sympathizers in Cincinnati and surrounding towns had formed an Anti-Abolition Society, whose purpose was to use the law "to repress and destroy the spirit of fanaticism which exists under the name of Abolitionism," according to its constitution. And, just as the antislavery societies had their own newspapers, so did this new society. It was called *The Cincinnati Post and Anti-Abolitionist.* In an early issue, its editors complained: "We find our markets for our manufactures diminishing and our best customers driven away by the intolerant and meddling spirit of the Abolitionists who by decoying the slave from his master and harboring the fugitive, make enemies of those who should be our friends. The slaveholder, who is passing, stops to rest in our city, or coming here to trade is robbed of his servants as certainly as a vessel wrecked on a savage coast is plundered by the barbarous inhabitants. A system of organized depredation is carried on by means of societies and agents who are continually employed in harboring, secreting and removing slaves and who thus while professing to be actuated by human motives are in fact kidnappers and negro stealers."

Consistent with the mimicking concept, slaveholders and their mercenaries effectively launched a reverse underground railroad that aided in the kidnapping of black people, bringing them back over the river into slavery regardless of their free status. Abducting free blacks and selling them back to Southern traders became a cottage industry. Slave catchers either reaped a reward from the slave owner to whom they returned the slave, or pocketed a goodly sum—usually far more than the reward—from a slave trader to whom they sold any free black they could catch.

In his columns, Rankin railed against the mounting numbers of abductions in the early 1840s. There was the free black woman near Cincinnati who, much like Eliza Jane Johnson, was snatched from her home in the middle of the day; she was seven months pregnant and had the measles. In her jail cell in Covington, she gave birth to a stillborn child and nearly died from untreated measles. There was the abduction of a dark-skinned white woman, taken out of Hamilton County and jailed in Mason County as an unclaimed runaway; the wife of a free black man, she was eventually returned to Brown County, after which the couple fled to Canada with their three children. In neighboring Clermont County, there was the shocking case of the Wigglesworth family. One late autumn night in 1842, around midnight, at least half a dozen white men broke into the farmhouse of Vincent Wigglesworth, a free black man who lived along Indian Creek and had been a citizen of Ohio for more than eighteen years. They tied him up and abducted his wife and their four children, one of whom was nine days old. The drama took many turns, and then, five or six months after the kidnapping, one of Clermont County's most active Underground Railroad conductors, Robert Fee, found the wife and children somewhere near Independence, Missouri, and brought them home.

By May 1843, *The Philanthropist* had begun to publish ads that looked much like the runaway-slave ads frequently found in newspapers south of the river. In an ironic twist, the abolitionists were now utilizing one of the tools of the slaveholders: newspaper ads to recover abducted black citizens. "$100 REWARD," one headline read. "$100 will be paid for the return of a mulatto girl named Lavinea, about nine years of age, enticed away yesterday morning from the house of Mr. Hawkins at the corner of 8th and Western Row, in Cincinnati." Another sought Catharine Morris, "about 11 years old, tolerably dark and slim made, a mark on her right shoulder from her birth and bites on her legs when stolen." And her sister Martha Morris, "about 9 years old, tolerably dark and chunky build, marked on the back from whipping."

That same month, the editors of the *Cincinnati Gazette* wrote: "KIDNAPPING: This crime is increasing all along the borders of the free states. Slavery in its mildest form is bad enough; but when the free are violently deprived of their liberty by a hellish thirst for lucre, and trafficked about as if they were logs of wood, every man possessed of human feeling should raise his voice against the crime and do what he may to overtake and bring to punishment the foul and fiendish perpetrators."

By the summer of 1843, much to the surprise and immense satisfaction of Thomas Collins, Alexander Campbell, James G. Birney, and Lowry Rankin, John Rankin had begun to raise his own voice in unison with the antislavery chorus of the nation's new third party: the Liberty Party. Each year since the 1840 election, the number of Liberty Party members in Brown County had increased: 51 in 1841, 108 in 1842, and 140 by 1843. Most, if not all of them, were participants in the Underground Railroad. Thomas McCague had recently joined the party, and so had John B. Mahan. With his legal burdens lifted, and with a stronger-than-ever passion to destroy the slave power, Mahan spent much of his time stumping for the Liberty cause and soliciting subscriptions for the party's media outlet, *The Philanthropist*. An April 1843 edition of that paper announced: "Our agents are stirring. Mr. Mahan, the victim of slaveholding rapacity and gubernatorial stupidity, is busy in Clermont, Brown and Adams and all neighboring counties." And in an April 24 letter to *The Philanthropist*, Mahan wrote, "I have just returned from a lecturing tour, made through the north-eastern part of Highland County and a neighboring portion of Adams [county]. . . . If traveling and local agents do their duty and others who are interested, ten thousand subscribers can readily be obtained. It is a small concern so far as money is concerned but a mighty engine so far as facts are concerned. Let every lover of liberty do his duty!"

Rankin's abandonment of the Whig Party and endorsement of a struggling new party devoted to the antislavery cause seemed like a shocking turn, especially to those who had read his adamant commentaries against the Liberty Party in 1840. Converting the members of an already established party was smarter than splitting off into a small, powerless new entity, he had said back then. But his change of heart came at the same time as his campaign to persuade the bureaucracy of the New School of the Presbyterian Church to take a public stand against slavery. The reluctance on the part of clergymen and church bodies to endorse abolitionism was abhorrent to Rankin, who saw how political the issue had become within the church. He had already witnessed the schism of 1837, when the church split into two factions: the Old School and the New School. And now he was painfully disappointed when the New School did not act on its convictions that slavery was wrong. Presbyterians—and Quakers and Methodists—had nurtured the antislavery movement in its infancy. But now, just as the nation feared that the fervor of the abolitionists would bring down the Union, many Presbyterians—when pushed to the edge, as Rankin pushed them—feared that abolitionism would bring down the church. Even to address the issue publicly could cause dissension and warring factions within the church. Heaving beneath the political body of the New School was a fault line that ran deep into the souls of every antislavery member. Many members opposed slavery, but they did not know how to end it and feared any sort of confrontation. Rankin chose to show them a way, which most did not take. Rankin had begun to believe that working toward change within sluggish, staid, and stubborn organizations—whether his church or the Whig Party—was not the way to abolish slavery.

In June 1843, Rankin sent a letter to *The Philanthropist* that began: "Through your paper, I desire to present to all anti-slavery Presbyterians, Old and New School, the following question: Ought not all anti-slavery Presbyterians withdraw from the present branches of the Presbyterian Church in the United States?" With this letter, which was republished in newspapers nationwide, Rankin stood at the edge of a high precipice, the highest point on the higher ground he had chosen years before.

CHAPTER TWENTY-FIVE

"A Victim of the Slave Power"

"The nefarious acts of the abolitionists of Ohio in aiding and abetting the escape of our slaves are producing their natural and inevitable results—hostility and bloodshed," wrote the editors of the *Lexington Gazette* in early December 1844.

A week or so later, on Dec. 12, Colonel Edward Towers, a Mason County slaveholder, rode into Red Oak looking for his six runaway slaves. With him were at least as many men from both sides of the river; some of the local men had been part of the gang of thugs that had stripped and mercilessly whipped Harbor Hurley, a black man from a highly respected family in Sardinia, a few months before. (Dr. Beck examined his back after the incident and found more than a hundred marks of the lash.) There had been no provocation for the attack on Hurley. Now the men were riding toward the home of Robert Miller, who had taken in Towers's slaves. When Miller heard the pounding of the hooves and the sounds of men's voices, he rushed out the back door of his house with two of the runaways. But he didn't act fast enough. Just as he mounted his horse, one of the band of slave hunters knocked him down. He fought back, but his oppressor stabbed him repeatedly. As the two slaves were recaptured, bound, and shoved onto the backs of horses, Miller died.

The posse then proceeded a few miles to the house of Absalom King,

226

one of Brown County's strongest supporters of the Liberty Party and a participant in the underground for at least five years. Five armed men stood at the door and informed the slave hunters that no one could enter without a warrant. This did not stop the posse, equally matched in pistols and knives. As if on the front lines of a major battle, gunfire erupted, and Colonel Towers's son fell to the ground, dead. While King was reloading firearms in the back part of his house, someone in the side yard shot through a window and hit him in the back. At this point, the sheriff of Georgetown arrived with his own posse at the King house and arrested both the abolitionists and the slave hunters. Some members of each group were able to ride away without being seen. An hour or so later, some of the men out of Colonel Towers's posse lynched one of the slaves who they believed had fought against Towers's son. They then burned down the houses of Miller and King. And before reaching the river, they stopped at the home of James Gilliland's son Alexander, forced him from his dinner table, dragged him out of the house into a thicket nearby, and beat him nearly to death.

"The number of Kentuckians is increasing loudly, and the whole neighborhood is up in arms!" editors at the Georgetown, Ohio, paper, the *Ohio Telegraph,* wrote two days later. "The Sheriff is actively engaged in attempting to quell the ongoing riot. Where it will end God only knows!"

Like the aftershocks of an earthquake, fistfights and skirmishes between abolitionists and their enemies continued to erupt in the days ahead in the vicinity of Red Oak. And in the midst of the conflict, word spread through the valley that John B. Mahan had died.

During his months in the Washington, Kentucky, jail, Mahan had suffered from a severe chest cold and cough—what turned out to be tuberculosis. He never completely regained his health, and often during the winter months he was again afflicted, even bedridden at times, with a severe cough and congestion. He had always recovered—until December 1844.

Although the official cause of his death was tuberculosis, some folks shook their heads and said that he had most certainly died of a broken heart. Others said it was likely the combination of the two, that John Mahan had lost the will to fight against his afflictions. His decline, they said, began during the summer of 1843, after his oldest daughter died. That was the summer when Mahan was away from home for two- and three-week stretches as he rode from village to village promoting the Liberty Party platform and selling subscriptions to *The Philanthropist.* An ardent Liberty Party supporter, he had worked with Absalom King, Alexander Campbell, Adam Lowry Rankin, and others in building the party membership in Brown County. In August that year, the *Cincinnati Weekly Herald,* a new incarnation of *The Philanthropist,* published a small notice, headlined "ZEAL": "J. B. Mahan wishes me to inform you that he pledges himself to be one of the hundred to obtain twenty-five subscribers each for the *Weekly Herald* and *Philanthropist.* He has almost redeemed his pledge. Who next?"

It was that August, too, that his oldest daughter, Mary Jane, who was teaching school in Manchester, Ohio, became critically ill. For days, family and friends tried to locate her father to tell him of her illness. But he was lecturing at some small town in a meeting hall in Illinois or Indiana, or perhaps speaking from the pulpit of a church somewhere in Ohio. Wherever he was, he could not be found. And on August 14, Mary Jane passed away. After her death, her body was taken to Sardinia, where her mother kept it for four days. The family continued to hope that the messenger whom they had already dispatched at least twice to find her father would finally succeed. But he did not, and by the time Mahan arrived home, friends and family had already sung "Unveil thy bosom, faithful tomb," at the grave of his daughter. Mahan was devastated. In the months ahead, he dropped out of the crusade to enlist party supporters and was rarely seen at abolitionist gatherings. By 1844, his commentary had ceased to appear in the antislavery newspaper *Zion's Watchman,* where he was well known. And the Rankin, Gilliland, and Hopkins families all knew not to bring runaways to his tavern; neither Polly nor John was up to the task. By the late autumn, Mahan was quite ill. His longtime friend and colleague on the underground, Dr. Beck, tried to prolong his life but was skeptical that he would live to see another Christmas. There was not even enough time for his brother William, who now lived in Illinois, to see him once more. Mahan died at his home on December 15.

On several occasions, John and Polly had discussed the possibility of joining their brother and sister in Lexington, in McLean County, Illinois, where there was an active Underground Railroad network. But they hadn't the funds to uproot and resettle. They could not sell their house and land, because they no longer owned it; Dunlop, the man who had bailed Mahan out of the Greathouse predicament, owned it. Worse still, despite the help of local abolitionists, they were still in debt from the enormous legal fees connected with the 1838 trial; Mahan had had to pay about $1,200. With John's death, Polly and the children were compelled legally to give up their land to Dunlop, who offered to sell it back at the discounted price of $960. But the family couldn't even afford that. The Mahans were now destitute.

Antislavery newspapers nationwide and regional mainstream papers noted Mahan's death, some in greater detail than others. On the day after Christmas that year, editors at the *Pennsylvania Freeman* wrote a piece that Garrison later published in *The Liberator*:

We have a letter from a friend in this city [Philadelphia], in which he says: "I have this morning received the sad intelligence of the decease of that true and long-tried friend of human rights, J. B. Mahan, of Ohio." Many of the readers of the Freeman will recollect the imprisonment and trial to which our friend Mahan was subjected in 1838. He was charged with felony—with aiding and assisting certain slaves to escape from their tyrant master. Being unable to procure bail, he was thrown into a Kentucky prison, and heavily ironed; after an incarceration of some weeks, he was brought to trial—the jury, after hearing his case for six days, brought in a verdict of acquittal, on the ground that the Kentucky courts had no right to sit in judgment on acts done in Ohio.—Our correspondent was personally acquainted with the deceased, and describes him as a man of energy and talent, and untiring zeal in the cause of universal liberty. The memory of such a man will live after him, and impart new energy to his surviving co-laborers in the cause.

In the weeks ahead, Mahan's friends wrote pieces for various newspapers asking for financial help for Polly and the seven children, who, as soon as they could afford to go, planned to join William and Cassandra in Illinois. In *The Philanthropist*, several men from Sardinia wrote:

Mr. Mahan has gone to the grave—robbed by the oppressor of everything necessary to rear his dear children and robbed too for doing what we do every opportunity afforded us. If only one or two had been doing that which awakened the ire of the oppressors, then had they not exposed themselves to the scorn of mankind and disgraced their courts of justice to glut their vengeance on him; but because we helped their fugitives on our own soil to a land of freedom they took vengeance on Mr. Mahan. You will see by the statement and resolutions accompanying this address that a committee is appointed to receive funds and appropriate them for the benefit of the family. Who will come to their relief? Who? The friends of justice and the slave are morally bound to restore to the bereaved and helpless family of that distinguished independent and worthy citizen and philanthropist all that he has been legally compelled to sacrifice in the great cause of justice and human rights."

Mahan's tombstone was erected on a shady slope at the far end of the Sardinia cemetery, and on it were engraved the words "In Memory of John B. Mahan, died December 15, 1844, aged forty-three years eight months and nine days. A victim of the slave power." By the time of his death, Mahan had conducted runaways on the Underground Railroad for nearly twenty years, first out of Clermont County—often with Levi Coffin, the Quaker merchant, who then lived in Indiana—and then out of Brown County. From the early 1830s to the autumn of 1843, he had worked with John Rankin and his sons, and with Dr. Beck, the McCoys, the Pettijohns, the Gillilands, the Huggins brothers, and the free black "conductor" John Hudson, among others on the Ripley line. His death was a palpable loss to a loose yet reliable network of people who had come together for many years to aid slaves. But as the network lost one great participant, it was soon to gain another: a former slave who called himself John Parker.

CHAPTER TWENTY-SIX

Parker's Ferry

The man said he was a barber from Maysville who had been forced to leave his home in a hurry. One day he was helping runaways cross the Ohio River, and the next he was fearing for his life. A free black man who was exposed for working with runaway slaves had no choice but to flee, he told the other black man who lived in the same boarding house. And so he had come to Cincinnati, where he hoped he could continue his underground work in the relative safety of more secrecy. But he was determined to return to Maysville to help two young slave girls whom he knew to be in trouble there. He needed help, he said, and certainly a man so confident and so sturdy as his new neighbor would be willing to work with him.

But the neighbor said no. So fiercely had the neighbor fought for his own freedom that he had no inclination to risk it. His life was good now. He was starting afresh in the bustling marketplace of Cincinnati, working hard at his trade as an iron molder.

Several evenings later, the barber again sought out his neighbor, this time to tell him the exciting news: He had made all the arrangements for the escape, and the girls were waiting for "them" to arrive with a skiff. His plan was to use the river town of Ripley as headquarters. There he would find a vessel to take across the river, and there too he would later hide the girls until it was safe to move them northward. But while he waited in the boat on the Kentucky shore, he needed a partner who would climb up the Maysville bank and alert another freeman to send for the girls. The plans were made; the girls were waiting. Now would the neighbor help him? No, said the neighbor, as if swatting a fly. No. No. No. But the barber, day after day, urged the tall, strong man to come along, for the sake of the slave girls who so desperately wanted their freedom.

Perhaps it was this persistence that swayed the neighbor or simply wore him down. Perhaps it was the vision of two young girls with dreams of a future in a free land. Or perhaps it was the neighbor's angry memory of the chains that once rubbed against his own wrists. Whatever the reason, the man, John Parker, finally agreed to the work with the barber. It would be Parker's first experience on the Underground Railroad—and his introduction to the town of Ripley.

Parker had been born into slavery in Virginia in 1827. At the age of eight, in 1835, he was sold by his plantation owner—who was also his father. Never again would he see his mother. That June, he crossed the mountains of Virginia, his ankles chafing against the shackles that locked him into a caravan of slaves walking all the way from Virginia to Alabama. As he walked, he struggled to keep up with the adults in front of and behind him. And he carried a stick that he used to thrash every flowering shrub he could reach from his place on the narrow, rock-strewn trail. As he waded through a mountain stream, he struck at the bubbles. When he emerged from the water, he saw a red bird perched on the branch of a chestnut tree in full bloom and he traded his stick for a rock, throwing it at the bird and shaking his fist when he missed. The other slaves laughed at his anger. What good did it do to flog a flower or strike a bird?

Parker's anger made him difficult, and he was beaten on several occasions because of it. But beatings never broke his defiant spirit. His anger would drive him to great accomplishments. In Alabama, at the home of his new master, a doctor in Mobile, he learned to read, secretly, with the help of the doctor's two sons. At age sixteen, he escaped the Mobile master and was caught, escaped again, was caught again, then for another two years, he dodged slave catchers, sheriffs, steamboat captains, and angry bosses to gain his freedom, which he finally purchased for $1,800. In 1845, Parker arrived in Cincinnati from Jeffersonville, Indiana, where he had worked as a molder in the iron foundries and as a free man for the first time in his life.

Parker had an abiding hatred for slaveholders and slave hunters. On his first underground venture, his co-conspirator, the barber, eventually abandoned the mission, largely because he and Parker were unable to find a skiff on the Ohio side. So determined was Parker to complete what he had set out to do that he devised a new plan of action and eventually succeeded by himself in freeing the girls. Although his first experience was fraught with mishaps, the knowledge that his actions subverted the institution he so despised would inspire Parker to many, many more incidents. He would soon become one of the most daring men on the Underground Railroad, even though he risked his own freedom every time he left Ohio.

In the months ahead, Parker connected with Levi Coffin, the Quaker merchant in Wayne County, Indiana, who had worked with both of the Mahan brothers and regularly connected with the Ripley line. Two years later, Coffin moved to Cincinnati and opened a dry-goods store that sold only products made with slave-free labor; it was a few blocks away from a general store owned by Andrew Coombs, a former student of Rankin's at Ripley College and an active member of the underground. Their stores were at the intersection of two runaway-slave routes: one leading from Cincinnati to Ripley, and another through New Richmond and Batavia in Clermont County. By then, Parker had used both routes on numerous occasions.

Parker was one of the few free blacks willing to work with either Coffin or Coombs. Though Cincinnati was indeed a hub of Underground Railroad activities, free blacks and whites often looked upon each other with great suspicion. In later years, Parker would say that he preferred working with the Ripley underground, where blacks and whites usually did work together, and where he felt the efficiency was greater. Ripley, Parker said, was "the real terminus of the Underground Railroad. The Ripley group was the intermediary between the spirit of the Revolutionary patriots and the fiery New England group who took this fire and inspiration about 1830 from the irrepressible firebrand William Lloyd Garrison."

In 1849, the year after his marriage, Parker and his wife, Miranda Boulden, a Cincinnati woman, moved to Ripley, where he continued to live a double life: by day an iron molder, and by night a conductor on the underground. Parker quickly became a powerful player on the Ripley line, where his bold style was unmatched: crossing the river, walking sometimes miles into slave territory, and working directly with slaves on a scheme for their escape. The *Commercial Tribune* of Cincinnati once said of Parker, "A more fearless creature never lived."

Of this period of time on the Ripley underground, Parker later told a journalist, "Every night of the year saw runaways, singly or in groups, making their way slyly to the country north. Every precaution was taken to prevent the fugitive from successfully passing through this forbidden land. The woods were patrolled nightly by constables and any man black or white had to give a good account of himself, especially if he were a stranger. Every ford was watched, while along the creeks and the river, the skiffs were not only pulled up on shore, but were padlocked to trees, and the oars removed. There were dogs in every dooryard, ready to run down the unfortunate. Once word came from further south that runaways were on the way, the whole countryside turned out, not only to stop the fugitives, but to claim the reward for their capture. Everything was organized against the slaves' getaway."

Slaves had a number of ways to find Parker, who was now known on the other side of the river for his willingness to go into Kentucky to bring slaves out. Sometimes free blacks traveled to Ripley and told the abolitionists about slaves who wanted to escape. More often, Kentucky slaves entrusted by their masters to carry out an errand in Ripley brought word of slaves wanting to leave. One evening shortly after Parker had moved to Ripley, Thomas Collins went over to Parker's house with a slave who had just called upon him to draw attention to a group of ten fugitives hidden in the woods twenty or so miles inside Kentucky. Their leader had been captured, and they were confused and scared about how to proceed. Waiting until it was dark, Parker took his small boat across the river to find them. Hours later, he brought the ten men and women to his boat, but there wasn't enough room for everyone. Knowing that slave hunters were not far behind, one slave gave up his seat to another whose wife was also in the party. As Parker vigorously rowed back across the black expanse of water, he could see the flickering of lanterns along the shoreline, like flashes of lightning, and in the next few moments, he could hear the unnerving screams of the man he had left behind. With his nine fugitives, Parker met Collins at the shore, and they agreed that, because of the master's pursuit, they would take the group immediately to Reverend Gilliland's house in Red Oak.

After Parker moved to Ripley, he operated a foundry at the northwest end of Front Street and lived in the house next to it with his growing family and library. His house quickly became known as a place for runaways to go in Ripley, and just as quickly Parker's name was added to the reward posters in northern Kentucky. Despite the growing suspicions about the black man on the riverfront, Parker's iron foundry thrived, and he began to employ workers from both sides of the river. One man, who was the son of a Kentucky slaveholder by the name of Shrofe, continually goaded Parker, daring him to run off with one of his father's slaves. Saying nothing in response, Parker secretly resolved to do just that.

Late one night, Parker crossed the river to locate the slave cabins at the Shrofe place and to persuade one of the slaves to escape. One man and wife were eager to work with him. A week later, as arranged, Parker returned to take the family, including their baby, beyond the river to Ripley. All week long, the parents, in anticipation of the journey ahead, were nervous, and their agitation drew the attention of their master. So suspicious was he that he took their baby into his own bedroom, where he and his wife kept two pistols next to their bed. On the night of the escape, Parker, undaunted by this new obstacle, took off his shoes and gave them to the baby's parents to hold for him while he crept across the yard and into the master's house. Shuffling silently across the rough kitchen floorboards, Parker swung open the bedroom door and heard the encouraging sounds of deep breathing. As he slid the bundled baby off the bed and into his arms, the master awakened and knocked the guns and a candle onto the floor. Parker ran with his prize. A bullet whistled overhead as Parker flew past the terrified slave couple, who both seemed paralyzed by the action before them. Parker shouted that he had the baby, and if they wanted it they had better follow him. In only moments, he was pulling the skiff into the river current with all three fugitives on board. They landed safely on Ripley's shore, but as Parker secured his skiff, the couple told him that they had dropped his shoes during their flight to the river.

In Ripley, Parker took the family to the home of Archibald Leggett on Main Street, where without question they would be sheltered and prepared for the journey north. Knowing the master and his men were in close pursuit, and nervous about what they might figure out because of the shoes, Parker ran home and crawled into his bed to await the expected pounding on the door. Soon enough, Shrofe and several others stood on Parker's doorstep, making threats and demanding to search the house. Parker allowed the search, and the men left, angry and empty-handed. The next day, Shrofe returned to Ripley—this time with Parker's shoes, which he took to every shoemaker in town to find out to whom they had been sold. Parker was worried, but no one in town shared any information with the slavers.

The Shrofe incident was only one of many close calls, but Parker seemed to revel in such "direct action" against slavery. One Sunday, just before dawn, one of the Rankin boys appeared at Parker's door to summon him to an emergency meeting at the Collinses'. "Bring all your guns," the boy told him. This was new. Parker had been asked to take small arms on a rescue but never his musket and larger firearms. At the Collins house, where Rankin, Dr. Campbell, Thomas McCague, Dr. Alfred Beasley, and others had gathered, Parker learned that a group of five fugitives had misjudged the timing of their journey to the river and were stuck at daybreak on the Kentucky shore. Worse still, they could be seen from the Ohio side. Rankin was extremely agitated about their vulnerability. His face was pale and his voice shook from the passion of his distress. In a bold, unprecedented move, he proposed that the Ripley men—specifically, six of his sons, himself, and any others who wished to join in—lead an armed expedition to Kentucky to rescue the fugitives in broad daylight, fight anyone who tried to interfere, and, after bringing the fugitives back to Ripley, walk them, with armed escorts, straight up Mulberry Street to Rankin's house and to safety beyond it. Such an organized show of force in the light of day had never before been done in Ripley.

At the "council of war," as Parker later called the meeting at the Collins house that day, a few people expressed fear about the potential for violence in such a plan. After all, the slave catchers would be willing to fight long and hard for the thousands of dollars in reward money they could collect from the capture of five fugitive slaves. No one could predict how the townsfolk in Ripley would react to such a bold act of defiance on the part of the "conductors." And no one could know when the slave hunters might discover the fugitives on the Kentucky side, or even if they would find them before dusk. In the end, cooler heads prevailed. Dr. Campbell and Dr. Beasley reminded Rankin of the midnight assassins at his house back in 1841 and how his plan could precipitate another such battle. They persuaded Rankin that it was better to wait until the sun had set to take action. All agreed that everyone should be fully armed. Of the discussion, Parker later said, "For a time the measure was in the balance, which indicates that there were other people who were thinking the same way John Brown was, except he went further and executed their ideas."

And so, when the sun began to disappear over the Kentucky hills that day, a tiny flotilla of rowboats moved swiftly across the river from Ripley: two for the rescue and one filled with armed guards for security. Among them were seven men with muskets, including Rankin and Parker. They picked up the anxious runaways and soon arrived back in Ripley, landed the skiffs just below Mulberry Street, then marched with the fugitives straight up the steep hill to Rankin's house, where Mrs. Rankin fed them all. The incident was pulled off without any violence, although the threat of it was hanging like humidity in the air along the river all that night. Parker later referred to the episode as Ripley's "Harper's Ferry." Everyone knew that the plan, both as imagined and as executed, represented an escalation in the conflict between slavery and freedom along the river.

These incidents, Parker told a journalist later, "were discussed in the streets of the city, the cabins of woodsmen, and they penetrated the remote corners of the Union. The southland became excited and swore vengeance on abductors and their abettors, and after every event there was an explosion of ill feeling, which found vent in angry threats."

Parker kept a journal of the names, dates, and details of every incident in which he was involved—until 1850. That year, he threw his journal into the iron furnace after he read the details of the new Fugitive Slave Law passed that September. As a black man who owned property—soon to own his home as well as a foundry—and ran a successful business, he had a lot to risk.

"My little memorandum book I dropped quietly in the cupola of my own iron foundry, so no one knew its existence, especially its damaging contents," Parker said. "But the work went on just the same, in fact, more aggressively than ever, which speaks well for the conscience and courage of the Ripley group."

CHAPTER TWENTY-SEVEN

WITH SPUR AND REIN

The first scourge to hit the Ohio Valley in 1850 was cholera. The second was the Fugitive Slave Law. Each was a plague with the daunting potential to touch anyone at any time.

In March that year, rumors rippled through the valley about the occurrence of cholera on steamboats moving upriver from New Orleans. By April, admonitions and advice abounded in the local newspapers. "Temperance, cleanliness and regularity of personal habits," might prevent the onslaught of the disease, the *Maysville Eagle* suggested. Above all, it said, maintaining courage and a cheerful spirit could fend it off. "Timidity and alarm, there is no doubt, have made victims of many, many, very many," the editors wrote. *The West Union Intelligencer,* out of nearby Adams County, Ohio, proposed a recipe for "THE" cure: a concoction of three-quarters of an ounce of opium, the same amount of gum myrrh, pulverized rhubarb, seed-bruised coriander, cayenne pepper, bruised aniseed, frankincense, and camphor, mixed in with five grains of musk, the same of skunk castor, and one quart of French brandy. "Put all in a bottle and let stand for two or three days, observing to shake it frequently and it is fit for use. As a preventive or curative, this medicine appears in its effects worldwide to be a specific if not an infallible remedy for cholera if taken at the commencement of the disease."

On June 30, Richard Dillingham, a young Quaker who had taught free blacks to read and write in Cincinnati and had been convicted the previous year of aiding fugitive slaves fleeing from Tennessee, died of cholera in the penitentiary at Nashville. By July, hundreds of crew members and deck passengers on northbound steamboats had been buried at different points along the river, and newspapers were now listing the names, ages, and hometowns of the dead. The disease was "raging violently" in Louisville, the *Ripley Bee* reported in late July, though there were no new cases in Brown County. On September 5, the *Maysville Eagle* reported that the cholera had moved upriver and had "assumed somewhat the form of an epidemic" in the counties along the river.

Two weeks later, on September 18, a blight of a different kind struck the region: a plague of prejudice, in the form of the Fugitive Slave Law. Much like the gradual approach of the cholera, the new federal law had been slowly evolving and gaining strength for many months. Henry Clay first proposed it on the floor of the Senate in January 1850 as part of a compromise package of legislation. Among other things, California would enter the Union as a free state, and the citizens of the territory acquired from Mexico would be allowed to choose whether or not they wanted slavery. To assuage the South's pain over what it perceived to be a series of losses, the 1793 Fugitive Slave Act would get a new set of teeth for reclaiming fugitive slaves and punishing those who tried to assist escapes.

Throughout the summer, fierce debates shaped and reshaped the controversial law. Southerners claimed they were losing hundreds of thousands of dollars yearly to the thieves in the North. Although there were no firm figures for the numbers of slaves that had escaped and the cost per slave, each state reported its estimates of the losses: Kentucky, $30,000; Virginia, $100,000; Maryland, $80,000; and South Carolina, $200,000. Who and what was at fault for this? The abolitionists and their underground system. And how to stop it? Shackle the abolitionists with laws that condemned their behavior and stymied their efforts.

Northerners fought the law, which they claimed demonstrated callous disregard for the personal liberties of all citizens of the North and at the very least stripped the black population of every protection against re-enslavement. Still, the law passed in the Senate on August 23 with 27 yeas and 12 nays; and on September 12 in the House, with 109 yeas and 75 nays. And then, on September 18, President Millard Fillmore gave his approval. Before the ink was dry, the law had begun to do exactly the opposite of its intent, which was to preserve the union. Instead, it was steering the nation into more sectional strife than ever before and onto a clear path toward a violent resolution.

"Future history will tell of the legislators of the present day whose sense of fear has been more potent than their sense of right and who have felt at liberty to be liberal with the money of their constituents rather than adhere to those unbending principles of justice and impartiality which are alone the attributes of the great and good," wrote the editors of the *New York Courier & Enquirer.*

The debates of the summer quickly became the intersectional war cries of the autumn. The South felt that it didn't get enough. This law would never be enforced, screamed Southern critics, who vowed to do everything in their power to ensure its enforcement. Northerners felt that the slave power had trampled their civil liberties to death. What did the North have to do with slavery? Now the question was moot. No Northerner could deny the presence of slavery and slave interests during every hour of the day. No free black person—whether free after crossing the river in the early hours of the previous day, free by birthright in a state such as Ohio, or, like John Parker, free after buying himself from his owner—could be assured that a slaveholder or mercenary would not at any moment steal away his freedom. By the same stroke of Millard Fillmore's pen, no white person could be safe from the demands for cooperation from slaveholders and mercenaries, who now could legally require the assistance of any person within sight of a struggle to apprehend an alleged fugitive slave.

From September 18 forward, anyone who obstructed the arrest of a fugitive or facilitated the slave's flight could be fined up to $1,000, be incarcerated up to six months, and be liable for $1,000 for each runaway whom the slaveholders could not reclaim. The first five clauses of the law called for the appointment of commissioners throughout the U.S. who had the legal authority to grant certificates to any claimant for the return of a black person to his or her alleged owner in another state. Any circuit or district court could appoint the commissioner, who had the power also to demand the aid of any bystander in the apprehension of an alleged fugitive slave under the penalty of a fine or incarceration. The sixth clause authorized a claimant to seize a man or woman without any kind of preliminary "process" and drag him before one of the commissioners, "whose duty it shall be to hear and determine the case of the claimant in a summary manner," based upon affidavits taken perhaps hundreds of miles away and other potentially false evidence, but not on any testimony from the alleged slave himself. Fugitives did not have the right to a jury trial, could not testify on their own behalf, and could not use the writ of habeas corpus to restrict the terms of their arrest. If the slave was returned to his or her owner, then the commissioner who had approved and ordered the return received $10. If there was no match, then he received $5. If a U.S. marshal or deputy marshal let the fugitive slip from his grasp, the marshal could be fined up to $1,000.

What was new about the law was that it struck down the right of habeas corpus, it demanded that every person in sight be responsible for the successful return of the slave to his or her alleged owner, it raised all fines and terms of imprisonment for violation of such procedures, it allowed any citizen to be appointed by a circuit court as a commissioner, and it provided financial incentives for the commissioner to retrieve the slaveholders' property. The law threatened the freedom of all people of color in the North, whether or not fugitives. And it obstructed the civil liberties of all persons, black or white, by demanding the participation of bystanders. Missing from the new law was any system of penalties against those who might make false claims and succeed, with the help of the law, in carrying off freemen and selling them as slaves.

The *New York Evening Post* called the Fugitive Slave Law "an act for the encouragement of kidnapping." And the New York mayor declared that his officers would not assist in the capture of fugitive slaves. The Common Council of Chicago—in a ten-to-three vote—refused "to aid or assist in the arrest of fugitives from oppression." In most Northern cities, citizens formed vigilance committees to protect free blacks and to assist runaways. Blood would flow through the streets of all the nation's cities, warned the representatives of free black communities, before former slaves or alleged slaves would be returned.

So repugnant was the law, and so angry were its critics that many antislavery advocates believed the law would unite the various spirits of the movement into one powerful force. "It will, not withstanding the alarm and distress it occasions, do great good in opening the eyes of the people," said New York abolitionist and philanthropist Lewis Tappan. To be sure, bonds within the antislavery movement quickly strengthened, factional divisions diminished, and new recruits suddenly appeared like buds bursting forth in a hothouse. The law may have struck like a plague of prejudice, but what it killed more than anything was indifference. It even had the effect of reviving the religiously fervent portion of the movement, which had dwindled throughout the 1840s. And it drew more attention to the antislavery clergy. After all, one justification for not obeying such a law was to move to higher ground and pledge allegiance to the higher laws of God.

As if speaking for the silent army that dwelled along the alleys of Ripley and amid the folds of its high hills, the *Ripley Bee* assailed the law. Its great vice, the editors wrote, "is the presumption in favor of Slavery. As soon as a man is claimed as a slave his fate is well nigh sealed. All those rules and provisions made in our Constitutions and laws in favor of innocence and liberty are disregarded and his right to liberty is determined as if he were a mere chattel. In a free state where Slavery is not tolerated, the presumption of law is in favor of liberty just as it is in favor of innocence. Every man is presumed to be innocent until his guilt is established by due process of law. Every man should be presumed to be free until the contrary is established in a like manner. Better is it that ninety-nine guilty persons should be acquitted than that one innocent one should be convicted and punished. Better that ninety-nine slaves should escape than that one freeman should be condemned to Slavery."

On the Ripley line, the new law forced men like John Parker, Thomas Collins, Dr. Isaac Beck, Thomas McCague, and James Huggins to fine-tune their secrecy skills.

"After the passage of the fugitive slave law, I enquired but little what my friends were doing and kept as ignorant as I could," Dr. Beck later wrote. "If they wanted help, I gave it. If not, I made no enquiry. I judge others did the same for in case of a prosecution or suit for damages against our neighbors 'ignorance was surely bliss.' "

Indeed, more people than ever seemed to be willing to make a few fast dollars helping errant mercenaries to snatch a black man or woman and threatening the lives and safety of workers on the underground. At the same time, Dr. Beck wrote, the law provoked some conversions among the townsfolk. People whom he least expected came to him to ask what they could do to assist the runaways—mainly younger people, "for the love of excitement and adventure." Most volunteered as informants, to scout the hills and tip off Dr. Beck about the locations of slave hunters. Some who now joined the clamor had watched their abolitionist neighbors, sometimes with disdain, for many years.

On November 10, Dr. Beck and Reverend James Gilliland called a meeting of concerned citizens of several Brown County towns at Sardinia to discuss the new law. Dr. Beck spoke, then Gilliland and James Huggins, and then the floor opened to the dozens of people who crowded the small meeting hall. Their fear was palpable. But in unity they found strength, and they channeled their fears into the wording of six resolutions. Number Six read: "Resolved that should a fugitive come to our doors, he shall not be turned away and that we will defend him to the same extent and with the same weapons as we would defend our wives and children and that the dark shadow of the kidnapper whether officer or private person shall never pass our threshold."

Rankin led the next Ripley Anti-Slavery Society meeting on December 25 at the Stone Church in Red Oak. "It is the deliberate determination of this meeting to agree not to assist in carrying out the provisions of this law, nor suffer it to be done if in our power we can prevent it," he said. Numerous resolutions brought unanimous votes. Among them: "Resolved, that it would better comport with the usages of this Government to resort to its old practice of employing blood hounds to hunt down its human prey than to command all good citizens to perform that service." And "Resolved, that the members of Congress who voted for said law deserve the scorn and contempt of the civilized world."

The following week, Rankin and Salmon P. Chase, the abolitionist lawyer from Cincinnati who would serve in Abraham Lincoln's cabinet, conducted a similar meeting in Highland County. Rankin closed the assembly with one lasting comment: "Disobedience to the enactment is obedience to God."

Soon after that meeting, the Ohio legislature passed a resolution "that the law commonly called the Fugitive Slave Law, being a law that makes ex-parte evidence conclusive of the master's right to recapture and return his slave: that denies a jury trial here or elsewhere; that provides for the appointment of swarms of petty officers to execute it; that gives a double compensation to find every claim set up in favor of the master and pays the expenses in any case from the public treasury—ought never to receive the voluntary co-operation and ought therefore to be immediately repealed."

To disobey the law, said the newly appointed U.S. secretary of state, Daniel Webster, in a speech in New York a few months later, and to pass resolutions denouncing the law, as conventions in New York, Ohio, and Massachusetts had just done, was "distinctly treasonable." And he called a recent rescue of a black waiter, apprehended as a fugitive under the new law, from a Boston courtroom during his trial, "an act of clear treason . . . and nothing less."

Politicians made their pronouncements, advocates passed their resolutions, and conductors on the Underground Railroad destroyed the records of their double lives. But the hateful law remained, pitting neighbor against neighbor, provoking cruel and preposterous suspicions, and riding with spur and rein over the freedoms of all who lived beyond the river.

CHAPTER TWENTY-EIGHT

NEIGHBORS

One March morning in 1852, Theodore Collins looked out a second story window of his house on Front Street and saw his neighbor, Ira H. Shaw, walking at a swift, determined gait with his family toward downtown. Shaw was a brother of Franklin Shaw, the bully arrested for beating Benjamin Templeton back in 1831, and Chancey Shaw, the slave hunter—now working as a butcher—who had helped the slave woman and her child out of the freezing river in 1838. All three were sons of Peter Shaw, the boat builder, who was now a hotelkeeper in town. Typically, for as long as Collins had known him, Ira Shaw left his house at precisely eight-thirty every weekday morning and also on Saturdays. But on Sunday mornings, Collins had never seen Shaw much before nine, when Shaw and his wife and their four children walked to the Methodist church. It was Sunday. It was barely dawn. And Shaw was in a hurry to leave.

Collins was up because he hadn't yet gone to sleep. He had just returned from a trip to Red Oak in the company of two runaway slaves. To see Shaw at this hour was extremely odd, Collins thought, though his exhaustion and his busy day spared him little time to think about it again. Then, later that day, something happened to jolt his memory. On March 13, the *Ripley Bee* published Collins's account of what happened:

Believing that what is the interest of one member of the community concerns the whole, I wish to give you an account of the descent of the Goths & Vandals of the patriarchal institution on Sunday night last, headed by King Alcohol in the persons of Capt. Samuel Owens (formerly clerk of Mason County, Ky), Lieut. Wm. Wood, (alias "Duck Wood") son of Dr. Wood, Ensign Joseph Gilpin, Corporal John Wilson (the roll not being present, the names of the privates were not known.)

About nine o'clock my family and myself having retired, I heard a knock at the door, thinking no ill I said "come in" when lo! The whole "army" was upon me with pistols and cowhides, the Capt. ordering me to lie still as they had been informed by one that had been watching, that there were runaway negroes secreted in the house and they had come with the intention of searching. I ordered them to stand back for I would get up. After I got up I inquired if they had a search warrant.

"No," they said.

"Do you know then that this is a penitentiary offence!" I said.

"Yes," said one of them. "But we could not get a warrant and have had to come in this way and if there are no 'niggers' here you have been much belied."

My son lit the lamp and proposed as they were in the house that if they had any two who they considered gentlemen in the crowd they might search, provided they would be satisfied and go off. They consented and "Capt." Owens and "Lieut." Wood were selected, the rest going out. I then told them that there was no one about the house blacker than they (which by the by would be hard to find anywhere if their color of character is taken into comparison) and the search commenced: Kitchen first, in the fireplace and loft, a small bedroom on the porch, and while "Lieut." Wood was under the bed I told him not to steal anything. Next my daughter's room, and as "Lieut." Wood was going to the bed I ordered him not to go there as it was my daughter's bed, and the next my wife's room and the "Lieut." looked under the trundle bed, my wife telling him that that was a good place to hide "niggers" wasn't it? The "Capt." by this time rather losing zeal, permitted the "Lieut." to take the lead; next, was the parlor after that my daughter in-law's room, she still being in bed. As the "Lieut." entered, my son was sitting on the bed [sic] she raised her head and named the "gentleman" when he started back with an "O, excuse me," next was the garret loft; having no permanent way of getting to it, but to satisfy them I pointed them to a ladder; afterwards the smoke-house, the privy, henhouse, barn, corncrib. This ended the search. As they left finally one of them said, "Let's go. We have been lied to."

Now the question is by whom! Who was Benedict Arnold pro tem? Is it our nearest neighbor? They came directly through his premises, they returned the same way. The watch was stationed there all day Sunday. He went to town remarkably early for him that morning. A certain tavern keeper told that he was at his house all day. Our neighbor was seen talking to Respess, McMillen & Co. [known slave hunters from Kentucky] early in the morning. His children say that his house was searched also. There were signs of horses being hitched in his lane and fence corners—nor has he ever made his appearance to sympathise with us although previously he was very sociable and the hunters knew I was a Presbyterian and knew which door to knock at.

I now take this means of notifying Benedict Arnold and company never to set their feet upon my place for I will consider it trespass. I have been a citizen of Ripley for near forty years and this is the first lie that I recollect of ever being told to injure me.

THEODORE W. COLLINS

Also to the "Capt.," "Lieut." and company, I would say that they came upon me and found me unprepared for entertaining them as they deserve but will be for all time to come. There was not a lock on a door nor a gun nor axe nor any weapon about the house save an old shot-gun that takes a half an hour to kill a chicken.

A few days later, Ira Shaw responded to Collins with a letter in the *Ripley Bee* that was headed "Who Is Benedict Arnold?":

Messrs. Editors:—In reply to Theodore Collins' communication, in the last Bee, I being his "nearest neighbor," I have only to say that every charge in it derogatory to my character is false.

I do not know any man he has named in the search of his house. I have not seen or spoken to McMillen for a month, and if I had, I consider it no concern of Mr. Collins', as I have a right to speak to any man on any subject; and simply because I am not suspected of stealing or secreting negroes, as he is, am I to be held up before the public as a traitor?

Negroes, having the appearance of runaway negroes, were seen going to said Collins' house, and I have no doubt that such is the fact, and I am prepared to prove it—they were seen by a certain person, not watching for such a thing. I charge said Theodore with falsehood in his article, and can prove that also.

If they were all asleep, how do they know the men passed through my place? To reach his house, they must pass through mine or his place.

No one was at my house on Sunday, other than connections of my family—a brother-in-law and his wife and friend from White Oak were on a visit. They and Calvin [no identity given] were the only persons at my house that day, the latter remained less than an hour.

As to sympathizing with him, I do not approve of stealing or harboring negroes, and have no sympathy for any such doings.

To return good for evil, I grant to said Theodore the privilege of passing through my place when convenient and he or any man may hitch his horse to my fences and I will not hold it as trespass.

I. H. SHAW

Next, on March 16, the editors of the *Maysville Eagle* responded to Collins's letter, accusing him of overreacting to what the editors called the "order and gentlemanly deportment" of the men who searched his house. "If the citizens of Ripley wish to shield themselves from having their town and houses searched for stolen negroes, the quickest and most efficient means is to quit concealing property which belongs to other people. The fact that Ripley is a place of concealment for fugitive slaves has long been notorious. It is time that reproach were wiped from the good name of the place. Its citizens should consider their obligations to the law and observe them. Until this begins, there can be no good neighborhood; and unless it be soon done, we fear a rupture that all may deplore. Will the people of Ripley seriously consider this matter?"

PART IV

Beyond the River

My father was always ready and quick to get through any difficulty. He firmly believed that a kind Providence assisted and guided those who earnestly tried to help themselves or others in dire trouble coupled with right.

—John Rankin, Jr.

I was a slave born in Mason County, Kentucky, two miles west of May's Lick. I made arrangements to buy myself for $900 and paid $725 and Wells, my owner, advanced $125 and I was to work for Wells one year in return. I worked for him near two years and then when I spoke to him about it, about my freedom, he wanted to sell me. I wanted a suit of clothes I pretended and got $50 from him and a colt, a bridle, a saddle and a pass. Then I went and got my nephews on the North Fork and was a goin' across the river that very night. I think it was 1858, the latter part of August. We started to Charleston Bottom on the river. They was a white man set us across the river. He lived right in Maysville and set others across by hundreds. We went to Ripley and I found a friend of mine there (black)—Johnson (Gabriel) and he took us up to Rankin's—up on the hill. We stayed there one day and a night. We went afoot from Rankin's through cornfields and woods to New Hope. . . .

—Horace Washington, Windsor, Ontario, Canada, 1895

CHAPTER TWENTY-NINE

Prison Doors

The month of March along the river is when the gods of winter declare war on the invading forces of spring. One day a dozen daffodils will bravely burst through the earth's surface and begin to reach for the sky, and on the next a strong wind moving up the valley will bring sheets of snow and punish them for being so bold. For many people who lived on the river, the 1850s were like one long, tormenting month of March.

By then, the struggle between oppression and conscience in the border counties seemed never-ending, and the hope of abolishing slavery anytime soon seemed dim—especially after politicians succumbed to the South's demand for tougher fugitive-slave legislation. What hope was there to topple a political force so powerful as to persuade Congress to pass such an unconstitutional and unconscionable law?

One hope in Brown County was that the roster of citizens willing to help runaways was growing, and new recruits bolstered the spirits of those who had labored for many years in the underground movement. On the Ripley line, newcomers included seventeen-year-old William Harris Snedaker, who in 1852 began the routine of riding to Red Oak, picking up slaves at the Gillilands' house behind the old stone church, and taking them back to his parents' home in Decatur, where a vast cornfield served as a hiding place until it was safe to take them farther north. Another new recruit was Martha West Lucas, who lived in a row house in Russellville, where, in the 1850s, the owners agreed to connect their attics as a way to thwart slave hunters. Runaways, often on their way to or from the Reverend Jesse Lockhart's house, also in Russellville, passed through the attics, while Lucas and her three daughters made every effort to confuse and delay the hunters.

Still, antiabolitionists and Southern-sympathizers in Brown County outnumbered those in sympathy with the conductors of the underground movement, and the work of sequestering runaways had become increasingly dangerous and complicated. With slave catching now a bustling enterprise along the river, more eyes watched and more dogs sniffed than ever before. There were far fewer places to hide on the Kentucky banks because farmers had chopped down the once-dense forests along the river to build their houses and expand their arable lands. And there were decreasing numbers of slaves along the northern Kentucky border to guide runaways to the river because by the 1850s many had escaped or been sold to Southern traders.

At the same time, the identities of Ripley-area conductors, including Parker, the Collins brothers, Beck, the Pettijohns, the Hugginses, and the Rankins, were well known among the mercenaries on both sides of the river—an unveiling that had begun with the Mahan trial. Although the activities of the underground were covert and its participants exercised more caution after the passage of the 1850 law, the existence of such a network was widely known. Because of this, there was a budding industry of con artists who told slaves they were part of the Underground Railroad and then turned them in for the reward. Trust was becoming more and more an issue throughout the underground movement. Near Ripley, just over the line into Adams County, for example, a scoundrel by the name of Fountain Pemberton was in the habit of searching the local papers for notices of cash rewards for runaways and then hunting them down. He had been able to buy a house and a small parcel of land with the proceeds from his betrayals. Then, one day, under the guise of kindness, he tricked a fugitive into his kitchen in order to capture him, but the fugitive pulled a razor, made his getaway, and by some accounts ended Pemberton's career. Also operating in and around Ripley for a number of years was a black man named Robert Russell, about whom many handbills were written and circulated in the 1850s throughout northern Kentucky and southern Ohio. "Beware the Rogue, Robert Russell!" said one handbill out of Covington, Kentucky, "who absconded from Ripley, Ohio, to evade the strong arm of the law he rightly deserved and who will as readily take ten dollars from any of your slaves to bring them to Cincinnati and again take ten dollars to return them to you, as he has no higher purpose than to serve his paltry self."

As in every decade since the early years of the century, slave escapes were on the rise, which meant three things: more midnight intrusions by friends and foes knocking at the doors of the homes of people known to help runaways; more rewards for the heads of abolitionists; and more oppressive legal efforts on the part of Kentucky politicians to please their slaveholding constituents and to stop the loss of their property. By the 1850s, Kentucky newspapers were running ads for the latest trend: slave insurance. And banks were no longer accepting the "property" of slaves as collateral.

In early October 1852, the *Maysville Eagle*—and the *New York Daily Tribune*—reported that thirty-two slaves from Mason and Bracken counties in Kentucky had escaped into Ohio. "Three of them were captured some 35 miles back of Ripley," the paper said, "but owing to the facilities afforded for flight in Ohio, the probability is that the residue will make good their escape. It is beyond question that fugitive slaves are afforded protection, means and facilities by people of Ohio."

A week later, at a mass meeting of slaveholders from Mason and Bracken counties, held in Maysville, a man who had recently interviewed runaways in Canada reported that one former Kentucky slave told him "that every slave he knew in Kentucky was 'making up their minds to leave,' that they had discovered it was 'wrong to serve a master,' and that they knew now that the Bible was against slavery." The man said he could verify the escape of two hundred slaves in the previous two months. He concluded, "We may rightfully apprehend that some disastrous undercurrent has been at work in the state which we as slaveholders must meet and meet it now!"

Later in 1852, the Kentucky legislature passed a law that called for the appointment of slave patrols of up to thirty men in the counties along the Ohio River, "whose duty it shall be to guard and watch the places for crossing the river, to notice the condition and situation of all water craft upon the Kentucky shore of the Ohio river," and who were given the power to arrest without warrant any "person found lurking about with intention to afford assistance by advice or otherwise to any slave to escape from his master."

During the same year in Kentucky, a law passed that prohibited ferry owners from allowing slaves on their boats without the owners or without a document of ownership certified and on file at a county courthouse. If any slaves were caught on the ferry without such authorization, the ferry operator would lose his license, be fined $200, and be liable for the value of the slave.

When the Kentucky legislators passed a bill to charter a company to build the first suspension bridge across the Ohio River, they inserted a provision making that company liable "for all slaves who escape through its connivance." "This, we suppose, means those who escape by crossing the bridge," wrote the editors of *The Anti-Slavery Bugle,* of Salem, Ohio. The *Bugle* went on to note that Kentuckians were ever suspicious that "fugitive slaves who sometimes find it difficult to cross the Ohio River either by swimming or otherwise, would doubtless rejoice in the building of such a bridge and use it more for their own than their masters' benefit."

Kentucky had made the legal system into a powerful weapon in the war against its own abolitionists and those north of the river. Chief among the state's deterrents to antislavery activism was the threat of incarceration in Kentucky's state penitentiary in Frankfort. As early as 1801, the state penal code had called for a penalty of two to nine years for "slave stealing," and in 1830 legislators voted to increase the penalty to twenty years for anyone guilty of "seducing or enticing a slave to leave his lawful owner." And the law was enforced, though more arrests were made than cases successfully tried. In one week in November 1853, two free blacks in Bracken County, Henry and Isaac Ramsey, were tried for helping a slave escape; Isaac was acquitted for lack of witnesses, and Henry was dismissed because of a hung jury. A few days later, two white men, both schoolteachers, who had come into the state to help two slaves at Brooksville were indicted, paid their bail, and then fled to Ohio.

Still, between 1844 and 1864, forty-four men and women in Kentucky would be convicted of the crime of helping runaways. More prisoners were likely serving time for the same crime, which instead of being specifically described in the record books as "assisting slaves," was listed as simply "a felony." Of those forty-four, twenty-four were white, of whom ten were from the free states; only one black prisoner had been born north of the Ohio. Seven of the forty-four were women. Fourteen of the prisoners were eventually pardoned. Twenty served their time. One escaped. One had his sentence overturned. And eight died in their cells.

Among those who died was a much-beloved resident of Augusta, Kentucky, who was arrested in September 1852 for assisting the slave of Blackstone H. Rankins and after a trial in 1853 was sentenced to three years in the penitentiary. Dr. Perkins, as he was called, was a seventy-six-year-old free black man who made his living baking breads and cakes for the people of Augusta. He also helped runaways any chance he could get. After he entered prison, the residents of Augusta began a campaign to urge the Kentucky governor to grant executive clemency for Perkins because of his age. But the governor rejected the petition, and eight months later the old man died.

In Brown County, residents of the Gist settlements and participants in the Ripley line were outraged when George Williams was arrested in the hills behind Red Oak in August 1856 and incarcerated in Kentucky. Slaves belonging to Dr. James E. McDowell in Mason County had escaped across the river, and slave hunters with dogs following the scent came upon Williams. One of the ruffians put a knife to Williams's throat, accused him of helping slaves, and threatened to "cut his guts out" if he didn't confess. Not surprisingly, he did. Later, in documents filed with the court, he stated that he had been forced to confess against his will. Still, he was convicted of assisting slaves and sent to prison in Kentucky on October 31, 1856. On December 29, 1858, the thirty-five-year-old free black man, serving time for a crime he didn't commit, died. The cause was listed as "consumption."

Another free black "conductor" who died in Kentucky's penitentiary was Elijah Anderson. Born free in Virginia, Anderson later moved to Madison, Indiana, downriver from Ripley, where he prospered as a blacksmith by day and worked as an active member of the "black underground" by night. In 1856, Anderson was arrested by Louisville policemen after another black man betrayed him for the reward money. A few years later, at age fifty-three, Anderson, who had helped hundreds of runaways, died in his cell, allegedly of a heart attack.

Conditions for abolitionist prisoners were reportedly worse than for others. Calvin Fairbank, an Oberlin student who became a well-known conductor of fugitive slaves across the Ohio, served a total of seventeen years and four months in the Kentucky penitentiary for two separate cases. In his autobiography, he wrote that in 1863 he was struck by a club with such force that he was temporarily blinded, and that during eight years of his incarceration he felt the lash upon his back 35,105 times. There was little difference, he wrote, between the life of the prisoner and that of an actual slave.

On May 18, 1855, a sixty-year-old Irishman, Thomas Brown, entered the Kentucky penitentiary after a conviction for "abducting slaves" in Union County, Kentucky. After his release, Brown recounted the brutality of his jail term in a book, *Three Years in Kentucky Prisons*. In it, he alleged that the warden, who had "a wish to be permitted to hang" all abolitionists, was out to get him from the start. Once a guard flogged him "till his blood ran upon the floor" because he had supposedly failed to perform a task properly. And when he complained of this to another prisoner, the same guard punched him so hard that he fell to the ground unconscious with two fewer teeth. A few weeks later, he was beaten again for not eating the crust on his bread. In his book, Brown told the story of another antislavery inmate, a free black man from Evansville, Indiana, who died in March 1857 "after receiving a severe blow from one of the keepers." The cause of death was listed as "congestion of the lungs."

If Kentucky politicians were intent on effectively making the state a prison for slaves and abolitionists, Kentucky citizens were to be its jailers. After the passage of the Fugitive Slave Law, reward posters for the heads of abolitionists were so commonly tacked to tree trunks in northern Kentucky that they seemed a natural part of every wooded glen. By the early 1850s, there was a price on just about every known conductor's head, the newest addition being John Parker.

Parker was one of the few abolitionists who dared venture into the South to guide slaves to the North, and as a free black he risked the loss of his freedom. His actions inspired hefty rewards for his capture or death, and sparked criticism among his colleagues in the movement. Rankin and other conductors, such as Coffin, did not approve of such aggressive forays. They believed it was their duty to help a slave who asked for their help, but they rarely would invade the land of slavery and take what was deemed in that land as the property of others—only if it was necessary for saving the lives of fugitives who, as in the "Parker's Ferry" case, had already taken the initiative to leave on their own. They also objected for political and practical reasons, because they knew as residents of border counties that such actions could escalate the violence in their own neighborhoods.

Parker was clearly in a tiny minority within the abolitionist minority, which by the 1850s included Harriet Tubman, the former Maryland slave who made an estimated nineteen raids into the South. Through swamps and thickets, sometimes in disguise, always with a pistol, often on a Saturday night, she brought hundreds of slaves out of bondage. And in the 1840s and 1850s, the Virginian John Fairfield sometimes pretended to be a slave trader to get close enough to organize groups of slaves. Once, in the 1840s, Fairfield, who was incarcerated several times but always escaped, spent a long, harsh winter in the Bracken County, Kentucky, jail and became quite ill from the cold and dampness of his cell. With the help of friends, he escaped to Ripley before his trial and lived with the Rankins for two weeks while recovering.

On one of Parker's excursions into enemy territory, he was walking along a tree-lined road after a meeting with slaves in Charleston Bottom, Kentucky, about four miles west of Maysville. And out of the corner of an eye, he kept seeing what appeared to be identical pieces of paper tacked to trees and fenceposts. They were so numerous that he was curious enough to strike a match and take a look. What he saw stunned him: a poster asking for his own capture or death for a price of $1,000. He later said, "I did not go off whistling after I had read that sinister offer for my head, because I knew how deadly in earnest the men were who authorized billeting me from every fence corner as being worth $1,000 to any rascal who saw me."

Such was the appeal of the large reward that Parker suddenly became a target for abduction and murder. In the days after he discovered the poster, he slowly awakened to the fact that he was being followed and watched, night and day. He and his colleagues back in Ripley met to discuss the problem and decided that for a while there must be a moratorium on Parker's work on the line. Further, until his stalkers backed off, Parker decided that going into Kentucky was too dangerous. His cohorts agreed to stop directing runaways to his house until they could determine that the spies had dispersed. Grounded from picking up slaves in Kentucky as well as from guiding them from his house up to Rankin's or on to Red Oak, Parker was frustrated. Eventually, his impatience exploded into action.

One night, two groups of fugitive slaves arrived at the Collins house on Front Street, one just after the other. While Thomas Collins was escorting the first group, someone in town led the other group to Parker's house. This person, though sympathetic to the cause, was unaware of Parker's vulnerable position. Parker and his wife assessed the group, applying their years of experience to determine whether or not this was a setup. Trusting both the guide and the slaves, they let the fugitives into the house. But Parker knew if he left with them the watchers in the shadows around his house would follow. So he decided this was the time to take action. He left the house alone and started up the alley next to his foundry, very slowly. At the corner of Second Street, he found a dark place near a house and waited. When his stalker made the turn, he grabbed the man by his arm, shoved him into the light of the moon, and pressed a knife to his chest. Parker informed him that he knew the man's Kentucky friends were paying him, that he was tired of being watched, and that he would kill the man and his friends if he ever found the man trailing him again. Parker was back to work on the Ripley line that night. And the stalker never returned to the shadows and alleys of Front Street.

CHAPTER THIRTY

THE QUICKENING FLOW

Early one February morning in 1856, a medley of moaning and cracking serenaded the people who lived on Front Street. During the night, Ripley's network of creeks had deposited immense quantities of ice in the river, and the floes were now pushing against each other as if in a race downriver to beat the inevitable lockup of a deep-freeze. At the same time, temperatures had plummeted. By daybreak, the sheets of floating ice were congealing, and what would be the deepest and longest freeze of the decade had commenced.

The river had already frozen from shore to shore several times during the 1850s, in the winters of 1850–51 and 1852–53. But the early-1856 freeze was by far the worst, lasting several weeks and resulting in hundreds of thousands of dollars in damage to steamboats and their cargoes. Kentucky slaveholders claimed their losses were just as dire: Dozens of their slaves, they claimed, had taken the "bridge of ice" to Ohio.

"The underground railroad has been doing an uncommonly thriving business," wrote the editors of the *Cincinnati Gazette* in February 1856. Another newspaper, the *Daily Columbian,* in Columbus, Ohio, told of three slaves who reached the river at Covington and, "on coming in sight of it, retreated in fear on account of the number of people on it. They came upon a horse and sleigh standing hitched at a residence, jumped into it, rushed off at lightning speed for the other side of Jordan, leaving the sleigh standing on the other side of the river." The *Maysville Eagle* noted, "A party of five slaves in Mason County borrowed their master's horse and sleigh for a ride three or four days ago and crossing the river upon the ice, they effected their escape."

On the first day when a firm sheet of ice appeared to connect Kentucky and Ohio, townsfolk in Ripley gathered on the riverbank to determine whether or not the time had come to walk upon the ice and test its strength. Children fetched their skates in rapt anticipation of a go-ahead gesture from one of the adults, who seemed to be more interested in talking about past years when the river had frozen. Repeating stories they had heard in their families every time the river froze, some spoke of the years when Kentucky was simply the other side of a river and not an almost separate nation. They talked in sentimental tones of the innocence and relative peace of bygone years. Some recalled 1838 and the incident of the horse and sleigh; they spoke of it "as a better time." So very much had changed. Jimmy Campbell, one of the first to test the ice back in 1838, was now Dr. James Campbell and, following his father's lead in more ways than one, he had long been an active member of the Ripley Anti-Slavery Society. Samuel Rankin, another skater that day, was now the pastor of a Presbyterian church in a small town in Connecticut. After graduating from Lane Seminary, John Rankin, Jr., was also a pastor, in Indiana. Ripley's double life, still a cherished secret in 1838, was now widely known. Even the *Ripley Bee* now openly discussed it. In a recent front page article, the "Bee" editors had written, "We learn from 'official sources' that the Underground Railroad, a big branch of which runs through this city, up to the Canadian frontier, has been doing an unusually large business this year. Some days the 'train' takes a dozen at a time, and the aggregate business of the year is counted by hundreds."

In 1856, John Rankin still had a price on his head and still, despite all that had happened, was clinging to the hope of a peaceful resolution to the slavery conflict. By now he had faced, and overcome, a multitude of disappointments and losses—among them, the typhoid death of his son David Wilmot, the loss of his congregation and resulting need to launch a new branch of the Presbyterian Church, and, most recently, on March 10, 1856, the death of his youngest daughter, Lucinda, in Urbana, Illinois.

But Rankin's most prolonged struggle in the 1840s and 1850s—his antislavery activities excluded—was with his congregation. The story was a common one among abolitionists. Just ninety or so miles away, in

Franklin, Ohio, the antislavery militant, John Brown, several years before, had drawn attention to the racial discrimination in seating at his church—the blacks forced to sit way in the back—and thus gave up his family's "slip" of seats to the blacks. He was soon the victim of a hitherto unknown rule that expelled him from the church. Rankin, in the early 1840s, had called upon his church to expel the slaveholders, and indeed had urged all Presbyterians to do this. Many among the 220 members of his own Ripley congregation agreed with him. Others did not. Two of the latter—one from Russellville and one from Georgetown—were proslavery men who were determined to rid their church of Rankin and his dangerous notions. But to banish him for his beliefs when so many others respected him was not smart, and so they obfuscated the issue, finding bogus reasons to call for his expulsion.

First, they lodged a complaint that Rankin spent too much time away from the pulpit. They specifically attacked his time at Ripley College, a thorny issue to begin with because Rankin had encouraged the enrollment of black students. And there were his many days on the road preaching against slavery—nearly a year, back in the mid-1830s. Next, they tried to prove that he had acted unethically—perhaps even illegally—regarding certain financial transactions. After all, Rankin was forever stitching together his income with creative combinations of real-estate deals, farm produce, and his published works to keep his family fed and clothed and to pay for his antislavery work. It wasn't hard to cull pieces of his financial puzzle and fabricate a story around them.

In the early 1840s, not long after Rankin had called for Presbyterians to consider leaving the church because of the slavery question, he had tried to ease his financial troubles by handing over parts of his land to a son and a son-in-law and in exchange giving them title bonds. Eventually, after the land was paid off, he would give them ownership. Their monthly payments would then provide him with enough money to make monthly installments to his creditors. But his two arch-enemies in the church distorted the story, telling members that he was hiding assets from his creditors. The men beat the drum of dishonesty and created enough skepticism of Rankin in the church that some members whispered among themselves about the possibility of his dismissal. His loyal followers knew that it was a trumped-up charge and that at the heart of the campaign against him was the fear of his commitment to the abolitionist cause and the alarm over knowing that their church's leader was, in the eyes of the public, fanatical about that cause. "I had no reason to believe that before these two men began their labors for Satan, there were three other persons in the whole church who desired me to leave it," Rankin later wrote.

At one point the two men came to him and said he should ask for a raise in salary from $350 to $500; if the congregation could afford it—it appeared that it could—then the money would be paid. But if the congregation could not afford it, he would agree to leave. Rankin was smart enough to see that the advice was meant to deceive him; if he indeed asked for the raise, the two men would block the raising of the funds to corner him into leaving.

One Sunday morning, Rankin asked his son Adam Lowry to preach in his place. At the close of the service, Lowry read his father's request that the congregation vote to release him from his obligations as pastor. And so, in the autumn of 1846, after twenty-four years of serving the Ripley Presbyterian Church, and after inspiring nearly two hundred people to join the congregation during those years, Rankin stepped down. He announced his resignation and walked out the door of his church for the last time. Seventy-four members of the congregation—one-third of the membership—followed him.

"This was one of the greatest afflictions of my life," he later wrote. "I never endured at any other time such agony of spirit. To see a church that I had brought from thirty-six to two hundred and twenty members, that had to a great extent controlled the morals of the town, that had always been harmonious, and for which I had labored twenty-four years and made for it every sacrifice in my power, now violently torn asunder was heart rending."

Following his resignation, Rankin started the Free Presbyterian Church and commenced gathering materials for the construction of a new building on August 1 that year. Among those who generously gave money for the building of the new church and who publicly stood by Rankin was Theodore Collins. To allow more money to be allocated to the building, Rankin served his first year at the new church without pay. By spring the following year, the building was completed and the fledgling branch of the Presbyterian church began to grow, though very slowly. Eventually, there would be seventy-two congregations in the Free Church, mostly in southern Ohio and western Pennsylvania, some as far away as Iowa and New York. For now, the task of attracting new members was intense, but Rankin approached it with hope and with the satisfaction that he had acted morally and with faith. Never dwelling on the past, he marched forward, trying not to think about the pain of what he had left behind. But just as he was recovering from one loss, he sustained another. On Christmas Day, 1847, his twenty-nine-year-old son, David Wilmot, died at his home in Ripley after struggling against typhoid fever.

In the late 1840s and throughout the 1850s, Rankin was hit by more and more attacks against his *Letters on Slavery* and other commentaries. Denigrating and ridiculing his fervent pleas to recognize the evils of slavery, the campaign against him was provoked partly by the inclusion of his work in Theodore Weld's widely distributed book *Slavery As It Is*. Weld called upon several writers, whom he called "witnesses," to describe in detail all aspects of slavery. As a witness, Rankin wrote six accounts in Weld's book. For many people who had not read Rankin's *Letters on Slavery,* the Weld book, which was more widely circulated than the letters and excerpted in various publications nationwide, was an introduction to Rankin. And so he gained a new audience of admirers and foes. It was his contribution to the Weld book that likely provoked Southern delegates in Congress in January 1849 to rip asunder Rankin's descriptions of slavery as it was.

"We presume that we are better acquainted with the fields of Alabama than Mr. Rankin," said one senator from Tennessee, "and we can assure him that we have never seen what he states 'that you may see their slaves in the cotton fields without so much as even a single rag upon them, shivering before the chilling blast of winter.' A greater lie than this, we believe, was never told. That a negro might have been seen naked at work in the summer at his own will and pleasure may be possible for they are very fond of throwing off most of their clothes in hot weather; but that Rankin ever saw or anyone else a negro or negroes either of his own will or by compulsion of his master laboring naked in the fields in winter shivering before the chilling blast of midwinter is grossly false, blatantly untrue. . . . That our ladies whip, beat and kick their servants and compel them to work when laboring under mortal disease. . . . Is it possible that Mr. Rankin could succeed in obtaining believers that such barbarity would be received in our community?"

In the 1840s, Rankin and other antislavery writers had begun to encounter obstacles to getting their pamphlets published by the American Tract Society. And so, at a large antislavery convention in Chicago, Rankin proposed the organization of "an Antislavery Tract Society." Everyone agreed, but nothing came of it until another convention a few years later, in 1851, in Cincinnati. At this one, Rankin again suggested the formation of a publication society that would publish tracts against all forms of oppression, including American slavery. The meeting took place in the Vine Street Congregational Church, and the small, enthusiastic audience voted unanimously to support Rankin's idea. Soon Presbyterians, Congregationalists, and Quakers joined in the cause. Rankin then went on the road to raise funds in New York, New Jersey, Pennsylvania, and even as far as Bangor, Maine. He spent a total of seven months traveling and raised $3,000. The name of the society became the Western Tract and Book Society.

Rankin wrote at least eight lengthy tracts for the new society, including one about the 1850 Fugitive Slave Law. The new law, Rankin wrote, was "a standing monument of the most high handed wickedness ever a nation did." His tract, published in English and German, was widely circulated and, as newspaper commentaries revealed, it was well received—except in Ripley, where his ardent denunciation of a law that he believed to be unconstitutional inspired threats of violence and, once again, the visits of thugs to his land. At one point in the autumn of 1855, two thousand copies of the tract were taken off a boat docked at Ripley's wharf and burned on the bank of the river.

In early 1857, the river froze yet again. "The ice continues to grow thicker and firmer daily. The landing presents a bleak and icy dreariness," reported a Cincinnati paper on January 10. On January 16, it reported, "No material change in the river since our last report. The ice is still increasing in solidity." And on January 21: "No favorable change to report in the river at this point. The water is gradually receding, but the ice remains firm and daily increasing in solidity. Yesterday snow fell to the depth of half an inch or more. During the night it again turned cold and this morning is nearly as cold as any day of the season." After weeks of oppressive weather, the river finally broke up on February 4, Rankin's sixty-fourth birthday. On February 8, when the river had cleared, navigation resumed.

In March of that year, Rankin received an invitation to speak at an antislavery convention planned for August in Cleveland. Its purpose was to organize a National Compensation Emancipation Society whose constitution would call for "the extinction of slavery by a system of compensation to the slaveholder." He consented to travel to Cleveland and to speak on behalf of a theory that, as he described, promoted a "generous and brotherly spirit between the peoples of the North and South so that the North should share liberally in the expense of putting an end to so great a moral and political evil as American slavery." At the convention he proposed several resolutions. Among them: that "the American people should make their common Government their agent in this matter and should call on

Congress to pay to each State that shall abolish Slavery a sum not exceeding two hundred and fifty dollars for each and every slave emancipated, each State providing for any additional remuneration that it may deem proper."

Rankin had promoted the compensation system for many years and was accustomed to the outrage that it often evoked, even from his abolitionist brethren, including William Lloyd Garrison, who railed repeatedly against the notion. As early as 1819, while he was still in Kentucky, Rankin had published an article in a religious paper from Chillicothe, Ohio, in which he urged the government to purchase the slaves and set them free. Now he was clinging to this idea and promoting it as he had never before, as one of the last hopes for averting the violence that seemed more inevitable to him each day. But he must have known how futile such a cause had become, for, by the mid-1850s, a series of events, like storm-whipped waves on the river, was sweeping hope from every region of the nation.

In May 1856, Charles Sumner, the esteemed U.S. senator from Massachusetts and an antislavery radical, delivered an ardent speech on the floor of Congress about the bitter divisions over slavery in the state of Kansas. Three days later, South Carolina Representative Preston Brooks marched into the Senate chambers and struck Sumner on the head with his cane, brutally beating the senator into a state of unconsciousness from which he would recover only with lasting injuries.

Worse still was the case of Dred Scott, the following year. A slave from Missouri, Scott had once accompanied his master, John Emerson, to live in Illinois, a free state since the 1787 Northwest Ordinance, and then into the Wisconsin Territory, free because of the 1820 Missouri Compromise. After returning to Missouri with Emerson, he believed himself to be free. Emerson, a U.S. Army surgeon, died in 1843, and in 1846 Scott put his convictions and his courage to the test: He sued Emerson's widow, claiming that he should be free because of the years he had spent living on free soil. Was Dred Scott a slave or a freeman? In 1857, the question finally came before the U.S. Supreme Court, where seven proslavery justices ruled that black people—including all free blacks—could not be U.S. citizens and therefore did not have the right to sue. Chief Justice Roger Taney said that black people were "so inferior that they had no rights which the white man was bound to respect." The ruling also struck down the part of the Missouri Compromise that banned slavery in the U.S. territories north and west of the state of Missouri. The federal government had no authority, the justices said, to control slavery in territories before they became states, effectively ruling that the Missouri Compromise was unconstitutional. In response, Frederick Douglass said, "This very attempt to blot out forever the hopes of an enslaved people may be one necessary link in the chain of events preparatory to the complete overthrow of the whole slave system."

The other links in that chain came together quickly. In early 1859, the Southern Commercial Convention called for the reopening of the African slave trade, which had been closed for decades. Later that year, John Brown and his followers seized the arsenal at Harper's Ferry, Virginia, as part of a grand scheme to incite a great slave revolt. In the 1860 election, slavery was the central issue, and South Carolina said it would secede from the Union if Abraham Lincoln won the vote. He did.

To avert secession, U.S. Senator John Jordan Crittenden of Kentucky proposed a compromise that protected slavery below latitude 36 degrees 30 minutes, allowed slavery to remain in the states where it already existed, and called on the government to compensate slaveholders for the loss of their runaway slaves if it could be established that they had in fact been assisted in their escape by men and women in the North. This proposal was rejected by Congress.

On December 20, South Carolina seceded from the Union, followed quickly by Mississippi, Florida, Alabama, Georgia, Louisiana, and Texas. On February 4, 1861, delegates from those states met in Montgomery, Alabama, to set up a provisional government for the Confederate States of America.

On that date, February 4, 1861, John Rankin turned sixty-eight, but there was little jubilation. On Ripley's highest hill, everyone could see the gathering clouds of war. And by March, the melting snows of a hard winter caused the nearby creeks to flood and the river to rage.

CHAPTER THIRTY-ONE

BROKEN VESSEL

When the Confederate forces opened fire on Fort Sumter on April 12, 1861, John Rankin had been denouncing the evils of slavery for forty-five years. With his fellow abolitionists, his wife, his children, and now even his older grandchildren, he had waged an undeclared war against its defenders. He had taught his nine sons how to march in a silent army, without parades, without uniforms, without flags. Now, in the spring and summer months of 1861, he would say goodbye to five of his sons and one grandson as they joined the forces of an official war. It was a war that Rankin had feared to be inevitable for a long while, perhaps since that night in 1841 when he first understood his own temptation toward violence to defend his family from the midnight assassins.

A week after the attack on Sumter, Ripley's town council, headed by one of the sons of Theodore Collins and one of Rankin's sons, Richard Calvin, called an emergency meeting in the Methodist church to discuss what to do about their neighbors across the river. Because Ripley had been plagued for decades by marauding mercenaries from Kentucky chasing down runaway slaves and punishing those who assisted them, and because Kentuckians were so very bitter over the loss of their property, the potential for an outbreak of unrestrained fighting on the banks of the Ohio demanded some sort of defensive treaty, Ripley's leaders thought. Besides, so many people in Ripley had a friend or a relative on the other side. And once in a while when the water was low, people remembered when the river had seemed like a mere road winding through the same hills and farmlands where people with the same dreams and fears had planted their fields, borne their children, and worshiped their God.

Earlier in April, Kentucky's governor had refused calls for volunteers from both the Union and the Confederacy. In the weeks ahead, he would issue a proclamation of neutrality for the state of Kentucky, where 20 percent of the population, or roughly 225,000 people, were slaves. But recruiters were already flooding the state from both sides. Kentucky would remain neutral throughout the war, but neither side would respect Kentucky's neutrality. However, the people of Ripley—both proslavers and antislavers—did; they showed their respect by initiating the "treaty."

There were thirty-seven hundred citizens in Ripley now. In the past twenty years, the town had more than tripled in size. There were four hotels, seven churches, four lawyers, eight physicians, twenty-five wholesale and retail groceries, three hardware stores, three billiard saloons, six shoestores, two breweries, three lumber yards, three coal yards, five pork-packing houses, five tobacco warehouses, and seven dry-goods stores with annual sales of at least $120,000 each. With the advent of the new gasworks in 1860, Front Street and its alleys now had gas lamps, and every night was as bright as a full moon over the river.

"Altogether this city may be considered as possessing all the requisites of wealth and comfort," wrote a visitor in 1861. "The climate salubrious, the water excellent, the general health of the people unsurpassed, and each year a reliable expansion in business and population."

Although nearly everyone in Ripley had anticipated war for months, if not years, its abhorrent ramifications had not begun to penetrate even the most perceptive minds. The resolutions that came out of the April meeting seemed like a naïve effort to control the horrors that war was sure to bring. The resolutions read that, although the townsfolk were determined "to defend themselves against invasions, attacks or unlawful interference from any quarter," they could not contemplate any "hostilities against their neighbors across the river and do not condone any movements hostile to them." The Ripley councilmen sent their resolutions to Maysville, Dover, and Augusta, and within days they received enthusiastic responses from each.

And then came the reality of war. Those who had fought in the wars against Britain were gone; their sons and daughters, some of whom were alive now, had been too young to remember war. And so it was that the grandsons of those who had fought for freedom more than eighty years before would be going to war to complete the job begun by their grandfathers: to gain freedom for all Americans. But they knew nothing of war.

There were no railroads yet through southern Ohio, so boats were the means of transporting troops there. As an important river port, Ripley became one of the main recruiting centers of the North. From Company E, Seventh Ohio Cavalry, to Company H, Twelfth Ohio Volunteer Infantry, to Company A, Fifty-ninth Ohio Infantry, most of the troops from the southern half of the state assembled in what became known as Camp Ripley.

Ripley men who were too old or too young to enlist formed their own Home Guard to defend the town, which was frequently threatened. When the Confederate John Morgan's brother moved his raiders through northern Brown County and the towns of Sardinia and Georgetown, it was the men of the Home Guard who removed the nails from the planks in all the bridges over the creeks surrounding Ripley, and who waited in the hollows for long hours in anticipation of the raiding party.

Many of the sons of the Ripley line enlisted in the Union Army, including boys from the Huggins, Beck, Collins, Campbell, Gilliland, and Pettijohn families, as well as the five sons of John Rankin. John Parker supervised the recruitment of Ripley's free blacks. His own three sons—Cassius Clay, Hale Giddings, and Horatio—were too young to serve.

Only a few days after the April 1861 meeting, Richard Calvin Rankin enlisted in the Twelfth Ohio Regiment; later, he joined the Fourth Independent Cavalry, where he became a captain. Adam Lowry Rankin served in the First Brigade of the Second Division of the Fifteenth Army Corps; Major General W. T. Sherman commanded the Second Division, and Major General U. S. Grant, whom Adam Lowry had known personally during Grant's days at Ripley College and through their mutual friend Jacob Ammen, commanded the Fifteenth Army Corps. Dr. Andrew Campbell Rankin served as a surgeon in several companies throughout the war. Prior to the war, he had ridden with John Brown and Brown's compatriot Jim Lane. William Alexander Rankin served as chief quartermaster of the cavalry command in Sherman's Atlanta campaign and was entrusted with the transportation supplies of the entire cavalry forces of the Army of the Cumberland; in August 1863, while he was waiting for his military assignment, he and his cousin John Knox Rankin had a scuffle with Confederate General William Quantrill's men on the streets of Lawrence, Kansas.

John Thompson Rankin—also referred to as John Rankin, Jr.—was a quartermaster in an Illinois regiment. And Rankin's grandson John C. Rankin—one of the children whom the Rankins had raised after their son David's death—was a private soldier who served in the Army of the Ohio, the Army of the Tennessee, and the Army of the Cumberland. He fought throughout the countryside of East Tennessee, and after the siege of Knoxville, he joined Sherman's army, remaining with it until the fall of Atlanta.

Back in Ripley, runaway slaves continued to find their way to Rankin's hill. Joseph Settles was one, in early 1863. A slave on the Wilson farm in Mays Lick—nine miles from Maysville—Settles, who drove the carriage for his master, had watched as his siblings were sold to Southern traders after the master's wife had died. Taking charge of the slaves was the owner's sixteen-year-old daughter, who often beat Settles's wife. One early spring night, Settles, with his wife, their baby daughter, and his brother-in-law, who was the overseer of the plantation, took off for the river. Slave catchers who routinely patrolled land near the river spotted them and began the pursuit. Hearing the pervasive sounds of hunters coming from somewhere behind them, the slaves moved quickly, until they came upon a high wooden fence at which time the baby started to cry—loudly. Settles scaled the fence and helped his wife over. Then without a word spoken, the brother-in-law threw the wailing baby over the tall structure. Settles caught his daughter and soon all four were piling into a skiff bound for the Ohio shore. To move as silently as possible over the water, they didn't dare use the oars. By dawn, the skiff had drifted to the mouth of Eagle Creek in Ripley, where Settles took his family to a white friend, John Greiner, with whom they would live for the next two years. Settles quickly learned of other families in Ripley who took in runaways and made arrangements for his friends in Kentucky to stay with them. Four nights later, Settles returned to the Wilson farm and helped eight more slaves across the river.

Around the same time, Arnold Gragston, the slave of Jack Tabb in Mason County, was routinely rowing slaves to Ripley. His first such venture was in 1859. "I never got anything from a single one of the people I carried over the river to freedom," he later said. "I didn't want anything. After I had made a few trips I got to like it and even though I could have been free any night myself I figgered I wasn't gettin' along so bad so I would stay on Mr. Tabb's place and help the others get free. I did it for four years."

And what did he do with the slaves once he arrived in Ripley? "Well, there in Ripley was a man named Mr. Rankins. I think the rest of his name was John. . . ." One night in 1863, shortly after the Emancipation Proclamation freed slaves in the warring Confederate states, but not in Kentucky, Gragston slipped quietly across the river with his wife and, after stopping at the Rankins', continued north to Detroit; he would later return to live in Ripley.

Also, in the early 1860s, one of Rankin's sons, Thomas Lovejoy, escorted four runaway slaves from Ripley all the way to Chatham, Canada. The fugitives sat inside the carriage while Rankin sat up with the driver, a black man who asked Rankin where he had come from. Without telling him his name, he said simply that he had brought the slaves up from the region of Mason and Bracken counties in Kentucky. The driver then told him that he himself had come up from Mason County twenty-nine years before.

When I was a pickaninny waiting on the table for my master at Carlisle, Nicholas County, Kentucky, my master had a friend that often called, a Mr. Rankin, and when they'd be dining together, I heard them talk on the slavery question as I had heard very few white folks talk and my slavemaster believed, he said, just like Mr. Rankin that the slavery business was all wrong. A little later on Mr. Rankin moved away from Carlisle. Some of the smart colored folks told me that he just had to move out of Kentucky, that they had passed laws that it was sedition and a penitentiary offence to teach against slavery in Kentucky. He was doing that all the time, and the niggers all knew that Mr. Rankin was their friend.

And my master, he had a brother-in-law doing a large business in hemp and tobacco, and he failed in his business. My master had to sign a whole lot of notes for him, and that broke up my good master, too. And we niggers was all sold by the sheriff, and I was bought by a man down in Mason County, Kentucky, when I was about 17 years old. I'd been there but a short time when the niggers all told me that my master's old friend, Mr. Rankin, lived only about seven miles from there across the Ohio River.

One Sunday, I walked up on to the hill on the Tuckyhopike and a colored man told me that there where the brick house on the hill stood, a light burned in the window at night, so that the colored man could see where to go to "catch the train on the underground railroad." When I was about 22 years old, I told my master, on Saturday night, that I wanted a pass until Monday morning, so that the patrol wouldn't catch me up on the road and give me ten lashes, as they had a right to give any negro found without a pass away from his plantation. I told him I wanted to go up on Beasley Creek and see me gal. I didn't intend to see no gal, but intended to use that pass to go over to that brick house on the hill, and see if Mr. Rankin could tell me how to get to Canada. If he couldn't, I'd be back home Monday morning all right, as I had plenty of time to make the trip both ways.

I went over to the river, stole a skiff, and paddled it across, went up to Mr. Rankin's house, knocked at the door. Mr. Rankin came to the door. I says, "I specs you don't know me, but I belonged to Mr. So and So, at Carlisle, Nicholas County, Kentucky, where I heered you and me master talk on the slavery question as few white folks talk, an' I jest want to know if you can tell me how to get to Canada? If you can't, I've got a pass until Monday morning and will get back home anyway."

He says, "Come right in," then went to the back hall and called up the stairs, "Samuel, Calvin, John, up like bucks, I have business for you."

Three big boys came down the stairs, saddled up four horses. I never will forget the names of them boys. We rode that night, I think about 21 miles, near the town, Sardinia, and they left me at the house of a man by the name of McFadden. The next night he took me to another station and the friends brought me from house to house in the night until I reached Detroit, and friends there rowed me over the river.

"Have you been about Ripley, lately?" the driver asked.

"Yes," answered Rankin. "I was there a few days ago."

"Is that old gentleman still living there?" asked the innkeeper.

"Yes, he's still there."

"You going back there?"

"Yes, I shall return to Ripley in a short time."

"Well, I'd just like to have that gentleman know that I am one of the colored men that prospered in Canada, as I owe it all to him that I ever got here. I own the hotel where you are going to stop these people tonight, and I own two business buildings nearby; but I own something across the Thames River that is far better than that. A farm and a wife and seven children. They are all Queen Victoria's subjects and there's no Kentucky whip cracking over that family. If you're sure you'll see that gentleman, I will drive you around and show you just what I've got. I think I'm worth $20,000."

When they arrived at their destination, Rankin handed the driver $1.50 in silver, to pay his bill. "You're sure you'll see that old gentleman when you get back to Ripley?"

"Yes," said Thomas Rankin, "yes, I surely will. That man is my father."

The driver broke down. "Take that money, take that money! It burns my hands."

Rankin and many of his fellow abolitionists thought that slavery would not be abolished until a constitutional amendment was passed, and that even then it could never really end until racial prejudice was eradicated. Still, the Emancipation Proclamation was the major turning point in the struggle to end slavery. Not only did it free three million slaves in the rebel states, but it provided military protection for them and enabled their enlistment in the Union Army. In *The Liberator,* Garrison described it as "sublime in its magnitude, momentous and beneficent in its far-reaching consequences, and eminently just and right alike to the oppressor and the oppressed."

Rankin commented on the epochal event in a letter to Garrison several months later. He wrote the letter in response to an invitation to attend the thirtieth anniversary meeting of the American Anti-Slavery Society at Concert Hall in Philadelphia that December. Hundreds of people gathered to celebrate a cause that had condemned abolitionists to the ranks of fanatics back in 1838, when mobs torched Pennsylvania Hall. The cause was now proved to be right. It was public sentiment, as Rankin had preached at the Lane debates, that had been wrong. And here were many of the people who had had the courage to go up against the public sentiment of their times. The hall was decorated with banners inscribed with the writings of John Greenleaf Whittier, among others, and large white posters bearing quotes from Washington, Jefferson, Madison, Monroe, and Clay. Speakers included William Lloyd Garrison, Frederick Douglass, Lucretia Mott, and Wendell Phillips. They cheered the proclamation, honored the early spirits of the movement, and recognized the religious visions that had effectively launched the movement so many years before. At one point, the letters of those who could not attend and would have been honored were read out loud to the audience. Garrison read Rankin's letter.

"The next letter is from one who entered into the anti-slavery field at an earlier period than almost any of us," said Garrison. "Long before my own mind was turned to this subject, he had fully comprehended it, and bravely and faithfully bore an uncompromising testimony for the abolition of slavery. His name deserves to be held in last remembrance. I allude to Rev. John Rankin, of Ohio." And then he read Rankin's letter of November 19, written the same day Lincoln gave the Gettysburg address.

Mr. Garrison—Dear Sir, Your invitation to attend the thirtieth anniversary of the American Anti-Slavery Society has been received. I regret that I am not in circumstances that will enable me to be present at your meeting. You and I have ever been united on the subject of immediate emancipation while we have widely differed in other respects. I feel that my labors must soon close. I am now in the seventy-first year of my age, and of course must soon go the way of all past generations. From my boyhood to the present time, I have opposed the abominable system of American slavery. For the liberation of the slaves I have labored long and suffered much reproach and persecution; but I regret none of the sacrifices I have made for the hapless millions that have been bought and sold as if beasts of the field and deprived of all that makes existence desirable. Nearly forty years have passed away since I began to warn this nation of the ruin that would result from this horrible system of oppression, but now the day of blood has come. The Son of God has come with his rod of iron and dashed those slaveholding governments in pieces as a potter's vessel is broken; and has made the General government tremble on its foundation. "True and righteous are thy judgments, O Lord."

I greatly rejoice in the President's proclamation. No other man ever had the privilege of making a proclamation so magnificent. It is to lift more than three million people from the deepest degradation and misery to dignified life and station as rational beings. And although it is not broad enough to cover the whole field of oppression, it is the fiat that will end the system. He that is higher than the heavens has ordained it, and our brave soldiers in the field are the armies of the Living God to enforce it. Let us thank God and take courage; and not relax our efforts while there is a slave in the land. John Rankin.

After the war, one of Lyman Beecher's sons, the renowned preacher Henry Ward Beecher, was asked, "Who abolished slavery?" His response: "Rev. John Rankin and his sons did it."

CHAPTER THIRTY-TWO

ECHOES

In 1886, on one of those frigid March nights when a beating gale churns up the waters of the river and winter's cruel reign seems endless, six black men with swaths of black crepe draped over their arms, rippling in the wind, waited on the Ripley wharf for the sounds of a boat chugging down the river and waves crashing against a bow. The boat, now late on its journey from Ironton, seventy miles upriver, carried the body of John Rankin.

The next morning, at the church that Rankin had helped to build, Rankin's eighth son, Arthur Tappan, now fifty-one years old, spoke of his father to an audience of blacks and whites who crowded into the pews and the aisles. "The colored people turned out in numbers," the *Ripley Bee* reported. The six black men who had stood on the icy wharf for hours the night before, as well as two of Rankin's sons-in-law and four of his sons—Arthur Tappan, John, Jr., Andrew Campbell, and Richard Calvin—served as pallbearers. Chambers Baird, Jr., wrote a poem in Rankin's memory; its last stanza read: "Dear Hero of our age, thy work is o'er, / Thou canst and needst no more thy warfare wage, / In peace and joy thou sawst thy latest sun; / Thou hast the victor's crown forevermore, / And leav'st to us for blessed heritage, / The faith well-kept, the good fight fought—and won!"

A horse-drawn hearse carried the coffin up Second Street to the cemetery. It was followed by a procession of men, women, and children who either had known John Rankin or had heard stories about him for all the years of their lives. Among them were the Settles family and other former slaves who had remained in Ripley or returned, with their families, years later.

Rankin was ninety-three years old when he died in Ironton from a painful, slow-moving cancer of the face. In the last few months of his life, the disease ate away a portion of his face and one of his eyes; in its final stages, it attacked his brain. He had spent his last years in Ironton, at the home of one of his granddaughters, after the death of his wife, Jean, in 1878. She had died in Lyndon, Kansas, where the Rankins had lived for several years with their youngest son, Thomas Lovejoy. Wherever Rankin lived and however old he was, he continued to preach, to lecture, and to write about racial equality. In his eightieth year, he wrote a fifty-page auto-biography. He was blessed, he wrote, that none of his children or grand-children was even wounded in the Civil War. But he felt pain for the rest of his life that there was a war at all. "I lived to see four million slaves liberated but not in the way I had long labored to have it done."

In later years, Rankin was never interviewed by a journalist or a historian about his activities on the Underground Railroad, but the news of his death may have drawn the attention of a Tennessee journalist who was born in Ripley. Sometime between 1886 and 1889, Frank Gregg, a writer for sev-eral years at the *Chattanooga News* and later for a Cleveland paper, returned to his hometown to find out the truth about Rankin, Ripley, and the story that he had heard for years about a runaway slave woman who crossed the frozen river in 1838 just as the ice was breaking up. Was this the story on which Harriet Beecher Stowe had based her character Eliza? Gregg was cu-rious about the role his town had played in the Underground Railroad and so he sought out those who might still remember, including John Parker, whom he knew as the man who had the habit of walking in the middle of the street. He also interviewed Mrs. Chambers Baird, the elderly wife of the Ripley attorney who had helped John Mahan; Mrs. Charles Campbell, a daughter-in-law of Alexander Campbell; Billy Marshall, a free black man who had lived in Ripley from the 1820s on; Lindsay Jackson, Polly Jackson's brother; and Richard Calvin Rankin, who now lived on Second Street up the alley from the house with the three front doors. His interviews began with John Rankin, Jr.

Gregg wrote in his notes:

I found John Rankin, Jr. living on his farm near Greensburg, Indiana. For some time I had been on the trail of a group of Cromwellian Presbyterians who had settled in the little riverside town of Ripley, Ohio, early in the 19th century. There they preached the abolition of slavery, long before William Lloyd Garrison and his Boston associates. The leader of this group of round-head Presbyterians was Reverend John Rankin, father of my host.

We had finished with the Campbells, McCagues, Gillilands, Collinses, and Beasleys when my host plunged headlong into the Eliza episode. I had heard rumors of the incident when I was in Ripley but no facts. But Mr. Rankin had first hand information on this dramatic episode which was not only interesting but convincing. He was fully aware of the historical significance of the event and so I sat and took notes and listened.

"My narrative opens in my own home which sat on top of a high hill just back of Ripley, Ohio," he began. "I was aroused by father calling up the stairs for my brother Calvin and myself. I had answered that night call too many times not to know what it meant. Fugitive slaves were downstairs. Ahead of us was a long walk across the hills in the dead of night, under a cold winter's sky.

"I was only a boy at the time and like all the boys of the town had been down on the ice that very afternoon, knew the ice was rotten, with air holes and cracks extending almost across the river. So when father said the woman in our home had crossed upon the ice, I could not believe the statement until I heard the woman's own story. . . ."

When Gregg returned to Ripley, he double-checked John, Jr.'s story, which included the detail that the next morning on the banks of the river "a woolen shawl" was found at the place where the woman described the moment when Chancey Shaw reached out to help her onto the land.

"Do you remember an incident of a slave woman carrying her baby crossing the river on the ice?" Gregg asked Mrs. Baird.

"Very well indeed. As it was against the law to give assistance to runaway slaves, no one ever admitted seeing them or rendering them aid. But the next morning after this woman did cross, the town was full of rumors. The poor condition of the ice was what made the people wonder how she did it and lived," said Mrs. Baird.

"There was no doubt in your mind about her crossing?" asked Gregg.

"None whatever, for the next morning someone found the woman's shawl, which she had dropped in her flight," Mrs. Baird said.

Gregg asked Mrs. Campbell the same question and she said, "I remember very distinctly the report of a slave woman escaping with her baby across the ice. Someone picked up her flannel skirt which she had dropped. The man who found the skirt saw her tracks on the ice. The town was full of reports at the time because it was so dangerous."

In turn, Richard Calvin Rankin and Billy Marshall all confirmed the Eliza story for Gregg. So did Lindsay Jackson.

John Parker was an eleven-year-old slave in Alabama when the woman crossed the ice at Ripley, but he told Gregg that John Rankin had personally told him the story. "Strange as it may seem no one placed any importance on the episode when it occurred." Rankin, said Parker, told few people, especially after the release of *Uncle Tom's Cabin* in 1852. "Rankin did not dare confess his knowledge of Eliza openly; nor could Mrs. Harriet Beecher Stowe associate him with the crossing. If she had, he and his sons would have been sent to jail, their property confiscated."

Gregg's interview with Parker, which lasted from sunset one day to sunrise the next, stretched far beyond the Eliza story to Parker's life and to other events in Ripley during the later years of the Underground Railroad. "A fearless man, quick witted and resourceful," Gregg wrote. Parker "went into the country of the 'Enemy,' as he designated it, read the posters for his reward, captured dead or alive, then went on to round up his runaways."

Although a reticent, distant man, Parker was willing to tell his story to Gregg with touching precision. He spoke of risky exploits, such as the time he and a runaway hid in one of Thomas Collins's coffins as slave hunters scoured Collins's workshop in search of them, and the time bounty hunters cornered him on a ferryboat from Cincinnati to Maysville, forcing him to jump into the river. He spoke of his utter hatred of slavery and how it had shaped his life. And he spoke of Rankin and his cohorts on the Underground Railroad.

These echoes, coming to me now and then, take me back to the days and nights when my blood ran fast. My years were few and hatred of slavery [of] which I was a victim prompted me to do what I could to serve my unfortunate brothers. No night was too dark or too cold for me to issue forth on a mission of relief and to those who came knocking at my door. A pair of rusty pistols and a hunting knife grown dull, as old friends whose presence I have not felt for years; with their work finished, they like their owner will soon be forgotten.

Occasionally as I walk down the curbs of the streets through sheer force of habit, I meet white-haired men, bent and stooped with age.

We nod and pass on. These are the few survivors of a group whom I knew in their youth and vigor, who answered my rappings in the dead of night. . . .

With the help of John Parker and John Rankin, Jr., Gregg uncovered a small part of Ripley's double life during the war before the war, but the truth of the Ripley line and all who participated, both slave and free, would surface only slowly over many decades.

One day in the summer of 1892, just after sunset, Dr. Isaac Beck heard that rapping at the door that was once a common sound in his household. Standing on Beck's porch was a gray-haired black man who said he was traveling through Ohio to solicit funds for the benefit of a freedmen's college near Memphis. He was a college professor. And he was a former fugitive slave. As he was coming through Brown County, he decided that he must take the time out from his work to find the people who had helped him escape many years before. Most of them, he learned, had already passed away. He remembered that Dr. Beck was one of the people who had carried food to him while he was hiding in a field outside of Sardinia. It had been fifty years, he said, but he could still recall the meal. He told Beck he had gone all the way to Canada and then later, some years after the war, had returned to Tennessee to raise his family. Beck was touched that the man would seek him out, but as the man was about to leave, he realized that all through the conversation he had never asked the man his name, nor had the man offered it.

"Sir, what is your name?" he asked as he shook the man's hand at the door.

The man smiled and said, "My name is Rankin, after the man who took me in my first night here."

ACKNOWLEDGMENTS

I could write a book about the writing of this book and the exceptional individuals with whom I connected, both living and dead. What a privilege it was to spend a good part of each day for nearly three years with John and Jean Rankin, John Parker, John B. Mahan, and Isaac M. Beck, among others. Their strength and courage are an inspiration to me, and I will always feel that John Rankin is now somehow part of my own spirit. The phrase "touching greatness" has new meaning for me. That greatness, it must be noted here, extends into the realm of the living, to those people who so generously contributed hearts, minds, and souls to helping me create *Beyond the River*.

I must begin such acknowledgments with my agent, Alice Martell. One day in January 1999, we met for lunch in Manhattan to discuss book ideas. I was excited about the two ideas I had developed, and as I eagerly described them, I watched Alice's face, waiting for that look of excitement that I knew so well and hoping for the praise that I was certain one of the ideas would inspire. But the praise never came, and her facial muscles seemed to sink into sullenness, while the piece of grilled salmon on her fork fell to her plate, unnoticed. Then she took a deep breath, regained her usual composure, and asked simply, "What is in your heart?" It was then that I expressed my interest in the Underground Railroad. "I can't stop thinking about these people," I told her, "these people who dedicated their lives to something larger than themselves. The Ohio Valley is especially intriguing to me, but I haven't thought of it as a book really. . . ." Then that look that every author hopes for, the smile, the eyes bright again. "Yes," she said. "*That* is your book." Thank you, Alice.

The next person to thank is Bob Bender, my editor at Simon & Schuster, who also saw the importance of the story from the very start, and who has been so very supportive of me throughout the years of my work on the book. He understood immediately when I said that I had to move to Ripley to do justice to the story, that the book could be more authentic if I knew the moods of the river, and that my research would be far better if I could network daily with the people along the river, many of whom have ancestors who are characters in the book. He advised me well about structure and content; his editing suggestions were always excellent. Every day I think how blessed I am to have an editor as skilled, as involved, as sensitive as Bob is.

It is impossible to say who is more or most important in helping an author with a book, but the next four people were truly indispensable and truly remarkable. The library in Ripley is a lovely prairie-style building that is not especially large, but because of its librarian, Alison Gibson, its resources are vast. I can honestly say that Alison is the most competent, creative, and resourceful research librarian I have ever worked with, and I have worked with many. She not only runs the Union Township library system, but she finds time to assist patrons in the great pastime of many Ripley citizens: local history. For the past three years, she's had an additional challenge: helping an author find books, articles, people, and newspapers. Alison was able to locate issues of the *Ripley Bee* from the 1850s and 1860s that I could not find at any library in the country; she also discovered some obscure issues of the *Maysville Eagle;* she connected with a Rankin relative who had Adam Lowry Rankin's Bible, inscribed with genealogical information; and she found a detailed article that told the heartbreaking story of John Mahan's daughter's death. She opened the library doors to me at odd hours so that I could read the reels of *The Philanthropist* late into the evening, and she listened to my woes when I couldn't find the details I was seeking, often trying to find them herself. I am indebted to her, and I hope that Ripley will always appreciate the national treasure that she is.

There is no one who better understood the themes of *Beyond the River,* the lessons to be learned from the lives of Rankin and his cohorts, and the ideological foundation of their work on the front lines of abolitionism than Allen Schwartz. Allen's knowledge of American history is remarkable, and his passion for teaching history through storytelling has been an inspiration to me throughout this book. I was blessed to have him as a reader whose editing skills were nothing less than brilliant; one chapter in particular, twenty-one, benefited enormously from his understanding of the abolition movement. He could always see the story of Ripley and Rankin in the context of the larger history of social movements in this nation. It was his idea to give the chapters titles—very much a nineteenth-century concept—and, as an experienced songwriter, he wrote several wonderful songs about the Ripley line, based on the book. Most of all, his belief in me as an artist—that nonfiction writing can indeed be art—encouraged me to move to a new level in my skills as a storyteller. I am eternally grateful.

On a daily basis, no one was more encouraging and helpful than June Zipperian, one of my neighbors on Front Street in Ripley. Weather permitting, June was my partner most days in walking up Rankin's hill, and she fed me on all those intense days when I was so engrossed in the book that I forgot to stock up on food. As a New Yorker transported to a small town, I had a tough time adjusting to life without takeout and delivery. June also was the first to read the completed manuscript and caught some inconsistencies; and she helped with the research throughout the project. The friendship and support of both June and Don Zipperian have made my time in Ripley exceptional.

From my first moments in Ripley, in the spring of 1999, through the completion of the book, Bob and Betty Campbell were consistently enthusiastic and helpful. They introduced me early to the spirit of Ripley's past, connected me with research sources in the area, loaned me books, sat with me late nights in the library reading through piles of papers and books, picked me up late at night at the Cincinnati airport, supplied tarps in the middle of the night for a roof leaking water, and even found a refrigerator for me. Betty Campbell has devoted her life to preserving Ripley's rich history and bringing its story to the rest of the world. I'm sure that Bob's great-great-grandfather Alexander Campbell would be proud of them both.

I had a tough time with the animal kingdom when I first arrived in Ripley from New York. From the hissing possums that hovered at my back door each night, and the feral cats that turned up one night in the basement, to the slugs on my office walls, the bats in my bedroom, and the three-inch spiders everywhere, I had quite an adjustment. Time was the teacher, but David Gray, my next-door neighbor, and his wife, Linda, helped me to resume a semblance of calm so that I could return to the writing of the book after interruptions from the wild kingdom. One morning, at 3 A.M., I was deeply into writing about the trial of John B. Mahan when a bat, frantically flapping its wings, suddenly appeared above my head. David, who always said to call if there was a problem, was soon at my doorstep, broom in hand, to take care of the problem. Being a retired history teacher, David also proofread the Ripley-history chapter to be sure it was correct, and he also did some research for me that was quite helpful. He knew where to find the people and the facts about the history of Brown County.

ACKNOWLEDGMENTS

Dorothy Prevost and Lanny Warren completed a half-renovated house for me to live in while I wrote the book. They were the best landlords a tenant ever had; they also housed me at their bed-and-breakfast during the early stages of research on the book. Their endless generosity was much appreciated. Dorothy, Linda Gray, Judith Gray, Alison Gibson, June Zipperian, and Roberta Gaudio often invited me to dinner. Roberta's peanut-butter pie fueled many long nights of writing, and Linda's hickory-nut cake was something to behold.

I am especially grateful to Lyn Boone at Denison University (head of Alumni Relations), who is a wonderful editor. She was one of my readers and did an exceptional job of advising me on the first ten chapters of the book. I thank Tom and Jane Zachman for their enthusiasm and support, and Miriam Zachman for her limitless knowledge about Ripley and its history. And I am grateful to the Reverend Lisa Corum Fox, in Texas, for sharing her research on Theodore Weld and his relationship with Rankin, and for her passionate appreciation of Rankin and his work to end racial prejudice.

I was fortunate to have excellent research assistance throughout the making of the book. Brent Cunningham, a journalist and graduate of the Columbia Journalism School, did research for me at the New York Public Library in the early stages of the book. His work at the Schomburg branch in Harlem was exceptional. Also, abundant thanks to the Reverend Kelly Flood, of Lexington, Kentucky, who worked for me during the first year of the book. While I was still living in New York, Lisa Reynolds did some good work for me in Ripley, especially genealogical research. Professor Julianna Mulroy at Denison University, a descendant of Thomas L. Hamer, one of the figures in the book, discovered great details in her research on the Internet. It was because of Julie and the network of Mahans she introduced me to that I eventually found a photo of John B. Mahan. I thank Gary Knepp, a lawyer in Batavia, Ohio, who is writing a history of the Underground Railroad in Clermont County. Gary shared with me some interesting stories that shed light on Brown County's history. Carl Westmoreland at the National Underground Railroad Freedom Center was an inspirational support. His brilliant knowledge of African-American history helped me enormously throughout the book. I thank him especially for reminding me of the importance of such details as the onerous Black Laws of Ohio. Lee Edwards, the curator of the Ripley Museum, was helpful in proofreading and in unearthing some gems from her manuscript collection. And I thank the Reverend Larry G. Willey for his excellent work on John Rankin and his well-organized research materials, now housed at the library in Ripley.

Pauline Kochanski, at the Chicago Metro History Fair at the Newberry Library in Chicago, did some excellent fact-checking for me. I am grateful also to the History Fair's Holly Campbell and Lisa Oppenheim for suggestions and encouragement throughout the book. Thanks also to Martha Wright. Thanks to Maggie Sanese and Duryea Kemp at the Ohio Historical Society. Flo Hoffman, the director of the Granville Historical Society, helped me find the facts for the 1836 story of the abolitionist gathering and subsequent riot in that town. Professor William Nichols, at Denison University, saw the importance of the story from the earliest stages of my research and was supportive throughout the writing of the book. Professor Richard Smith at Ohio Wesleyan University and Professor Larry Gara at Wilmington College were both helpful. I thank Professors Clark Wilhelm, Tony Stoneburner, Jack Kirby, and Dennis Read at Denison University; Professor Michael S. Perdreau at Ohio University; and Professors Emeriti William Preston, Jr., and Blanche Wiesen Cook at John Jay College of Criminal Justice. I thank John Aubrey at the Newberry Library in Chicago; James Prichard at the Kentucky State Historical Society in Frankfort, Kentucky; and Margaret Wilson at the University of Kansas Libraries. Margaret's research on the Rankins in Kansas was especially helpful as was Jim Prichard's excellent study of the Kentucky State Penitentiary. I also thank Patricia Donaldson-Mills for her genealogical help regarding the Shaw family, and Barry Hopkins at the McCormick Theological Seminary in Chicago. And I thank the Settles family, especially Reverend Jim Settles and his father, Eugene, who told me the story of his grandfather's escape from slavery.

I also want to thank the congregation of Ripley's First Presbyterian Church, the Reverend Nancy Bassett, and Thelma and Nathan Poff; Katie Johnson, transcriber of Wilbur Siebert's interview with John Rankin, Jr.; Union Township Library staffers Jerry Daniel, Mary Catherine List, and Carol Cooper; Stephanie Reed; Mae Case; Dr. Jon E. Zufelt; Judith M. Nagata at Hanover College; Kenneth Woods, nephew of Glenn Woods; John C. Harris; Liz and Rick Franklin (who found the photo of their ancestor John B. Mahan); Hylda and Jerry Strange; Ellen Seibert at the Supreme Court of Ohio Law Library; and John E. Leming, Jr. I am grateful, as always, to the New York Public Library for its excellent resources and the inspiring atmosphere of the Main Reading Room on Forty-second Street. I also thank the Amistad Research Center, Tulane University; the American Missionary Association Archives; Duke University Library; Stanford University Library; Harold Washington Library; Carter G. Woodson Library; the Wright Public Library in Dayton, Ohio; Transylvania University Library; Denison University Library; the Presbyterian Historical Society in Philadelphia; the Mason County Historical Society and Library; the Augusta Public Library; the William T. Young Research Library at the University of Kentucky; the Kentucky State Historical Society; Berea College; Cincinnati Historical Society; Cincinnati Public Library; McLean County Historical Society; Augusta County Historical Society; Southeastern Ohio Regional Library Systems; Adams County Historical Society; Brown County Genealogical and Historical Society; Springboro Historical Society; Western Reserve Historical Society; Virginia Historical Society; the Library of Congress; and the Tennessee Historical Society. I also thank James Mahan; Jeffrey Sroufe; Melody Sroufe; Sidney Wells; Elayne Thompson; Elizabeth Rankin, and all other Mahan and Rankin family members; Pat Stoneburner; Nancy Nichols; Neil Chetnik; Charles Nuckles; the late Stuart Sprague; Russell Wilhoit; Clare Coss; Ann Veith; Rorie Sherman; William Nack; Kathy Layford; Peggy Mills Warner; Jerry Gore; Paul Young; Stephen Kelly; Carolyn Wilson; Caroline Miller; my neighbors Jane and Gordon Scott; Larry and Joanne May; Dr. Consuelo Alley; Clint Polley; and the movers at The Padded Wagon.

As always, I thank my mother, Elizabeth Hagedorn, my sister Sarah Byers, my nephew Scott Byers, and John Auerbach for their belief in me as a writer and for understanding that I had to leave New York to write this book. Lastly, I honor the memory of my father, who would have loved the story of Ripley and its forgotten heroes.

NOTES

In researching this book, I relied on primary sources such as court records, letters, pre–Civil War newspapers, pamphlets, unpublished memoirs, newspaper ads, land surveys, property deeds, tombstones, tax records, and certificates of freedom as well as county histories, census records, genealogical records, family Bibles, marriage licenses, and obituaries. Many of these documents are at the Union Township Library in Ripley, the Ohio Historical Society, the Kentucky State Historical Society, the Mason County Historical Society, the Brown County Historical Society, the Schomburg Center for Black Culture (a branch of the New York Public Library), and the Brown County Administration Building, where the old legal records for the county are stored. Other research sites are noted in the acknowledgments of this book. Copies of these documents that I gathered from individuals, courthouses, libraries, and historical societies nationwide are now housed at the library in Ripley, Ohio. It is my hope that these sources will be helpful and even inspiring to students of the abolitionist period as well as to general readers. Although transcribing the old court records and the many letters was tedious and often frustrating, it was also enthralling. And, indeed, it was the richness of the primary sources that seemed to bring the nineteenth century into my writing room, making this book one of the most exciting research experiences in my career as a writer.

In these notes, I have cited the secondary and primary sources that I used in each chapter. Citations for direct quotations are noted with page numbers. In a few instances, such as the account of the slave woman crossing the icy river in 1838, I have discussed the various sources I found, and which ones I chose to use. With the exception of newspapers, many of the primary sources were handwritten. If there was a problem deciphering words, and guesswork regarding the transcription, I have noted that. The sources are listed in the order in which the information based upon them appeared in each chapter. The Bibliography that follows the Notes consists largely of secondary sources and is not comprehensive.

I looked for at least two independent accounts for each incident included in the book. If I found a story in a letter, I searched newspapers and court records for another account to validate it. For example, in his 1892 recollection, Isaac Beck told the story of the murder of a free black woman, Sally Hudson. I was able to find several newspaper accounts backing up and expanding upon his account. If I found the first reference to an event in an antislavery newspaper, then I sought corroboration in local newspapers, in court records, in autobiographies, and/or letters. For example, I discovered several references to the 1844 assault at Red Oak, and at least three versions of the attempted barn burning and assault against John Rankin in 1841. In such cases, I studied each version and culled the facts that were common to each. When there were contradictions in the facts, I considered the credibility of each source in past accounts and chose the details and the story that seemed the most logical and authentic. If I could not find corroboration, I did not include the incident. For example, I discovered a great detail in a letter written by a Ripley citizen about the animosity between Kentucky and Ohio in the 1850s, in which he recalled a time when a resident of Augusta, Kentucky, who was infected with smallpox came to a Ripley town meeting with the intention of spreading the disease among the abolitionists. I couldn't find any record of an outbreak of smallpox in Augusta for that period, and no articles in local papers about such an incident. And so, intriguing as the story was, I chose not to use it.

There are numerous monetary references in the book. For example, the reward offered for the assassination of John Rankin was $2,500 at one point. His salary was $500 a year for his first seven years in Ripley. And when John B. Mahan lost his civil case to William Greathouse, he owed Greathouse $1,600. I considered trying to convert those amounts to today's currency values in the narrative, but decided that it would interrupt the flow of the text and that the source notes were the best place for such explanations. According to the *Handbook of Labor Statistics* published by the U.S. Department of Labor, one dollar in 1850 would have been worth $21.34 in the year 2001. This means that Rankin's salary would be about $10,670 in 2001; the reward for his life would be roughly $53,350, and Mahan's debt to Greathouse for the value of the slaves Mahan was accused of stealing was $34,144.

It must be noted that, in this same time period, there was another John Rankin who was an abolitionist. He was a merchant from New York and at one point served as the treasurer of the American Anti-Slavery Society. Note also that the newspaper begun by James G. Birney was called *The Philanthropist* from 1836 to 1843; from 1843 to 1846, it was the *Cincinnati Weekly Herald and Philanthropist;* and it was the *National Era* from 1847 to 1860.

Dates for some incidents were difficult to establish. I typically employed a combination of letters, court records, and dates from tombstones. For example, in the story of the Settles family's escape, Eugene Settles said that the baby girl—who was his aunt Mary Alice—was "a few months old" when she was thrown over the fence. Jim Settles and I found the gravestone for Mary Alice at the cemetery in Ripley. She was born on November 13, 1862, and so I placed the incident in the early months of 1863.

Also important to note is that this book is not meant to be a comprehensive account of the Underground Railroad in Ripley and Brown County. Many incidents and individuals are not included in this story. Among the names I saw mentioned at least once in accounts and letters are the following: Dobbins, Evans, Steele, Burgess, Carothers, Rodgers, Colonel Keys, Kincaid, Kirkpatrick, (Ramsey) Lowry, Betts, McClanahan, Frazier, Pangburn, Crane, Moore, Graham, and Shephard. I have also chosen not to refer to all of John Rankin's published works. Rankin was a prolific writer and published four books, at least ten tracts (pamphlets), six of his sermons, and dozens upon dozens of newspaper articles in antislavery papers as well as local and regional papers. The list of newspapers to which he contributed includes: *The Philanthropist, The Liberator, The Emancipator, The Advocate of Freedom, Friend of Man, Pennsylvania Freeman, The Anti-Slavery Bugle, The National Anti-Slavery Standard, Cincinnati Weekly Herald and Philanthropist, National Era,* the *Cincinnati Gazette,* the *Alton Observer,* and the *Free Presbyterian.*

Throughout the research and writing of the book, I heard persistent rumors that John Rankin had a black mistress with whom he had at least one child. Some people said the mistress was in Kentucky during Rankin's years in Carlisle and that this explains the heritage of the African American families now named Rankin in that region. Others said the woman had lived in Ripley. I acknowledge the possibility of this and I, of course, respect the work that the African Americans who now have the name Rankin are doing to find the truth about their ancestry. But I did not include this detail in the book because no definitive proof of it ever surfaced.

At the beginning of this project, I encountered skeptics who cautioned me that the Underground Railroad story had already been told as much as it could be, because most of the records were destroyed after the Fugitive Slave Law of 1850 was passed. Indeed, many people, including

John Parker, did burn their personal accounts at that time or otherwise destroy them. But many accounts can be found in the newspapers, court records, letters, and memoirs of the period. Newspapers in towns such as Lexington, Louisville, Cincinnati, Maysville, Ripley, and Georgetown, as well as Parkersburg, West Virginia, Marietta, Ohio, and Madison, Indiana, are rich with the stories of the undeclared war over runaway slaves on both sides of the river. For the purposes of storytelling, I left out many stories and characters that I discovered. Indeed, I have only scraped the surface of what is available. I invite historians and students to expand upon the research and storytelling that I have begun here. It is my hope that this book will inspire many more books about the remarkable social movement known as the Underground Railroad.

xv   "Thus have I been attacked": John Rankin, letter dated Sept. 13, 1841, *The Liberator,* Oct. 22, 1841.

Preface
1   How the river freezes: Interview with Dr. Jon E. Zufelt, U.S. Army Corps of Engineers, Hanover, N.H.
2   The horse-and-sleigh incident on the Ohio River in 1838: John Rankin, Jr. (John Thompson Rankin), in Greensburg, Ind., letter dated Feb. 15, 1912, to Mr. J. C. Nucomb, editor of *Ripley Bee,* in Ripley, Ohio.

Part I: The War Before the War
5   "There was a time": John Parker, quoted in Stuart Seely Sprague, ed., *His Promised Land: The Autobiography of John P. Parker, Former Slave and Conductor on the Underground Railroad* (New York: W. W. Norton, 1996), pp. 74, 75. This autobiography is based on an interview that Frank Gregg conducted with John Parker in Ripley in the 1880s.

Chapter One
7   Roughly a thousand feet: Richard Swainson Fisher, M.D., *A New and Complete Statistical Gazetteer of the United States of America* (New York: J. H. Colton, 1853).
8   The description of early days on the Ohio River, Ripley, and its settlers was put together by studying a variety of sources, including the original plat maps of Ripley (at the Brown County Administration Building in Georgetown, Ohio) and the following: Alice Adams, *The Neglected Period of Anti-Slavery in America, 1808–1831* (Boston: Ginn and Company, 1908); Michael Allen, *Western Rivermen, 1763–1861* (Baton Rouge: Louisiana State University Press, 1990); Thomas Ashe, *Travels in America; performed in the year 1806* (New York: N. p., 1811); Thomas Baldwin and J. Thomas, M.D., *A New and Complete Gazetteer of the United States; giving a full and comprehensive review of the present condition, industry, and resources of the American Confederacy* (Philadelphia: Lippincott, Grambo & Co., 1854); R. E. Banta, *The Ohio,* with new foreword by Thomas D. Clark (Lexington: University Press of Kentucky, 1998; originally published in 1949); Rev. S. R. Beggs, *Pages from the Early History of the West and Northwest; embracing reminiscences of settlement and growth and sketches of material and religious progress of the states of Ohio, Indiana, Illinois and Missouri* (Cincinnati: N.p., 1868); Tiffany Brockway, Jr., Diary of Tiffany Brockway, Jr., describing trip to Ripley in 1837 to settle the estate of his father, Nathan Brockway, in the Brockway family collection, George Arents Research Library for Special Collections, E. S. Bird Library, Syracuse University, MS 68-1715; Charles D. Campbell, letters to Chambers Baird, 1936, Union Township Library, Ripley, Ohio [Campbell, a for-

mer Front Street dweller, was ninety-six years old when he wrote this letter with a West Virginia address; among other details, he called Ripley the "mecca" for fugitive slaves]; Zadok Cramer, *The Navigator,* 10th ed. (Pittsburgh: Cramer, Spear and Eichbaum, 1818); "Gilbert F. Dodds, First Abolitionist Minister in Brown County, O.," in *Columbus Sunday Dispatch,* Sept. 12, 1943; Nelson W. Evans and Emmons B. Stivers, *A History of Adams County, Ohio, From Its Earliest Settlement to the Present Time* (West Union, Ohio: E. B. Stivers, 1900); Gerald Fowke, "The Origin of the Ohio River," in *Who's Who on the Ohio River and Its Tributaries,* by Ethel C. Leahy (Cincinnati: E. C. Leahy Publishing Co., 1931); Charles B. Galbreath, *History of Ohio* (Chicago and New York: American Historical Society, 1925); William W. Gilliland, account of his father's life, as told to Prof. Wilbur H. Siebert, in the 1880s, Wilbur Siebert Collection, Ohio Historical Society, Ohio Box 115; *The History of Brown County* (Chicago: W. H. Beers & Co., 1883); Henry Howe, *Historical Collections of Ohio* (Columbus, Ohio: Henry Howe and Son, 1891); R. Douglas Hurt, *The Ohio Frontier: Crucible of the Old Northwest, 1720–1830* (Bloomington: Indiana University Press, 1996); "Indian Land Cessions in the United States, 1784–1894," in U.S. Serial Set, no. 4015, 56th Cong., 1st sess., pp. 654–55; John A. Jakle, *Images of the Ohio Valley: A Historical Geography of Travel, 1740 to 1860.* Cartographer, Miklos Pinther, (New York: Oxford University Press, 1977); Richard K. MacMaster, *Augusta County History* (Staunton, Va.: Augusta County Historical Society, 1987); Original surveys, Brown County, Ohio, Bk. 1, survey no. 418, Brown County Archives, Georgetown, Ohio; J. Lewis Peyton, *History of Augusta County, Virginia* (Staunton, Va.: Samuel M. Yost & Son, 1892); John Thompson Rankin, also called John Rankin, Jr., interview with Frank Gregg. Handwritten, The Rankin-Parker Collection, Special Collections Library, Duke University, also a copy at Union Township Library, Ripley, Ohio; Robert L. Reid, *Always a River: The Ohio River and the American Experience* (Bloomington: Indiana University Press, 1991); Wilbur H. Siebert, *The Underground Railroad from Slavery to Freedom* (New York: Macmillan, 1898); William B. Sprague, *Annals of the American Pulpit, or Commemorative Notices of Distinguished American Clergymen of Various Denominations from the Early Settlement of the Country to the Close of 1855,* intro. by Wm. B. Sprague, vol. 4 (New York: Robert Carter & Bros., 1858); Eliese Bambach Stivers, *Ripley, Ohio: Its History and Families* (Ripley: Ripley, Ohio Historical Committee, 1965); Henry Louis Taylor, "The Northwest Ordinance and the Place of Ohio in African-American History," *Old Northwest: A Journal of Regional Life and Letters,* vol. 14, no. 2 (Summer 1988); Carl N. Thompson, compiler, *Historical Collections of Brown County* (Piqua, Ohio: Hammer Graphics, 1969); Reuben Gold Thwaites, *On the Storied Ohio* (New York: Arno Press, 1975); William T. Utter, *A History of the State of Ohio,* vol. 2, *The Frontier State: 1803–1825* (Columbus: Ohio State Archaeological and Historical Society, 1942); Father William, *Three Days on the Ohio River* (New York: Carlton & Porter, 1854).

12 Tice Davids story taken from: Henrietta Buckmaster, *Let My People Go* (New York: Harper & Brothers, 1941).

12 Samuel Gist: Michael Trotti, "Freedmen and Enslaved Soil: A Case Study of Manumission, Migration, and Land," *Virginia Magazine of History and Biography,* vol. 104, no. 4 (Autumn 1996); *Sentinel,* Georgetown, Ohio, July 18, 1878; Wilbur Siebert Collection, Ohio Historical Society, Ohio Box 115; Wayne L. Snider, *All in the Same Spaceship: Portions of American Negro History* (New York: Vantage Press, 1974); *Journal of Negro History,* Jan. 1916; "A List of Manumitted and Free Blacks Who Paid Tax in Brown County, Ohio, 1838," transcribed from the auditor's tax-transfer book, Brown County Archives, Georgetown, Ohio.

13   "Much as we commiserate": *Chillicothe Supporter,* June 16, 1819.

14   "Hell is about to enlarge": Elihu Embree, in *The Emancipator,* published by Elihu Embree, Jonesborough, Tennessee, 1820, in *The Emancipator (Complete)* (Nashville: B. H. Murphy, 1932).

14   "The title page": John Quincy Adams, quoted in Buckmaster, *Let My People Go,* p. 39.

14   Ohio legislators passed a law: William C. Cochran, "The Western Reserve and the Fugitive Slave Law," *Western Reserve Historical Society,* no. 101, 1920, pp. 72–73.

15   "I can remember": Adam Lowry Rankin, "The Autobiography of Adam Lowry Rankin," unpublished, handwritten in the early 1890s; typewritten copy by one of Adam Lowry Rankin's granddaughters, Belle Rankin, in 1931, available at Union Township Library, Ripley, Ohio; original available in Special Collections Department, Stanford University Library.

Chapters Two and Three

16   Details about the life of John Rankin: William Birney, *James G. Birney and His Times: The Genesis of the Republican Party with Some Account of Abolition Movements in the South Before 1828* (New York: D. Appleton & Co., 1890); Lyman Chalkley, *Chronicles of the Scotch-Irish Settlement in Virginia* (Baltimore: Genealogical Publishing Co., 1974); Dwight L. Dumond, ed., *Letters of James Gillespie Birney, 1831–1857* (New York: D. Appleton–Century, 1938); Paul R. Grim, "The Rev. John Rankin, Early Abolitionist," *Ohio Archaeological and Historical Quarterly,* vol. 46 (1937), pp. 215–56; letters and accounts of five of John Rankin's sons—Adam Lowry, Samuel Gardner Wilson, Richard Calvin, John Thompson (or John Rankin, Jr.), and Thomas Lovejoy—available at Union Township Library, Ripley, Ohio; Adam Lowry Rankin, "The Autobiography of Adam Lowry Rankin"; John Rankin, "The Life of Rev. John Rankin: Written by Himself in His 80th Year (ca. 1872)," text from a manuscript in the collection of Lobena and Charles Frost, reproduced and copyrighted in 1998 by Arthur W. McGraw; Lloyd R. Rankin, Jr., compiler, *The Rankin Tercentenary* (Tampa, Fla.: Lloyd R. Rankin, 1984); Rev. Andrew Ritchie, *The Soldier, the Battle, and the Victory; being a Brief Account of the Work of Rev. John Rankin and the Anti-Slavery Cause, 1793–1886* (Cincinnati: Western Tract and Book Society, 1868), typescript, available at Union Township Library, Ripley, Ohio; Wilbur H. Siebert, Underground Railroad materials for Illinois, Indiana, New Hampshire, New York, and Ohio, Ohio Historical Society, Columbus, Ohio. [Material collected between 1891 and 1948 on American loyalists, East Florida, and Underground Railroad; includes correspondence, typed transcripts of official documents, letters, portions of articles and books; about 45 percent of it is about the Underground Railroad, and a large portion of that is about Ohio]; Hazel Timblin Townsend, *Rankin Roots in East Tennessee* (Sevierville, Tenn.: Back Home Printing, 1997); Larry Gene Willey, "The Reverend John Rankin, Early Ohio Antislavery Leader," Ph.D. thesis, Department of History, Graduate College of the University of Iowa, May 1976; Larry Gene Willey, "John Rankin, Antislavery Prophet, and the Free Presbyterian Church," *American Presbyterians: Journal of Presbyterian History,* vol. 72, no. 3 (Fall 1994).

16   The Fugitive Slave Act of 1793: "The Rendition of Fugitive Slaves: The Acts of 1793 and 1850, and the Decisions of the Supreme Court Sustaining Them; the Dred Scott case—what the court decided," published by the National Democratic Campaign Committee, 1860; William C. Cochran, "The Western Reserve and the Fugitive Slave Law"; Dwight L. Dumond, *Antislavery: The Crusade for Freedom in America* (Ann Arbor: University of Michigan Press, 1961); the act itself, "Act of Congress of 1793: An Act Respecting Fugi-

tives from Justice, and Persons Escaping from the Service of their Masters," signed by Jonathan Trumbull, Speaker of the House of Representatives, and John Adams, Vice President of the United States and President of the Senate, and George Washington, President of the United States, approved Feb. 12, 1793, *Congressional Record,* "The Debates and Proceedings in the Congress of the United States; with an appendix containing important state papers and public documents, and all the laws of a public nature," 2nd Cong. Oct. 24, 1791–March 2, 1793.

16   Article IV, Section 2: U.S. Constitution. Exact wording: "No person, held to service or labour in one State, under the laws thereof, escaping into another, shall, in consequence of any law or regulation therein, be discharged from such service or labour; but shall be delivered up, on claim of the party to whom such service or labour may be due."

18   About rebellions, throughout chapter: Herbert Aptheker, *American Negro Slave Revolts* (New York: Columbia University Press, 1943); Ira Berlin, *Many Thousands Gone: The First Two Centuries of Slavery in North America* (Cambridge, Mass.: Belknap Press of Harvard University Press, 1998); Joseph C. Carroll, *Slave Insurrections in the United States, 1800–1865* (Boston: Chapman & Grimes, 1938); Douglas R. Egerton, *Gabriel's Rebellion: The Virginia Slave Conspiracies of 1800 & 1802* (Chapel Hill: University of North Carolina Press, 1993); C.L.R. James, *The Black Jacobins: Toussaint L'Ouverture and the San Domingo Revolution* (New York: Vintage Books, 1989; originally published by Random House, 1963).

18   "Throw away the symbol": C.L.R. James, *The Black Jacobins,* p. 87.

18   "They write from Charleston": *New York Journal & Patriotic Register,* Oct. 16, 1793.

19   Of the Southern states and territories: "Return of the Whole Number of Persons Within the Several Districts of the U.S.," Washington, D.C., 1791 (numbers in the text are rounded off).

19   About Tennessee and slavery: Stephen V. Ash, ed., *Secessionists and Other Scoundrels: Selections from Parson Brownlow's Book* (Baton Rouge: Louisiana State University Press, 1999); Merton L. Dillon, *The Abolitionists: The Growth of a Dissenting Minority* (Dekalb: Northern Illinois University Press, 1974); Durwood Dunn, *An Abolitionist in the Appalachian South: Ezekiel Birdseye on Slavery, Capitalism, and Separate Statehood in East Tennessee, 1841–1846* (Knoxville: University of Tennessee Press, 1997); Robert William Fogel, *Without Consent or Contract: The Rise and Fall of American Slavery* (New York: W. W. Norton, 1989); *Knoxville Gazette,* June 1797; Chase C. Mooney, *Slavery in Tennessee* (Westport, Conn.: Negro Universities Press, 1957); "A Society Formed in 1815," *American,* Nashville, Tenn., June 3, 1901.

22   About religious revivals: Gilbert Hobbs Barnes, *The Antislavery Impulse, 1830–1844* (New York: D. Appleton–Century, 1933); Dillon, *Abolitionists;* Albert Bushnell Hart, *Slavery and Abolition 1831–1841* (New York: Haskell House, 1968).

25   About the New Madrid earthquake, from eyewitness accounts and commentary out of the Cincinnati newspaper *Western Spy,* Dec. 1811–March 1812; *Knoxville Gazette,* Feb. 10, 1812; *Wilson's Gazette,* Knox County, Tenn., Dec. 23, 1811; *Nashville Clarion,* Dec. 3, 1811; extract of letter from "a gentleman of great respectability" at Natchez, Miss., to a friend in Knoxville, Jan. 7, 1812. Basic facts from: David Stewart and Ray Knox, Drs., *The Earthquake America Forgot* (Marble Hill, Mo.: Gutenberg-Richter Publications, 1995).

28   About Samuel Doak, from: Janie Preston Collup French (Mrs. J. Stewart French), *Notable Southern Families,* vol. 6, *The Doak Family* (Spartanburg, S.C.: Reprint Company, 1974); William Gunn Calhoun, compiler, *Samuel Doak* (Washington College, Tenn.:

Pioneer Printers 1966); William B. Sprague, *Annals of the American Pulpit, or Commemorative Notices of Distinguished American Clergymen of Various Denominations from the Early Settlement of the Country to the close of 1855; with historical introductions by Wm. B. Sprague*, vol. 3 (New York: Robert Carter & Bros., 1858).

32   "The feelings of that parting": Rankin, "Life of Rankin," p. 12.

33   "If the slave has a right": ibid., p. 16.

Chapter Four

37   Some were "stript naked, stretched and tied across barrels": John Rankin, *Letters on American Slavery*, p. 52.

37   References to early slave escapes: *Petersburg, Va., Gazette & Intelligencer,* ads for fugitives, Nov. 17, 1797; *Clermont Sentinel,* July 19, 1819; *Clermont Courier,* Oct. 19, 1837.

38   John Finley Crowe quote: Dwight L. Dumond, *Antislavery,* p. 118.

38   About escapes, runaways, and the Ohio River as the River Jordan: Herbert Aptheker, *American Negro Slave Revolts;* R. E. Banta, *The Ohio;* Dr. Isaac M. Beck, unpublished letters, Union Township Library, Ripley, Ohio; Ira Berlin, *Many Thousands Gone;* Alexander Black, *The Story of Ohio* (Boston: D. Lothrop, 1888); Henrietta Buckmaster, *Let My People Go;* Levi Coffin, *Reminiscences of Levi Coffin* (New York: Arno Press and New York Times, 1968); J. Winston Coleman, Jr., *Slavery Times in Kentucky* (Chapel Hill: University of North Carolina Press, 1940); Douglas R. Egerton, *Gabriel's Rebellion;* Philip S. Foner, *History of Black Americans: From Africa to the Emergence of the Cotton Kingdom* (Westport, Conn.: Greenwood Press, 1975); John Hope Franklin and Loren Schweninger, *Runaway Slaves: Rebels on the Plantation* (New York: Oxford University Press, 1999); Larry Gara, *The Liberty Line: The Legend of the Underground Railroad* (Lexington: University Press of Kentucky, 1961); Eugene D. Genovese, *Roll, Jordan, Roll: The World the Slaves Made* (New York: Random House, 1972); Peter P. Hinks, ed., *David Walker's Appeal: To the Coloured Citizens of the World* (University Park: Pennsylvania State University Press, 2000); R. Douglas Hurt, *The Ohio Frontier;* Charles Johnson, Patricia Smith, and WGBH Series Research Team, *Africans in America: America's Journey through Slavery* (New York: Harcourt Brace, 1998); Adam Lowry Rankin, "The Autobiography of Adam Lowry Rankin"; John Rankin, "The Life of Rev. John Rankin"; Robert L. Reid, ed., *Always a River;* Stuart Seely Sprague, ed., *His Promised Land.*

38   Pete Driscoll quote: A. L. Rankin, "Autobiography," p. 105.

39   "The North Star": William Wells Brown, letter, *National Anti-Slavery Standard,* April 21, 1855, Schomburg Library, New York.

39   Regarding "The Drinking Gourd": I was concerned about whether this song was written after the war and then reputed to be used by slaves to communicate ways to escape, or actually written before the war and indeed authentic. The answer came from the Smithsonian Institution, where Jeff Place guided my fact-checker Pauline Kochanski to H. B. Parks, "Follow the Drinking Gourd," in J. Frank Dobie, ed., *Follow de Drinkin' Gou'd* (Austin: Folklore Society of Texas, 1928), vol. 7, pp. 81–84. From the research that Parks did around 1912, it is very likely that the song was sung by slaves and that a sailor with only one leg, Peg Leg Joe, inspired it. Parks's research certainly strengthens the probability of the song's authenticity, but it must be understood that the only way to be certain would be to find the song in a slave narrative, which I have not yet done.

39   William Lloyd Garrison quote from: *The Liberator,* Sept. 3, 1831.

40   The meanings of the name Ohio River: Richard Swainson Fisher, M.D., *A New and Complete Statistical Gazetteer of the United States of America* (New York: J. H. Colton,

1853); Wills De Hass, "History of the Early Settlement & Indian Wars of Western Virginia," *Western District of Virginia,* 1851, p. 624.

40 Countywide meetings regarding escaping slaves: *Maysville Eagle,* from 1824 onward; quote in text is from July 11, 1827. Other examples of the early impact of "slave stealing" can be found in Kentucky newspapers of the 1820s, including *Western Citizen, Western Luminary,* and *Louisville Courier.* More on the rising fears in Kentucky regarding slave escapes in *Niles' Weekly Register,* Sept. 7, 1822; Coleman, *Slavery Times in Kentucky.*

40 For the 1820 law giving slaveholders the right supposedly to remove their slaves from other states: Mason Brown and C. S. Morehead, *Digest of the Statute Laws of Kentucky,* 2 vols (Frankfort, Ky.: N.p., 1834).

40 "Between the slaveholding and non-slaveholding States": *Liberty Hall,* June 22, 1820; letters from congressmen in Feb. 12, 1821, issue.

41 "They was all kinds of white folks": Gara, *Liberty Line,* p. 58; Gara got it from B. A. Botkin, *Lay My Burden Down: A Folk History of Slavery* (Chicago: N.p., 1945).

41 "Black Laws": W. C. Cochran, "The Western Reserve and the Fugitive Slave Law," pp. 55–56.

41 Underground Railroad participants at this time: Dr. Isaac Beck's own account of his life, Union Township Library, Ripley, Ohio; *U.S. Census for 1820* (Washington, D.C.: 1821), p. 34; Brown County and Clermont County histories, *The History of Brown County* (Chicago: W. H. Beers & Co., 1883); and geneaological information from John B. Mahan's descendants, based on years of their own research into his life.

Chapter Five

43 Ripley as "abolitionist hellhole": The origin (sometimes referred to as an "abolition hellhole") is most likely in Calvin Fairbank, *Reverend Calvin Fairbank: During Slavery Times* (Chicago: N.p., 1890), in which Fairbank, who served seventeen years in the penitentiary in Frankfort for helping slaves escape from Kentucky, tells the story of meeting slaveholder and slave hunter Pete Driscoll on the ferry ride to Ripley in August 1844. Fairbank recognized Driscoll, who was renowned by then as a slave hunter, and so pretended that he too was hunting down slaves. At one point he asked Driscoll about Ripley, at which time Driscoll called it an "abolition hellhole," Fairbank wrote. This is the earliest reference I could find in a primary source. Some secondary sources say that the term was used by Kentucky slaveholders as early as the 1820s, but I have found no proof of that.

43 Rankin's first days in Ripley: John Rankin, "The Life of Rev. John Rankin"; Adam Lowry Rankin, "The Autobiography of Adam Lowry Rankin."

44 Denmark Vesey: Douglas R. Egerton, *He Shall Go Out Free: The Lives of Denmark Vesey* (Madison, Wisc.: Madison House, 1999). The stats regarding those arrested come from the record of the Vesey trial found in *A Narrative of the Conspiracy and Intended Insurrection; amongst a portion of the Negroes in the state of South Carolina, in the year 1822,* intro. by John Oliver Killens (Boston: Beacon Press, 1970), pp. 140–46 [lists the names of the slaves and what happened to them]; *Niles' Weekly Register,* Sept. 7, 1822.

45 Southern editorials and other quotes: Egerton, *He Shall Go Out Free,* pp. 204–6, 210–11.

45 "The fruits of abolitionists": *Maysville Eagle,* March 12, 1823.

45 Pinckney and Desaussure quotes: Egerton, *He Shall Go Out Free,* p. 210.

46 "Infatuation . . . cruelties inflicted upon slaves": Rankin, "Life of Rankin," p. 39.

47 "My Dear Brother": John Rankin, *Letters on American Slavery Addressed to Mr. Thomas*

Rankin, Merchant at Middlebrook, Augusta Co., Va., 5th ed. (Boston: Isaac Knapp, 1838). There are thirteen letters in the book version, as against twenty-one published in *The Castigator.* Rankin himself did the editing, as the book's preface indicates.

Chapter Six

51 On the burning of Rankin's books and the publication of the letters on slavery in book form: John Rankin, "The Life of Rev. John Rankin"; Adam Lowry Rankin, "The Autobiography of Adam Lowry Rankin." Some newspaper accounts in later years on the burning of the books noted the warehouse as being in Cincinnati, as did Rankin himself in his autobiography. Adam Lowry Rankin wrote that the books were stored with a bookseller in Maysville, and all of what Adam Lowry wrote could be verified through city directories and ads in 1825. His story is the only one that can be verified with other primary sources, and so I have chosen that. What is beyond dispute is that the books were burned, whether in Maysville or in Cincinnati. Either is logical, considering the provocative nature of the letters and the proslavery forces in both towns, but the details and the logistics of the selling, storing, and burning of the books make it far more logical that it occurred in Maysville. There is no mention of the fire in any contemporary newspapers in either town.

51 Details about the printing and publishing of the letters: Rankin, "Life of Rankin"; A. L. Rankin, "Autobiography"; Larry Gene Willey, "The Reverend John Rankin, Early Ohio Anti-Slavery Leader."

52 "A slave was lately murdered in Henry County": *Castigator,* March 22, 1826, and again on October 10, 1826.

52 Edward Stone: *Genius of Universal Emancipation* [newspaper], Nov. 14, 1826; J. Winston Coleman, Jr., *Slavery Times in Kentucky,* pp. 145–46, 173–75.

53 About the U.S. efforts toward Canadian "return policy": James F. Hopkins and Mary W. M. Hargreaves, eds., *The Papers of Henry Clay,* vol. 5, *Secretary of State, 1826* (Lexington: University Press of Kentucky, 1973), pp. 234–37, 344–45, 441, 472–73, 588–89, 612, 750, 1,016, 1,072–73; vol. 7, p. 482.

53 "Ignorant, infatuated barbarians": *Maysville Monitor,* Sept. 24, 1827.

54 Presbyterian minister from Ohio: Incident described in several different sources, including the *Cincinnati Gazette,* 1826, and the History of Adams County (both similar accounts except for the dates). The version in the History of Adams County said that it happened to the Reverend Dyer Burgess, a compatriot of John Rankin and James Gilliland. The story also appears in *The Philanthropist* much later, in the July 16, 1839, edition, in which the minister is referred to as "Rev. B" and his rescuer as "J——— R———"—possibly John Rankin.

55 "Unconstitutional and wicked": James D. Richardson, *Messages and Papers of the Presidents, 1789–1897* (Washington, D.C.: Richardson, 1897), p. 175.

55 New Kentucky law: Mason Brown and C. S. Morehead, *Digest of the Statute Laws of Kentucky.*

56 Details about Rankin's new house: Rankin, "Life of Rankin"; A. L. Rankin, "Autobiography"; "Report on the Restoration of the Dr. Rankin Home, Ripley, Ohio," prepared by Ohio State Archaeological and Historical Society, Columbus, Ohio, Oct. 1946.

56 About Rankin's salary: Rankin, "Life of Rankin," pp. 18, 20.

57 Arnold Gragston quote: James Mellon, ed., *Bullwhip Days: The Slaves Remember, an Oral History* (New York: Avon Books, 1988), pp. 266–67.

57 "I supposed it would never": Rankin, "Life of Rankin," p. 34.

58   Second edition of letters: Ibid.

58   William Lloyd Garrison quote: A. L. Rankin, "Autobiography," p. 26; event also covered in *Daily Cincinnati Gazette,* April 20–24, 1853.

58   Garrison's inscription: Copy on file at Ohio Historical Society. Also of interest is a letter Garrison wrote in 1835 to Henry E. Benson regarding another antislavery publication: "I have read Channing's work. . . . I would not give one dozen of Rankin's letters for one hundred copies of Channing's essay." (In Walter M. Merrill, ed., *I Will Be Heard! The Letters of William Lloyd Garrison,* vol. 1, *1822–1835* [Cambridge, Mass.: Belknap Press of Harvard University Press, 1971], letter 233. See also, at Union Township Library, Ripley, Ohio, a copy of the card Garrison sent to John and Jean Rankin on their fiftieth wedding anniversary.)

Chapter Seven

59   William Lloyd Garrison quote: *The Liberator,* Jan. 1, 1831 [first issue].

59   Nat Turner: Albert Bushnell Hart, *Slavery and Abolition 1831–1841;* John Hope Franklin, *From Slavery to Freedom: A History of American Negroes* (New York: Alfred A. Knopf, 1947).

60   Details of Benjamin Templeton's life: Personal communications from Professor Michel Perdreau and Connie Perdreau at Ohio University, who so generously shared some of the findings from their extensive research into the life of John Newton Templeton, Benjamin's brother; Connie Perdreau, *A Black History of Athens County and Ohio University* (Athens: Ohio University, 1988); will and estate papers of Thomas Williamson, file 2228, Spartanburg County Records, S.C.; Adams County History; Book of Common Pleas, 1830–1840 at Brown County Archives in Georgetown, Ohio.

61   Details about Ripley College: Numerous ads and articles in *The Castigator* throughout 1830 and 1831 and on Sept. 18, 1832, and Aug. 31, 1836; *Hillsborough Gazette,* Oct. 15, Oct. 22, and Oct. 29, 1831; *Ripley Bee,* Feb. 2, 1850; handwritten record books of Ripley College debate society, original records at Cincinnati Historical Society, microfilm copy at Union Township Library, Ripley, Ohio; handwritten roster of students, Union Township Library; *The History of Brown County;* Carl N. Thompson, compiler, *Historical Collections of Brown County;* Adam Lowry Rankin, "The Autobiography of Adam Lowry Rankin"; John Rankin, "The Life of Rev. John Rankin."

62   Franklin Shaw: Thanks to genealogist Patricia Donaldson-Mills in Georgetown, Ohio, who has done extensive work on the Shaw family.

64   The frozen river: Contemporary Cincinnati newspapers; Lewis Collins, *History of Kentucky,* vol. 1 (Covington, Ky.: Collins & Co., 1878).

Chapter Eight

65   Flood of 1755: R. R. Jones, compiler, *The Ohio River, 1700–1914: A Brief Account of Its Early History* (Cincinnati: U.S. Engineer Office, 1914), p. 159.

66   Cholera: "Chronology of Cholera," *West Union Intelligencer,* Jan. 10, 1849; "Foreign News," *Niles' Register,* Sept. 3, 1831; *Cincinnati Gazette,* Aug. 20, 1831; "Progress of the Cholera," *Niles' Register,* Oct. 27, 1832; Charles E. Rosenberg, *The Cholera Years* (Chicago: University of Chicago Press, 1962), and Adam Lowry Rankin, "The Autobiography of Adam Lowry Rankin."

67   Theodore Weld: Benjamin P. Thomas, *Theodore Weld: Crusader for Freedom* (New Brunswick, N.J.: Rutgers University Press, 1950); Robert H. Abzug, *Passionate Liberator: Theodore Dwight Weld and the Dilemma of Reform* (New York: Oxford University Press,

1980); Gilbert Hobbs Barnes, *The Antislavery Impulse, 1830–1844;* Hart, *Slavery and Abolition, 1831–1841;* Merton L. Dillon, *The Abolitionists;* Staughton Lynd, *Intellectual Origins of American Radicalism* (New York: Pantheon Books, 1968); Charles Stowe and Lyman Stowe, *Harriet Beecher Stowe: The Story of Her Life* (Boston: Houghton Mifflin, 1911).

67   Lane Theological Seminary and Lane debates: Lane archives, McCormick Theological Seminary Library, Chicago, Ill., including the minutes of the executive committee in the months preceding the student exodus; accounts in various issues of *The Liberator* during the autumn of 1834 and Jan. 1835, including "Statement of the Faculty Concerning the Late Differences at Lane Seminary," Jan. 17, 1835; Lewis Tappan, *The Life of Arthur Tappan* (New York: Hurd and Haughton, 1871); Gilbert H. Barnes and Dwight L. Dumond, eds., *Letters of Theodore Dwight Weld, Angelina Grimke Weld and Sarah Grimke, 1822–1844* (Gloucester, Mass.: Peter Smith, 1965).

68   Rankin, Gilliland, and Lockhart attended: Larry Gene Willey, "The Reverend John Rankin, Early Ohio Anti-Slavery Leader"; Dwight L. Dumond, *Antislavery: The Crusade for Freedom in America.* Also in this source, great details about the Lane students who rebelled; more about them in *Friend of Man,* Utica, N.Y., Sept. 8, 1836, and Jan. 3, 1838.

69   Accounts of debates by Allan and Benton: *The Legion of Liberty! And Force of Truth; containing the thoughts, words and deeds of some prominent apostles, champions and martyrs,* 2nd ed. (New York: American Anti-Slavery Society, 1843).

70   "The Lord has done": Barnes, *Antislavery Impulse,* p. 67.

70   "The business of Egypt": Thomas, *Theodore Weld,* p. 78.

70   "Our temple of God": *Cincinnati Journal,* July 11, 1834.

71   Lane trustees' new resolutions: *Cincinnati Daily Gazette,* Aug. 30, 1834.

71   "Far better for the Seminary": Rankin's editorial published first in *Cincinnati Journal* and then in pamphlet form; excerpts are taken from the pamphlet, *Review of the Statement of the Faculty of Lane Seminary in Relation to the Recent Difficulties in that Institution by John Rankin, Pastor of the Presbyterian Church of Ripley and Author of "Letters on Slavery"* (Ripley, Ohio: Published by the Author, Campbell & Palmer, Printers, 1835).

71   Students walked out of Lane: Tappan, *Life of Arthur Tappan,* says there were fifty-one. There are discrepancies in secondary sources regarding the number of Lane rebels. The Lane records in combination with this secondary source and several others concur that it was fifty-one; others say seventy-five, forty-two, fifty, and sixty-one. I have settled on fifty-one because of the credibility of the secondary sources that use that number and the Lane records.

71   Harriet Beecher Stowe's description of John Rankin: Forrest Wilson, *Crusader in Crinoline: The Life of Harriet Beecher Stowe* (New York: J. B. Lippincott, 1941).

73   Weld's speeches: I could not find any of the speeches that Weld gave in Ripley, but I did want to give the reader a sense of Weld's intensity and passion. The examples in the text come from, Barnes, *Antislavery Impulse,* p. 79; *Legion of Liberty! And Force of Truth.*

Chapter Nine

76   Story of Adam Lowry Rankin's awakening: Adam Lowry Rankin, "The Autobiography of Adam Lowry Rankin."

81   Antislavery cause a "family business": Byron Williams, *History of Clermont and Brown Counties, Ohio* (Baltimore: Gateway Press, 1987), vol. 1; cemetery records in Brown County towns, mainly those on the Ripley line; *The History of Brown County;* Carl N. Thompson, compiler, *Historical Collections of Brown County;* files for Brown, Adams, Clermont, and Highland counties, Siebert Collection, Ohio Historical Society; U.S.

Census records for Adams, Brown, Clermont, and Highland counties; newspaper ads [e.g., ad for Thomas W. Collins, *Ripley Bee,* confirming his coffin-making business and hence giving credence to the stories that he had hidden fugitive slaves in the coffins]; real-estate deeds [land survey no. 3,389, e.g., revealed the earliest presence of the Pettijohn family in Brown County, near Sardinia]; newsletter abstracts of Brown County, Ohio, 1977–82, Brown County Genealogical Society, Georgetown, Ohio; certificates of freedom and bills of sale for slaves, Mason County Historical Society, Maysville, Kentucky; Edward O'Conner Purtee, "The Underground Railroad from Southwestern Ohio to Lake Erie," Ph.D. dissertation, Graduate School of Ohio State University, 1932; Wilbur H. Siebert, "The Underground Railroad in Ohio," *Ohio Archaeological and Historical Society Quarterly,* vol. 4 (1895), pp. 44–63. That particular individuals were part of the Underground Railroad was often confirmed through newspaper accounts of incidents, court records, property records, and tax records in combination with interviews with people in the region today.

81 Rankin's family: John Rankin, "The Life of Rev. John Rankin"; obituary of Jean Rankin, *Ripley Bee,* Jan. 30, 1879; the Ripley Museum files; A. L. Rankin, "Autobiography."

82 Stagecoach stop outside of Decatur: The current owners of this site were well aware of its history. The Ripley line, from Ripley to Red Oak to Russellville to Sardinia (and sometimes to Decatur instead of Russellville), is apparent from the interviews in the Siebert Collection, Ohio Historical Society. Lisa Reynolds, a Ripley resident, was able to confirm a rumor about the row houses in Russellville. We knew from county accounts and relatives that Martha West Lucas had been active in the Underground Railroad, and we had also heard that the attics in the row houses on North Columbus Street in Russellville had been used to sequester slaves. By corresponding with a relative of Lucas's and checking property deeds in Russellville, Lisa made a match: Martha West Lucas had indeed lived in one of those row houses.

83 John M. and Marshall Nelson: Elsie Johnson Ayres, *The Hills of Highland* (Springfield, Ohio: H. K. Skinner & Son, 1971); *Transactions of the McLean County Historical Society* (Bloomington, Ill.: Pantagraph Printing and Stationery Co., 1899), vol. 1. The Huggins family details were in the obituary of James E. Huggins, *News Democrat,* Aug. 20, 1898; Isaac M. Beck, letters; cemetery records; land deeds; genealogical work done by Lisa Reynolds on the Internet.

83 "Dear Sir": Committee of the Home-Coming Association, ed., *Greene County, 1803–1908* (Xenia, Ohio: Aldine, 1908), p. 69.

83 The Rankins kept fugitives: Rankin, "The Autobiography of Adam Lowry Rankin," p. 154.

84 "Julia would deny herself": Samuel Rankin, as told to John Rankin, Jr., who told it to Wilbur Siebert. At Ohio Historical Society, Rankin Papers (VFM 2137), p. 27.

86 About Sardinia: Gladys Kincaid Kilmer, "Brief History of Sardinia," unpublished typescript; *History of Brown County.*

86 Isaac M. Beck: His 1892 letter, in Union Township Library, Ripley, Ohio, in which he offers an autobiographical sketch; *History of Brown County;* Thompson, compiler, *Historical Collections.*

87 A free black man, John Hudson: Isaac M. Beck, account of life on the Underground Railroad in Brown County, 1892, Union Township Library, Ripley, Ohio; "Free Blacks of Brown County, Ohio in 1830," Union Township Library [this list was taken from the 1830 U.S. Census and Carter G. Woodson "Free Negro Heads of Families in 1830"]; Brown County Census Records for Washington Township, 1850.

87　John B. Mahan: His birthplace, in Fleming County, Kentucky, revealed through his father's property records in that county, bk. A, p. 330, Land Records. Marriage records in Brown County (license says Dec. 8, 1820, but marriage was actually Dec. 19, 1820, Georgetown, Ohio; also 1840 U.S. Census records in Washington Township, Brown County, Ohio. See also Mrs. Reba Mahan Stevens, Mrs. Ramah Clawson, Mrs. Ruth L. Harris of Fostoria, Michigan, and John C. Harris, compilers, "Lines from the Rev. Jacob Mahan and from William Mahan," unpublished manuscript; *Transactions of McLean County Historical Society,* vol. 1; Erasmus Mahan, "Friends of Liberty on the Mackinaw," in *Transactions of McLean County Historical Society,* vol. 1, p. 396; *Portrait and Biographical Album of McLean County, Illinois* (Chicago: Chapman Bros., 1887); Ezra M. Prince and John H. Burnham, eds., *Historical Encyclopedia of Illinois and History of McLean County,* vol. 2 (Chicago: Munsell, 1908); G. Glenn Clift, *History of Maysville and Mason County* (Lexington, Ky.: Transylvania Printing Co., 1936).

Chapter Ten

90　Amos Dresser: Dresser's own account of the incident in *Cincinnati Gazette,* Aug. 25, 1835; *Zion's Watchman,* Feb. 10, 1836. Commentary on the incident in *Anti-Slavery Record,* Sept. 2, 1835.

98　"The American Anti-Slavery Society aims": American Anti-Slavery Society's Second Annual Report, pp. 62–63.

98　The "great pamphlet campaign of 1835": Dwight L. Dumond, *Anti-Slavery;* Margaret L. Coit, *John C. Calhoun: American Portrait* (Boston: Houghton Mifflin, 1960); William Lee Miller, *Arguing About Slavery: The Great Battle in the United States Congress* (New York: Alfred A. Knopf, 1996); Gilbert Hobbs Barnes, *The Anti-Slavery Impulse;* Albert Bushnell Hart, *Slavery and Abolition 1831–1841;* Stephen B. Oates, *The Approaching Fury: Voices of the Storm, 1820–1861* (New York: HarperCollins, 1997); Merton L. Dillon, *The Abolitionists;* Leonard L. Richards, *"Gentlemen of Property and Standing":* in *Anti-Abolition Mobs in Jacksonian America* (New York: Oxford University Press, 1970); and Gilbert H. Barnes, "Introduction," in Barnes and Dwight L. Dumond, eds., *Letters of Theodore Dwight Weld, Angelina Grimke Weld and Sarah Grimke, 1822–1844* (1934 ed.); *Niles' Register,* Aug. 20 and 22, 1835.

98　"Incendiary publications": President Andrew Jackson, seventh annual State of the Union address, delivered Dec. 7, 1835, in Robert Vincent Remini, *Andrew Jackson and the Course of American Democracy, 1833–1845* (New York: Harper & Row, 1984); also in James D. Richardson, *Messages and Papers of the Presidents, 1789–1897,* pp. 147, 174–76.

99　"Frivolous, absurd": John C. Calhoun, in Coit, *John C. Calhoun,* p. 310.

99　About the Ohio Anti-Slavery Society: Benjamin P. Thomas, *Theodore Weld.*

100　Cholera struck the region again: *Ripley Bee,* July 22, 1835.

100　Ripley Anti-Slavery Society: "Records of Anti-Slavery Society Preserved in Old Volume," *Columbus Dispatch,* June 11, 1948; "Ripley Anti-Slavery Society Minute Book." The latter is a handwritten book that contains the constitution of the society, the names of 337 members, and minutes of meetings from 1835 through 1848. The original passed through several generations of the family of Chambers Baird, landing in the household of Baird descendant Nellie Baird Haggerty, whose sister-in-law was the last person to own it. Mrs. Maude Haggerty Ervin gave it to the Ohio Historical Society, where it was transcribed. The typescript is available at Union Township Library, Ripley, Ohio; the original is at OHS. All excerpts and resolutions from the society come from this source.

101 Delegate to Ohio Anti-Slavery Society convention: John Rankin, "The Life of Rev. John Rankin"; Adam Lowry Rankin, "The Autobiography of Adam Lowry Rankin"; Larry Gene Willey, "The Reverend John Rankin, Early Ohio Anti-Slavery Leader"; accounts in the Siebert Collection, Ohio Historical Society.

Chapter Eleven

102 Granville in 1836: Generous research efforts of Florence Hoffman, Lyn Boone, and Julianna Mulroy, as well as "Daybook of A. P. Pritchard," Jan. 1, 1839–May 16, 1846; photo of Broadway in 1842; letters of Rev. Henry Bushnell, all available at the Granville Historical Society, Granville, Ohio; Rev. Henry Bushnell, *The History of Granville* (Licking County, Ohio: Press of Hann & Adair, 1889).

102 Granville Literary and Theological Institution: Now called Denison University, it was called Granville Literary and Theological Institution 1831 to 1844. From 1845 to 1853, it was Granville College, and then, in either 1853 or 1854, the name was changed to Denison University. The Granville Female Seminary opened in 1832 and was incorporated in 1835. In 1861, it became the Young Ladies' Institute, and was renamed Shepardson College in 1886. This Baptist women's school later became part of Denison. In 1836, there was also a Granville Female Academy, an Episcopal school incorporated that year. (This information provided by Lyn Boone, Denison University, who was one of the readers of the manuscript for this book.)

103 "We consider": William T. Utter, *Granville: The Story of an Ohio Village* (Granville, Ohio: Denison University, 1956), p. 171.

104 Proclamation of citizens of Granville: *Newark Gazette,* March 31, 1836.

104 Meeting in the Bancroft barn: Letters, personal accounts, and other sources, Granville Historical Society Archives, Granville, Ohio, including: William Birney, *James G. Birney and His Times;* Bushnell, *History of Granville;* Dwight L. Dumond, ed., *Letters of James Gillespie Birney, 1831–1857,* vol. I., esp. p. 320 and the letter to *Anti-Slavery Record* in footnote; Henry Howe, *Historical Collections of Ohio* (Columbus: Ohio State Archaeological and Historical Society, 1896), vol. II [for complete account of the incident in Granville]; a letter to Rev. H. Bushnell from L. Barnes of Delaware, Ohio [describing Weld's visit to Granville in 1835 and the antislavery convention the following year], Aug. 31, 188[7] [presumably the letter was in response to Bushnell's fact-finding mission for his history of Granville]; Robert Price, "The Ohio Anti-Slavery Convention of 1836," *Ohio State Archaeological and Historical Society Quarterly,* 1887.

105 Rankin's speech: Rev. John Rankin, *An Address to the Churches; in relation to slavery* (Medina, Ohio: Printed at the Anti-Slavery Office, 1836).

109 Letter from Thome to Weld: Gilbert H. Barnes and Dwight L. Dumond, eds., *Letters of Theodore Dwight Weld, Angelina Grimke Weld and Sarah Grimke, 1822–1844,* vol. 2, p. 301.

109 Underground Railroad in Granville: Granville Historical Society Archives; of particular interest, an undated letter from Theophilus Little to H. E. Nottingham.

109 Rankin on the ride from Granville to Ripley: John Rankin, *The Emancipator,* Sept. 6, 1836.

110 Report from August Wattles: Dated April 28, 1836, in *The Liberator,* May 14, 1836.

111 Destruction of *The Philanthropist* press: Birney, *James G. Birney and His Times; The Philanthropist,* July 15, 22, and 29, 1836; "Introduction," Dumond, ed., *Letters of Birney,* vol. 1.

112   Resolutions of Ripley Anti-Slavery Society: Minutes of the Society, Aug. 11, 1836, Union Township Library, Ripley, Ohio.

Chapter Twelve

113   "The Seventy": Gilbert Hobbs Barnes, *The Anti-Slavery Impulse, 1830–1844;* John L. Myers, "The Agency System of the AntiSlavery Movement, 1832–1837, and Its Antecedents in Other Reform and Benevolent Societies," Ph.D. dissertation, Department of History, University of Michigan, 1948; *Friend of Man,* Sept. 8, 1836.

114   Violence inflicted on antislavery speakers: Benjamin P. Thomas, *Theodore Weld: Crusader for Freedom.*

114   Rankin's 1836 tour for American Anti-Slavery Society: *The Philanthropist,* Dec. 15, 1836, Jan. 12, 1837, Feb. 3, 1837, March 15, 1837, Dec. 23, 1837; *The Emancipator,* Dec. 15, 1836; Rankin letter dated Sept. 6, 1836, in *The Emancipator,* Sept. 29, 1836; *Advocate of Freedom,* Augusta, Maine, Sept. 6, 1836; John Rankin, "The Life of Rev. John Rankin."

117   Adam Lowry Rankin's Underground Railroad experiences at Lane Seminary: Adam Lowry Rankin, "The Autobiography of Adam Lowry Rankin."

121   Antislavery petitions: Dwight L. Dumond, *Antislavery;* Margaret L. Coit, *John C. Calhoun;* Merton L. Dillon, *The Abolitionists.*

122   "Speech on the Reception of Abolition Petitions": Eric L. McKitrick, ed., *Slavery Defended: The Views of the Old South* (Englewood Cliffs, N.J.: Prentice-Hall, 1963), pp. 12–16.

Chapter Thirteen

123   Story of Eliza Jane Johnson: Transcript of county court records for "October Term 1831, 1ˢᵗ Day. The Commonwealth of Kentucky against Eliza Johnson, a woman of color," Kentucky Department for Libraries and Archives, Kentucky State Historical Society, Frankfort, Ky.; various newspaper commentaries, e.g., *Cincinnati Journal and Luminary,* Sept. 30, 1837; *Maysville Eagle,* Oct. 18, 1837; *The Philanthropist,* Nov. 14, 1837; *The Liberator,* April 20, 1838; records of debates in the Ohio state legislature later, March 1838, over the fate of Eliza Jane Johnson, in *The Philanthropist,* March 3, 6, and 13, 1838.

124   Thirty-two-year-old: 1830 census records.

124   Member of the Ripley Anti-Slavery Society: Society's roster, in the Minute Book.

126   Judge Reid issued his judgment: "Judge Reid's Opinion," *Maysville Eagle,* Nov. 4, 1837.

127   "Citizen of Kentucky" letter: *Maysville Eagle,* Nov. 1, 1837.

127   Morris's letter to Campbell: Dated Nov. 13, 1837, *Political Examiner,* Nov. 16, 1837, reprinted in *The Philanthropist,* Dec. 26, 1837.

128   Evansville, Indiana, incident: *Evansville Journal,* reprinted in *The Liberator,* Oct. 20, 1837.

129   Elijah P. Lovejoy was shot and killed: *Observer,* Nov. 7, 1837; Merton L. Dillon, *Elijah P. Lovejoy, Abolitionist Editor* (Urbana: University of Illinois Press, 1961); David W. Blight, "The Martyrdom of Elijah P. Lovejoy," *American History Illustrated,* vol. 12, no. 7 (Nov. 1977); Leonard L. Richards, "Gentlemen of Property and Standing."

130   William Herndon, John Brown, and Wendell Phillips quote: Blight, "Martyrdom of Lovejoy."

131   "Resolved that": "Ripley Anti-Slavery Society Minute Book," Union Township Library, Ripley, Ohio.

PART II: 1838

133 "My dear children": John B. Mahan, letter to his children, *Cincinnati Weekly Herald and Philanthropist*, Feb. 12, 1845.

133 "As I marked": *Trial of Rev. John B. Mahan, for Felony, in the Mason Circuit Court of Kentucky, Commencing on Tuesday, the 13ᵗʰ and Terminating on Monday the 19ᵗʰ of November, 1838* [pamphlet].

Chapter Fourteen

135 The ice was breaking: For reports of when the river froze in 1838, see *Liberty Hall and Cincinnati Gazette,* all issues for Feb. and March. By Feb. 22, the river was frozen; a week later, it began to thaw and break up; and then, by the first days of March, it was frozen again, not to break up until March 11.

135 "All the boys": This story of a woman and child crossing the ice and arriving in Ripley is taken from the accounts of three of the sons of John Rankin; it is a compendium of Adam Lowry, Samuel, and John Jr.'s accounts from respectively, Adam Lowry Rankin, "The Autobiography of Adam Lowry Rankin"; Rev. S. G. W. Rankin, in Connecticut, as told to a reporter, *Hartford Daily Courant,* Nov. 23, 1895 (reprinted Nov. 30, 1895, in *Boston Transcript*); and two accounts by John, Jr. (John Thompson), one told to Frank Gregg and one to William Siebert, and both filed in Rankin Papers, Ohio Historical Society, and also at Union Township Library in Ripley. When I found inconsistencies in the accounts, the default account was John, Jr.'s, because his version as told to Gregg and to Siebert, is the most detailed and the details are the most logical and accurate. John Parker confirms the role of Chancey Shaw, but Parker did not live in Ripley at the time of the incident, and so I did not rely on his account for the entire story. Numerous secondary sources claim the authenticity of the escape of this slave, who was Harriet Beecher Stowe's inspiration for her character Eliza in *Uncle Tom's Cabin.* There is no way to know with certainty exactly what happened that night in 1838, or even when the woman returned to get the remainder of her family. There is considerable confusion in the primary sources about whether the children she retrieved on her return trip were her own or her grandchildren; again, I relied on John, Jr.'s accounts. Despite such confusion, I am persuaded by the accounts that I read that a slave woman with a child did indeed cross the Ohio River while the river was frozen during 1838, that she returned to retrieve the remainder of her family, and that John Rankin told the story to Harriet Beecher Stowe at some point between 1838 and the time when Stowe moved away from Cincinnati. It is easily documented that the Stowes, Beechers, and Rankins spent time together, and that John Rankin and/or Adam Lowry Rankin related to the Stowes, at the very least, stories of slaves escaping across the Ohio River. Rankin could have told Stowe at his own home, or in New York, perhaps at the 1839 anniversary meeting of the American Anti-Slavery Society, or at Lane Seminary that same year. One of Rankin's sons documented a meeting between Stowe and Rankin at Lane in 1839 and said it was there that his father shared the story with her. Clearly Stowe protected Rankin when she published her book *A Key to Uncle Tom's Cabin,* because the story was well known by then, and Rankin could have been incarcerated and fined heavily if Stowe revealed that he had told her the story.

137 That Chancey Shaw helped the woman out of the river and directed her to Rankin's hill comes from several independent sources: from John Parker's account, as told to him by John Rankin, in Stuart Sprague, ed., *His Promised Land;* in the accounts of the three Rankin sons on file in the Ohio Historical Society; and A. L. Rankin's "Autobiography."

139 Levi Coffin in Newport, Indiana: Levi Coffin, *Reminiscences of Levi Coffin;* from the John Rankin, Jr., accounts; and various nineteenth-century secondary sources, such as George S. McDowell, "Harriet Beecher Stowe at Cincinnati," *New England Magazine,* March 1895.

Chapter Fifteen

140 Eighteen hundred and thirty-eight was the year: Philip S. Foner, *Frederick Douglass* (New York: Citadel Press, 1964); *History of Pennsylvania Hall; which was destroyed by a mob, on the 17th of May, 1838* (Philadelphia: Merrihew and Gunn, 1838).

140 School in Red Oak: This fascinating story can be re-created through the issues of *The Philanthropist,* and the *Ripley Bee,* May–Dec. 1838. The school was burned on July 1, 1838 by "haters of the colored man" (*The Philanthropist,* Sept. 25, 1838). It was rebuilt by the late autumn, and then burned down again.

141 Eliza Jane Johnson: W. C. Cochran, "The Western Reserve and the Fugitive Slave Law," *Western Reserve Historical Society,* no. 101, 1920; *The Philanthropist,* March 6 and 13, 1838.

142 "This case has some attendant circumstances": *Cincinnati Gazette,* Feb. 27, 1838.

142 March 12, the day after the thaw: *Liberty Hall and Cincinnati Gazette,* March 16, 1838.

142 "Upon the motion": Court record books, March 12, 1838, on microfilm, Mason County Historical Society, Maysville, Kentucky.

142 John Rankin, letter of March 14, 1838: regarding Eliza Jane Johnson, in *The Philanthropist,* March 20, 1838.

143 Rewards up to $2,500: Translates to $53,350 in 2001 dollars.

Chapter Sixteen

144 Flash floods killed one man: *Liberty Hall and Cincinnati Gazette,* June 28, 1838; in the same edition, notice of the earthquake; for the temperatures throughout June, see July 11, 1838, edition of the same paper.

145 "Our neighborhood": Minutes, June meeting of Sardinia Anti-Slavery Society, reprinted in *The Philanthropist,* Dec. 12, 1838.

145 Alfred Beasley brought a black man: Adam Lowry Rankin, "The Autobiography of Adam Lowry Rankin," p. 79.

147 "Muscular, raw-boned and stalwart": William Birney, *James G. Birney and His Times,* p. 166.

147 John the slave remained with Mahan: Depositions in the Mahan civil case (see chapter twenty) and trial testimony (see chapter eighteen).

147 Details of the account of the Mahan entrapment: Court testimony, Nov. 1838 trial; accounts of that testimony, *Philanthropist,* Nov. 20, 1838; depositions in the Mahan civil case, 1839, 1840, and 1841.

148 Greathouse property: Tax records at the Mason County Historical Society, Maysville, Kentucky.

148 "A wicked and depraved person": The Aug. 9, 1831, indictment "Commonwealth vs. William Greathouse" at the Kentucky Department for Libraries and Archives at the Kentucky State Historical Society in Frankfort, Kentucky.

148 "After searching through the country": Eli Huggins, deposition in the Mahan civil case, and also from his account in *The Philanthropist,* Oct. 30, 1838.

148 The drama regarding William Greathouse and the Pettijohns and the arrest of John B. Mahan: an account written by Mrs. Lewis Pettijohn and later published in *The Philan-*

thropist on July 20, 1838; and minutes of the Sardinia Anti-Slavery Society for November 1838, at Union Township Library, Ripley, Ohio.

150 "In the last three months," *Parkersburg Gazette,* Aug. 1, 1838.

151 Nelson's escape encounter between "Mr. Rock" and Mahan: Depositions in the Mahan civil case and trial testimony with the Mahan criminal case: Mahan's letters.

151 "Dear Sir": Letter dated Aug. 4, 1838, that John Mahan allegedly wrote for the slave John to take to the next stop, from exhibit at the trial, with the trial transcript and depositions in the *Commonwealth of Kentucky* v. *John B. Mahan,* Kentucky State Historical Society Library, Frankfort, Kentucky.

Chapter Seventeen

153 "In September 1838, Greathouse returned": Minutes of the Sardinia Anti-Slavery Society for November 1838; and *The Philanthropist,* Oct. 30, 1838.

154 Polly Mahan sat: Scene from account by Eli Huggins, then president of the Sardinia Anti-Slavery Society; from letter by "A Friend of the Oppressed," *The Philanthropist— Extra,* reprinted in *The Philanthropist,* Oct. 30, 1838; and from *The Philanthropist,* Dec. 18, 1838.

154 "Before he left": *The Philanthropist,* Oct. 30, 1838.

154 Reward of up to $2,500 and "$500 to any responsible man": Depositions of Joseph and Zachariah Pettijohn, late Nov. 1838, *The Philanthropist,* Dec. 18, 1838.

155 Account of Mahan's arrest from: Testimony at upcoming trial (see chapter eighteen); from depositions in the Mahan civil case, 1839, 1840, and 1841 (see chapter twenty).

156 The grand jury of Mason County issued two indictments: Frankfort, Kentucky, *Commonwealth of Kentucky* v. *John B. Mahan,* Kentucky State Historical Society Library, reprinted in *The Liberator,* Nov. 2, 1838.

156 Clark sent letter to Vance: *The Liberator,* Nov. 2, 1838.

158 Rankin wrote a letter: *The Philanthropist,* Sept. 18, 1838.

158 "A Citizen of the State of Ohio": *The Philanthropist,* Sept. 24, 1838. Some newspapers later claimed that the Mahan case was a plot on the part of abolitionists to get attention to their cause; see especially the *Ohio Star,* reprinted and commented on in *The Philanthropist,* Nov. 20, 1838. Similar commentary from the *Ohio Sun* was discussed in the *Clermont Courier,* March 2, 1839.

158 Newspaper reports about the Mahan case: *The Liberator, Pennsylvania Freeman, Morning Star* of New Hampshire, *Christian Witness, Cincinnati Daily Gazette,* and *Worcester Christian Reflector,* all reprinted in *The Philanthropist,* Oct. 30, 1838.

162 "Gov. Vance upon such a demand": *Pennsylvania Freeman,* reprinted in *Cincinnati Journal,* Oct. 11, 1838.

162 Gov. Vance tried to repair: Letter to governor of Kentucky, reprinted in *The Philanthropist,* Oct. 23, 1838; in that same issue is the quote from *Ohio Statesman* (the organ of the Democratic Party in Ohio).

163 Ohio gubernatorial election returns: *Journal and Register* of Columbus, Ohio, Oct. 26, 1838.

163 Mahan's letters: To Gov. Vance, to his friend, to his wife, to his children, respectively, from *The Philanthropist,* Nov. 6, 1838; *The Liberator,* Nov. 16, 1838 (also in *Pennsylvania Freeman,* Nov. 1, 1838); *Pennsylvania Freeman,* Nov. 1, 1838; and *Cincinnati Weekly Herald and Philanthropist,* Feb. 12, 1845.

164 Greathouse's proposal for a compromise: Letter by Mahan to editor of *Zion's Watchman,* Dec. 22, 1838.

165   Mahan's will: *Cincinnati Weekly Herald and Philanthropist*, March 26, 1845.

165   She knelt at her husband's side: There are two versions of Mrs. Mahan's visit to her husband's jail cell. One is that she tore her own underclothes to make him bandages, and the other that she tore his underclothes to do the same. I chose the former, which was more logical. *Transactions of the McLean County Historical Society*, (Bloomington, Ill.: Published for the McLean Historical Society by Pantograph Printing and Stationery Co., 1899) vol. 1.

165   "WHO WILL CONTRIBUTE?": *The Philanthropist*, Nov. 6, 1838; an appeal on behalf of Rankin's appeal appeared in ibid., Nov. 20, 1838.

Chapter Eighteen

166   In late October: *Philanthropist*, Nov. 4, 1838; response of editors in same edition.

167   Slave insurrection in Boone County: *Warsaw Patriot* in Kentucky, Nov. 3, 1838; *Liberty Hall and Cincinnati Gazette*, Nov. 14, 1838; *Western Citizen*, of Paris, Ky., Nov. 16, 1838.

167   Walker Reid was a prominent figure: *Lawyers and Lawmakers of Kentucky*, pp. 699–700; *Biographical Encyclopaedia* (Cincinnati: Galaxy Publishing, 1876).

168   "I cannot believe": Judge Walker Reid, charge to jury, trial testimony, and closing arguments from *Trial of Rev. John B. Mahan, for Felony, in the Mason Circuit Court of Kentucky, Commencing on Tuesday, the 13th and Terminating on Monday the 19th of November, 1838;* also in *Western Citizen* of Paris, Ky., Nov. 30, 1838; and in edition of *Maysville Eagle*, Nov. 20, 1838. Commentary throughout the trial in *Maysville Eagle*, original copies at Union Township Library, Ripley, Ohio.

169   Details about Mason County Courthouse in Washington, Kentucky, and about Harriet Beecher Stowe's 1833 visit: Mrs. Lula Reed Boss, "Mason County's First Temple of Justice," Maysville, Kentucky. Publication date unknown. Available at the Mason County Historical Society in Maysville, Kentucky; and in *Kentucky Ancestors*, vol. 3, no. 3, January 1968.

170   Defense team and prosecutors: *Biographical Encyclopedia;* lawyers' ads in *Maysville Eagle*, autumn 1838.

175   "Fifteen slaves had passed through his hands": this allegation and the first media mention of "a line of posts" from Kentucky to Canada, are from *Maysville Eagle*, Nov. 21, 1838, as reported from the Mahan testimony.

178   Not guilty: Mahan's acquittal was announced nationwide, e.g., *The Liberator*, Nov. 30, 1838, and *N.Y. Journal of Commerce*, Nov. 29, 1838.

179   Mahan was still not free: *Cincinnati Gazette*, reprinted in *The Philanthropist*, Nov. 7, 1838.

179   William Dunlop posted security: William Birney, *James G. Birney and His Times*.

179   Mahan's release announced in *The Philanthropist*, Dec. 4, 1838; and *The Liberator*, Dec. 28, 1838.

Chapter Nineteen

180   "Developments in the case": *Maysville Monitor*, Nov. 20, 1838, reprinted in *Clermont Courier*, Dec. 19, 1838; concurring opinion in *Cincinnati Gazette*, Nov. 28, 1838; response in *The Philanthropist*, Dec. 4, 1838.

181   Governor Clark publicly bemoaned: James Clark, speech, December 1838, *The Philanthropist*, Dec. 18, 1838.

182   Letter to Ohio Governor Wilson Shannon: "Special Message of the Governor, Transmitting a Communication from Mssrs. Morehead and Smith, Commissioners from Ken-

tucky, from the National Hotel in Columbus, January 26, 1839," at Schomburg Center for Research in Black Culture, New York Public Library, New York City.

182 "Ohio Fugitive Slave Law": Ohio—Documents of the Thirty-seventh General Assembly, pt. 2 of vol. for 1838–39, doc. no. 84, p. 1 [Columbus, Ohio, 1852]; also in *Niles' National Register,* March 30, 1839.

182 *Christian Witness* wrote: Reprinted in *The Philanthropist,* Aug. 6, 1839.

183 "Brown County is becoming quite celebrated": Ibid., May 14, 1839.

Chapter Twenty

184 "Citizen of Ripley" incident: *The Philanthropist,* April 23, 1839.

185 "These hateful and groveling": Ibid.

185 The details of the incident that led to the criminal case against John Mahan and quotes in the incident description: "Indictment for a Riot, State of Ohio vs. John B. Mahan, Amos Pettyjohn [sic] and Joseph Pettyjohn [sic]," Brown [County] Court of Common Pleas, April Term 1839, Brown County Administration Building, Georgetown, Ohio; Sept. 30 trial testimony, in the same file; for the sentencing, see transcript for Oct. 11, 1839; and *The Philanthropist,* May 21, 1839.

187 Sally Hudson's death: Isaac M. Beck letter, 1892, at Union Township Library, Ripley, Ohio; *The Philanthropist,* June 18, 1839.

188 Mahan petitioned the Ohio legislature: *Western Citizen,* Paris, Kentucky, Feb. 1, 1839.

188 Mahan offered $10 for chains: *Clermont Courier,* Feb. 16, 1839; June 25, 1860.

190 The sentence was reversed on appeal: *John B. Mahan, Amos Pettijohn, and Joseph Pettijohn v. The State of Ohio,* in *Reports of Cases Argued and Determined in the Supreme Court of Ohio in Bank,* vol. 10, [compiled] by P. B. Wilcox (Cincinnati: Robert Clarke & Co., 1873), at Ohio State Supreme Court Archives, Columbus, Ohio.

190 Mahan deposed: The depositions in the Mahan civil case, including the interview regarding the question of John Rankin's ownership of a carriage, in *William Greathouse* v. *John B. Mahan,* case in Mason [County] Circuit Court, in Kentucky Department for Libraries and Archives, Kentucky State Historical Society, Frankfort, Kentucky.

196 "Now the question": "A Citizen of Brown County, Ohio," *The Philanthropist,* April 28, 1840. There are numerous versions of this incident, especially in secondary sources, such as Ripley's own history, Eliese Bambach Stivers, *Ripley, Ohio; The History of Brown County;* Carl N. Thompson, compiler, *Historical Collections of Brown County;* and various articles in *Ohio Archaeological and Historical Society Quarterly* (see its index at the Ohio Historical Society, Columbus, Ohio). I trusted the version in Adam Lowry Rankin, "The Autobiography of Adam Lowry Rankin," and the very detailed letter from "A Citizen of Brown County, Ohio." And after reading Lowry's "Autobiography" and becoming familiar with his style and cadence of writing, I consider it very probable that that letter was written by Lowry.

PART III: MIDNIGHT ASSASSINS

199 "We feel the hand of oppression": John Rankin, *Sixth Annual Report of the Executive Committee of the American Anti-Slavery Society, with the Speeches Delivered at the Anniversary Meeting Held in New York City, on the 7th of May, 1839, and the Minutes of the Meetings of the Society for Business, Held on the Evening and the Three Following Days* (New York: American Anti-Slavery Society, 1839).

199 "It evidently was the purpose:" Adam Lowry Rankin, "The Autobiography of Adam Lowry Rankin," p. 108.

Chapter Twenty-One

201   Ripley in the 1840s: Eliese Bambach Stivers, *Ripley, Ohio; The History of Brown County.*

202   Thomas McCague and the Panic of 1837: *History of Brown County;* Carl N. Thompson, compiler, *Historical Collections of Brown County.*

202   Rankin advocated boycotting: John Rankin, "The Life of Rev. John Rankin."

202   Thirty-foot pole: It is impossible to confirm without a doubt that Rankin erected a pole with a fish-oil lantern near his house in the early 1840s. And because neither Rankin nor his sons mention it in their accounts or letters, I was hesitant to include this detail. Yet I did find references to it in four independent sources. Frank Gregg clearly believed there was a pole, and in 1912 he re-enacted the lighting of the lantern on the pole and took a photo of the re-enactment. He must have interviewed someone who told him about it, but no record of that interview can be found. However, the pole was mentioned in the obituary of Thomas Lovejoy Rankin, *Quenemo News* in Kansas, Nov. 25, 1915; and Thomas was present in Ripley at the time of the re-enactment. In addition, there is a photo of the Rankin house that shows a faint image of a pole on the far side of the house. The photo is in a pamphlet written by Wilbur H. Siebert, *A Quaker Section of the Underground Railroad* (Columbus: F. J. Heer, 1930), reprinted from *Ohio Archaeological and Historical Quarterly.* And Arnold Gragston mentions the pole in James Mellon, ed., *Bullwhip Days* (see chapter six).

202   "Never-failing fountain": John Rankin, *Letters on American Slavery,* p. 5.

202   By 1840, the movement was less unified: Gilbert Hobbs Barnes, *The Anti-Slavery Impulse, 1830–1844;* Albert Bushnell Hart, *Slavery and Abolition, 1831–1841;* esp. Merton L. Dillon, *The Abolitionists.* In Dillon's work, the chapter "No Union with Slaveholders" is excellent regarding this topic.

203   "In discussing the subject of slavery": Theodore Weld, letter to a friend, J. F. Robinson, in Dillon, *The Abolitionists,* p. 145.

203   "Come-outerism": Dillon, *Abolitionists,* pp. 150, 157, 158.

203   "Considered so much a matter": James G. Birney, letter to Salmon P. Chase, Feb. 2, 1842, in Dwight L. Dumond, ed., *Letters of James Gillespie Birney,* p. 670.

203   "There is no reason": James G. Birney, letter to Lewis Tappan, Jan. 14, 1842, in Dumond, ed., *Birney* Letters, p. 658.

203   Rankin at sixth annual meeting: *Sixth Annual Report of the Executive Committee of the American Anti-Slavery Society, with the Speeches Delivered at the Anniversary Meeting Held in New York City, on the 7ᵗʰ of May, 1839, and the Minutes of the Meetings of the Society for Business, Held on the Evening and the Three Following Days."*

204   "I feel that great care": William Lloyd Garrison, in Dillon, *The Abolitionists,* p. 147.

204   Whig Party rally in Ripley in autumn 1840: Stivers, *Ripley, Ohio;* Thompson, compiler, *Historical Collections;* Adam Lowry Rankin, "The Autobiography of Adam Lowry Rankin"; and "Letter from an Old Timer Who Heard General Harrison Speak in Ripley in 1840," in *Ripley Bee,* January 8, 1919.

205   New allegiances of Adam Lowry: A. L. Rankin, "Autobiography." See also *The Philanthropist,* throughout summer and fall of 1840, for commentary from John Rankin regarding the antislavery movement and the election of 1840.

205   Resolution "that while we recognize": news accounts in newspapers (e.g., *Cincinnati Weekly Herald and Philanthropist,* Dec. 13, 1843, April 23, 1845); Philip S. Foner, *History of Black Americans,* p. 538.

206   Rankin's dwindling funds: Rankin, "Life of Rankin"; A. L. Rankin, "Autobiography."

Chapter Twenty-Two

209 "What has brought you back?": This account combines the versions of three of John Rankin's sons: Adam Lowry Rankin, "The Autobiography of Adam Lowry Rankin"; John, Jr., in his interviews with Wilbur Siebert and with Frank Gregg, respectively, on file in the Rankin Papers at the Ohio Historical Society in Columbus, Ohio, and in the Rankin-Parker Collection at the Special Collections Library at Duke University; Samuel Rankin, in the Connecticut newspaper, *Hartford Daily Courant,* Nov. 23, 1895. Richard Calvin Rankin claimed that "Eliza" returned in 1839, but his brothers say the year was 1841. In addition, based on other evidence in John Rankin's autobiography, Adam Lowry's, and Rankin's travel activities as noted in his letters to *The Philanthropist* during 1839, he would not have been home during June 1839, and he was home in June 1841. See also the notes for Chapter Fourteen.

214 Approximately fifteen thousand former runaways in Canada: *The Philanthropist,* May 12, 1840; backed up by account of a man who regularly went to Canada to try to find former slaves, *Maysville Eagle,* Feb. 20, 1844.

214 "It will no doubt": Reprinted in *The Philanthropist,* May 12, 1840. It is possible that the *Agitator* was an individual and not a publication—I could not find such a publication. However, the style and tradition of *The Philanthropist* and the placement of the name after the column indicates that it is likely a piece reprinted from a publication with that name.

Chapter Twenty-Three

215 Outcome of *Greathouse* v. *Mahan:* Record books of Mason County Circuit Court, Kentucky State Historical Society, Frankfort; *Cincinnati Weekly Herald and Philanthropist,* Feb. 12, 1845.

216 "The bringing of slaves": from the *Cincinnati Gazette,* June 26, 1841. June 1841 ruling from Ohio Supreme Court; Leonard L. Richards, *"Gentlemen of Property and Standing,"* p. 124.

216 The 1829 riot: Ibid.

216 Details of the summer of 1841 Cincinnati riot in Cincinnati daily newspapers Sept. 1–11, 1841. Leonard L. Richards, "Gentlemen of Property and Standing," writes about the newspaper sources in a footnote on p. 125: "The *Gazette,* the *Chronicle* and especially the *Republican* sympathized with the Negroes and the abolitionists. All were Whig papers. The *Enquirer* blamed the riot on the Negroes and the abolitionists. The *Gazette,* which had tendencies toward anti-Catholicism and nativism, implied that the white rioters were predominantly Irishmen. The *Enquirer* published several denials. Among the wounded, only a few names were Irish." *The Philanthropist* published its version of the riot on Sept. 8, 1841. Because of the prejudices of the local papers, as Richards points out, accuracy was a challenge. I relied mostly on the version found in Richards, pp. 122–29, in combination with *The Philanthropist,* and with the aid of a city map of Cincinnati in 1840.

217 "Our city is infested with kidnappers": *The Philanthropist,* Sept. 8, 1841.

Chapter Twenty-Four

219 Account of the assassination attempt is from John Rankin letter, Sept. 13, 1841, widely distributed to most local newspapers and every antislavery publication in the nation— including *Pennsylvania Freeman,* Nov. 3, 1841; *The Liberator,* Oct. 22, 1841; and *Ripley Telegraph,* Sept. 14, 1841—and from John Rankin, "The Life of Rev. John Rankin";

Adam Lowry Rankin, "The Autobiography of Adam Lowry Rankin"; Samuel Rankin, interview in *Hartford Daily Courant,* Nov. 23, 1895. There are also accounts by Richard Calvin Rankin of that night in *The History of Brown County;* and Carl N. Thompson, compiler, *Historical Collections of Brown County.* The account in this book, *Beyond the River,* is a combination of Rankin's and Lowry's.

222   Anti-Abolitionist Society in Cincinnati: *Cincinnati Post and Anti-Abolitionist,* Jan. 22, 1842.

223   "We find our markets": Ibid.

223   Nearly died from measles: *The Philanthropist,* Nov. 12, 1842.

223   Vincent Wigglesworth: *The Philanthropist,* Dec. 21, 1842; April 12, 1843.

224   Newspaper ads: See, e.g., *The Philanthropist,* May 3, Aug. 12, 1843.

224   "KIDNAPPING": *Cincinnati Gazette,* reprinted in *The Philanthropist,* May 3, 1843.

224   Rankin and antislavery chorus in support of Liberty Party: *The Philanthropist,* Aug. 27, 1842; *Cincinnati Weekly Herald and Philanthropist,* June 12, 1844.

224   So had John B. Mahan: *The Philanthropist,* April 14, 1843.

224   "I have just returned from a lecturing tour": *Cincinnati Weekly Herald and Philanthropist,* May 10, 1843.

225   About the struggle in the Presbyterian Church: Larry Gene Willey, "The Reverend John Rankin, Early Ohio Anti-Slavery Leader"; Larry Gene Willey, "John Rankin, Antislavery Prophet, and the Free Presbyterian Church"; R. C. Galbraith, *The History of the Chillicothe Presbytery, from Its Organization in 1799 to 1899* (Chillicothe, Ohio: Sciotto Gazette Book and Job Office, 1899).

225   "Through your paper": John Rankin, in *The Philanthropist,* June 21, 1843; reprinted in *Anti-Slavery Standard,* July 13, 1843.

Chapter Twenty-Five

226   "The nefarious acts of the abolitionists": *Lexington Gazette,* Dec. 12, 1844; reprinted in *Democratic Standard,* Georgetown, Ohio, Dec. 31, 1844.

226   Harbor Hurley: *Cincinnati Weekly Herald and Philanthropist,* July 17, 1844.

226   Robert Miller and Absalom King: *Ohio Telegraph,* Dec. 15, 1844; reprinted in *The Liberator,* Dec. 20, 1844. For another incident at Red Oak involving slave hunters and two white women who tried to protect a slave named Lewis, see *Cincinnati Weekly Herald and Philanthropist,* Feb. 5, 1845.

227   Mahan's daughter died: *Cincinnati Weekly Herald and Philanthropist,* Nov. 15, 1843. (Mary Jane Mahan, his eldest daughter, died August 14 that year.)

227   Mahan's public speaking tour in the summer of 1843: *Cincinnati Weekly Herald and Philanthropist,* May 10, 1843. About Mahan being an active agent for the Liberty Party and *The Philanthropist,* see *The Philanthropist,* April 19, 1843.

228   Legal fees about $1,200: *The Philanthropist,* Dec. 11, 1838.

229   "We have a letter": *Pennsylvania Freeman,* Jan. 2, 1845; *The Liberator,* Jan. 17, 1845; *Democratic Standard,* Georgetown, Ohio, Dec. 24, 1844.

229   Asking for financial assistance for Polly: *Cincinnati Weekly Herald and Philanthropist,* Dec. 3, 1845; minutes, meeting of Sardinia Anti-Slavery Society, Jan. 11, 1845, in which it was resolved that the Mahan family must be helped, reprinted in *Cincinnati Weekly Herald and Philanthropist,* Feb. 12, 1845.

Chapter Twenty-Six

231   The account of John Parker and the incidents in this chapter all came from John Parker's own words, as told to Frank Gregg in the late nineteenth century. The original transcript is in the Rankin-Parker Collection, Special Collections Library, Duke University, and the published version is in only one source—Stuart Seely Sprague, ed., *His Promised Land.*

Chapter Twenty-Seven

238   "Timidity and alarm": "The Cholera," *Maysville Eagle,* April 9, 1850.

238   The recipe for the cure for cholera: *West Union Intelligencer,* beginning Jan. 10, 1849, and continuing off and on for the next two years.

239   Richard Dillingham died of cholera: *The Liberator,* Aug. 23, 1850; also in Harriet Beecher Stowe, *A Key to Uncle Tom's Cabin* (Boston: John P. Jewett & Co., 1853).

239   On the progress of the disease as it came closer and closer to the Ohio Valley: *Maysville Eagle,* April 9, 1850.

239   "raging violently": *Ripley Bee,* July 16, 1850.

239   "assumed somewhat the form": *Maysville Eagle,* Sept. 5, 1850.

239   Southern states' estimates of losses: Henrietta Buckmaster, *Let My People Go.*

239   The law passed: *Ripley Bee,* Sept. 21, 1850.

240   "Future history": *New York Courier & Enquirer,* reprinted in *Ripley Bee,* Oct. 12, 1850.

240   From September 18: The Fugitive Slave Law of 1850 is reproduced verbatim in *Ripley Bee,* Oct. 12, 1850; see also W. C. Cochran, "The Western Reserve and the Fugitive Slave Law," *Western Reserve Historical Society,* no. 101, 1920; Dwight L. Dumond, *Antislavery;* J. Winston Coleman, Jr., *Slavery Times in Kentucky.*

241   "The encouragement of kidnapping": *New York Evening Post,* reprinted in *Ripley Bee,* Oct. 12, 1850.

241   "To aid or assist": Chicago City Council Resolution, Nov. 29, 1850, from original document in Robert E. Bailey and Elaine Shemoney Evans, *Early Chicago, 1833–1871: A Selection of City Council Proceedings Files* (Springfield: Illinois State Archives, 1992).

241   Vigilance committees: Merton L. Dillon, *The Abolitionists.*

241   "It will, not withstanding": Lewis Tappan, quoted in ibid., p. 178.

242   "Is the presumption in favor of Slavery": *Ripley Bee,* Nov. 23, 1850.

242   "After the passage": Isaac M. Beck, letter, 1892, Union Township Library, Ripley, Ohio.

243   "Resolved that": *Ripley Bee,* Nov. 23, 1850.

243   "It is the deliberate determination": *Ripley Bee,* Jan. 18, 1851.

243   "Disobedience to the enactment": *National Era,* Dec. 5, 1850.

243   Ohio legislature passed a resolution: *The Liberator,* April 11, 1851.

243   "Distinctly treasonable": Daniel Webster, *Works of Daniel Webster* (Boston: C. C. Little and J. Brown, 1851), vol. 2, pp. 577–78, quoted in Dillon, *The Abolitionists,* p. 183.

Chapter Twenty-Eight

245   Saw his neighbor, Ira H. Shaw: Theodore W. Collins, letter, *Ripley Bee,* March 13, 1852; editors of *Maysville Eagle* respond to Collins letter published in the March 13 *Ripley Bee,* in *Maysville Eagle,* March 16, 1852; I. H. Shaw, "Who Is Benedict Arnold?," *Ripley Bee,* March 20, 1852; editors of *Ripley Bee* respond to *Eagle* editors' response, in *Ripley Bee,* March 20, 1852.

PART IV: BEYOND THE RIVER

249   "My father was always ready": John Rankin, Jr., interview with Frank Gregg, Greensburg, Indiana, late nineteenth century, transcribed copies at Ohio Historical Society in Columbus, Ohio, and Union Township Library, Ripley, Ohio; original in the Rankin-Parker Collection, Special Collections Library, Duke University.

249   "I was a slave": Horace Washington, Aug. 2, 1895, in Ohio–Brown County file, Siebert Collection, Ohio Historical Society.

Chapter Twenty-Nine

251   Newcomers, Snedaker and Lucas: See notes for Chapter Nine, noting sources regarding participants in the Ripley "line."

252   Fountain Pemberton: Letter by Pemberton's grandson to Wilbur H. Siebert, in Adams County file, Siebert Collection, Ohio Historical Society.

252   Robert Russell: J. Winston Coleman, Jr., *Slavery Times in Kentucky,* p. 256. Also, J. Winston Coleman, Jr. Collection, Transylvania University, Lexington, Kentucky.

253   Thirty-two runaways: *Maysville Eagle,* reprinted in *Ironton Register,* Oct. 14, 1852; also in *New York Daily Tribune,* Oct. 2, 1852.

253   "that every slave he knew": *Maysville Eagle,* Nov. 8, 1852, reprinted in *The Liberator,* Dec. 17, 1852.

253   "whose duty it shall be": *Revised Statutes of Kentucky,* chap. 73, "Patrols," articles 1 and 2, pp. 520–23.

253   Law prohibiting ferry owners: *The Liberator,* Feb. 14, 1851.

254   First suspension bridge over the Ohio River: "Aid and Comfort to Fugitive Slaves," *Anti-Slavery Bugle,* March 7, 1856. Earlier discussions in *Journal,* of Covington, Ky., Feb. 23, March 2, April 6, 1849, and March 2, 1850; and in *The Liberator,* March 9, 1849.

254   Kentucky's state penitentiary: Details on inmates, and the concept that Kentucky used its legal system as a powerful weapon, from interview with James M. Prichard, Kentucky Department for Libraries and Archives, Kentucky State Historical Society, Frankfort; also from his excellent, well-researched paper "Into the Fiery Furnace: Anti-Slavery Prisoners in the Kentucky State Penitentiary, 1844–1870." Mr. Prichard generously provided me with his paper early in my own research. His sources for the inmates are available at the Kentucky Department for Libraries and Archives at the Kentucky State Historical Society, Frankfort, Ky. They are: Mason Brown and C. S. Morehead, *Digest of the Statute Laws of Kentucky,* 2 vols (Frankfort, Ky.: N.p., 1834); Kentucky Penitentiary Registers (1848–1866); Report of the Keeper and Lessee of the Kentucky Penitentiary, Sept. 13, 1861. Frankfort, Ky., 1861; William C. Sneed, *Report on the History and Mode of Management of the Kentucky Penitentiary from its Origins in 1798 to March 1, 1860.* Frankfort, Ky., 1860.

254   Henry and Isaac Ramsey: *Ripley Bee,* Nov. 26, 1853.

255   George Williams: *Ripley Bee,* Aug. 28, 1856.

255   Calvin Fairbank and his 35,105 lashes: Calvin Fairbank, *Reverend Calvin Fairbank.*

255   Thomas Brown: Thomas Brown, *Brown's Three Years in the Kentucky Prisons* (Indianapolis: Courier Company, 1857).

256   John Parker and the reward: Stuart Seely Sprague, ed., *His Promised Land.*

256   Harriet Tubman: Henrietta Buckmaster, *Let My People Go.*

256   John Fairfield: I have done considerable research regarding Fairfield, who is truly one of the most fascinating individuals of his era, and one whose story has not yet been told. Unfortunately, the many details of his life could not be part of this book because he was not a major player on the Ripley line. After escaping from the Bracken County jail, he

convalesced with Rankin for about two weeks. This story is validated through Adam Lowry Rankin, "The Autobiography of Adam Lowry Rankin"; and Levi Coffin, *Reminiscences of Levi Coffin*.

Chapter Thirty

259 That the Ohio River had frozen in 1856: *Cincinnati Gazette*, February 1856 issues; *The Liberator*, March 7, 1856.

259 "The underground railroad has been doing," and other accounts in the same paragraph about escapes over the frozen river in 1856: from *Daily Columbian, Louisville Democrat, Maysville Eagle*, all reprinted in *The Liberator*, March 7, 1856.

260 Some recalled 1838: *The History of Brown County.*

260 "We learn from 'official sources' ": *Ripley Bee*, Nov. 12, 1859.

260 Death of David Wilmot Rankin: Obituary, *National Era*, Feb. 3, 1848.

260 Death of Lucinda: Rankin family Bible discovered in autumn 2001 by Russ Wiley, a descendant of Rankin's now living in Walnut Grove, Calif.; also in *Ripley Bee*, March 15, 1856.

261 "I had no reason to believe": John Rankin, "The Life of Rev. John Rankin," p. 27.

262 John Rankin and the Free Presbyterian Church: John Rankin, "The Life of Rev. John Rankin"; Adam Lowry Rankin, "The Autobiography of Adam Lowry Rankin"; Larry Gene Willey, "The Reverend John Rankin, Early Ohio Anti-Slavery Leader"; Larry Gene Willey, "John Rankin, Antislavery Prophet, and the Free Presbyterian Church"; and "Buckeye Presbyterianism," prepared by Committee of the United Presbyterian Synod of Ohio. E. B. Welsh, Chairman, 1968.

263 Rankin's work in Weld's book: Theodore Weld, *Slavery As It Is* (New York: American Anti-Slavery Society, 1839).

263 Southern delegates in Congress: "Slavery and the Abolitionists: Address of the Southern Delegates in Congress, January 15, 1849," *Southern Quarterly Review*, vol. 40 (1849) (Charleston, S.C.: James S. Burges, 1849), pp. 200–205.

264 Rankin's pamphlet on the 1850 Fugitive Slave Law: Rankin, "Autobiography of Rankin."

264 National Compensation Emancipation Society convention: *The Liberator*, Sept. 4, 1857; also in Louis Ruchames, ed., *The Letters of William Lloyd Garrison*, vol. 4, *From Disunionism to the Brink of War: 1850–1860* (Cambridge, Mass.: Belknap Press of Harvard University Press, 1975), pp. 483–84.

265 Charles Sumner: "Assault on Mr. Sumner: Speech of Hon. T. S. Bocock, of Virginia, Delivered in the House of Representatives, June 11, 1856."

265 Dred Scott: Thomas H. Benton, *Examination of the Dred Scott Case* (New York: D. Appleton & Co., 1857).

266 "This very attempt": Frederick Douglass, quoted in Henrietta Buckmaster, *Let My People Go*, p. 246.

266 Southern Commercial Convention: *Report of Mr. Henry Hughes, of Mississippi: Read Before the Southern Convention at Vicksburg, May 10, 1859, on the Subject of the African Apprentice System; pending the discussion of the resolutions of Mr. Spratt, of South Carolina, in favor of the repealing of the laws of Congress prohibiting the African Slave Trade. . . .* [pamphlet, with no more publishing information].

Chapter Thirty-One

267 Ripley emergency town meeting and "treaty": *Ripley Bee*, April 25, 1861.

268 Ripley had more than tripled: "All the Requisites of Wealth and Comfort: Ripley in 1861," *Ripley Bee*, Aug. 25, 1989.

268 "Altogether this city": Letter from "visitor," *Ripley Bee,* Feb. 14, 1861.

269 Camp Ripley: "Great Recruiting Center of North at Ripley During Civil War Days," *Ripley Bee,* Aug. 6, 1942; personal communications, Lee Edwards, director of the Ripley Museum, and David Gray, local historian, both experts on Camp Ripley.

269 Richard Calvin and other Rankin sons: *United States Biographical Dictionary* (Kansas, 1879; Chicago: S. Lewis & Co., 1879); Geo. W. Martin, ed., *Collections of the Kansas State Historical Society, 1911–1912* (Topeka, Kans.: State Printing Office, 1912); *Correspondence of Thomas Ebenezer Thomas; mainly relating to the anti-slavery conflict in Ohio, especially in the Presbyterian Church, 1834–1874* (republished, N.p.: Arthur W. McGraw, 1997); *Albuquerque Daily Citizen,* Jan. 23, 1900; *Ironton Register,* Sept. 5, 1905; obituary of Rev. Arthur Tappan Rankin, minutes of the Synod of Indiana of the Presbyterian Church, Held at Sullivan, Oct. 9–11, 1911 (published by the Synod Under the Direction of the Stated Clerk), p. 49; *Quenemo News,* Kansas, Nov. 25, 1915; Adam Lowry Rankin, "The Autobiography of Adam Lowry Rankin"; *The History of Brown County.*

270 Joseph Settles: Information from the Settles family in Ripley from an interview with Joseph Settles's grandson, Eugene, and from "The Settles Family," unauthored typescript, Brown County Genealogical Society, Georgetown, Ohio.

270 Arnold Gragston: Ira Berlin, Marc Favreau, and Steven F. Miller, eds., *Remembering Slavery: African Americans Talk About Their Personal Experiences of Slavery and Freedom* (New York: New Press, 1998).

271 Story of former slave in Chatham, Canada: verbatim account by Thomas Lovejoy Rankin, one of John Rankin's sons, in the late nineteenth century, now at Union Township Library, Ripley, Ohio.

273 "Sublime in its magnitude": William Lloyd Garrison, quoted in Henry Mayer, *All on Fire: William Lloyd Garrison and the Abolition of Slavery* (New York: St. Martin's Press, 1998), p. 547.

273 Meeting at Concert Hall in Philadelphia, "The next letter," and John Rankin's Nov. 19 letter: "Celebration in Philadelphia," *National Anti-Slavery Standard,* New York, Dec. 19, 1863.

274 "Rev. John Rankin and his sons did it": Henry Ward Beecher, quoted in William Birney, *James G. Birney and His Times,* p. 168.

Chapter Thirty-Two

275 Death of John Rankin, on March 18, 1886: Diary of Mrs. Cora Young Wiles, noted in *Ripley Bee,* April 15, 1937. Mrs. Wiles was born in Ripley and later known as a writer from Indianapolis. The information regarding Rankin's cancer is from Mrs. Wiles. Other details come from *Ripley Bee,* March 22, 1886.

276 "I lived to see four million slaves": John Rankin, "The Life of Rev. John Rankin," p. 50.

276 Frank Gregg: *Ripley Bee,* Aug. 14, 1912; his obituary, *New York Herald Tribune,* Jan. 7, 1937.

276 Gregg's interviews with John Rankin, Jr., with the four citizens of Ripley (Baird, Campbell, Jackson, and Marshall), with John Parker: All in Union Township Library, Ripley, Ohio; originals in Rankin-Parker Collection, Special Collections Library, Duke University.

278 Collins's coffins: Confirmation in ads in *Ripley Bee,* e.g., July 16, 1859.

278 "These echoes": John Parker, original of autobiography, in Rankin-Parker Collection, Special Collections Library, Duke University [this quote not included in *His Promised Land*].

279 "My name is Rankin": Dr. Isaac M. Beck, letter, 1892, Union Township Library, Ripley, Ohio.

SELECTED BIBLIOGRAPHY

Abzug, Robert H. *Passionate Liberator: Theodore Dwight Weld and the Dilemma of Reform.* New York: Oxford University Press, 1980.

Adams, Alice. *The Neglected Period of Anti-Slavery in America, 1808–1831.* Boston: Ginn and Company, 1908.

Allen, Michael. *Western Rivermen, 1763–1861.* Baton Rouge: Louisiana State University Press, 1990.

Aptheker, Herbert. *Abolitionism: A Revolutionary Movement.* Boston: Twayne, 1989.

———. *American Negro Slave Revolts.* New York: Columbia University Press, 1943.

Banta, R. E. *The Ohio.* New foreword by Thomas D. Clark. Lexington: University Press of Kentucky, 1998. (Originally published in 1949.)

Barnes, Gilbert Hobbs. *The Antislavery Impulse, 1830–1844.* New York: D. Appleton–Century, 1933.

Barnes, Gilbert H., and Dwight L. Dumond, eds. *Letters of Theodore Dwight Weld, Angelina Grimke Weld and Sarah Grimke, 1822–1844.* Gloucester, Mass.: Peter Smith, 1965.

Berlin, Ira. *Many Thousands Gone: The First Two Centuries of Slavery in North America.* Cambridge, Mass.: Belknap Press of Harvard University Press, 1998.

Berlin, Ira, Marc Favreau, and Steven F. Miller, eds. *Remembering Slavery: African Americans Talk About Their Personal Experiences of Slavery and Freedom.* New York: New Press, 1998.

Birney, William. *James G. Birney and His Times: The Genesis of the Republican Party with Some Account of Abolition Movements in the South Before 1828.* New York: D. Appleton & Co., 1890.

Black, Alexander. *The Story of Ohio.* Boston: D. Lothrop, 1888.

Blassingame, John W. *Slave Testimony.* Baton Rouge: Louisiana State University Press, 1977.

Blockson, Charles L. *The Underground Railroad: Dramatic Firsthand Accounts of Daring Escapes to Freedom.* New York: Simon & Schuster, 1987.

Breyfogle, William Arthur. *Make Free: The Story of the Underground Railroad.* Philadelphia and New York: J. B. Lippincott, 1958.

Brown, Thomas. *Brown's Three Years in the Kentucky Prisons.* Indianapolis: Courier Company, 1857.

Buckmaster, Henrietta. *Let My People Go.* New York: Harper & Brothers, 1941.

Campbell, Stanley W. *The Slave Catchers: Enforcement of the Fugitive Slave Law, 1850–1860.* Chapel Hill: University of North Carolina Press, 1970.

Carroll, Joseph C. *Slave Insurrections in the United States, 1800–1865.* Boston: Chapman & Grimes, 1938.

Coffin, Levi. *Reminiscences of Levi Coffin.* New York: Arno Press and New York Times, 1968.

Coit, Margaret L. *John C. Calhoun: American Portrait.* Boston: Houghton Mifflin, 1950.

Coleman, J. Winston, Jr. *Slavery Times in Kentucky.* Chapel Hill: University of North Carolina Press, 1940.

Cover, Robert M. *Justice Accused: Antislavery and the Judicial Process.* New Haven: Yale University Press, 1975.

Cramer, Zadok. *The Navigator,* 10th ed. Pittsburgh: Cramer, Spear and Eichbaum, 1818.

Dillon, Merton L. *The Abolitionists: The Growth of a Dissenting Minority.* Dekalb: Northern Illinois University Press, 1974.

———. *Elijah P. Lovejoy, Abolitionist Editor.* Urbana: University of Illinois Press, 1961.

Douglass, Frederick. *My Bondage and My Freedom.* New York: Miller, Orton & Mulligan, 1855.

Duberman, Martin, ed. *The Anti-Slavery Vanguard: New Essays on the Abolitionists.* Princeton: Princeton University Press, 1965.

DuBois, W. E. Burghardt. *John Brown.* New York: International Publishers, 1996. (Originally published in 1909.)

Dumond, Dwight L. *Antislavery: The Crusade for Freedom in America.* Ann Arbor: University of Michigan Press, 1961.

Dumond, Dwight L., ed. *Letters of James Gillespie Birney, 1831–1857.* New York: D. Appleton–Century, 1938.

Egerton, Douglas R. *Gabriel's Rebellion: The Virginia Slave Conspiracies of 1800 & 1802.* Chapel Hill: University of North Carolina Press, 1993.

———. *He Shall Go Out Free: The Lives of Denmark Vesey.* Madison, Wisc.: Madison House, 1999.

Evans, Nelson W., and Emmons B. Stivers. *A History of Adams County, Ohio, from Its Earliest Settlement to the Present Time.* West Union, Ohio: E. B. Stivers, 1900.

Fairbank, Calvin. *Reverend Calvin Fairbank: During Slavery Times.* Chicago: N. p., 1890.

Father William, *Three Days on the Ohio.* New York: Carlton & Porter, 1854.

Fogel, Robert William. *Without Consent or Contract: The Rise and Fall of American Slavery.* New York: W. W. Norton, 1989.

Foner, Eric, compiler. *America's Black Past: A Reader in Afro-American History.* New York: Harper & Row, 1970.

Foner, Philip S. *Frederick Douglass.* New York: Citadel Press, 1964.

———. *History of Black Americans: From Africa to the Emergence of the Cotton Kingdom.* Westport, Conn.: Greenwood Press, 1975.

Franklin, John Hope. *From Slavery to Freedom: A History of American Negroes.* New York: Alfred A. Knopf, 1947.

Franklin, John Hope, and Loren Schweninger. *Runaway Slaves: Rebels on the Plantation.* New York: Oxford University Press, 1999.

Galbreath, Charles B. *History of Ohio.* Chicago and New York: American Historical Society, 1925.

Gara, Larry. *The Liberty Line: The Legend of the Underground Railroad.* Lexington: University Press of Kentucky, 1961.

Genovese, Eugene D. *Roll, Jordan, Roll: The World the Slaves Made.* New York: Random House, 1972.

Glazer, Walter Stix. *Cincinnati in 1840.* Columbus: Ohio State University Press, 1999.

Hart, Albert Bushnell. *Slavery and Abolition 1831–1841.* New York: Haskell House, 1968.

Hickok, Charles Thomas. "The Negro in Ohio, 1802–1870." Ph.D. dissertation, Western Reserve University, Cleveland, 1896.

Hinks, Peter P., ed. *David Walker's Appeal: To the Coloured Citizens of the World.* University Park: Pennsylvania State University Press, 2000.

The History of Brown County. Chicago: W. H. Beers & Co., 1883.

Hopkins, James F., and Mary W. M. Hargreaves, eds. *The Papers of Henry Clay.* Vol. 5, *Secretary of State, 1826.* Lexington: University Press of Kentucky, 1973.

Howe, Henry. *Historical Collections of Ohio.* Cincinnati: C. J. Krehbiel & Co., 1888.

Hurt, R. Douglas. *The Ohio Frontier: Crucible of the Old Northwest, 1720–1830.* Bloomington: Indiana University Press, 1996.

Jakle, John A. *Images of the Ohio Valley: A Historical Geography of Travel, 1740 to 1860.* Cartographer, Miklos Pinther. New York: Oxford University Press, 1977.

James, C.L.R. *The Black Jacobins: Toussaint L'Ouverture and the San Domingo Revolution.* New York: Vintage Books, 1989. (Originally published by Random House, 1963.)

Johnson, Charles; Patricia Smith; and WGBH Series Research Team. *Africans in America: America's Journey Through Slavery.* New York: Harcourt, Brace, 1998.

Kolchin, Peter. *American Slavery, 1619–1877.* New York: Hill & Wang, 1993.

Lacour-Gayet, Robert. *Everyday Life in the United States Before the Civil War: 1830–1860.* New York: Frederick Ungar, 1972.

The Legion of Liberty! And Force of Truth; containing the thoughts, words and deeds of some prominent apostles, champions and martyrs. Second edition. New York: American Anti-Slavery Society, 1843.

Lowance, Mason, ed. *Against Slavery: An Abolitionist Reader.* New York: Penguin Books, 2000.

Lynd, Staughton. *Intellectual Origins of American Radicalism.* New York: Pantheon Books, 1968.

Mayer, Henry. *All on Fire: William Lloyd Garrison and the Abolition of Slavery.* New York: St. Martin's Press, 1998.

McKitrick, Eric L., ed. *Slavery Defended: The Views of the Old South.* Englewood Cliffs, N.J.: Prentice-Hall, 1963.

McKivigan, John R. *The War Against Proslavery Religion: Abolitionism and the Northern Churches, 1830–1865.* Ithaca, N.Y.: Cornell University Press, 1984.

McKivigan, John R., ed. "History of the American Abolitionist Movement," in *Abolitionism and American Law.* Garland series, 1999.

McPherson, James M. *Battle Cry of Freedom: The Civil War Era.* New York: Ballantine Books, 1989.

Mellon, James, ed. *Bullwhip Days: The Slaves Remember, an Oral History.* New York: Avon Books, 1988.

Miller, William Lee. *Arguing About Slavery: The Great Battle in the United States Congress.* New York: Alfred A. Knopf, 1996.

Mooney, Chase C. *Slavery in Tennessee.* Westport, Conn.: Negro Universities Press, 1957.

Myers, John L. "The Agency System of the AntiSlavery Movement, 1832–1837, and Its Antecedents in Other Reform and Benevolent Societies." Ph.D. dissertation, Department of History, University of Michigan, Ann Arbor, 1948.

Oates, Stephen B. *The Approaching Fury: Voices of the Storm, 1820–1861.* New York: HarperCollins, 1997.

Purtee, Edward O'Conner. "The Underground Railroad from Southwestern Ohio to Lake Erie." Ph.D. dissertation, Graduate School of the Ohio State University, 1932.

Quarles, Benjamin, ed. *Narrative of the Life of Frederick Douglass: An American Slave, Written by Himself.* Cambridge, Mass.: Belknap Press of Harvard University Press, 1960.

Rankin, Adam Lowry. "The Autobiography of Adam Lowry Rankin." Unpublished, handwritten in the early 1890s. Typewritten copy by one of A. L. Rankin's granddaughters, Belle Rankin, in 1931, available at Union Township Library, Ripley, Ohio.

Rankin, John. *Letters on American Slavery: Addressed to Mr. Thomas Rankin, Merchant at Middlebrook, Augusta Co., Va.* Fifth edition. Boston: Isaac Knapp, 1838.

———. "The Life of Rev. John Rankin: written by Himself in His 80th Year (ca. 1872)." Text from manuscript in collection of Lobena and Charles Frost, reproduced and copyrighted 1998 by Arthur W. McGraw.

Reid, Robert L. *Always a River: The Ohio River and the American Experience.* Bloomington: Indiana University Press, 1991.

Remini, Robert Vincent. *Andrew Jackson and the Course of American Democracy, 1833–1845.* New York: Harper & Row, 1984.

Renehan, Edward J., Jr. *The Secret Six: The True Tale of the Men Who Conspired with John Brown.* Columbia: University of South Carolina Press, 1997.

Review of the Statement of the Faculty of Lane Seminary in Relation to the Recent Difficulties in That Institution, by John Rankin, Pastor of the Presbyterian Church and Author of *Letters on American Slavery.* Ripley, Ohio: Published by the Author, Campbell & Palmer, Printers, 1835.

Richards, Leonard L. "Gentlemen of Property and Standing." In *Anti-Abolition Mobs in Jacksonian America.* New York: Oxford University Press, 1970.

Ritchie, Rev. Andrew. *The Soldier, the Battle, and the Victory; being a Brief Account of the Work of Rev. John Rankin and the Anti-Slavery Cause, 1793–1886.* Cincinnati: Western Tract and Book Society, 1868. Typescript. Available at Union Township Library, Ripley, Ohio.

Ruchames, Louis, ed. *The Letters of William Lloyd Garrison.* Vol. 4, *From Disunionism to the Brink of War: 1850–1860.* Cambridge, Mass.: Belknap Press of Harvard University Press, 1975.

Siebert, Wilbur H. *The Mysteries of Ohio's Underground Railroads.* Columbus: Long's College Book Co., 1951.

———. *The Underground Railroad from Slavery to Freedom.* New York: Macmillan, 1898.

———. Underground Railroad materials for Illinois, Indiana, New Hampshire, New York, and Ohio. At Ohio Historical Society, Columbus, Ohio. [Material collected between 1891 and 1948 on American loyalists, East Florida, and Underground Railroad. Includes correspondence, typed transcripts of official documents, letters, portions of articles and books. Most of the collection is about the Underground Railroad, and a large portion of that is about Ohio.]

Sprague, Stuart Seely, ed. *His Promised Land: The Autobiography of John P. Parker, Former Slave and Conductor on the Underground Railroad.* New York: W. W. Norton, 1996.

Stampp, Kenneth M. *The Peculiar Institution: Slavery in the Ante-Bellum South.* New York: Vintage Books, 1989.

Stampp, Kenneth M., ed. *The Causes of the Civil War.* New York: Simon & Schuster, 1959.

Stewart, James Brewer, and Eric Foner, consulting ed. *Holy Warriors: The Abolitionists and American Slavery.* New York: Hill & Wang, 1996.

Still, William. *The Underground Railroad.* Washington, D.C.: N.p., 1871.

Stivers, Eliese Bambach. *Ripley, Ohio: Its History and Families.* Ripley: Ripley, Ohio, Historical Committee, 1965.

Stowe, Harriet Beecher. *A Key to Uncle Tom's Cabin.* Boston: John P. Jewett & Co., 1853.

———. *Uncle Tom's Cabin.* New York: Bantam Books, 1981.

Strangis, Joel. *Lewis Hayden and the War Against Slavery.* North Haven, Conn.: Shoe String Press, 1999.

Styron, William. *The Confessions of Nat Turner.* New York: Random House, 1966.

Tappan, Lewis, *The Life of Arthur Tappan.* New York: Hurd and Haughton, 1871.

Thomas, Benjamin P. *Theodore Weld: Crusader for Freedom.* New Brunswick, N.J.: Rutgers University Press, 1950.

Thomas, Hugh. *The Slave Trade: The Story of the Atlantic Slave Trade, 1440–1870.* New York: Simon & Schuster, 1997.

Thompson, Carl N., compiler. *Historical Collections of Brown County.* Piqua, Ohio: Hammer Graphics, 1969.

Trial of Rev. John B. Mahan, for Felony, in the Mason Circuit Court of Kentucky, Commencing on Tuesday, the 13th and Terminating on Monday the 19th of November, 1838. Reported by Joseph B. Reid and Henry R. Reeder, Esqs. Cincinnati: Samuel A. Alley, 1838.

Walker, David. *Walker's Appeal.* Boston: N.p., 1819.

Watson, Harry L. *Liberty and Power: The Politics of Jacksonian America.* New York: Hill & Wang, 1990.

Weisenburger, Steven. *Modern Medea: A Family Story of Slavery and Child-Murder from the Old South.* New York: Hill & Wang, 1998.

Weld, Theodore. *Slavery As It Is.* New York: American Anti-Slavery Society, 1839.

Willey, Larry Gene. "John Rankin, Antislavery Prophet, and the Free Presbyterian Church," *American Presbyterians: Journal of Presbyterian History,* vol. 72, no. 3 (Fall 1994).

———. "The Reverend John Rankin, Early Ohio Anti-Slavery Leader." Ph.D. thesis, Department of History, Graduate College of University of Iowa, May 1976.

Wilson, Forrest. *Crusader in Crinoline: The Life of Harriet Beecher Stowe.* New York: J. B. Lippincott, 1941.

Wittke, Carl. *The History of the State of Ohio.* Columbus: Ohio State Archaeological and Historical Society, 1941.

INDEX

Abingdon Presbytery, 28, 29, 30

Abolition Intelligencer and Missionary Magazine, 15, 38

abolitionism:
  arson used by opponents of, 51–52, 140, 149–50
  colonization movement and, 55, 68, 70, 103–4
  criticism and violent opposition to, 13, 34, 43–44, 45, 51–55, 92–100, 103–12, 114–16, 127–30, 140, 149–50, 165, 180–82, 184–88, 215–18, 252–58
  emergence of national movement for, 67–74, 80, 113–22
  ethical and moral principles of, 14–15, 16, 18, 19, 28, 30–31, 67
  evangelical vs. political points of view in, 202–6, 225
  free black workers in support of, 5, 10, 13, 18, 44–45, 88–89, 119, 182–83, 232–37, 254–58
  fund-raising in, 105, 110, 114
  gradual emancipation advocated in, 68, 103, 130
  guilt as component of, 70
  immediate emancipation advocated in, 69, 70, 80, 86, 204
  multiracial society associated with, 55, 149
  proselytizing for, 68–74, 90–98, 113, 263–64

schisms in, 203–6, 225
severe penalties advocated for activists in, 55–56, 96–98, 140
white martyrs of, 130, 159, 187–88, 202, 226
white supporters of, xv, 9–15, 16, 18, 19–21, 23, 28, 32–33, 41–42, 54–55, 61, 67–74
women recruited for, 105
see also antislavery societies

Adams, John Quincy, 14
Advocate of Freedom, 116
Africa, 55, 104
Agitator, 214, 306*n*
Alabama, 27, 68, 69, 70, 92
Allan, William T., 68, 69, 70, 71, 99
Allen, Abram, 118
Allen, Mr., 147
Alton, Ill., 129–30, 131
American and Foreign Anti-Slavery Society, 204
American Anti-Slavery Society, 58, 71, 73, 90, 94, 96, 140, 273, 274
  1835 pamphlet campaign of, 98–99
  JR as agent of, 74, 113–17, 120–21, 206
  women's issues and, 203–4
American Colonization Society, 55, 103–4
American Tract Society, 263
Ammen, David, 36, 46, 47, 50, 51, 76
Ammen, Jacob, 269